Reconstructing Individualism

Autonomy, Individuality, and the Self
in Western Thought

EDITED BY THOMAS C. HELLER,

MORTON SOSNA, AND DAVID E. WELLBERY

with Arnold I. Davidson, Ann Swidler, and Ian Watt

STANFORD UNIVERSITY PRESS

Stanford, California 1986

Stanford University Press, Stanford, California

© 1986 by the Board of Trustees of the Leland Stanford Junior University

Printed in the United States of America

CIP data appear at the end of the book

Reconstructing Individualism

Contributors

CHRISTINE BROOKE-ROSE

STANLEY CAVELL

NANCY JULIA CHODOROW

JAMES CLIFFORD

NATALIE ZEMON DAVIS

JOHN FRECCERO

MICHAEL FRIED

CAROL GILLIGAN

STEPHEN GREENBLATT

IAN HACKING

WERNER HAMACHER

NIKLAS LUHMANN

JOHN W. MEYER

MARTHA C. NUSSBAUM

J. B. SCHNEEWIND

PAOLO VALESIO

In memory of Michelle Zimbalist Rosaldo (1944–1981)

Acknowledgments

Given the paradox inherent in the subject, it is appropriate that a book on individualism should be so collective an enterprise. The three coeditors and the sixteen contributors are not the only ones who played a vital role in creating it. First, we owe particular thanks to Arnold Davidson, Ann Swidler, and Ian Watt, fellow members of the committee that conceived and planned the February 1984 Stanford Humanities Center conference out of which this book grew; their spirit, ideas, and support pervade the enterprise. Second, we are truly grateful to the Exxon Education Foundation, the Georges F. Lurcy Charitable Trust, and the Stanford Humanities Center for their indispensable financial support.

We also wish to mention several people who were involved with the conference but whose contributions, stimulating as they were, could not be included here. Harvey Leibenstein and John Perry spoke on economic and linguistic aspects of individualism, respectively; only the editorial decision to concentrate on papers that emphasized the subject's more historical aspects kept us from including their essays. We also benefited from the thoughts of Leo Lowenthal, who, though unable because of illness to speak at the conference, nonetheless conveyed his reflections on the subject to us. Although he, too, was in the end unable to participate in the conference, Richard Poirier generously shared his proposed paper. We are very grateful to each of them.

Many others have contributed to our efforts. We want especially to thank Susan Asch for her superb job in handling the administrative arrangements for the conference and Dee Marquez for typing the final versions of the manuscript. Among those who also assisted with various phases of the conference were W. B. Carnochan, Albert H. Hastorf, Van A. Harvey, Larry N. Horton, John R. Kates, Thomas C. Moser, Jr., Michael Oman, John Prostko, Renato Rosaldo, Michael T. Ryan, and Robert Tilton. Sara Blair provided valuable multilingual assistance with the final proofreading. Finally, we owe much to Helen Tartar of Stanford University Press for her steady encouragement and editorial skills in seeing this multi-authored volume through to publication, and we also wish to thank Paul Psoinos for his careful copyediting.

December 1985

T.C.H.
M.S.
D.E.W.

viii

Contents

Contributors   xi

Introduction   1
THOMAS C. HELLER AND DAVID E. WELLBERY

Autobiography and Narrative   16
JOHN FRECCERO

Fiction and Friction   30
STEPHEN GREENBLATT

Boundaries and the Sense of Self in Sixteenth-Century
France   53
NATALIE ZEMON DAVIS

The Use of Autonomy in Ethical Theory   64
J. B. SCHNEEWIND

Courbet's Metaphysics: A Reading of *The Quarry*   76
MICHAEL FRIED

"Disgregation of the Will": Nietzsche on the Individual
and Individuality   106
WERNER HAMACHER

On Ethnographic Self-Fashioning: Conrad and Malinowski   140
JAMES CLIFFORD

Contents

The Beautiful Lie: Heroic Individuality and Fascism   163
PAOLO VALESIO

The Dissolution of Character in the Novel   184
CHRISTINE BROOKE-ROSE

Toward a Relational Individualism: The Mediation
of Self Through Psychoanalysis   197
NANCY JULIA CHODOROW

Myths of Socialization and of Personality   208
JOHN W. MEYER

Making Up People   222
IAN HACKING

Remapping the Moral Domain: New Images of the Self
in Relationship   237
CAROL GILLIGAN

Love and the Individual: Romantic Rightness and
Platonic Aspiration   253
MARTHA C. NUSSBAUM

Being Odd, Getting Even: Threats to Individuality   278
STANLEY CAVELL

The Individuality of the Individual: Historical Meanings
and Contemporary Problems   313
NIKLAS LUHMANN

Notes   329

Index   357

Contributors

CHRISTINE BROOKE-ROSE is a widely published novelist, critic, translator, and reviewer; as a university professor, she teaches literary studies at the University of Paris, VIII. Her fictional writings include *Amalgamemnon* (1984), *Thru* (1975), and *Between* (1968), and a collection of short stories, *Go When You See the Green Man Walking* (1969). Among her best-known critical writings are *A Grammar of Metaphor* (1958; 1970), *A ZBC of Ezra Pound* (1971), and *A Rhetoric of the Unreal* (1981). She has written extensively about modernist and contemporary fiction in many leading European literary reviews and journals.

STANLEY CAVELL is Walter M. Cabot Professor of Aesthetics and the General Theory of Value at Harvard University. His general interest is in the philosophy of language, especially the connections between philosophy and literature. His books include *Must We Mean What We Say?* (1969), *The Claim of Reason: Wittgenstein, Skepticism, Morality and Tragedy* (1979), *Pursuits of Happiness: The Hollywood Comedy of Remarriage* (1981), and *Themes Out of School* (1984).

NANCY JULIA CHODOROW is Associate Professor of Sociology at the University of California, Santa Cruz, and Associate Research Sociologist at the Institute of Personality Assessment and Research at the University of California, Berkeley. She is the author of *The Reproduction of Mothering: Psychoanalysis and the Sociology of Gender* (1978) and of many articles on feminist theory and psychoanalytic social theory. She is now working on a study of early women psychoanalysts.

JAMES CLIFFORD, a historian, is Associate Professor in the History of Consciousness Program at the University of California, Santa Cruz. His special interest is the history, politics, and poetics of cultural description. He is the author of *Person and Myth: Maurice Leenhardt in the Melanesian World* (1982) and coeditor of *Writing Culture* (1986). His articles on ethnographic authority and ethnographic surrealism have appeared in *Representations* and *Comparative Studies in Society and History*.

NATALIE ZEMON DAVIS is Henry Charles Lea Professor of History at Princeton University. Her interests are religion and society in sixteenth- and seventeenth-century France, sex roles in early modern Europe, and popular culture. She is the author of *Society and Culture in Early Modern France* (1975) and *The Return of Martin Guerre* (1983), and she is currently completing *The Gift in Sixteenth-Century France*.

JOHN FRECCERO is Rosina Pierotti Professor of Italian Literature at Stanford University and former Chairman of Stanford's Comparative Literature Program. He is the author of several studies on Dante, Petrarch, and John Donne.

MICHAEL FRIED is Professor of Humanities and the History of Art and also Director of the Humanities Center at The Johns Hopkins University. He is the author of *Morris Louis* (1970), *Absorption and Theatricality: Painting and Beholder in the Age of Diderot* (1980), and *Realism, Writing, and Disfiguration in Thomas Eakins's "Gross Clinic"* (forthcoming). The present essay is part of an almost-completed study of the art of Gustave Courbet.

CAROL GILLIGAN is Associate Professor at Harvard University, Graduate School of Education. Her studies of identity and moral development have focused on the ways people think about experiences of conflict and choice. She is the author of *In a Different Voice: Psychological Theory and Women's Development* (1982); her more recent writings include "The Conquistador and the Dark Continent: Reflections on the Psychology of Love" (*Daedalus*, Summer 1984).

STEPHEN GREENBLATT is Professor of English at the University of California, Berkeley, where he specializes in Renaissance literature and critical theory. He is an editor of *Representations* and the author of *Sir Walter Ralegh: The Renaissance Man and His Roles* (1973) and *Renaissance Self-Fashioning* (1980).

IAN HACKING, a philosopher, teaches at the Institute for the History and Philosophy of Science and Technology in the University of Toronto. His books include *Logic of Statistical Inference* (1965), *The Emergence of Probability* (1975), *Why Does Language Matter to Philosophy?* (1975), and *Representing and Intervening* (1983). He has just completed *The Taming of Chance*, which is about the erosion of determinism in the nineteenth century.

WERNER HAMACHER is Professor in the Department of German and the Humanities Center at The Johns Hopkins University. His publications include an edition of G. W. F. Hegel, *Der Geist des Christentums*, with an accompanying book-length study *'Pleroma'—zu Genesis und Struktur einer dialektischen Hermeneutik bei Hegel* (1978), and essays on Kant, Schlegel, Schleiermacher, Kleist, Yeats, Célan, and others. He is currently preparing a book of essays on literary hermeneutics entitled *Entferntes Verstehen*.

NIKLAS LUHMANN is Professor of Sociology at the University of Bielefeld, West Germany. Since his important debate with Jürgen Habermas in 1971 (published under the title *Theorie der Gesellschaft oder Sozialtechnology—Was leistet die Systemforschung?*), he has emerged as a major sociological theoretician and has written important books on the sociology of religion, the sociology of knowledge, and the sociology of law. In addition to his many publications in German, some of his works have recently been translated into English: *Trust and Power* (1979), *The Differentiation of Society* (1982), *Religious Dogmatics and the Evolution of Societies* (1984), and *A Sociological Theory of Law* (1985).

JOHN W. MEYER is Professor of Sociology at Stanford University. His primary interests are in the sociology of education, the study of formal organizations, and the social consequences of modernization in developing countries. He has written several books and numerous journal articles on these subjects.

MARTHA C. NUSSBAUM is Professor of Philosophy and Classics at Brown University. Her main interests are Ancient Greek philosophy, ethics, and the relationship between philosophy and literature. She is the author of *Aristotle's De Motu Animalium* (1978) and *The Fragility of Goodness: Luck and Ethics in Greek Tragedy and Philosophy* (1985), and the editor of *Language and Logos* (1982); her writings have also appeared in various classical, philosophical, and literary journals.

J. B. SCHNEEWIND is Professor of Philosophy at The Johns Hopkins University and Chairman of his department. Since publishing *Sidgwick's Ethics and Victorian Moral Philosophy* (1977), he has been working on eighteenth-century views of morality. He is coeditor with Richard Rorty and Quentin Skinner of *Philosophy in History* (1984).

PAOLO VALESIO is Professor of Italian at Yale University. His work has emphasized comparative rhetorics, literary theory, and the relationship between religion and literature. His books include *Strutture dell' allitterazione* I: *Grammatica, retorica, e folklore verbale* (1968); *Novantiqua: Rhetorics as a Contemporary Theory* (1980); and two novels and a volume of poetry.

Reconstructing Individualism

Introduction

THOMAS C. HELLER AND
DAVID E. WELLBERY

The essays that follow originated in a conference entitled "Reconstructing Individualism," held at Stanford University, February 18–20, 1984. The conference planners took as their leading idea the notion that the Humanities represent not a methodologically circumscribed domain of inquiry but rather an open and evolving conversation in which voices from many disciplines work out shared views and differences in a common labor of edification. The concept of individuality, in relation to the historical phenomenon of "individualism," seemed an especially appropriate theme for such a conversation both because of its relevance to all the "human sciences" and because of its centrality in the post-Renaissance world, in which the Humanities as such emerged.

Three very general assumptions informed the organization of the conference, the choice of format, the selection of speakers, and the delineation of themes. The first was that some form of individualism—broadly conceived as the view that the individual human subject is a maker of the world we inhabit—has been a key factor in the life of the West for the last five hundred years. Modern definitions of the self and psychology, of ethical responsibility and civic identity, and of artistic representation and economic behavior all rest on the notion of an individual whose experience and history, whose will and values, whose expressions and preferences are essential constituents of reality. Our second assumption was that, from the latter half of the nineteenth century to the present, the individualist order of the modern Western world has met with challenges that have rendered its beliefs and doctrines problematic. Historical developments in the material and social realms, such as in-

individual-ism, broadly defined

I

dustrialization and the emergence of mass society, have altered the ontological foundations of individual identity. Parallel changes have been apparent in the domain of theory, where—in psychology, linguistics, the social sciences, and other fields—fundamental and once seemingly necessary propositions about the unity and autonomy of human individuals have been questioned or recast. Although the resulting challenges to individualism must be reflected in any adequate contemporary account of social relations, they by no means relieve us of the responsibility of reflecting anew on the status of the individual in our contemporary world. Consequently, the third and animating assumption of the conference was that the concept of the individual, which has played such a central role in the formation of the post-Renaissance world, needs to be rethought in the wake of the severe criticisms which have been directed against it. In the conference title, "Reconstructing Individualism," reconstruction does not imply a return to a lost state but rather an alternative conceptualization of the experience of subjectivity, enriched by the chastening experiences of the last century. Considered together, the essays begin to map out the terrain for a future discussion of individuality that would enhance our understanding of both the fruitfulness and the limitations of that concept. We believe that such a discussion, like the one embodied in this volume, will take the form of humanist conversation.

It would be inconsistent with our understanding of the process of reconstruction to assert that the volume conveys a single unitary theme or consensual core. Instead, the essays collected here offer diverse representations of individualism, as is altogether appropriate to the complexity of the theme and to the variety of perspectives brought to the conference. This diversity stems in part from the fact that the sixteen contributors represent at least eight distinct disciplines, each with its own local history of academic practices in which the concept of individuality has assumed different boundaries in response to the genealogy of the field. But this interdisciplinary refraction of our theme is further complicated by internal plurality: each combines historical, critical, and reconstructive dimensions; each addresses questions of both subject matter and method; and each reflects, more or less explicitly, on the tensions and ironies involved in interdisciplinary discussions. As a result, the papers do not fall readily into any single classification, nor can they be organized into any one compelling narrative. Our arrangement of the essays, then, is necessarily contingent, reflecting one of several possible readings. And our introduction is likewise selective and partial: rather than summarizing or listing results, it describes one of many paths into the complex network of problems at issue.

In the West, individualism has been contingent and paradoxical. The centering of the imagery of individuality upon the topography of modern social discourse took place over an extended period of time, was halting in the elaboration of the boundaries between the individual and collective institutions, and was often mediated by indirect and exotic representations of the emergent figure. The prominence of autobiographical narrative may be one indication of the reorganization of experience around individual life. Looking at the origins of such narrative, John Freccero points out that the Augustinian prototype of confessional autobiography is marked by a severe moral ambivalence. Augustine's work, while establishing a narrative form that was to become commonplace in the post-Renaissance world, also illustrates a displacement of autobiography by allegory. Individual autobiography involves an immanent temporal history, whereas allegory refers to the ideal, and therefore static, time of the salvation scheme. Sin—the illicit assertion of selfhood and autonomy—is avoided only when conversion integrates the self within the transcendent order instituted by divine will. Thus Augustine's narrative can be read both as the creation of a modern self who establishes his coherent life story (a story, in this instance, of the supercession of self) and, paradoxically, as a premodern denial of the validity of such a creation. What survives for us is the literary genre, transvalued and secularized. Interestingly, modernist accounts of autobiography as the artificial construction of an integrated self against the background of the fragmented history of any actual life demand a return to a type of idealized time. The claim that autobiography must again dissolve into allegory testifies to the recent closure of an era marked by the normative figure of the autonomous individual.

Kindred ambiguities are discussed in the papers by Stephen Greenblatt and Natalie Zemon Davis. Opposing the view of Burckhardt, both stress that the moral passage toward individualism was fraught with conflict. Burckhardt had written that in the Middle Ages "man was conscious of himself only as a member of a race,

3

people, party, family, or corporation," whereas in the Renaissance "man became a spiritual *individual*, and recognized himself as such." Greenblatt shows, on the contrary, that the initial representations of individuality appearing in the interstices of the disintegrating medieval order cannot be recognized as figures of the mature cultural system of individualism. Rather, stabilized images of individuality were preceded by its representation in the prodigious and the perverse. The prodigy is the monstrous oddity, the individual in hyperbolic form, which calls the prior cultural order into question by exposing new possibilities. Its perverseness assaults the naturalness of preexisting classifications by drawing attention to their contingency. Fascination with the monstrous, excessive, and aberrant opened up the social space that was later to be organized by the norm of individuality. Especially for the prodigy, who longed for reabsorption into the community, this liminal phase in the cultural representation of the individual was violent and traumatic. Its conflicts reverberate, Greenblatt suggests, in the greatest tragedies written in our language.

For Davis, as well, the presentation of the self by women in sixteenth-century France, although undergoing experimentation and change, was not yet that "of a nineteenth-century individualist, testing himself against others and wholly self-determined." A normative ideal of self-expression and autonomy developed within an uncertain struggle with traditional religious obligations and patriarchical family relationships. Davis shows that the boundaries of the self were always redefined in relation to existing, collective institutions. The creation of identity was less a global phenomenon than a range of exploratory exercises within local semiotic fields. As is especially apparent from the study of women, the ongoing interplay between single persons and the collective institutions that circumscribed individuality points to two phenomena. First, individuality emerged within the constraints of local politics. Second, the discourse of individuality, with its greater applicability to the lives of men, has always been entwined with the social deployment of power.

The papers of J. B. Schneewind and Michael Fried describe a period in both moral philosophy and the fine arts when the figure of the autonomous, self-representing individual had become central to the cultural order. Mature individualism developed within the intellectual framework of a dualistic epistemology and was insti-

4

tutionalized in an increasingly elaborate network of economic, political, and legal structures. The language of individual self-representation was essentially a phenomenology of subjective experience. Descartes had postulated that each individual has a unique or privileged access to his or her own inner discourse—an access that could not legitimately be contradicted by any collective process or external authority. Inasmuch as the substantively grounded, theological foundations of prior normative orders had already been undermined in the early modern period, the validity of normative claims was relocated in the decentralized individual judgments emerging from this internal or subjective discourse. As an indeterminate number of possible lives across an open expanse of narratable time replaced the stasis of medieval hierarchy, so autonomy of choice and moral responsibility for self-initiated action replaced collectively defined status and social duty. Both moral and political authority were decollectivized and relocated in the personal projects of free individuals undertaken within the protected space created for them by the law.

Schneewind illustrates aspects of the mature discourse of individualism in terms of the Kantian transcendental subject. The creation of an institutional order consonant with the decentralization of authority presented a critical problem in the eighteenth century. The basic imagery of social contract presupposed that individual identity was not the product of some external order; rather, the experience of consciousness constituted the basis of social reality. The agreement of presocial, autonomous subjects to better their autarchic existences by cooperative interaction remains the ideological core of the contemporary Western political economy. However, it was perceived that fully individuated subjects, immersed in the particularities of their historical existences, would be unlikely to arrive at the reflective or generalized position required to originate just institutions. Man had to rise above his life history in order to achieve the dispassionate exercise of reason that full autonomy required. Kant's solution to this dilemma, the transcendent figure of the subject as a nonindividuated potential for self-actualization, still appears repeatedly in our most enshrined collective practices. Its current manifestations include the welfare-defining maximizer in economics, the democratic voter in politics, the socially mobile role selector in functionalist sociology, and the maturing moral actor in developmental psychology. Despite the criticisms that have

5

been directed at the ontological grounding and the political consequences of this individualist imagery, it continues to prevail in institutionalized culture.

Fried's study of Courbet's metaphysics emphasizes both the
epistemological split characteristic of classical individualism and
the conceptual tensions that increasingly destabilized these representations as they matured. Although Courbet's *oeuvre* focuses on
the self-representation of the individual artist, his realism was ori-
ented toward the portrayal of an objective natural world. Even as access to the normative was being fully decentralized, or transferred
to the inner discourse of the subject, there was an equal cultural
commitment to direct and collective access to the facts of empirical reality. An essential aspect of the individualist world view
was the belief that the objective domain was available to scientific
or logical representation. The province of public or collective knowledge, distinct from the private knowledge of the normative and
motivational spheres, was behavioral and mathematical. The conjunction of liberal individualism and technical accomplishment became evident in the growing use of economics, itself modeled on
thermodynamics, as the paradigm of valid method throughout the
social sciences and law. The determination of value preferences in
economics is individualized and therefore not susceptible to scientific analysis, since the normative power of economic conclusions
is derived from the subjective autonomy of the constituent actors.
Yet once these normative judgments are articulated in behavior, the
objective role of the technician is to analyze the aggregate data,
which alone legitimately define public welfare.

The concluding phase of Fried's interpretation alludes to some
later attempts, which Courbet's artistic practice anticipates, to resolve the dualist dilemma regarding qualitatively separate domains
of knowledge or being. On the one hand, certain radical phenomenologies of the early twentieth century suggested that the path to
reunification lay in the extension of the domain of spirit: "Should
we not then imagine nature, in this form, as an obscured consciousness and a dormant will? Habit thus gives us the living demonstration of this truth, that mechanism is not sufficient to itself: it is, so
to speak, only the fossilized residue of a spiritual activity." On the
other hand, the overcoming of dualism was also envisioned as a sit-
uating of the individual will within a more encompassing objectivity, such as that of the Freudian scenario to which Fried finally

6

assimilates Courbet's work. Schneewind echoes this second alternative when, pointing to the theoretical decline of mature individualism, he suggests that the commitment to an individualistic ethos is itself a social project open to substantive moral evaluation. The abandonment of an originary phenomenological discourse, whether achieved by asserting the validity of collective normative criteria or by elaborating structural accounts to reduce autonomy from an ontological state to an artifactual condition, marks a step toward more contemporary representations of individuality.

The modern crisis of individualism is an enormously complex historical phenomenon, which could be analyzed from various perspectives. For the purposes of this introduction, it can perhaps most fruitfully be approached in terms of theoretical developments in the human sciences. Since the late nineteenth century, theoretical work within these areas—one need only think of Marxist political economy, psychoanalysis, cultural anthropology, and Saussurian linguistics—has increasingly relied on models and methods incompatible with the fundamental terms of individualism. The internal logic of these structuralist (in a broad sense) arguments negates the normative power of autonomous individuality by reducing subjective consciousness to the artifact of a self-replicating, superpersonal mechanism. Accounts of conscious experience are denaturalized and shown to be determined by class, family, culture, and language. The papers of Nancy Chodorow, John Meyer, and James Clifford all reflect on the deep entrenchment of the structuralist paradigm in their respective fields and are principally concerned with a critical evaluation of what has become conceptual orthodoxy. In her treatment of the dissolution of character, Christine Brooke-Rose describes the workings of this structuralist paradigm within the domain of narrative fiction. The representation of the individual in modern and postmodern literature surrenders the wholeness of personality that had marked the narrative of autonomous lives; character becomes flattened or fragmented as it is reduced to an incarnation of the inanimate or of an idea. Drained of its distinctive substance, character returns as a ghost—a mannered replication of the premodern allegorical form left behind in the Renaissance. In this sense, the structuralist critique of the traditional referent—liberal society and its constituent individuals (characters)—leaves literature literally without a subject.

The privileging of objective discourses in the description of premodern societies emerged initially as an ideological aspect of modern individualism. In anthropological accounts of the primitive, especially in connection with the colonial administration of native social orders, to speak of a cultural determination of collective existence did not seem to intrude upon the norm of autonomy reserved for metropolitan societies. This discursive segregation of the premodern and the modern mirrored a representation of the passage from childhood to maturity that imagined the natural evolution of a full, free adult subject from a child in need of administration. In a like manner, the development of societies from the premodern to the contemporary would transfigure those describable as objective cultural orders to those composed by the agreement of autonomous individuals. However, the restriction of objectivist discourse to the account of the strange and exotic, as Clifford's discussion of Malinowski shows, proved a strategy of limited effect. As one moves from Frazer to Freud or from Lévy-Bruhl to Lévi-Strauss, the border between the archaic and the modern becomes increasingly porous.

The theoretical and literary attack on the autonomous subject has its counterpart in the social sphere, although here it is paradoxically the triumph of individualism that brings about the individual's demise. Incorporated within an administrative apparatus, classical individualism is transformed into a mass artifact institutionally produced and reproduced. John Meyer insists that, although liberal individualism began as a representation of the private or autonomous realm of the subject, this realm was gradually depleted as the liberal social order advanced. Increasingly, modern society is characterized by bureaucratic management of the economic and political behavior of replicable units. By the schooling of acceptable personalities and lives (careers) and by the technically efficient organization of work (Taylorism), choices (like sex and food) that started out as matters of private taste have become the objects and products of a discipline. Politically, the logic of the relation between state and society has been inverted. In the modern situation, it is a nexus of centralized authorities that manufactures reality and the populace which inhabits it. This is an exact reversal of the classical proposition that the subject, expressing his autonomy, constitutes the collective order. Recently, this administered form of individualism has expanded globally, supplanting indige-

8

nous modes of social organization. In the West, indeed throughout the world, the subject increasingly appears as the empty, ideological image of mass culture, the legitimating myth of an administrative discourse.

Of course, the ideological character of classical individualism was apparent early in the modern period. The removal of the philosophical and natural-law underpinnings that had supported the individualist ontology exposed the secularized subject of the mid-nineteenth century to conceptual assaults from various quarters. The notion of autonomy could no longer be made to fit the sense of determinism, the lack of effective control, that registered at the level of felt experience. Novelists from Flaubert on began to subvert and finally to abandon the paradigm of the coherent biographical narrative. Especially in the context of the widespread misery and lack of opportunity that followed the industrialization of Europe, to define the lives of the bulk of the population in a vocabulary that stressed free choice and moral responsibility seemed callous, a transparent political ploy. As the century progressed, there developed an intellectual revulsion at the vacuity of the dominant bourgeois culture. And not surprisingly the emergent positive sciences contributed their share to the destruction of the individualist self-understanding.

But the same period produced some compelling attempts at a refiguration of the individual, for which the names of Nietzsche and Conrad can be taken as emblematic, and which continue to the present day. Werner Hamacher stresses Nietzsche's aversion to the homogenizing or flattening potentialities implicit in the emergent discourse of the positive human sciences, which, in Nietzsche's words, "want nothing less—whether they admit it to themselves or not—than a fundamental transformation, indeed a weakening and cancellation of the individual: they do not tire of enumerating and accusing the evil and malignance, the wastefulness, the costliness, the extravagance of the previous form of individual being: they hope to administer more cheaply, less dangerously, more homogeneously, and more uniformly, when only large bodies and their limbs remain." Authentic individuality for Nietzsche took on an epistemological, discursive, and artistic character removed from its former ontological foundations. Individuality implied an "unaccountable surplus element of experience," a sort of willed prodigiousness that echoes the phenomena described by Greenblatt.

The individual assumes an impossible position on the far side of what is manageable and reproducible, in the interstices of objective knowledge.

Much of the intellectual history of the present century can be read in terms of a fundamental tension in the representation of the individual, a dismantling of the classical figure and a simultaneous effort to reconceive it. For structural analysts from various disciplines, the development of autonomous individuality has passed from its initial characterization as the telos of modernity to become the principal ideology of an illegitimate mass culture. For a time, systemized knowledge of the objective determinants of consciousness appeared to offer a theoretical bulwark against the ethical anarchy of radical subjectivism. As structures proliferated, however, their manifestly relative character drew attention to their production by individual analysts as well as to their role in a regime of knowledge and power. Thus, strategies emerged to relocate the experience of individuality in the indeterminacies left around the edges of competing structures. Of course, the sense of selfhood that appeared in these gaps could not assume the coherence and consistency of the classical representation; the claim of an unproblematic and substantial individuality is, in the modern period, inevitably an index of ideology. Nevertheless, a major theme of many of the conference papers is that the modern crisis of the individual involves not merely negation but also complex and often subtle efforts to reconceptualize the role of individual experience, choice, and initiative.

One theme that organizes many of these endeavors is the modern notion of authenticity. This theme is common to many domains, from psychoanalysis to social theory, and from existentialism to ethnography and literature; it is likewise a component in several modern political ideologies. Although its coloration and significance vary from one field to another, it inevitably revolves around an opposition between, on the one hand, the inauthentic life produced by the economic and administrative mechanisms of modern mass society and, on the other, the possibility of moral responsibility and autonomous choice that follows from an authentic appropriation of one's own existence. The problem, then, is to resolve the contradiction between structured determination and the potential for a free expression of self. Chodorow points out that twentieth-century psychoanalysis, especially in its more ego-oriented variants, postulated that analytical procedures could mediate the transformation to self-realization. In effect, this strategy imagines a temporal sequence moving from an initial, inauthentic prehistory characterized by the reproduction of structure toward the development of a capacity to experience selfhood as a progressive narrative. A similar temporal division of qualitatively distinct modes of existence was adopted in radical political theory, which viewed revolution as the transition point between the collective prehistory of class determination and the future domain of a liberated humanity. A second strategy for the differentiation of authentic and inauthentic forms of individuality involved limiting the realization of autonomy to an exceptional subset of persons. Authenticity is imagined to be possible by spatial segregation from the administered mass. This divorce between the potential for reformation and the actuality of the given, homogenizing order leads to a language of mass versus elite politics, whose ramifications are complex and troubling. To move beyond the administered mass, to overcome the condition of existences unaware of their own unmanageability, was a real possibility only for a small group and was therefore of limited social and political significance. Indeed, where exceptionality becomes a political creed it inevitably implies, as its collective support, mass manipulation. Paolo Valesio notes with regard to D'Annunzio and others that one moment in the origins of fascism was a connection to a poetics of heroic individuality. Fascism recast the mass from an impediment to individual action to a political object for the few who will their own destiny.

It would be difficult to claim that the strategies for differentiating authentic from inauthentic individualism provide a happy solution to the modern problem of reconceptualizing the individual. The contributions of Brooke-Rose, Clifford, and Martha Nussbaum all point toward a different strategy, likewise problematic, which approaches the problem of subjectivity and indeterminacy by assuming a consciously ironic stance toward individuality. Brooke-Rose argues that contemporary critics "steadily subverted what was left of the mimetic and expressive theories of literature, killing the referent in favor of the floating signifier, the author in favor of the reader, and the work in favor of textuality as an activity, an endless dissemination or even . . . a *jouissance* of infinite codes. Above all, they deconstructed the self into a disintegrating play of selves." Clifford describes a similar pluralized representation of self in the lives and works of Conrad and Malinowski. What begins to take shape is an unstable individuality, always circling among the alternative descriptions it deploys to reflect on its own condition. Subjectivity is experienced simultaneously as dependent on a cultural order and as an undetermined, productive instance. The individual is actor when observer and artifact when observed. It is a self in motion that makes use of the discourse of autonomous individuality in conjunction with an ongoing series of displacements of its position in order to reinterpret the history of its own behavior from continuously shifting vantage points. In an extreme form, this transitory self, which experiences a coherent sense of individuality and uniqueness as one of several competing but mutually vivid accounts of existence, may undergo a kind of intellectual vertigo. Nussbaum's alternation of romantic and platonic meditations upon love suggests a modernist representation of individuality as an unceasing journey through the possibilities of signification. Replacing ontology with discourse as the foundation of individuality yields, in its recursive logic, an ironic stance in which change threatens to collapse into mechanical repetition.

Although classical representations of autonomous individuality were able to bear the weight of a network of social institutions built upon them, it is unlikely that a fragile modernist individuality, weakened by the instability of its linguistic and epistemological foundations, can do so. Recently, a somewhat mannerist reaction to this tenuous situation has emerged, a reaction that reflects basic political concerns. If all representations, including individuality, are held to be fleeting figures in an open-ended game, aesthetic, moral, and intellectual standards appear threatened by cultural chaos. In such circumstances, the response is often to cling to the forms of the preexisting order—in this case, the autonomous individual—precisely because its substantive basis has disappeared. However well motivated, the revival of a discourse emphasizing intention, autonomy, and responsibility echoes the "jargon of authenticity" that Adorno perceived in the rhetoric of the existentialists. The fact is that, especially in America, the poststructuralist critique of individuality has had only a feeble impact on the persistently individualist imagery of our institutions and popular culture. In the political, economic, and artistic spheres of public life, these images have remained unshaken by the theoretical trauma that has led to the subtleties of poststructuralist theory. Nor are they likely to decompose because of *jouissance* in the academy. This is not to denigrate the importance of theoretical discourse or the validity of its diagnosis. It is only to point out that, since cultural disorder is not upon us, alarmist turns to mannerism are an inappropriate response to current conceptual dilemmas. Reactionary recreations of classical individual forms drastically simplify the present situation and thus are reabsorbed into the institutionalized representation of individualism in the West.

The contributions of Ian Hacking, Carol Gilligan, Stanley Cavell, and Niklas Luhmann illustrate the diversity of contemporary thinking about the status of the individual. Together they reveal that in all fields of humanistic study—from epistemology to the theory of moral development, from hermeneutics to sociology—the concept of individuality maintains both the centrality and the intractable complexity that have characterized its history. Although the first three of these presentations certainly do not fit into a single pattern, they do display a range of related concerns that might be characterized by the terms "local" and "political." The concept of the locality of practice is epitomized in Hacking's dictum: "I do not believe there is a general story to be told about making up people." As in the work of Foucault, the emphasis on "locality" bespeaks a general disillusionment with the political and theoretical implications of global or totalizing accounts of identity or other objects of study. Knowledge is no longer to be integrated into a comprehensive unity but rather is viewed as discontinuous and domain specific. Hacking describes the constitution of a social practice that creates new possibilities for being. These emergent categories or recategorizations do not determine identity; rather, they open up spaces where both autonomous development and varieties of control are possible. The set of descriptions of possible lives is always evolving, historically specific, and local. Gilligan also insists that identity is a collective product that is nonreproducible, or historically unique. This individuality is to be distinguished both from the timeless artifacts produced by structural mechanisms and from the individualist vision of singular lives autonomously generated. Individuality derives from the politics of interactive inclusions and exclusions. It is constituted within an ongoing process of differentiation in which we, in taking positions, clothe ourselves in personal attributes historically asso-

13

ciated with diverse locales. In this perspective, individuality is the outcome of collective controversy.

Cavell's paper recalls the importance in the American philosophical and literary tradition of a discourse attending to oddity and opposed to the disciplinary force of normalization. But the development of this local tradition now depends on the resituation of individuality within an evolutionary process that creates, and constantly recreates, intelligibility and sense. Individuality, the stance of self-reliance, is attained only by a discursive interaction that returns to language and history what language and history have given one. In this view, authorship is not absolute creation but rather an interplay of appropriation and rendering intelligible in which we mean more than we say, in which thought, by our very engagement with the words we write and read, takes place in us. Luhmann would agree that the substance of individual identities is defined interactively in local, historically specific systems. Accounts of the individuality of individuals, like that of the individuality of individualism, do not begin in the logic of structural orders but in the evolution of cultural and political practices. However, Luhmann also seeks to clarify the formal theoretical conditions that permit the question of individuality to emerge. Referring to work in contemporary biology and artificial intelligence, he suggests that individuality is not an ontological category but a standpoint or locale within an architecture of complex systems of information. Descriptions of phenomena like consciousness and autonomy are no less real or valid than objective explanations that purport to reduce them to the status of artifacts. Both constitute discrete perspectives by which we can examine the multiple levels of possible representations that allow information to be organized as meaningful.

Individuality is a formal expression in which an element of a more comprehensive system reflexively imagines its particular, indeterminate trajectory within the system. Luhmann's understanding of subjectivity bridges the orthodox dualism between natural and human science because this type of account is not logically restricted to our level of representation. Each neuron, cell, species, or suprahuman unit of a still more multilevel system would speak about itself as an individual had we access to its reflexive descriptions. But such a depriveleging of the traditional representation of individuality does not devalue the experience of subjectivity. The local standpoint it describes is *our* standpoint as human beings. At

14

the volume's close the figure of the individual has not been discredited or dissolved so much as displaced and transposed. Resituated in a field of images that call attention to the discontinuous, evolutionary, and dissipative character of all patterns of signification, contemporary thought continues to offer a rich and diverse topography for individuals to explore.

Autobiography and Narrative

JOHN FRECCERO

The great nineteenth-century medievalists were not famous for their literary sensitivity. Perhaps the most famous anecdote illustrating the point is told about Gaston Paris, who ridiculed the legend about how the unicorn is attracted by the milk from a virgin's breast: with impeccable positivist logic, he pointed out that, as everyone knows, virgins do not lactate. Such remarks would seem to deserve the description Henri Marrou gave Jeanroy's work on the troubadours—the most exacting science applied to an object that the investigator has not yet located.

St. Augustine is an object that has been particularly hard to locate, precisely because he may be said to be the first subject. His work therefore belongs as much to the twentieth century as to the fifth and does not easily lend itself to the empirical analysis to which troubadours and unicorns have been subjected. St. Augustine is as important in the study of modern literature as he is for the study of Western Christendom. His relevance to a conference entitled "Reconstructing Individualism" is that his *Confessions* presents for the first time the literary self-creation of an individual seen both as object and as subject, with all of the contradictions that those aspects imply. If in Nietzschean terms individuality is achieved only by its own destruction, then it may be said that Augustine's is the paradigm for all such achievement, inasmuch as conversion, the theme of the *Confessions*, was theologically defined as the destruction of a former self. Whatever the psychological bases for the theological claim, in this paper I shall try to show that this theme is inherent in the autobiographical genre, which, when it claims to be true, definitive, and concluded, implies the

16

death of the self as character and the resurrection of the self as author. In theological terms, conversion is the separation of the self as sinner from the self as saint; but in logical, or narratological, terms, this separation founds the possibility of any self-portraiture, a separation between the self as object and the self as subject when the two are claimed to be the same person.

When Pierre Courcelle assembled his repertoire of the posterity of the *Confessions,* ending with André Gide, one of the effects was doubtless to show modernists how scholarly light could be shed on a field usually explored only by critics and other dilettantes. A curious effect of Courcelle's book, one he perhaps did not intend, is that it reveals the influence of the *Confessions* to have been greater in the Renaissance and in the modern period than in the Middle Ages. Themes and influential passages from that great work were cited continually throughout the Middle Ages, of course, but it was always *Magister Augustinus* who was cited; not until Petrarch did it occur to anyone to take the bishop of Hippo as a literary role model. If the modern era may be said to begin with the Petrarchan cult of personality, when Cicero and Virgil ceased being *auctores* and became pen pals, then it may be said that the *Confessions* came to be regarded only in the modern era for what it is: not simply the life of a saint, but also the paradigm for all representations of the self in a retrospective literary structure. This monument of Western Christianity paradoxically achieved its literary significance at the beginning of a distinctly more secular age.

What was thematized in Christianity as the conversion of the sinner into the saint who tells his story may be thematized in a modern narrative in a variety of ways that need have very little to do with the Christian experience. The essential paradigm is unchanged, for it springs from the formal exigencies of telling one's life story rather than from any explicit experience. To state the matter hyperbolically, we might say that every narrative of the self is the story of a conversion or, to put the matter the other way around, a conversion is only a conversion when it is expressed in a narrative form that establishes a separation between the self as character and the self as author. When he told his life story in terms of a conversion from paganism to Christianity, Augustine was at the same time establishing a literary genre, the confession, or narrative of the self.

One reader who found Augustine's conversion difficult to understand was at the same time one of his most assiduous followers. St. Teresa of Avila mentions no other author in her autobiography. Having been given the book to read by her confessor, she is genuinely stirred by some of the ecstatic passages in the narration. Nevertheless, she feels a certain frustration, wondering how someone could have been such a terrible sinner, then seen the light, never to sin again, whereas her own life seems a perpetual series of ups and downs. In her own quest for sanctity she seems disheartened by what she takes to be episodes of backsliding.

If we think of other and later memoirs of saints, particularly in the Renaissance, we too will be struck by the definitiveness of Augustine's conversion. He does list in Book 9 some of the temptations to which he remains subject, but these are not sins properly speaking. There is of course no reason for the bishop to recount every peccadillo—his confession is meant more as witness, which is one of the senses of the word, than as confession in the sacramental sense. But my point here is not the sincerity but the completeness of the story, the starkly definitive crisis that conversion seems to represent.

In order to suggest that this is not a small point, I should like to mention that the contrast between the linear conversion story of Augustine and the fragmentary, dispersed account of Teresa's life may correspond to a distinction that some have made between life stories told by men and those told by women. Male versions seem to be linear, conflictual, and, in a word, oedipal, marked by a struggle for separation. Female versions seem less obsessed with separation and struggle, less linear and more global in their recounting of a life story.

Whatever the value of such a distinction, a question that I have no grounds or competence to decide, it does seem that, historically, in religious memoirs crisis conversions are a male genre—perhaps because the opportunity for sinful behavior, like other opportunity, has traditionally been greater for men. One of the greatest narratives in the Augustinian tradition by a woman, the *Golden Notebook* by Doris Lessing, seems a deliberate refutation of the Augustinian pretense of writing a definitive life story—the red notebook and the black notebook are partial views of the definitive golden notebook that, by implication, can never be completed short of death. Lessing seems to represent as gender specific this view of the writer's attempt to capture her life.

18

It may be, however, genre specific: Augustine may also be considered the first to have written a story of oedipal separation that resembles the myth of male coming of age. Just as a conversion narrative suggests a separation between the sinner and the saint who tells his story, and as any story of the self implies a separation between the self as protagonist and the self as narrator, so the myth of male maturation is represented as a separation from the parents, which is to say, the separation of a nondifferentiated self from the self that thereby gains an irreducible identity. This pattern, named after Oedipus since Freud, also finds expression, perhaps its first narrative expression, in the *Confessions*. Whatever else is recounted in that story, its plot is clearly oedipal: a struggle to reject the "father of the flesh," as Monica refers to her husband, in favor of the true father and an authentic identity. The basis of the struggle is also clearly sexual, played out in symbolic terms, marking the evolution of the mother from obscure object of desire to frail human being, with all of the faults of any other.

In Augustine's story, the separation of the self from the self is undeniably the central theme; my remarks thus far have interpreted that theme both theologically and psychosexually. The instrumental use of literature would permit either reading: a theological or traditional interpretation, or a Freudian or Eriksonian explanation of the theme. My purpose here, however, is to privilege narrative form in order to show that the autobiographical structure demands this separation, regardless of how theologians, sociologists, or psychologists may use that literary exigency.

The contribution of narrative form to the phenomenology of conversion or maturation becomes apparent when we contrast St. Teresa's observation of her conflicting moments of sin and sanctity with the strict linearity of Augustine's crisis. If we were trading observations about the psychology of everyday living we would probably have to admit that conflicting states of consciousness are what we in fact experience—the "yes" and "no" of what romantic theorists described as "ironic consciousness"—and so we find the Spanish mystic's account of her inner life more true to real life. There is probably no escape from these conflicts in real life, but in literature there does seem to be a way to transform discontinuous moments into linear trajectory: by taking one moment of contradiction and transforming it into a narrative, from *Augustinus* to *alter Augustinus*, so that alternating atemporal moments are transformed into a single temporal sequence and the observing self is segregated from the observed, with which in real life it is constantly confused. In the terms of a now-classic article by Paul de Man, this is the transformation of irony into allegory, the creation of ideal narrative time.[1] We learn in Book 11 of the *Confessions* that time is an extension of the self, just as a literary text is a spatial extension of time; it would not be too bold, perhaps, to turn Augustine's formula around and suggest that the self, the individual, is an extension of inner conflict into an idealized, narrative time.

The literary representation of the self that originates with St. Augustine implies conversion as a logical precondition for the coherence of such a story. The representation of the self in confessional literature involves a reduplication of the self, a separation between the self that was, whose story is narrated, and the self that is, who narrates the story. When the story pretends to be true, definitive, and concluded, it implies simultaneously a continuity between the narrator and the protagonist, so that the intimate details of the story may be known, and a discontinuity, providing an Archimedean point from which the story of that former self may be judged with apparent objectivity and detachment. Any autobiography rests on this logical contradiction. The Pauline doctrine of conversion as a death and resurrection provides a thematic basis for an otherwise-absurd pretense: the story of one's life is definitively concluded, yet one survives to tell the tale. Conversion is therefore not only the subject matter of confession but also the premise that makes the telling of such a story possible. Like the legendary drowning man who sees his whole life panoramically, the storyteller pretends somehow to have survived his own death.

At the same time, the idea of conversion is inconceivable without its narrative expression, the testament that gives an at least rhetorical answer to the question of Nicodemus in the Gospels (John 3:4): "How can a man enter into his mother's womb and be born again?" When the subject is the self, then a retrospective literary structure, with its formally imposed closure, provides a simulacrum of death in its ending and a simulacrum of survival in its very existence. The phenomenon of conversion can be adequately represented as definitive only by extending what may be simply a moment of self-consciousness into a temporal sequence, which is to say, into narrative form, in which the observing self is separated from the observed.

There are, of course, many wry variations on the allegory of the self in modern literature, and all of them depend on the lack of verisimilitude of linear narrative. For example, the arbitrary ending that places an indeterminate time between living the story and telling it, as in Jean-Paul Sartre's *The Words* or in James Joyce's *Portrait of the Artist as a Young Man*, where the qualifying phrase might almost be underscored in order to make a fictive assertion of authenticity. Again, the absurdity may be thematized by infinite regression, as in Gide's *Counterfeiters* (a novel that calls forth a journal and then the journal of the journal), or by alternate versions of a life story, as in Doris Lessing's *Golden Notebook*. Finally, aesthetic distance may be substituted for spiritual distance in the secularized form of conversion exemplified by Proust's *Remembrance of Things Past*. All of these may be said to be attempts to borrow the structure of conversion narrative or to reveal its impossibility while avoiding its theological theme.

Such a borrowing marks the beginning of irreducible individuality in literary self-portraiture. Petrarch, for example, arguably the most influential poet in the history of European literature and an assiduous Augustinian, based his self-proclaimed uniqueness on a reading of the *Confessions*, turning Augustine against himself, making sin the principle of individuation. The historical fact is that Augustine the sinner, radically other in his own terms—*alter Augustinus*—turned out to be far more fascinating than the disembodied episcopal voice that judged him so severely.

It is in the nature of the narrator's role to be without individuality—"Call me Ishmael," as Melville put it. From the standpoint of the theme of conversion, nothing further can happen to the person who has faced death and survived. The sinner, however, has historicity. All that happens in a confession has happened to the sinner; as every reader of Dante knows, the truly interesting people are in hell. Similarly, Petrarch's portrait of himself as sinner is essential for his characterizing himself as unique. By the time the genre reaches Rousseau and uniqueness seems more and more elusive, the claim to sinfulness requires virtuoso efforts. This turning-around of Augustine's avowed purpose marks the origin of what might be called the hagiography of the sinner. Because saints are meant to represent the image of God, they all look pretty much alike.

Saints are dull, however, also because in conversion stories they must function as narrators. Every quality attributed to a narrator transforms that function into a character or a persona. The author is a pure function and is discovered only when all qualities are refined away. One is reminded of Chaucer's straight-man narrator of *Troilus and Criseyde* copying out the story that he finds written in his author, Lollius. To arrive at Chaucer through that series of reduplications would require further ironization of the narrator until his only characteristic would be writing. When the story is autobiography, this progressive attenuation of the storytelling function to pure writing is thematized to represent an authorial self without individuality.

If we were to translate the struggle between author and character, saint and sinner, into modern terms, it might recall a dialectic of consciousness, the self aware of itself, sometimes as totally other. In the field of rhetoric, as Paul de Man has shown, the same separation is characteristic of the figure of irony, a turning back or away from normal signifying processes. What is characteristic of these processes, according to de Man, is that they are endlessly repeated and seem to provide for no escape. The same may be said for Augustine's analysis of conversion and aversion: since the process of turning to God in this life is endless, it is constantly in danger of blockage. No story of the self can be built on such a threat. If, however, the two moments were placed in temporal sequence, aversion from the self and conversion to God, so that in a single turning the reified self led to the self as sign, it would then be possible to transform irony into allegory, specularity into linearity, and the story could be told.

This is in fact what happens in the *Confessions*. Two specular moments are juxtaposed, and an arbitrary period of time is said to separate them: the first is the theft of pears in a nearby orchard; the second is the conversion proper, which takes place under a fig tree in a garden in Milan.

The theft of the pears in Book 2 of the *Confessions* is perhaps the most memorable moment of Augustine's early life and has become part of the standard repertoire of autobiographical narration. Not only is Rousseau's theft of a piece of ribbon in his *Confessions* obviously modeled on this incident, but so are incidents recounted in far less Augustinian stories, as, for instance, the theft of apples in the autobiography of Charles Darwin. What all of these incidents have in common is the relative unimportance of the object stolen and the gratuitousness of the act. The pears in Augustine's story were misshapen, he was not hungry, and he had far better pears at home: "But it was not the pears that my unhappy soul desired. I had plenty of my own, better than those, and I only picked them that I might steal. For no sooner had I picked them than I threw them away, and tasted nothing in them but my own sin, which I relished and enjoyed. If any part of one of those pears passed my lips, it was the sin that gave it flavor."[2] The extraordinary fact about this incident is that Augustine goes on for pages analyzing it, whereas he seems to treat much more briefly several far more serious sins in his life that, even by contemporary standards, should have provoked considerably more guilt or at least more space. For example, he mentions in a few lines his casting-off of a common-law wife with whom he had lived for many years and by whom he had had a child. He abandoned her and took her child, and whereas she went back to Africa swearing she would never know another man, he waited barely two months before he took another mistress.

Even Jean-Jacques Rousseau may have been shocked by the disproportionate amount of time Augustine spends on pears as compared to the paragraph he grants to his treachery. In Rousseau's *Confessions* scholars seem not to have noticed that the two Augustinian episodes are conflated: Jean-Jacques steals the ribbon to give to the servant girl under circumstances in which only she or he could be suspected of the crime. When he is publicly accused, he falsely accuses her, knowing she will be sent back home in terrible disgrace. Although, as de Man has suggested, he reflects on her pain and his guilt with considerable relish, he has at least managed to elevate petty thievery to the rank of a monstrous deed. By contrast, Augustine seems scrupulous over a peccadillo and callous about a crime.

From the standpoint of apologetics, it is easy enough to see why Augustine concentrates on such a minor incident: the purpose of confession in his day was almost diametrically opposed to Rousseau's. Presumably anyone could be guilty of adolescent willfulness as Augustine describes it; the theft of the pears establishes a certain solidarity between him and his readers and provides a control for analyzing sin at its most elementary level. Jean-Jacques's crime, although also petty larceny, is a *tour de force* of evil. The implication is that not even in his wildest imagination could a reader forge such an injustice out of such trivial material.

The two stories also have in common the public nature of the theft: Jean-Jacques is surrounded by the members of the household when he is accused of the crime, and he says that, had he been alone with the father, he would not have lied about his responsibility. Shame paradoxically induced him to compound his guilt. In a different vein, Augustine also attributes his act to shame before his companions, who might have thought him cowardly if he had not gone forward with the theft: "Alone, I would not have done it." The voices of his companions seduce him into the otherwise-unmotivated theft so that he may prove himself.

The real motivation for Augustine's apparently gratuitous act is his desire to be God-like: "All who desert you and set themselves up against you merely copy you in a perverse way" (2.6; p. 50). Herein lies the importance of the gratuitous nature of the theft: to have a motive is to be in need and therefore to be contingent. The appropriation of the pears is a self-appropriation, an illicit assertion of one's selfhood and one's autonomy. At the same time, this is the essence of all sin. The context of the episode makes it clear that the pears might be metonymically replaced with any other object of desire and its structure would be the same: sex for the adolescent, riches and ambition for the adult, all are conversions to the self. A passage from *On the Trinity* presses the analogy between any human action, for good or ill, and the inner life of the Trinity, inasmuch as both generate a word, defined as the union of knowledge and love: "Now a word is born, when, being thought out, it pleases us to the effect either of sinning or of doing right. Therefore love, as it were a mean, conjoins our word and the mind from which it is conceived, and without any confusion binds itself as a third with them, in an incorporeal embrace."[3] The word of sin is averted from God and directed toward materiality in a parody of power, "like a slave," says Augustine, "who ran away from his master and chased a shadow instead" (2.6; p. 50).

There is a sexual overtone in the theft of the pears that is never made explicit. It derives from the fact that the episode is virtually contemporaneous in the narrative with Augustine's sexual coming of age: "The brambles of lust grew high above my head and there was no one to root them out, certainly not my father. One day at the public baths he saw the signs of active virility coming to life in me and this was enough to make him relish the thought of having grandchildren." (2.3; p. 45.) Fortunately, from the standpoint of the narrative, even Monica stays her hand: "For even my mother . . . did not act upon what she heard about me from her husband with the same earnestness as she had advised me about chastity. She saw that I was already infected with a disease that would become dangerous later on, but if the growth of my passions could not be cut back to the quick, she did not think it right to restrict them to the bounds of married love." (2.3; p. 46.) The phallic associations were doubtless as obvious to the author as they are to us, so that it seems ponderous to insist on the threat of castration manqué suggested in that passage. For the moment, it is enough to say that the assertion of selfhood by shaking down and carrying off the pears and the suggestion of nascent sexuality are contiguous in this text, whereas theft and adolescent sexuality are conflated in Rousseau.

If there is a suggestion of sexuality hovering about the pear tree, there is more than a suggestion of maternity associated with the fig tree. In Book 3, Augustine makes fun of some Manichean beliefs that he once shared: "I was gradually led to believe such nonsense as that a fig wept when it was plucked, and that the tree which bore it shed tears of mother's milk. But if some sanctified member of the sect were to eat the fig—someone else, of course, would have committed the sin of plucking it—he would digest it and breathe it out in the form of angels." (3.10; p. 67.) Immediately following this passage, Augustine returns to the subject of his mother, precisely to her tears: "You . . . rescued my soul from darkness because my mother, your most faithful servant, wept to you for me, shedding more tears for my spiritual death than other mothers shed for the bodily death of a son. . . . You heard her and did not despise the tears which streamed down and watered the earth in every place where she had bowed her head in prayer." (3.11; p. 68.) The episode of the fig tree itself, in Book 8, is preceded by a series of female apparitions. First, Augustine's former mistresses pluck at the "garment of [his] flesh" and ask, "Are you going to dismiss us? . . . Will you no longer be allowed to do *hoc et illud?*" They keep plucking at his back, trying to make him turn his head although he wishes to go forward. Habit then asks, "Do you think you can live without these things?" Finally Lady Continence appears, beckoning him: "She stretched out loving hands to embrace me, holding up a host of good examples to my sight. With her were countless boys and girls, great numbers of the young and people of all ages, staid widows and women still virgins in old age. In their midst was Continence herself, not barren but a fruitful mother of children . . . saying, 'Can you not do what these men and these women do?'" (8.77; p. 176.) Reinforcing the association of Continence and the tree is the fact that the catalogue of innocents in the arms of Continence is strongly reminiscent of a Virgilian simile in Book 6 of the *Aeneid* comparing generations of men and women to leaves.

Amid the head-high brambles of lust, Augustine was called to the pear tree by a band of roughnecks: "Come on, let's do it!" He is summoned to the fig tree by the voices of children, perhaps from a nearby house, calling, "*Tolle, lege*"—"Take it and read." He wonders whether children ever say such words in their games, and not being able to recall ever having heard such words before, he interprets them as a command to take up the Bible and to read the passage that leads to his conversion. He reads the book because he remembers hearing the story of St. Anthony, who was converted when he heard the Gospel. The interpretive process does not stop here, however, for he passes the book to his friend Alypius, who reads on and is also converted. That touch has the effect of extending the trajectory of the reading proleptically to us, the readers of a text about someone who was interpreted by a text after someone was interpreted by a text in a regress that for Augustine goes back to the Gospels. Finally, Book 8 ends when the two friends go back to tell an overjoyed Monica about their experience, and she is pleased more than she could have been by grandchildren begotten by the flesh.

The insistence upon the fruitfulness of Lady Continence and the mention of the conversion as the spiritual equivalent of Monica's grandchildren marks the end of Augustine's sexual identity and the beginning of the narrator's ideal existence. In Augustine's terms, it marks the turning around of the inner word from the creature to the Creator, for the fruit of the tree are like words: "The words of scripture are a leafy orchard, where some see hidden fruit. They fly about in joy like birds, breaking into song as they gaze at the fruit and feed upon it." (13.20; p. 328.)

It is tempting to read the *Confessions* as an oedipal drama, in which the "father of the flesh," as Monica referred to her husband, is at last defeated and replaced by his son. The narrative even provides a godfather in the person of St. Ambrose, ready to play the

26

part of Creon in order to make the drama complete. The psyche thereby revealed, however, would not be that of St. Augustine the individual but rather that of Latin Christianity. Augustine's father, still a pagan, is rejected as Rome is rejected in favor of Mother Church. Ambrose the bishop is at once spiritual godfather and spiritual husband of the Church. The roles for the drama had been established by Scripture; if the *Confessions* are oedipal in structure, then so is the *City of God*.

The same may be said for the psychosexual drama of the two trees, for they are clearly allegorical: for all of the dramatic realism that seems to be conveyed by the incident of the theft of the pears, there are several suggestions in the text that the pear tree is meant to be the Tree of the Knowledge of Good and Evil. Not only are the pears referred to as *poma*, the Vulgate's generic word for fruit in the Garden of Eden, but the themes of hiding and temptation are prominent as well. Augustine's description of his relationship with his mistress also recalls Genesis, for when she is torn away from him, it is as if he has lost his rib: "The woman with whom I have been living was torn from my side . . . and this was a wound which left my heart bleeding." Finally, even the highly suspicious allusion to castration can be subsumed under the authority of Christ's words in the Gospel of Matthew, cited by Augustine immediately before the anecdote about the onset of adolescence. The text of the Gospel (Matt. 19:12) is as follows: "For there are some eunuchs which were so born from their mother's womb: and there are some eunuchs which were made eunuchs by men: and there be eunuchs which have made themselves eunuchs for the kingdom of heaven's sake."

A similar series of allusions surrounds the episode of the fig tree in Book 8. The fig tree represents the ultimate aspiration of the Jews in the Old Testament. The prophet Micah looks forward to the day when "he shall sit every man under his vine and under his fig tree" (Mic. 4:4). Undoubtedly the writer of the Gospel of John had this in mind when he began his narration with a calling-forth of Nathanael the Jew, who had been sleeping under the fig tree (John 1:45–48). Philip summons him to Jesus: "We have found him of whom Moses and the prophets did write, Jesus of Nazareth, the son of Joseph." Nathanael answers with what is probably the only joke in the Gospel of John—"Can anything good come out of Nazareth?"— but goes to Jesus, who says, "Before Philip called you, when you were under the fig tree, I saw you." The episode is traditionally read as the vocation of the Jews to begin the struggle again where the Old Testament had left off.

Genesis and John were the two portions of the Bible upon which St. Augustine commented most often and on which he became the interpretive authority. They were linked, as far as he was concerned, by their tracing of the history of the word. Genesis begins, "In the beginning God created heaven and earth"; the Gospel of John begins, "In the beginning was the Word." For him, these were equivalent statements that summed up the rationale of all of history, a movement from the uncreated word before time to the incarnation, the word made flesh. Readers of the *Confessions* will remember that the book ends with a reprise of this favorite theme.

If I am correct in my identification of the pear tree and the fig, then they are nothing less than the poles of human history, from the interdiction in the beginning to the conversion at the end. Far from being simply anecdotes drawn from an irreducibly individual human life, they are intended as the embodiments in Augustine's life of the pattern of the Redemption. Furthermore, if my hypothesis is correct, then this reading may help to explain what the autobiographical books of the *Confessions* have to do with the exegetical books that close the work, dedicated to an understanding of the words "In the beginning God created heaven and earth." It is as if the historical Augustine had been refined away by his conversion and had become the commentator on the very structure that retrospectively seemed to be the principle of his own life's organization. In other words, the conversion marks the transformation of autobiography into biblical allegory.

I have spoken of the transformation of ironic impasse into allegorical temporality at the level of autobiography and of universal history. What binds these together is the very nature of narration, the fact that a sentence, a life, or a book must have an ending. In an extraordinary passage in Book 11, in the midst of a discussion on the nature of time, Augustine makes a poem the paradigm of understanding linearity and separation in all of the realms we have been discussing. We may extend his observation in a thoroughly secular way by suggesting that his own idealized self-portraiture is a result of its presentation in narrative form. The *Confessions* remains the exemplary autobiography because it makes coextensive the book and the life that the book was meant to illustrate. Theme and form are one. The important implication for this conference is that individualism, with all its contradictions, is inconceivable, in the Augustinian tradition, without its literary expression. This is the meaning that subsequent generations of writers took from Augustine's work, long after they had rejected what he considered to be its substance.

Fiction and Friction

STEPHEN GREENBLATT

In 1601 in a small town near Rouen, a 32-year-old widowed mother of two, Jeane le Febvre, had a very odd experience. For nearly five weeks she had been sharing her bed (not at all an odd experience) with a fellow servant named Marie le Marcis, a woman in her early twenties who was recuperating from a long illness. Then one evening, while they were doing the laundry together, Marie whispered that she was in fact a man—a claim she (or rather he) graphically demonstrated—and precipitously proposed marriage. Jeane at first refused, but during the following weeks the two fell in love.

The couple did not intend to keep their relationship clandestine; they wished to get their parents' permission and have a proper wedding, sanctified by the church. Indeed, despite the wildly irregular circumstances in which they found themselves, they seem to have been immediately caught up in the ordinary social problems and strategies that attended marriage negotiations in the Renaissance. Jeane had been raised in the Reformed faith; Marie, though he had been converted to that faith by an employer, wished now to return, as his mother had long been urging, to the Catholic Church. Jeane agreed to join him. We may assume that Marie's parents were gratified, but there is no record of their reaction, nor is there, oddly enough, any record of their reaction to the revelation that their daughter was a son. We are told, however, that they strenuously objected to his decision to marry a penniless widow with two small children. The dutiful son consented not to see Jeane, but, finding the separation unendurable, he returned to his beloved's bed. There,

30

after making vows to one another, they consummated their passion—three or four times, we are told, on the first night alone.

Not content with secret pleasures, Marie and Jeane were steadfast in their desire for the public confirmation of a recognized marriage. But to achieve this confirmation, of course, Marie needed to acquire a new sexual identity in the eyes of the community; he had been baptized, named, dressed, and brought up as a girl. His was a personal and pressing instance of the need to reconstruct individualism, or rather, since individualism did not yet exist, to reconstruct an individual identity that was at the same time an inescapably social identity. To accomplish this, he changed his clothing, asked that he be called Marin le Marcis, and publicly declared his matrimonial intentions. Not surprisingly (though the lovers themselves, preoccupied perhaps with the drama of parental disapproval, appear to have been surprised), there was an immediate public scandal; the two were arrested, tried, and condemned, Marin to be burned alive, Jeane to watch the execution, then to be beaten and banished from Normandy. (After an appeal for mercy, the sentence was humanely moderated: Marin was only to be strangled to death; Jeane merely to be whipped.) The crime of which they were convicted was sodomy, for both the wife and the mother of the man in whose household the couple had served testified that Marie le Marcis had regularly had her menstrual period (*ses purgations naturelles*),[1] and a medical examination revealed no signs of masculinity. The accused maintained that terror at imprisonment had caused his penis to retract, but the court dismissed his claim. Marie, it was charged, was not a man but a *tribade*—a homosexual seductress who had, with her unnaturally enlarged clitoris, abused the all-too-willing Jeane.

Marin appealed his conviction to the Parlement of Rouen, which appointed a panel of doctors, surgeons, and midwives to renew the medical examination. One of the doctors, Jacques Duval, had a learned interest in hermaphroditism, to which he saw this case as allied, and consequently he pursued the examination much farther than his colleagues. Where they were willing only to stay on the surface, Duval was determined to probe within, recalling, as he later wrote in a book inspired by the case, that Aristotle had reproached philosophers who foolishly held themselves aloof from things vulgarly thought to be indecent. Duval's determination was

31

rewarded: responding to his finger's pressure was "a male organ, rather large and hard" (p. 403). A second examination left no doubt, for the friction of the doctor's touch caused Marin to ejaculate; the semen, he reports, was not thin and watery like a woman's but, like a man's, thick and white (pp. 404–5). Medical authority had masturbated Marin's identity into existence.

On the strength of Duval's expert testimony (with which the rest of the medical panel did not concur), the lovers' conviction was overturned. Marin and Jeane were released. The court evidently remained guardedly skeptical about his claim: Marin was ordered to wear women's clothes until he reached the age of 25 and was forbidden, on pain of death, to have sexual relations during this period with members of either sex. What would happen thereafter— whether Marin would be allowed to marry Jeane or be forced to remain Marie—the court left undecided. Perhaps, like me, the judges hadn't the vaguest idea what Marin's sex really was.[2] They did not, in any case, feel certain enough to let him either marry or burn. We should be grateful, I suppose, that they let him live.

This cheerfully grotesque story and the long book in which it is recounted, Duval's *On Hermaphrodites, Childbirth, and the Medical Treatment of Mothers and Children*, may serve at once to advance and to complicate an inquiry into the origins of individualism. Such an inquiry has traditionally been rendered difficult by the overpowering presence of individualism itself. Though the term "individualism" is relatively recent, a nineteenth-century coinage, the existence of individuals has long seemed to be a constitutive, universal element in the natural structure of human experience and hence more the basis than the object of historical investigation. But the belatedness of the general term for the phenomenon of individuals should make us wary of assuming the stable existence of individualism as a category of human life; we may note the presence of distinct individuals in every historical society, but we may not at all find a corresponding concept of individualism, even in latent or half-conscious form. Such a concept would at a minimum entail what we may call a principle of entitlement: a sense that each person, however bound up by the surrounding codes governing behavior, however fashioned internally by the spoken and unspoken laws of feeling, perception, and action, is nonetheless unique and entitled to that uniqueness.

Within the broad doctrine of a legitimated uniqueness, there may then be sharply divergent accounts of the origin and development of each embodiment of the principle. The individual may be seen as the initial and natural condition of humankind, so that societies are constructed out of large numbers of distinct monads. Let us call this account genetic individualism. Alternatively, the individual may be seen as a cultural product, the result of a prolonged paideia or exercise of differentiation. Let us call this account teleological individualism. Both genetic and teleological individualism require a theory of protection, a mode of securing the entitlement. The genetic account tends to appeal to nature; that is, the individual is protected by being a constitutive part of the order of things. When pressed, this account appeals to a metaphysical principle: the natural order of things itself embodies a divine plan for the salvation of individual souls. The teleological account tends to appeal to law; that is, any society, however rudimentary, develops rules that foster and protect the emergence of individuals. When pressed, it appeals to language: the rules that govern the emergence of individuals are as basic and unavoidable as those that allow for the acquisition and transmission of language. We should add that these accounts are often blended together, as in the familiar theory that individuation is a birthright, a portion of which is ceded in exchange for a social protection that safeguards individuation.

As the title of this volume wittily suggests, individualism has in recent years been at least partially deconstructed. Even though we still inhabit a moral and psychological system based upon our legitimate existence as individuals, that existence has come to seem strange—as if the very basis of our idea of nature were itself revealed to be a cunningly wrought artifice, or as if our property rights to ourselves had been called into question, or as if the male "I" in our society were incommensurate with the female "I," or as if the goal of social life could no longer be trusted to be the protection of individuals. "Since the history of the individual," writes Bourdieu, "is never anything other than a certain specification of the collective history of his group or class, *each individual system of dispositions* may be seen as a *structural variant* of all the other group or class habitus." In such an account, the individual is merely the trace of a class trajectory, and the experience of uniqueness, "personal" style, "is never more than a *deviation* in relation to the *style* of a period or class so that it relates back to the common style not only by its conformity . . . but also by the difference which

33

makes the whole 'manner.'"[3] Even deviation, then, is revealed to be a collective strategy, and the individual as origin or goal virtually vanishes.

Now that the ideology of individualism has become so suspect, our attention has been redirected to social structures, of which the individual is merely a variant: to kinship patterns, economic systems, political institutions, cultural networks. Further, and more pertinent to the concerns of this book, attention has been displaced from the individual to what we may call the individual effect. That is, we have a heightened interest in the historically contingent categories by which our sense of individuation is constituted and a consequent concern with those moments when individuals appear to be in the process of disintegration or production, moments when we can historicize what Shakespeare calls "great creating nature"— the timeless and universal principle of generativity. Empowered by this interest we can understand a text like Duval's not as bizarre static on the margins of normative individualism—sexless, colorless, and above all cultureless—but as part of the particular and contingent discourse out of which individuals in a specific historical period were constructed.

On Hermaphrodites participates in a larger field of sexual discourse that in the early modern period included marriage manuals, medical, theological, and legal texts, sermons, indictments and defenses of women, and literary fictions. Any one text in this field is rarely of decisive importance (for even the strongest tradition generates countertraditions), but taken as a whole a culture's sexual discourse plays a critical role in shaping individuality. It does so by helping to implant in each person an internalized set of dispositions and orientations that governs individual improvisations. In any given life-experience it is the quality of the particular improvisation that is most acutely registered, but improvisation itself is inconceivable without what Michelle Rosaldo in her book on Philippine headhunters calls shared "structures of opportunity and constraint," against which each individual marks off a more or less deviant course.[4] The concrete individual only exists, then, by virtue of forces that pull against spontaneous singularity and that draw any given life, however peculiarly formed, toward communal norms. Even Marin le Marcis's highly original improvisation, we might note, had the most conventional of goals: a publicly recognized name and gender, an officially sanctioned marriage. Indeed the drive to be reabsorbed into the communal is sufficiently strong in his case to make us doubt that individualism—a principle of entitlement, a genetic or teleological account of the autonomous self, a mode of protection for licensed particularity—had any meaning or value to Marin or anyone involved with him. It has been customary since Jacob Burckhardt to trace the origins of individualism to the Renaissance. In the Middle Ages, in Burckhardt's famous, much-disputed formulation, "man was conscious of himself only as a member of a race, people, party, family, or corporation—only through some general category," whereas in the Renaissance "man became a spiritual *individual*, and recognized himself as such."[5] But the material we are considering here suggests that individual identity in the early modern period served less as a final goal than as a way station on the road to a firm and decisive identification with normative structures.

Of these structures, the most powerful appear to be those that governed sexual identity. Male writers in the Renaissance regard gender as an enduring sign of distinction, both in the sense of privilege and in the sense of significant differentiation. A male in Renaissance society had symbolic and material advantages no woman could hope to attain, and he had them by virtue of separating himself, first as a child and then as an adult, from women. All other significant differential indexes of individual existence (social class, religion, language, nation) could at least in imagination be stripped away, only to reveal the underlying and immutable natural fact of sexual difference. The Renaissance delighted in stories of individuals transformed out of all recognition: the king confused with the beggar, the great prince reduced to the condition of a wild man, the pauper changed into a rich lord.[6] Only the primary differentiation given by God himself—"male and female he made them"—would seem to be exempt from this swirling indeterminacy. Even here, of course, there was the possibility of confusion, for as the many stories of cross-dressing suggest, apparel may deceive the eyes of the most skilled observer. But beneath the apparel the body itself cannot lie, or so we might expect.

Yet paradoxically the apparently fragile and mutable social codes are almost always reinscribed in Renaissance stories (despite his savage upbringing, the true prince reveals his noble nature), whereas sexual difference, the foundation of all individuation, turns out to be at its origin unstable and artificial. To help us understand this paradox let us return to Duval's fascination with hermaphrodites. This fascination was not, for the late sixteenth century, eccentric, but was an instance of a widespread cultural concern with prodigies. Prodigies could be viewed both as signs—monitory messages to be read by those who understood the art of divination—and as wonders, as marvelous instances of the inexhaustible variety of things. Prodigies challenge conventional classifications, but they do not make classification itself impossible. On the contrary, as the voluminous accounts of monsters, earthquakes, eclipses, unnaturally heavy rains, physical deformities, and so forth, affirm, by means of these marvels people achieve a sense of the differences—the system of gradations and distinctions and variations—that make possible the dynamic order of individuation. That is, whereas the post-Enlightenment world tends to sharpen its sense of individuation through a grasp of the normative, the Renaissance tended to acquire an understanding of the order of things through a meditation upon the prodigious. Thus the modern interest, fueled by sociology, in the impersonal structures that govern individual improvisation finds its paradoxical Renaissance equivalent in an interest in prodigies: like sociological structures, prodigies organize individual variations around a norm or, in Renaissance terms, intensify a sense of decorum by revealing the inexhaustible fecundity of nature.

Nature in Renaissance thought is not a static entity but a life force that must constantly generate, create, reproduce individuals in order to exist. If this force should cease for an instant, all life would cease, and matter would sink back into primal confusion and disorder. This ceaseless generativity is epitomized in the production of prodigies, which by their very existence affirm the variety of things and mark out ineradicable differences. At the same time, prodigies paradoxically represent the disorder that their existence helps to negate. The monstrous is virtually defined by excess, by the improper, disordered fashioning of matter into misshapen lumps, uncanny conjunctions, gross and unnecessary excrescences. Hence in the moment that they celebrate nature's fecundity in producing prodigies, Renaissance scholars hasten to meditate upon the principle of order that may be discovered within the most uncanny oddity.[7]

The presence of both male and female sexual organs in a single person is a resonant occasion for such meditation. Hermaphroditism was at once a bizarre anomaly, violating the most basic of natural categories, and a sign of the deep, underlying structure of natural order, the structure enabling the very generativity that produced the anomaly. Hence, in the "Mutabilitie Cantos," the note of androgyny in Spenser's allegorical depiction of nature (*Faerie Queene* 7.7.5):

> Then forth issewed (great goddesse) great dame *Nature*,
> With goodly port and gracious Maiesty;
> Being far greater and more tall of stature
> Then any of the gods or Powers on hie:
> Yet certes by her face and physnomy,
> Whether she man or woman inly were,
> That could not any creature well descry:
> For, with a veile that wimpled euery where,
> Her head and face was hid, that mote to none appeare.

It is fitting, then, that Duval's book, in which the strange case of Marin le Marcis occupies so important a place, is not a mere compilation of the bizarre but a serious medical treatise on fertility, the care of pregnant women, and the safe delivery of babies. Discourse on hermaphroditism and discourse on normal sexuality and childbirth do not for Duval in any way conflict; on the contrary, they are in effect the same, for the knowledge that enables one to understand the monstrous conjunction in one individual of the male and female sexes is the same knowledge that enables one to understand the normal experience of sexual pleasure and the generation of healthy offspring.

Duval's task, as he understands it, is to display and explain the hidden riches of the human organs of generation, particularly of the womb, which he sees, in effect, as a fantastic treasure house to which he has acquired the key (p. 159). But why should the case of Marin le Marcis seem to give him this precious key? The answer lies in the central event that saved Marin's life: empowered by the court of law, the physician reaches in behind the woman's secret fold of flesh and feels with his finger's end a swelling penis.

Marin is an oddity, but for Duval his body encodes in its strangeness a universal natural paradox: on the one hand, a single individual is in reality double, since all bodies contain both male and female elements; on the other hand, there are not two radically different sexual structures, but only one—outward and visible in the man, inverted and hidden in the woman. Neither of these beliefs is

37

unique to Duval; they reflect ancient and accepted anatomical wisdom, at once elaborated and challenged by Renaissance physicians. Like many of his peers, Duval is in the awkward position of accepting beliefs with which he is not altogether comfortable; the case of Marin le Marcis serves him by simultaneously reaffirming and marginalizing these beliefs.

At least since the time of Galen, it had been widely thought that males and females alike were fashioned from both male and female seed; the predominance, rather than the exclusion, of the one or the other (along with position in the womb and other factors) helped to determine sexual identity and to make sex accord with gender. This predominance was never, or at least only rarely, absolute. Nor, in the opinion of most, was it definitively established in the womb: males made a transition during childhood from a state close to that of females—indeed often called "effeminate"—to one befitting an adult man; conversely, if less frequently, the predominance of the appropriate female characteristics could take some time to establish itself. If the female seed was dominant but still insufficiently strong, the woman would be a virago; a man in whom male seed was weaker than it should be was likely to remain effeminate. In the rare cases, as Duval notes, where the competition between male and female sperm was absolutely undecided, a hermaphrodite could be born.

All of this implies the persistent doubleness, the inherent twinship, of all individuals. Perceptions of such gender doubleness were usually closely linked to a belief in an internal power struggle between male and female principles. Proper individuation occurred when the friction between the competing seeds was successfully resolved; that resolution was almost entirely bound up in medical manuals, as in theological tracts, with patriarchal ideology: "By how much the more the Masculine Atomes abound in a Female Infant," writes Nathaniel Highmore, a seventeenth-century English physician, "by so much the more the Foetus is stronger, healthier, and more Man-like, a Virago. If the Female Atomes abound much in a Male Infant, then is that issue more weak and effeminate."[8] One peculiar consequence of this view was that normal women had in effect to submit to the weaker internal principle, to accept a certain debility, in order to achieve full female identity, an identity that, of course, entailed submission to a man. Women were *by definition* the weaker sex. A further consequence was that women had momentarily to overcome their inherent defect, and hence their female nature, in order to produce the seed necessary for generation. Not surprisingly, overcoming nature was thought to be difficult; accordingly, the medical texts prescribe extended foreplay as an integral part of sexual intercourse and, for cases where caresses and lascivious words fail, provide recipes for potions and vaginal douches designed to "heat" women beyond their normal body temperature.[9]

But if the Galenic heritage brought with it the notion that human singleness was achieved out of an inherent doubleness, it also brought with it a very different notion: since Galen it had been believed that the male and female sexual organs were altogether comparable, indeed, that they were mirror images of each other. Though Fallopius published in the 1560's his celebrated description of the female genitalia, and though belief in female testicles gave way in the later seventeenth century to the discovery of the ovaries, the specific functioning of the ovaries was not well understood until the nineteenth century. In the sixteenth and seventeenth centuries, physicians and laymen of sharply divergent schools agreed that male and female sexual organs were fully homologous. "The spermatic vessels in women," writes the celebrated French surgeon Ambroise Paré, "do nothing differ from those in men in substance, figure, composure, number, connexion, temper, originall and use, but only in magnitude and distribution. . . . For their Testicles, they differ litle from mens but in quantity [i.e., size]; for they are lesser and in figure more hollow and flat, by reason of their defective heat which could not elevate or lift them vp to their just magnitude."[10] The womb seems unique to women, but in fact it is "given by nature in stead of the *Scrotum*, as the necke thereof, and the annexed parts in stead of the yard; so that if any more exactly consider the parts of generation in women and men, he shall finde that they differ not much in number, but onely in situation and use" (p. 128).

Centuries earlier, Galen had invited his readers to engage in the topographical analysis Paré's description of the genitals implies: "Turn outward the woman's, turn inward, so to speak, and fold double the man's, and you will find them the same in both in every respect." Hence if you imagine the male genitals inverted, you find that the penis has become the cervix and the vagina, and the scrotum has been transformed into the womb, with the testicles on either side. Conversely, Galen suggests, think of the "uterus turned

39

outward and projecting. Would not the testes [ovaries] then necessarily be inside it? Would it not contain them like a scrotum?
Would not the neck [the cervix], hitherto concealed inside the per-
ineum but now pendent, be made into the male member?" In fact,
he concludes, "you could not find a single male part left over that
had not simply changed its position; for the parts that are inside in
woman are outside in man."[11]

This exact homology does of course imply a difference, because
the female is colder, and hence less perfect, than the male. This defect keeps the female genitals from, as it were, being born, a fate
Galen images in an astonishing metaphor: "You can see something
like this in the eyes of the mole, which have vitreous and crys-
talline humors and the tunics that surround these . . . , and they
have these just as much as animals do that make use of their eyes.
The mole's eyes, however, do not open, nor do they project but are
left there imperfect and remain like the eyes of other animals when
these are still in the uterus."[12] This double analogy gives a vertiginous twist to the topographical argument: the female genitals
are not only an inverted version of the male genitals, they are like
the perfectly formed but functionally useless eyes of the mole,
which are in turn like the blind eyes of creatures that have not
yet emerged from the womb. But, of course, by invoking birth the
metaphor implicitly acknowledges the functional utility it is intended to deny, and this paradox, far from embarrassing Galen, enables him to sustain a double vision of the female body, a vision
that endured for centuries. For Paré and most other Renaissance
physicians, the delicate balance of sexual identity and difference simultaneously expresses the providential order of generation and
the defectiveness of women, their failure to reach nature's goal: a
penis. "For that which man hath apparent without, that women
have hid within, both by the singular providence of Nature, as also
by the defect of heate in women, which could not drive and thrust
forth those parts as in men."[13]

One consequence of this belief in differential homology is a fascination with the possibility of sex change, almost always from female to male, that is, from defective to perfect. Paré recounts several such cases, including that of a fifteen-year-old peasant girl
named Marie who one day was "rather robustly" chasing her swine,
which were going into a wheat field. When Marie in mid-pursuit
leaped over a ditch, "at that very moment the genitalia and male

rod came to be developed." After consulting with physicians and the bishop, Marie changed her name to Germain and went on to serve in the king's retinue.[14] On his voyage to Italy, Montaigne stopped to see Germain for himself—he had not married, Montaigne was told, but he had "a big, very thick beard"—the prodigy was not at home, however. In the town, Montaigne noted in his journal, "there is still a song commonly in the girls' mouths, in which they warn one another not to stretch their legs too wide for fear of becoming males, like Marie Germain."[15]

Here again the prodigious is of interest because it unveils the natural. After all, such a spectacular change merely repeats or represents the normal development of males through the healthy operation of bodily heat. Like the two-seed theory, this developmental account suggests that men grow out of or pass through women, though now the formulation is reversed: where the two-seed theory imagines an individual identity emerging from a struggle between conflicting principles, the topographical account imagines gender as the result of the selective forcing out by heat of an originally internal organ—like reversing a rubber glove—so that where there was once only one sex, there are now two.

Duval's work obviously reflects this fascination with sex change, but it also registers and uneasily accommodates the anatomical discoveries that were beginning to cast serious doubts upon the notion of homology. There cannot truly be a sexual metamorphosis, argues Duval, for despite the great resemblance between the male and female sexual organs, the latter cannot simply be converted into the former, or vice versa. If you try to represent such a transformation, you discover its impossibility: "If you imagine the vulva completely turned inside out . . . you will have to envisage a large-mouthed bottle hanging from the woman, a bottle whose mouth rather than base would be attached to the body and which would bear no resemblance to what you had set out to imagine" (p. 375).

Like others of his generation, Duval is balanced uneasily between maintaining the ancient concept of homology and recognizing that it does not quite work. The recognition does not lead him to give up this concept, upon which the traditional psychology and physiology of sex depend, but it does shape his account of Marin le Marcis: not really a case of hermaphroditism, not an instance of sexual metamorphosis, but an embodied transvestism that momentarily confounds sexual categories, only in the end to give way to the clarification of gender and hence to proper, communally sanctioned identity. (Duval's fascination with Marin expresses his own uneasiness with the inherited medical traditions, which Marin seems at once to confirm and to push toward grotesquery.) Transvestism represents a structural identity between man and woman, dramatically disclosed in the penis concealed behind the labia, but it does not present this identity as real. Rather the case serves to marginalize, to render prodigious, the old wisdom. There has not in fact been a transformation from woman into man; Marie was always in some sense Marin, whose true gender was concealed by his anomalous genital structure. But the myth of such mobility is preserved in the very form of the account that denies its anatomical possibility.

The fascination with all that seems to unsettle sexual differentiation—hermaphroditism, gender metamorphosis, women who conceal the inward form of men, men who conceal the inward form of women—never actually threatens the proper generative order, which depends upon the stable distinction between the sexes. To be sure, Duval writes, "many women have been transformed into men." But, he continues, it is more accurate to say that "the male genitals, formerly hidden, have been discovered in many who were once thought to be women; whereupon they changed their names, clothing, and vocations" (p. 372). Even the much rarer cases of authentic hermaphroditism are not permitted to remain ambiguous; judges order that such people decide which sex arouses them more and on this basis choose their gender once for all (p. 302). Thereafter any violation of these sexual bounds will be severely punished, indeed, treated as a capital crime.

Despite this insistence on a determinate sexual identity, Duval and others cling to a notion of deep-structural homology between male and female genitals. Even when the belief that the woman was a defective male was abandoned by most physicians and the form of the female anatomy was attributed to function rather than inadequate heat, the notion of an alignment between the sexes proved surprisingly durable. It was supported by the drawings of the anatomists, who found what they had expected to find: that the uterus was analogous to the scrotum and the vagina to the penis. And if by the early seventeenth century Duval, for example, recognized that this analogy was by no means perfect, he could easily shift the grounds of comparison to the clitoris, "a particle in the shape of a small penis" ("vne particule representant la forme d'vn petit membre viril").[16] By the close of the century, the immensely popular *Aristotle's Masterpiece* informed its readers that "to say that Woman has true Seed, is false and erroneous"; what Galen and Hippocrates had taken to be testicles are in reality ovaries.[17] But this does not mean, the manual argues, that there is a "vast difference between the Members of the two Sexes" (p. 93); the clitoris "suffers erection and falling in the same manner" as the penis, and "both stirs up lust and gives delight in copulation, for without this, the fair sex neither desire nuptial embraces nor have pleasure in them, nor conceive by them."[18] In some lascivious women, the clitoris grows to the size of a male organ and can be used to seduce women and girls; hence the suspicion that almost led to Marin le Marcis's execution.

Like all of nature's gifts, this feminine penis could be abused, but its proper function was to help provide the "delectable pleasure" necessary to enable the woman to "yeeld forth" her seed. At least in Galenic thought, which dominated sixteenth- and seventeenth-century medicine, female ejaculation was at the center of the homology between the sexes; as Ambroise Paré declared, "generation or conception cannot follow without the concourse of two seeds, well and perfectly wrought in the very same moment of time" (p. 887). Everything in the process of conception hinges on sperm, which is the sole generative principle in a world without eggs, and sperm cannot be produced by either sex without intense sexual delight.

There is an elaborate medical literature on the purpose of erotic pleasure—as what enables men to overcome their natural revulsion at the defectiveness of women, what enables women to overcome their natural reluctance to endure pain and put their lives at risk in childbearing, what compensates for the Fall of Man. Sexual pleasure may be thought to link us to the beasts, writes Duval, but in fact in its specifically human form it is one of the marks of God's special favor. The Sovereign Creator was not content that his best-beloved creatures mate as the other animals do, with the male mounting on the female's back or, in the case of elephants, camels, and other heavy beasts, with the male and female turning their backs to one another. For human coition God ordained a different practice: men and women look into each others' faces—"the beautiful lines and features" of the human face—so that they may be

43

aroused to a more fervent desire to generate images of themselves, to make those beloved faces live again in their offspring. And as they look upon one another and make love, drawn into the genital "labyrinth of desire" that God created specially for them and obeying the "tacit commandments" engraved as a benediction in their very bodies, men and women avenge themselves upon their enemy, death. For to leave behind one's own image—"drawn to the life in one's child" ("vif et naïuement representé en son successeur")—is not to die.*

Following an ancient medical tradition, Duval offers simultaneously and bound together two apparently contradictory accounts of the origin of gender: in one a determinate sexual identity emerges when a double nature becomes single, that is, when either male or female seed, co-present in every person, establishes dominance; in the other a determinate sexual identity emerges when a single nature becomes double, that is, when the unitary genital structure (identified as male in its perfect form) divides into two distinct forms, internal and external. Why two accounts? If there were only one authentic structure—outward and visible in the man, inverted and hidden in the woman—gender difference would be reduced to a mere illusion, a trick performed with mirrors, and generation would be difficult to imagine. If there were two interlaced structures, from which gender emerged only by means of domination and submission, differentiation would also be threatened, since we would always discover two persons where we thought to find one. Identity is at once made possible and dissolved by the slippage between these conflicting theories: to this extent, though gender for the Renaissance has everything to do with determinate boundaries, it has equally to do with the friction between boundaries.

The link between these two accounts is heat: by heat the

---

*The interest and complexity of this account depend on the fact that the lovers are looking at the other as they strive to recreate images of themselves; or perhaps they are simultaneously looking at the other and at their own reflection in each other's eyes. In either case, the representation of oneself—one's reproduction and hence triumph over death—depends upon self-abandonment, upon giving oneself over to the image of the other. One might recall the moment in Milton when God draws Eve away from her narcissism, her potentially dangerous and prodigious individuation, toward a proper bonding with another. The narcissism is symbolized by her peering at her reflection in the water, a reflection that would be unstable and perpetually unsatisfying; the proper bonding is symbolized by her steady gazing into the face of another—Adam—and by the production of other images in the offspring they will generate.

struggle between the male and female seed is determined, and again by heat the genital structure of the male emerges from its hidden place, and again by heat ejaculation and orgasm is produced. This caloric model of sexuality is not exclusively genital; breast milk, for example, is also generated by the heating of the blood, and blood itself is produced by the heating of food. Sexual warmth is not essentially different from other warmth; it is only a particularly vehement instance of the principle of all animate life and therefore can be generated in some measure by food, wine, and the power of imagination.[19]

Duval is unusually idealizing, but the essential elements of his account of coition are widely shared: seed is produced and emitted by means of the concoction, or cooking, of blood, which is accomplished by erotic friction between men and women. Hence the recurrent images in the medical literature of what a seventeenth-century English gynecologist calls "the *Fervour* of a very *Libidinous Tickling.*"[20] For, as Thomas Vicary puts it in *The Englishman's Treasure; or, The True Anatomy of Man's Body*, "by the labour and chafing of the testicles or stones, [the best and purest] blood is turned into another kinde, and is made sparme,"[21] and by still further chafing the "sparme" is released into the heated womb. Hence too Duval's account of how his rubbing in the course of the medical examination caused Marin le Marcis's hidden penis to yield forth its seed and produce proof of his sexual identity. And this chafing is an official, public repetition and confirmation of the erotic friction, in bed with Jeane le Febvre, that originated Marin's transformation from Marie.

Marin le Marcis is an object of public interest, concern, and scrutiny because of this transformation. Hence his socially articulated individuality—his emergence from the anonymous mass of men and women into the differentiating light of representation—is for the Renaissance a passing moment of prodigious instability on the way to reintegration into the normal structures of gender and reproduction. Those structures are not, however, secure, ontologically grounded bases for identity; they are themselves necessarily built up out of sexual confusion, friction, and transformation.

We may object that such an account is far too peculiar to address the question of the individual. Our sense of "Renaissance individualism" is based not upon bizarre medical tracts but upon the great historical and literary landmarks of the period. I propose in

45

the rest of this essay briefly to look at literature, and, in literature, at the work of Shakespeare, for Shakespearean theater virtually defines in our literary tradition the representation of individuals. With Shakespeare we may seem to be far indeed from the world of Doctor Duval, until we recall once again some of the features of the story of Marin le Marcis: a love that cannot at first declare itself and that encounters, when it finally does so, life-threatening obstacles; a dizzying confusion of identity centered on cross-dressing; an intense experience of desire—the biological imperative—that seeks to satisfy itself in a sanctified union; the intervention of authority initially to block this union but eventually to resolve all problems and enable the happy couple to marry; the wildly unconventional drive toward conventionality. This is, of course, the plot outline of a prototypical Shakespearean comedy, and I want to propose briefly that the resemblance is more than fortuitous.

I hasten to disclaim any suggestion that Shakespeare took a lively interest in the medical discourse about sex, or that he favored one theory of generation over another, or, most unlikely of all, that he had read Paré, let alone had heard of Marin le Marcis and Jacques Duval. But Shakespeare's knowledge of medical science is not the important issue here. The relationship I wish to establish between medical and theatrical practice is not one of cause and effect or source and literary realization. We are dealing rather with a shared code, a set of interlocking tropes and similitudes that function not only as the objects but as the conditions of representation. Shakespearean comedy constantly appeals to the body, in particular to sexuality, as the heart of its theatrical magic; "great creating nature," the principle by which the world is and must be peopled, is the comic playwright's tutelary spirit. But there is no unmediated access to the body, no direct appropriation of sexuality; rather, sexuality is itself a network of historically contingent figures that constitute the culture's categorical understanding of erotic experience. These figures function as modes of translation between distinct social discourses, channels through which cultural power is circulated. How does a play come to possess sexual energy? What happens when a body is translated from "reality" to the stage or when a male actor is translated into the character of a woman? What does it mean for a Renaissance comedy, that most artificial of forms, to invoke nature? Or for nature, in the reified form of medical discourse, to assume the artificial form of a Renaissance comedy? The answers we are seeking lie not in a theory of causality or influence, but in a historical understanding of Renaissance modes of discursive negotiation and exchange. If we reconstruct the tropes of the body, we can perhaps not only develop a richer sense of the representational resources with which Shakespeare worked but discover some of the primary routes along which trade between theatrical representation and other modes of cultural representation took place. We can improve our grasp of why the bickering or chafing between lovers so fascinated Shakespeare's audience; we can newly gauge the significance of the transvestite transformations that resolve the plot complications of such plays as *As You Like It* and *Twelfth Night*; we can begin to understand why all memorable representation of individuality in Shakespeare—from the gross, monumental fat of Falstaff to Richard III's hunchback, from Macduff's untimely birth to Viola's uncanny twinship—is marked by the prodigious. And we can look with increased comprehension at the fact that Shakespeare wrote all of his women's parts—Kate, Portia, Juliet, Cleopatra, all of them—for boys.

Accounts of Shakespeare's plays constantly appeal, most often at the climactic point in the argument, to natural forces that underlie both social customs and literary models and give the characters their special power. These critical invocations of nature are not themselves a misreading; the plays solicit them. But the mistake is to imagine that the natural forces invoked are timeless and freefloating. Between Shakespeare's culture and our own there has been at least a partial shift in gender perception, from a search for the hidden penis in women to a search for the hidden womb in men, and with this shift the "natural forces" invoked in the representation of individuals have themselves changed. This change has been intensified by a major transformation of our understanding of the relation between sexual pleasure and generation. A culture that imagines (or, better still, knows as an indisputable biological fact) that women need not experience any pleasure at all to conceive will offer different representational resources than a culture that knows as a widely accepted physical truth that women have occulted, inward penises, which must for the survival of mankind be brought by the heat of erotic friction to the point of ejaculation. More specifically, a conception of gender that is teleologically male and insists upon a verifiable sign to confirm nature's final cause finds its supreme literary expression in a transvestite theater; a conception of gender that is symbolically female by contrast insists upon a genetic rather than a teleological account of identity, interests itself in the inward material matrix of individuality, and finds its supreme literary expression in the novel.

The medical texts we have been examining suggest that the generative power of nature centered on fruitful, pleasurable chafing. I want to propose that this notion—which functions less as a technical explanation than as a virtually irresistible assumption upon which technical explanations are built—is extremely resonant for the fashioning of individuals in Shakespeare, particularly in comedy. The theatrical representation of individuality is in effect modeled upon what the culture thought occurred during sexual foreplay and intercourse: characters in such plays as *The Taming of the Shrew, A Midsummer Night's Dream, Much Ado About Nothing, As You Like It,* and *Twelfth Night* both realize their identities and form loving unions mainly by erotic chafing.

The enemies of the Elizabethan and Jacobean theater charged that the playhouse was "Venus' palace," a place of erotic arousal.[22] For all its insistence upon solemn ceremony of marriage, Shakespearean comedy curiously confirms the charge, not only by gesturing forward to the pleasures of the marriage bed but by staging its own theatrical pleasures. "Men and women," wrote the great anatomist William Harvey, "are never more brave, sprightly, blithe, valiant, pleasant or beautiful than when about to celebrate the act."[23] Shakespeare's enactment of the celebration confers upon his comic heroes and heroines something of the special beauty of sexual arousal.

More than any of his contemporaries, Shakespeare discovered how to use the theater's erotic power, how to generate plots that would not block or ignore this power but draw it out, develop it, return it with interest, as it were, to the audience. This Shakespearean discovery, perfected over a six- or seven-year period in the comedies from *Taming* to *Twelfth Night,* entailed above all the representation of the emergence of identity in the experience of erotic heat. This Promethean heat, the crucial practical agent of sexuality in the Renaissance, seems to be precisely what is excluded from theatrical presentation—it takes place internally, out of sight, in the privileged intimacy of the body. But sexual heat, we recall, is not different in kind from all other heat, including that produced by the imagination. Shakespeare realized that if sexual

48

chafing could not be literally presented on stage, it could nonetheless be figuratively represented: friction could be fictionalized, chafing chastened and hence made fit for the stage, by transformation into the lovers' witty, erotically charged sparring.

We should remark that the representation of chafing is not restricted to Shakespeare's lovers; it is diffused throughout the comedies as a generalized system of foreplay. This diffusion is one of the generative principles of comic confusion: hence, for example, in *Twelfth Night* Viola/Cesario's cheeky replies arouse Olivia's passion as Orsino's sighs and groans cannot. Moreover, for Shakespeare friction is specifically associated with verbal wit; indeed at moments the plays seem to imply that erotic friction originates in the wantonness of language and thus that the body itself is a tissue of metaphors or, conversely, that language is perfectly embodied. Take, for a single instance, the following, rather unremarkable exchange between Viola and Feste the clown:

> *Viola.* Save thee, friend, and thy music. Dost thou live by thy tabor?
> *Clown.* No, sir, I live by the church.
> *V.* Art thou a churchman?
> *C.* No such matter, sir. I do live by the church; for I do live at my house, and my house doth stand by the church.
> *V.* So thou mayst say, the king lies by a beggar, if a beggar dwell near him; or, the church stands by thy tabor, if thy tabor stand by the church.
> *C.* You have said, sir. To see this age! A sentence is but a chev'ril glove to a good wit. How quickly the wrong side may be turned outward!
> *V.* Nay, that's certain. They that dally nicely with words may quickly make them wanton.
> *C.* I would therefore my sister had had no name, sir.
> *V.* Why, man?
> *C.* Why, sir, her name's a word, and to dally with that word might make my sister wanton.

The brief, almost schematic enactment of verbal friction leads to a perception of the suppleness of language, particularly its capacity to be inverted, a capacity imaged by the chev'ril glove. It is as if the cause of Marin le Marcis's sexual arousal and transformation were now attributed to the ease—the simple change of one letter—that turns Marie into Marin: "Her name's a word, and to dally with that word might make my sister wanton."

Dallying with words is the principal Shakespearean representation of erotic heat. Hence his plots go out of their way to create not only obstacles in the lovers' path but occasions for friction between them; to select but a single example, in *As You Like It*, when Rosalind escapes from the danger posed by her uncle and finds herself on her own in the woods with Orlando, she does not throw herself into her beloved's arms but initiates a playful tension between them: "I will speak to him like a saucy lackey, and under that habit play the knave with him" (3.2.282–83). Critics have often remarked that the scenes of chafing that follow—Rosalind's supposed "cure" for the madness of love—symbolically test the strength of Orlando's love, but that love is never really in doubt. Even more, the chafing symbolically enacts the lovers' mutual desires and wittily, experimentally fashions Rosalind's identity. We should add that the unique qualities of that identity, what gives Rosalind her independence and her sharply etched individuality, will not endure, or so Shakespeare conceives the play: they are bound up with exile, disguise, and freedom from ordinary constraint, and they will vanish, along with the playful chafing, when the play is done. What begins as a physiological necessity, then, is reimagined as an improvisational self-fashioning that longs for self-effacement and reabsorption in the community.

Why should that fashioning be bound up with cross-dressing? (Rosalind, you will recall, is pretending to be a boy named Ganymede.) In part, I suggest, because the transformation of gender identity figures the emergence of an individual out of a twinned sexual nature. That emergence, let us recall, begins in the womb, but it never extends to the absolute exclusion of the other seed; and the presence of both genders remains particularly evident through adolescence. The audience's sense of this co-presence must have helped to make the transvestite performances in the Elizabethan theater more convincing and powerful. It seems significant that the English stage, unlike the Chinese or Japanese, never developed a tradition of adult female impersonation; it was only boys who could, as it were, naturally play the woman's part. (Or perhaps—and, if so, equally significant—the English called anyone who played a woman's part a "boy.")

Shakespeare's own representations of twinned sexual nature focus on adolescents; his most ingenious version, in *Twelfth Night*, involves male and female identical twins who are at the borders of adulthood: "Not yet old enough for a man nor young enough for a boy" (1.5.150–51). With the change of a few conventional signals, the exquisitely feminine Viola and the manly Sebastian become indistinguishable: hence perhaps the disquieting intensity of Antonio's passion for Sebastian and the ease with which the confused Olivia is "betrothed both to a maid and man" (5.1.254). Near the play's opening, Orsino nicely captures the gender confusion in an unintentionally ironic description of his young page, Cesario—actually Viola in disguise:

> thy small pipe   (1.3.32)
> Is as the maiden's organ, shrill and sound,
> And all is semblative a woman's part.

At the play's close, Orsino has not yet seen Viola—whom he intends to marry—in woman's clothes; she remains in appearance Cesario and therefore still the mirror image of her brother:

> One face, one voice, one habit, and two persons, (5.1.216)
> A natural perspective that is and is not.

But beneath her "masculine usurped attire" there is a body in which the feminine elements are dominant, and the "true" mettle of her sex resolves the play's ambiguities by attaching Orsino's desire to an appropriate and "natural" object. Viola will in the end—but only when the play is done—put off her assumed male role and become "Orsino's mistress and his fancy's queen." But this transformation is not enacted. It remains "high fantastical," and the only authentic transformation that an Elizabethan audience could anticipate when the play was done was Viola's metamorphosis back into a boy.

Though Shakespeare characteristically represents his women characters—Rosalind, Portia, Viola—as realizing their identities by cross-dressing, this conception of individuation seems to me bound up with Renaissance conceptions of the emergence of male identity. Viola in disguise is said to look like one whose "mother's milk were scarce out of him" (1.5.154): in effect a boy is still close to the state of a girl and only passes into manhood when he has put enough distance between himself and his mother's milk. Separation from the female, the crux of male individuation, is inverted in the rites of cross-dressing; such characters as Rosalind and Viola pass through the state of being men in order to become women.[24] Shakespearean women are in this sense the representation of Shakespearean men, the projected mirror images of masculine self-differentiation. I should add that in the tragedies these mirror images become night-mares, and self-differentiation gives way to dreams of self-slaughter.

In Renaissance theater there is a further dimension to trans-vestism, one that returns us for the last time to the case of Marin le Marcis. Beneath the imaginary women's bodies, there are other bodies, the bodies of the actors playing the parts of Shakespearean women. From the perspective of the medical discourse we have been exploring, this final, authentic transvestism serves to secure theatrically the dual account of gender: plays insist upon the chaf-ing between the two sexes and the double nature of individuals, but the theater reveals, in the presence of the man's (or boy's) body be-neath the woman's clothes, the ultimate sexual reality.[25] Since on stage there is in fact but a single gender, the open secret of identity, that beneath or within differentiated individuals is a single struc-ture, identifiably male, is quite literally presented—presented, but not represented, for the play (plots, characters, and the pleasure they confer) cannot continue without the fictive existence of two distinct genders and the friction between them.

Boundaries and the Sense of
Self in Sixteenth-Century France

NATALIE ZEMON DAVIS

I want to argue, in contradiction to Jacob Burckhardt's famous dictum, that the exploration of self in sixteenth-century France was made in conscious relation to the groups to which people belonged; that in a century in which the boundary around the conceptual self and the bodily self was not always firm and closed, men and women nonetheless could work out strategies for self-expression and autonomy; and that the greatest obstacle to self-definition was not embeddedness but powerlessness and poverty.[1] "In myself lies all my hope," said Montaigne, quoting Terence. "This is something that each can find in himself, but more easily those whom God has sheltered from natural and urgent necessity."[2]

Virtually all the occasions for talking or writing about the self involved a relationship: with God or God and one's confessor, with a patron, with a friend or a lover, or especially with one's family and lineage. This last setting will be my focus in this essay, since the boundaries it established were maintained in the sixteenth century even when those of nation or occupation had been weakened by forced emigration or religious persecution. Children died young, widowers remarried, stepsisters jostled with sisters, widows and older brothers were left to manage. Despite all this slippage of life, the image of the patriarchal family stayed firmly in place. Marriage customs varied considerably from province to province and from class to class, and rules of succession were even more diverse, but everywhere the family was conceived as a unit from which one took identity, dowry, or inheritance and then passed these on, enhanced if possible, to the next generation. A man's rise in fortune was rarely perceived as due to his talents alone: a goldsmith's skill or a judge's learning would be noted, but as the result of collective effort—wife and in-laws helping husband, brother helping brother, patron intervening for client. And if a man's fortunes declined, then his close kin were affected also. Even the family quarrels that busied lawyers and notaries attest to the power, not the weakness, of the unit: they concern shares in the patrimony, the thing to which each person was entitled, if to nothing else.[3]

Thus even Benvenuto Cellini—for Burckhardt a man "who carries his measure in himself"—talked of his pride in "having laid some honorable foundation for my family" and claimed that the death of his illegitimate son "gave me greater grief than I have ever had in my whole life."[4] Priests not only maintained ties with their families of origin (as we learn from their wills) but set up kin-like connections with chambermaids and with fellow clerics. The printer-scholar Thomas Platter, who spent his boyhood as a shepherd and his teens wandering in Germany with a gang of students, thought God had turned his life to the good when at last he married and had a son.[5] The adventurous impostor Arnaud du Tilh reached his goal when he settled into the family life of peasant Martin Guerre.[6]

The family's role in shaping the individual's vision was double, stemming both from its patriarchal structure and from its power as a social field for placing people. This means that parents could sometimes look at their children as if there were barely boundaries between them. In Gargantua's moving letter to his son Pantagruel, Rabelais has the giant father say that through children one's name and seed are perpetuated to the Last Judgment: "Through you and by you I remain in my visible image in this world living, seeing, and conversing . . . as I used to do. . . . I have helped you as if I had no other treasure in this world than to see you once in my life absolute and perfected in virtue and honor . . . and in all liberal and honest knowledge, and to leave you after my death as a mirror representing the person [représentant la personne] of me, your father."[7] "Think, my daughter, that you can be greater than I," the royal midwife Louise Bourgeois says to a daughter just learning her craft. "You are a child in a family where your sister's husband is a doctor of medicine and your own husband is becoming one; one of your brothers is a pharmacist, your father a surgeon, and I a midwife. The body of medicine is complete in our house."[8] Montaigne's ironic essay "The Affection of Fathers for Their Children" informs readers of the many limitations on that sentiment, fathers showing more delight in their sons when they are young than when they are grown up "treading on our heels," reminding us that they can "live only at the expense of our being and our life." Montaigne says nonetheless that love for those we have engendered is natural, imprinted in us universally and second only to our instinct for self-preservation.[9]

In sorting themselves out from their parents, children would be operating within the framework of these oft-repeated cultural assumptions, and they would also have to contend with the injunction to obey their parents. Sixteenth-century French laws set the age of majority high for both sexes: in most regions it was 25 for a son unless otherwise "emancipated" by his father, and in the last part of the century parental consent to a marriage was required for women up to the age of 25 and for men up to the age of 30. In cases of extreme disobedience it was possible for parents to disinherit a son or give a daughter only a token dowry. When she married, a daughter was freed from the formal obligation of obedience to her parents because she was then legally subject to her husband. She brought rights into the marriage, too, however: her husband could not shed her blood, though he could correct her by a beating, and her dowry and whatever else had been promised her in her marriage contract had first claim on her husband's estate if he predeceased her. But as a member of the less worthy sex in a hierarchical society, as a member of the disorderly sex, whose wet bodily humors and wandering womb would weaken her will and her mind (so physicians and theologians said), she was required to undertake no actions without her spouse's permission. A contract of sales by a married woman, unless she had the special status of *marchande publique*, public merchant, could not hold up in court if it did not say "with the knowledge and consent of her husband."[10]

As one might expect, the structuring of the family as a hierarchy held together both by love and by contract encouraged the skills of manipulation and calculation in older children, and in wives. In practice, the wife's subordination to the husband was often tempered by common experience and common goals: the payment of the marriage debt (as sexual pleasure was called), child-rearing, and economic survival or advancement. But come what might, the image of hierarchy was maintained.

Having looked at the embedding of the person in the powerful and structured field of the family, let us now consider for a moment the boundary around the individual. In sixteenth-century French society, property boundaries were always blurred by the multiple rights that overlords, proprietors, and users could claim in the same house or field. Work was often perceived as collective even when the profits from it were distributed unequally, and objects moved as often by gifts as by sales; likewise, the line drawn around the self was not firmly closed. One could get inside other people and receive other people within oneself, and not just during sexual intercourse or when a child was in the womb. One could be possessed by someone else's soul; a magician or a sorceress could affect one's thoughts, feelings, and bodily movements, sometimes even without physical contact; indeed, the simplest little woman could change other people's loves and hates by breaking a thread in her daily spinning or by preparing herbs from her garden.[11] The Catholic liturgy had moments, especially during the ritual of exorcism, when the faith and prayers of a group were thought to change one person's inner state; so too, during the sacrifice of the mass, one person, the priest, ate for many. The Protestants of course had strongly rejected this collective dependency in favor of a direct relation between the believer and God, but they still thought one could cheer another up with psalms and Scripture. The Calvinist noblewoman Charlotte Arbaleste and the Calvinist textile manufacturer Jérome Desgouttes both used a metaphor of openness in writing to their children: you are blessed by God to have lived in a time when papal idolatry was overthrown. You have sucked in your faith with your mother's milk.[12]

Such writings for one's children bring me back to my initial focus, the relation of the strong pull of family to the exploration of the self. To begin with, family prompts people to tell and write about the self—even people who, not being spiritual heroes like Teresa of Avila, would never have an excuse to do so otherwise. "My dear son Felix," says the printer Thomas Platter in opening his memoirs, "you've often asked me to describe my life . . . because you've heard me tell about how great was the poverty in which I lived . . . and how great the dangers. . . . And in order that you may thank the Lord that you were born from me so well endowed and have not had to suffer poverty as I did . . . I want to tell everything, insofar as my memory allows, how I was born and how I was raised."[13] Much later Felix Platter writes an account of his student years for his younger brother, starting with his departure from home for medical school and ending with his return home to marry.[14] Stephen Greenblatt might argue that this illustrates the movement from prodigious back to pattern—Felix falls silent when his wanderings are over—but I would point out that only in the family setting could a man give an ordering to the unusual turns his life took.[15]

Montaigne presents his reflections on himself and others as a consolation for the loss of a cherished friend (Etienne de La Boétie), a friend with whom he could share secret thoughts that a father could never communicate to his son lest he engender an unsettling intimacy, a friend whom he could reproach and correct, as a son never would a father. But in some of Montaigne's most important pages of self-exploration and self-disclosure, he plays himself off against his father (in height, appearance, agility, temperament), recalls how his father raised him—"his design has not succeeded so badly"—and talks about his feelings for his own child, some of them surely difficult for Léonor de Montaigne to read later.[16] The Platters *père et fils* too reveal themselves through their relations with their parents, Thomas hurt by his mother's gruffness but admiring her strength, Felix both savoring and resisting Thomas's many letters of fussy concern for him and his activities.[17] In a remarkable and rare biography of a wife by her husband, the Breton nobleman Charles Gouyon, Baron de la Moussaye, speaks about himself on almost every page: his long pursuit of the beautiful, ardent Protestant Claude du Chastel despite royal opposition, his delight in her presence, his unceasing regret that he was absent and could not care for her during her last illness, his devotion to her memory.[18]

Women's memoirs are less common than men's (though women seem to have often told stories about their past, training in composition and rhetoric was much less usual for them), but those that exist are deeply enmeshed in considerations of family. Charlotte Arbaleste briefly presents her life up to her second marriage to the noble Protestant publicist Philippe du Plessis de Mornay, and then devotes hundreds of pages of her manuscript ostensibly to him, so that their son can have his father as a model for the service of God. We have a few glimpses of her character in the early pages: her loyalty to her religion when her mother and other kinfolk flinch, her bravery in a dangerous trip into exile, and her cleverness, good morals, and faith—these last told in a remark quoted from her husband, thus preserving the convention of modesty—and then she re-cedes. But this is a convention too, for she is everywhere in her husband's book—not just having babies and arguing with pastors, but receiving his letters, sending off dispatches, and especially or-dering his life. She is the one who decides when it stops being told, because their son dies, and the book was meant for him alone.[19]

This is a way a woman could reflect on and write about herself while retaining unthreatened the image of the patriarchal family. (It should be added that Charlotte had daughters too, who must have read the manuscript, but she did not dedicate it to them.) Her self-presentation is certainly not that of a nineteenth-century individu-alist, testing himself against others and wholly self-determined (if such a thing ever existed outside the thought of Nietzsche and a few others), but it does derive a sense of her worth and her qualities from service to God, the Reformed cause, and husband. In contrast to Baron de la Moussaye, who can easily fit his political trips, his hunting, and his lawsuits into his account of his wife, there are some subjects that a subjected wife could not think of approaching directly.

A more striking example—albeit by a woman of much less lit-erary talent—is Jeanne du Laurens's manuscript "The Genealogy of Messieurs du Laurens."[20] Jeanne's title does not mention the daughters and wives in the du Laurens family, but only the male line founded by her father, Louis, who rose from a Savoy village to be an important physician in Arles, whose sons became royal phy-sicians, judges, and archbishops, and whose grandchildren were fol-lowing suit. Yet Louis died when most of the children were still young, and Jeanne's history is really the story of her well-born mother, Louise, who used limited means with remarkable inge-nuity to arrange eight sons' careers and two daughters' marriages. (She is like the Widow d'Estissac, whom Montaigne depicts at the opening of his "On the Affection of Fathers for Their Children" as the "most forthright example of maternal affection in our time.")[21] Widow Louise maintains the genealogy, but always does it, in her own words and in her daughter's, as her late husband's agent, in-spired by his life. Jeanne gets around to herself late in the story; after the *enfants,* the children, come *les filles,* the daughters. Un-like the sons, Jeanne and her sister are kept close to their mother until they are married off and have children. Jeanne portrays herself as both like her mother—bustling between brother and widow to straighten out a career choice—and unlike her mother, laughing at childish pranks that the unbending Louise insists on punishing. Readers may think they are hearing little about Jeanne's values and feelings—until they realize this 71-year-old woman, the survivor, has put the words in everyone's mouth: her father's deathbed speech, her mother's scolding and exhortations. "You will tell me," she says to her descendants, "that I am boasting about my genealogy. I admit it, but everything I'm putting down is true."[22]

Michelle Rosaldo says in an essay published in 1980, "We must begin . . . to ask just how it comes about—in a world where people of both sexes make choices that count—that men come to be seen as the creators of collective good and the preeminent force in local politics."[23] Jeanne du Laurens's "Genealogy" shows how women may have helped perpetuate the image while maneuvering for some sense of self within it.

I have been describing how a patriarchal family unit could stimulate people within its borders toward self-discovery and self-presentation. Now let us consider a few strategies for achieving some personal autonomy in a world where in principle parents and husbands ruled and where, because of openings into other people's bodies and minds, it was not always certain where one person ended and another began.

The young were assisted in dealing with their elders by the oft-repeated prescription that parents should rule with justice and firm love, not as tyrants. In reference to sons, this meant that a career was chosen partly with regard to the boy's *naturel*, his "nature"—a wide-ranging word, which could include temperament, character, and talent—and with regard to the boy's vocation, something God called him to, but whose signs were in him, in his gifts and inclinations.[24] As a practical issue, this choice could come up only in better-off peasant families, in which parents could consider sending sons to the city, in artisanal and wealthier urban families in which a craft or profession was being decided, and in some noble families. The concepts of *naturel* and vocation offered young men in these social strata a language in which to think about themselves and argue legitimately with their parents. Thus three of Jeanne du Laurens's brothers could change the paths on which their parents had set them: Honoré, who after a year of doing nothing in medical school said that he did not want to be a physician, that God had called him to the vocation of law, "plus conforme à mon naturel"; Gaspard, who after passing his law exams wanted to "suivre son inspiration" and become a priest; and André, who said he had no "volonté" to be a monk but desired to be a physician like his late father.[25]

Even outright disobedience was possible for such young men as Thomas Platter, whose father was dead and whose family was too poor to make disinheritance a threat.[26] As Thomas recounts it, he ran away from an uncle who was training him for the priesthood and later from a vagabond cousin who was using him as a beggar; hungry for learning, he began to study, and, persuaded by Zwingli's preaching—"I felt like someone was pulling me up in the air by my hair"—he became a Protestant.[27] His son Felix had no such excuses for developing a sense of autonomy. He was another one who had sucked in the new religion with his mother's milk, and he had no conflict about his calling: "From my childhood I had always dreamed of studying medicine and of becoming a doctor. My father desired it as much as I did, for he had himself once approached the same study." So Felix simply used his five university years in Montpellier, far away from his home in Basel, to experiment timidly with forbidden things—to dance with Catholic women while writing home to his father to rejoice in his Protestant fiancée, to mask at Carnival and New Year's though this was forbidden by strict Reformed standards, and to refuse to come back, despite his father's pleas, until he had learned enough medicine to satisfy himself. Equally important, he wrote all this down for a nephew, thus establishing a family tradition of allowing a young man his breathing space.[28]

Interestingly enough, Montaigne affirms his autonomy, his individuality, without drawing any sustenance from a vocational identity (if anything, he presents himself as uncomfortable with his early profession as a judge), and he talks about his life, with his lazy and do-nothing *naturel* and "a soul all his own" (*une ame toute sienne*), as if it were one long vacation. He has passed beyond those authors who communicate themselves to people "by some particular and strange mark" (*marque particuliere et estrangere*). "I the first to do it [communicate] by my universal being, as Michel de Montaigne, not as a grammarian or a poet or a jurist."[29]

Would we expect a sixteenth-century woman to be able even to think about herself this way, not to mention communicate to others by her "universal being"? Women would have had to struggle merely to have a "particular and strange mark": they had diverse natures, but no vocation other than marriage (or alternatively, for Catholic women, the religious life). Being a female poet required some shuffling of concepts and finding of special muses, since cold and wet humors were supposed to put a damper on inspiration.[30] Outside the women of letters, one of the few cases I know of a woman with an unabashed vocational identity is the royal midwife Louise Bourgeois; she could write easily of how Socrates' mother and Lucina, goddess of childbirth, had come to summon her, because midwifery was tied to the secrets of women.[31] As for other women, they had skills, of course, and it was recognized that they could make gold thread, or run a linen shop or a manor house well or badly, but their calling was to put those skills to use in whatever household they found themselves, adjusting to father, stepfather, first husband, second husband. One was not Michel de Montaigne, *tout court*, but Charlotte Arbaleste, daughter of so-and-so, widow of so-and-so, wife of so-and-so. If women's natures were universal, it was not a sign of self-possession, but of being given away.

I would like to suggest paradoxically that a strategy for at least a thread of female autonomy may have been built precisely around this sense of being given away, that women sometimes turned the cultural formulation around, and gave themselves away. For one thing, they were helped by the oft-repeated prescription that daughters must consent to an arranged marriage, that indeed this was essential. If they refused to agree—as did the princess Jeanne d'Albret, who had to be carried to the altar in 1541—the act could be annulled.[32] For another, many women made their own marriages: most widows, for example, or serving girls who lived far from home or whose parents were deceased.

But let me make a more complicated case, that of the Catholic princess Marguerite de Valois, daughter of Catherine de Médicis and wife of the Huguenot Henri de Navarre, later Henri IV. Her memoirs are among the most interesting of sixteenth-century France. Marguerite presents her girlhood as a struggle with her brother, the future King Henri III, for the attention and favor of their widowed mother. She begins to change her sense of herself as a person "living without design, thinking only of dancing and hunting, not even having the curiosity to appear beautiful" when she realizes she is important to Catherine for a marriage alliance. Though she speaks of having accepted betrothal to Henri de Navarre in deference to

her mother—"I told her I had not will or choice other than hers"—
her subsequent behavior (as she reports it) shows her fully aware of
the high politics of marriage and her role in it. She will not let her
mother annul her marriage and employs all her power as an intermediary to forge an alliance between her Catholic brother and her
Protestant husband. Though now in opposition to Catherine, she is
consciously using her body and her kin ties to further a policy of
accommodation that had once been her mother's.[33]

Because Marguerite de Valois was a princess, one might well
ask whether we can transport into other families her reconcep-
tualization of the exchange in women. But think about it: marriage
at every social level was considered an alliance between families,
not just between individuals, and other wives could have taken initiative in the politics of local peacemaking and family advancement.

At any rate, my last example of women's deriving some sense of
autonomy from the experience of giving themselves away rests on
much firmer evidence. It is connected with a belief in the openness
of one body to another, here especially the female body, and is
drawn from hundreds of marriage contracts and wills. Women came
into marriage with clothing and jewels, and their husbands promised them more of the same. When they died, their wills were
much more likely than men's to have made gifts to specific women
and girls of their rings, necklaces, and rosaries, or their capes, skirts,
petticoats, shirts, and other items of intimate apparel. (The men just
left their clothing unspecified, with the rest of their goods, to their
universal heir, who would either keep items or dispose of them to
a second-hand dealer.) The women's wills carefully describe the
gifts—"my fur-lined gray cape," "my third-best petticoat"—and
the items are distributed according to the status and closeness of
the recipients. The pattern is the same for wealthy women and for
artisans, so it cannot be argued that women did this only because
they had no other property to give away.[34] Rather, by these elaborate
gifts from the body, women expressed their individuality as they
left the world—and demonstrated as well their neighborhood ma-
tronage systems.

Let me take a last leap here. If women can think of giving themselves away, then they can also begin to think of having stronger
ownership rights in their bodies, at least for the purposes of this
world. I used to believe that such a notion was possible only with
the spread of Lockean ideas in the eighteenth century. But a Lyon

woman, called before the Reformed Consistory of Geneva in the mid-sixteenth century for sleeping with her fiancé, has persuaded me otherwise: "Paris est au Roy et mon corps est a moy," she had snapped, "Paris belongs to the king and my body belongs to me." The rhyme suggests this was a proverb, perhaps cited by women and men trying to improvise strategies for autonomy in other circumstances also.[35]

I have been arguing that an examination of ideas of the self must not be universalizing, but rather must be located within a precise culture. (Here my method has been like Stephen Greenblatt's in his analysis of Renaissance sexuality above, and it makes me want to insist that readers interpret Carol Gilligan's findings about women's sense of responsibility and sacrifice primarily in terms of modern American categories and predicaments rather than simply link them linearly with what I have said about women giving themselves away.)[36] For sixteenth-century France I have mapped the boundary of the partriarchal family beyond the individual person and have pointed to apertures in the boundary of the person as important conditions in defining the self. Especially I have urged the view that embeddedness did not preclude self-discovery, but rather prompted it—common experience may feed the sense of one's own distinctive history—and that women and young men, grounding themselves in experience, sometimes turned cultural categories and images to their own independent uses. The example of the sixteenth century suggests the importance of seeing the person as part of a field of relations and of being open to paths and modes for the constitution of the self different from those in nineteenth-century thought. It also suggests how delicate is the balance between concern for the self and concern for others, even in the most privileged case (I take that to be Montaigne's), and that our most important task may not be to reconstruct individualism, but to keep it constantly in assay.

The Use of Autonomy in Ethical Theory

J. B. SCHNEEWIND

The basic features of morality do not change much over the centuries, any more than do the basic features of the natural world in which we live. There are far more changes in the stories we tell ourselves about morality, the stories by which we make it intelligible to ourselves in the light of whatever else we take to be known about the world. Those stories provide the vocabularies we use to express and criticize our moral feelings and convictions. But despite important historical changes in those vocabularies, we can trace certain similarities in structure, certain aspects of the morality of one time that are replicated, in other terms, in the morality of another. When such structural similarities can be detected in a wide variety of stories or theories about morality from differing but connected periods, it seems likely at the least that they reflect some very deep feature of a tradition. Studying the history of moral philosophy may thus help us to understand matters that still concern us. I propose to look at the notion of autonomy in this way.

The term "autonomy" came into moral philosophy rather late. It was taken over from political discussion, where it referred straightforwardly to the ability of a society or group to make its own laws. The responsibility for its adoption lies with Kant, who used it for the central idea of his ethical theory, namely, that morality is constituted by the requirement that we act out of respect for a moral law that we ourselves make. As an early nineteenth-century German philosophical lexicographer pointed out, however, the idea goes back at least as far as the Christian Scriptures. He cites the relevant text, the great dictum from St. Paul's Epistle to the Romans (2 : 14): "For when the Gentiles, which have not the law, do by

64

nature the things contained in the law, these, having not the law, are a law unto themselves." This was the text cited for centuries to explain how those who lived outside the community of revelation could nonetheless form a moral community with those who lived within it, the text that justified Christianizing the Roman Stoic theory of natural law and made the idea of self-legislation central to Western culture. Luther and Calvin used the passage to explain our ability to know what we ought to do even when we no longer have the ability to do it; and Bishop Butler published two sermons on it that until Kant were the most penetrating, philosophically acute, and widely read analysis of self-legislation as the core of morality. Butler came close to anticipating Kant's fundamental alteration of the tradition. In seeing just how he fell short of doing so, we can see both what Kant altered and what, more importantly, he preserved from the Pauline view of morality.

Butler claims that there is within us a voice that speaks with authority about what we are to do. Authority here is contrasted with strength: "conscience" or "reflection," as Butler calls this voice, may not succeed in controlling our desires and impulses, but we all admit that it has a right to do so. Though he opposes Hobbes's mechanistic account of deliberation and choice, Butler offers no alternative explanation of how authority is translated into effective control. He nonetheless makes it clear that we cannot view ourselves in the Hobbesian way, as simply the psychic place where our desires and needs come to an equilibrium. Our conscience approves and disapproves proposed courses of action regardless of how strongly we may want to pursue them or of how they will affect our long-term interests. Its dictates are thus what Kant later called "categorical demands" on us.

Conscience is for Butler as much a part of our nature as the desires and needs it controls. If you ask how you are obliged to obey the law of conscience, the answer, Butler says, is simply this: "Your obligation to obey this law, is its being the law of your nature." Asking what reason I have to do what my conscience tells me to do is as foolish as asking what reason I have to eat when I feel hungry.

Butler finds his evidence in the phenomena of morality itself: our understanding and acceptance of categorical demands on our action, and our shared ability to distinguish gratitude from simple gladness, or resentment and indignation from annoyance. Moreover, Butler uses no other evidence for his contentions. He is showing us how our own morality requires us to see ourselves, and he takes this to be sufficient to indicate that the Hobbesian picture is mistaken.

The independence of conscience or reflection from the calls of desire and passion is shown as much in its dictates about other people as it is in its directives about oneself. Against the nascent utilitarianism he found in contemporaries like Hutcheson, Butler argues tellingly that we have other obligations than to respond to needs and wants. Benevolence is not the whole of virtue. We are to be benevolent, he holds, but only "within the bounds of veracity and justice." This is evident, he thinks, if we reflect upon the moral judgments we are surest of. We know perfectly well in particular cases that we ought to tell the truth or return a piece of property to someone, even though we do not know whether our doing so will "produce an overbalance of happiness upon the whole," and even sometimes when we are sure it will not.

Butler believes that each person is an immortal being, designed by God to play a proper role in the larger creation and equipped with a conscience so as to be able to do so. He sees the authority of conscience as stemming from its ability to discover rights and wrongs that are independent of its working, though accessible to us only through that working. Kant showed that these two beliefs, in a substantial soul and in conscience as recognizing what is morally required, are not essential to an autonomy-centered view of morality. At the moral core of Butler's view, however, is a position Kant shared: that to explain the phenomena of morality—both the form and the substance of our enduring moral feelings and of our considered moral judgments—we must suppose the self to be capable of giving itself authoritative direction that is not determined by wants and demands arising from our existence as needy and dependent beings.

The defining feature of an autonomous agent, in Kant's view, is its ability to guide its own action by the choices of a will that is such that whatever it wills is good simply because it is willed by it. The point is not that the autonomous will unerringly homes in on what is independently and antecedently good, as Butler's conscience does. The point is rather that when something is chosen or pursued by such a will, that very fact makes the object of the will good. An agent so guided is not led by anything outside himself. Now the idea that the good or the right is constituted by the choice

66

of a will was not original with Kant. It had a long history in voluntarist theology, and Pufendorf's theory of natural law brought it much closer to home for Kant. But Kant always rejected such voluntarism on the grounds that it seemed to imply that the will in question was purely tyrannical. Could one explain how there might be a will whose choices constitute the good, even though the will is not dependent on anything but itself for guidance? Kant's answer, of course, was to claim that the will, for moral purposes, must be seen as practical rationality, as inherently working in a purely rational manner. And the simplest feature of rationality, he held, would suffice: a rational will has merely never to act in such a way that its modes of action are self-contradictory.

To found a moral theory on this concept, Kant had to show that it could lead us to specific moral judgments not at odds with our understanding of morality and its requirements. There has been heated debate about his success in this venture, and I do not intend to review the subject here. I think it is now clear that at least some of our ordinary moral convictions can indeed be derived using the categorical imperative as a test and that many of the things we think wrong are ruled out by it. But what interests me is a question that arises rather on the supposition that Kant could succeed in this part of his enterprise: why did Kant think so much else had to go along with this notion of autonomy, in particular a transcendental self possessed of a remarkable ontological status? I suggest that much of what we find untenable in the Kantian view of autonomy springs from the historical problematic that led Kant to the idea and that his moral thrust in this doctrine is not essentially different from Butler's, with one vital modification. To support this claim, I will indicate very briefly how Kant came to his view.

Kant several times uses a metaphor that gives a major clue for understanding his vision of morality. "When we are speaking of laws of duty," he remarks in the *Doctrine of Virtue*, ". . . we are considering a moral (intelligible) world where, by analogy with the physical world, attraction and repulsion bind together rational beings (on earth)." Love draws us together, yet moral respect keeps us at a proper distance, like centripetal and centrifugal forces in a Newtonian universe. Love here stands for our human desires and needs, and respect represents the action of moral law, which displays our autonomy.

This analogy between the physical and the moral worlds seems to have come to Kant in the course of some very early thinking about the problem of evil. In the early 1750's he sketched some ideas for a prize essay on the comparative merits of the theodicies of Leibniz and Pope. Leibniz held the much-parodied view that when God created the world he first contemplated all possible worlds and then, being good, chose the best one available. But even in the best world, given the kinds of things that can possibly co-exist, some evil occurs. This seemed to Kant to set unacceptable limits to the Almighty's powers. Pope's thesis—that "whatever is, IS RIGHT"—seemed to point to a more satisfactory position. The question was, how to defend it? Kant tried to work out the remarkable idea that God creates not just the world as it exists but the possibilities that are made real in it. If this is so, there will be no evil, because the limits on the possibilities of things and events that can coexist will already express God's infinite goodness and justice, as well as his power. But this position is hard to comprehend: it seems that in such a view to think of God as just or good is no more than to think that God does what he does. Is his will not purely arbitrary? To resolve this problem Kant hit on the idea of a will whose inner nature or structure is such that its outcomes must be good by definition; with this he was but a step away from the autonomous will of his ethical theory.

The idea of an autonomous will helped Kant complete his theodicy by accounting for moral evil. A will wholly determined from within must plainly be completely free; hence if we have wills of this kind, we, and not God, are responsible for what we do. Since our wills are like God's in that whatever they choose is by definition good, then if each of us always expressed this rational will in action, the resulting world would necessarily be good. The world God creates by himself, the natural world, is perfect: its laws and the events determined by them perfectly express his good will. The world we create is not perfect because we scarcely ever express our good will. But it could be made perfect if we so willed: the responsibility either way is entirely ours. Kant's views on ethics, politics, and history show how he thinks a morally perfect world would come to be created by us: within each individual self, in society by the slow creation of a republic in each country, globally and through history by the creation of a world federation of republics that, guaranteeing peace, would enable humanity to develop all its potentials.

For this extraordinary vision to work as a theodicy, Kant had to think of the moral self as functioning in a way analogous to a physical cause. But because he had to make such a sharp disjunction between nature, made by God, and the moral world, made by us, he had to think of that self as inhabiting a realm wholly other than the natural. Thus the transcendental self, no longer a Butlerian substance but still uncomfortably close to behaving like one, comes on the scene. There is, however, another reason for making that self the source of value, the bearer of moral autonomy. The Popian theodicy effectively removes all value from the natural world. Any condition or occurrence in it must be exactly as perfect or as good as any other. In the moral world, however, distinctions of value are essential. Thus value cannot be derived from the natural world— not from pleasure and pain, not from our sociable human nature, not from any fact about the way things are. Kant thus offers the moral counterpart to a Newtonian world, in which distinctions of value are allowed no role; and so Kant's earliest thinking anticipated the problems he was later to face.

One of the most fascinating developments to follow in Kant is his growing conviction that the autonomy of the self is always and only to be argued from the evidence of morality. At one point during the critical period Kant tried to argue to the autonomy of the will, and so to the categorical imperative, from general conditions of acting or even perhaps of thinking. But his later view, as made evident in the *Critique of Practical Reason,* is that for moral purposes we are to draw conclusions about the nature of the self from our experience of categorical obligations alone. Because such obligations undeniably exist, we must conclude that we are free agents, and only autonomy as self-legislation yields for Kant an intelligible account of that freedom. Thus, like Butler, Kant insists first that morality allows needs and desires to be satisfied only within limits set independent of any consideration of them, and next that we can draw a proper view of the moral self from the phenomena of morality alone. Both agree also in thinking self-governance a necessary feature of human beings, one not dependent on or created by society. Kant's crucial innovation is this: where Butler sees in self-governance only the explanation of our responsibility for our actions, Kant sees in it as well our responsibility for the principle that makes them right or wrong.

I turn now to a view of autonomy that carries far less metaphysical baggage than Kant's or Butler's but that displays again the positions I take to be essential to an autonomy-centered ethical theory. The main points of John Rawls's *A Theory of Justice* are too well known to need rehearsing. My aim will only be to bring out some distinctive functions of autonomy in his theory.

Rawls is mainly interested not in the actions of separate individuals, as Butler and Kant are, but in the social and political structure of society. His aim is to find a way of determining rationally what features these structures must have if society is to be fundamentally just. Kant sought a principle each person could use in making moral decisions case by case, believing that the cumulative effect would eventually be a just society. Rawls thinks the complexities of decision-making are too great for individuals to handle in this way. His thought is that the complexities of deciding what is right will be reduced to manageable proportions for individuals only if they can rely on their basic social structure as being just; he does not offer a procedure that will determine more than the principles for the justice of that structure. It is quite feasible, he holds, for people with a wide variety of views about the good life to live together within a well-ordered society. The kind of complete and necessary determination of the right that Kant thought requisite for a moral world to exist is not, in Rawls's view, needed.

Autonomy for Rawls is tied to the rational decisions people would make under certain conditions and not, as for Kant, to the actual choices they do make. If the basic structure of the society I live in is such that under appropriate conditions I would rationally ratify it or choose it to be as it is, then I am autonomous. It must be possible for me to raise and think through this question at any time. But I need not spend my life thinking about it in order to be autonomous. And while the citizens of the well-ordered society will have a standing concern for the maintenance of the features that make it just, their motivations in most cases will be those that arise from their pursuit of the good life as they see it.

Our autonomy itself, not merely the expression of it in action, is for Rawls contingent. We might not live in a well-ordered society; indeed, by Rawls's principles we certainly do not. Insofar as we do not, we are not autonomous. We can and ought to try to make our society more just, and if we succeed we will be increasing the degree of our autonomy. Thus Rawls does not accept the Butlerian and Kantian view that autonomy is the condition of our having any obligations at all. But he is in a deeper sense continuing Kant's line of thought: he holds that we are responsible not only for the standards by which justice is to be judged but also for continuing to be, and to educate, persons who can sustain a society judged by those standards. Nature alone no more does this than it provides the standards.

Rational choice under specific conditions is the core notion of Rawls's theory. His stipulations of those conditions bring out most clearly what he thinks is essential to an autonomy-centered ethic: what makes a basic structure just is not merely being rationally chosen but being rationally chosen under conditions that model our moral convictions. In order properly to reflect what morality requires, I must think of myself as one of a group of free and equal persons each of whom has an idea of the good life that each can follow and revise after reflection. But I must not bring my personal idea of the good life into play, and I must consider irrelevant any individuating information about myself, such as my sex, age, race, generation, religion, class, or abilities. Rational acceptance by a group so constituted determines the principles of justice. Thus the self, as morality requires us to think of it, is the person considered as able to take part in such a group's discussions and to live up to its decisions. It is important to understand why Rawls imposes all these conditions, but I will comment only on one, the exclusion from the moral self of benevolence or any other form of immediate concern for the well-being or happiness of others. This is not excluded because Rawls cynically thinks no such concern exists. But including a concern for the well-being of others in the moral self would entail that morality must allow its conclusions to be dictated by the way nature and society have made people respond to the conditions under which they live. Because of inheritance or upbringing, some people are more sensitive than others, some require more help to enjoy life at any level than others, some have more ability to fend for themselves than others. Both the veil of ignorance, which rules out considering my own real position, and the exclusion of altruistic motivation are meant to model what any autonomy-centered ethic takes to be a central requirement of morality: that the natural or historical distribution of sensibilities and personal powers or talents by itself carries no moral weight. Only after ratification by us may they count in moral deliberation.

I hope that these accounts of Butler, Kant, and Rawls, though brief and crude, have made clear what I mean by claiming that an enduring Western tradition of autonomy-centered interpretation of morality, reaching back to a central idea within Christianity, portrays morality in recognizably similar ways despite radical changes in vocabulary and theory. If this tradition locates what is important about the idea of autonomy, then it becomes clear that certain kinds of objections to autonomist views of morality are either beside the point or mistaken.

It should be obvious, to begin with, that metaphysical, epistemological, sociological, psychological, or language-based theories of the self's nature and formation have no bearing on the validity of the idea of autonomy. The defender of autonomy need have no views about the existence of an enduring substantial self, the immortal soul, the Cartesian subject, or the transcendental ego. The autonomist need not deny that the self is a cultural product, rather than a divine or natural one. Her claim is that the culture itself requires us to think of ourselves as able to look at our lives and actions from, among others, the point of view of a self-legislator. It is of course of interest to see if we can discover how the ability to do this is transmitted from generation to generation, because we no longer think that it is a necessary and unavoidable attribute of every mature person like, for example, sexuality. But it is one thing to ask how society shapes its members to continue its morality and another to ask what that morality is; the autonomist is answering only the latter question. To have a relevant objection to autonomy-centered views of morality and to the self as portrayed in them, it is necessary to object to them on moral grounds.

One such objection asserts that because autonomy-centered theories require the self to be completely unindividuated they must be reflecting and supporting a view that sees morality as centrally a matter of abstract universal rules. It is supposed that since these rules must be the same for everyone alike they must therefore be incapable of reflecting our deep moral conviction of the importance of unique personal relations, of the rightness of our caring more about some people than others just because they are who they are. But autonomy-centered views do not exclude this. The universalisability of moral judgments is at best a logical or conceptual matter and does not entail that only crude general rules can be morally acceptable. The unindividuated self in autonomy-centered theories is not meant to account primarily for this formal feature of

72

morality but represents the moral importance of not considering ourselves to have special privileges or exemptions we would not grant to other people situated and identified as we are. This is perfectly compatible with thinking that the circumstances that give us special privileges or responsibilities concerning another are so complicated or unusual that in fact no one else will ever stand in the identical relation to anyone. Autonomy-centered theories of morality are as well able to sanction unique personal ties as any other kind of theory.

Another objection comes from the opposite direction. It is held that autonomy-centered theories make too much of the individuality and separateness of persons. Such views are said to threaten communal life and the values of tradition, custom, group activity, and loyalties to larger wholes. Or they are taken to imply anarchic views of government or such instability in personality that anomic disorientation is the likely outcome. To be sure, if we follow some writers in supposing that autonomy means simply the refusal to be ruled or that it means the habit of constantly assessing our personal goals, abilities, circumstances, and resources with the aim of always maintaining maximum conscious control over our own lives, we will have difficulty in turning away such objections. We will also have some difficulty in explaining the value or importance of autonomy so conceived. But it is surely clear that ideals of this sort are neither the same as nor required by autonomy as conceived within the tradition I have tried to trace.

This point must, however, be pursued further. If morality is as it is seen by the autonomist tradition, then it does indeed require a culture in which each of us can look critically at our own social position and the institutions and customs of our society, and the moral self must provide us with the standpoint from which such a look is possible. It is now frequently said that the moral self as conceived by the autonomist is too impoverished to serve such a purpose and that a morally adequate idea of the self must allow it to be far more richly endowed with individuating attributes than the autonomist is willing to allow. These are objections of some complexity, and I can only suggest one or two points to keep in mind when considering them.

We must remember that the moral self is not thought by the autonomist to be the whole self, nor is it even held that the moral self alone could direct our actions. Butler argued that conscience only judges the projects and plans put before it by the particular passions or by long-range prudence. Kant, seeing the moral law as providing the form for material arising from the phenomenal self, held that the categorical imperative primarily gives us a procedure to test any proposal for action coming from the empirical self. On Rawls's view, we at any time can think ourselves into the original position behind the veil of ignorance, where the moral self operates. What gives point to the deliberations we go through in that frame of mind is the diversity of goods we know people actually pursue. So the claim that the moral self of autonomy theories is too sparely individuated to provide a standpoint for assessing social institutions or courses of action is either a mistake about the way the moral self is supposed to function in such theories—the mistake of thinking that the moral self is to generate moral policies solely from its own resources—or else it is the claim that the procedures and the information allowed the moral self are inadequate to produce any moral conclusions at all. But this claim, as I noted in discussing Kant, is simply mistaken. The question must really be whether autonomy-centered theories allow morally adequate conclusions.

Critics claim that only an inadequate morality can emerge from such a view and that the fault lies with the impoverished conception of the self embedded in it. The autonomist, it is said, cannot give a satisfactory account of the deepest roots of action and of personal character, because the theory requires us to view all of our projects and our ties to people and to groups as only contingently part of the self. Since we must give them up if morality requires us to do so, the self must have its identity even without them. Hence the self cannot be essentially constituted by any of its projects or attachments. But then, it is argued, the self cannot be closely and loyally tied to these activities, people, and groups and cannot engage all its energies in them or serve to ground a strong character.

It is hard to see the force of this objection. It might be meant as the claim that it is not possible to be fully committed to some long-range plan of action, or to be a loyal citizen, a devoted member of a group, or a true friend, if one is at the same time committed to impersonal principles of morality or justice and if as a result one is willing in case of conflict to weigh seriously the need to act as those principles require rather than as the more particular tie would demand. But that is the sort of *a priori* claim that only adherence to a theory leads one to make. It looks very much like the

74

once frequently heard claim that no atheist can possibly be a good man, and it has about the same degree of credibility.

Another, and more plausible, way of taking this objection is as making a moral point, namely, that it is not morally possible to question certain aspects of the self, that some part of our identity must simply be accepted as justified or as carrying moral weight. Taken one way, this is the naturalistic claim that something about human nature—for example, our being susceptible to pleasure and pain or our having preferences—must be taken as determinative of morality. On this interpretation we are back to well-known consequentialist views, facing not a new objection but a very old one. This criticism will be novel only if it means that some socially determined constitutive aspect of our identity is to be accepted as carrying moral weight and as not open to moral question. How such a view could be plausible in societies as morally erratic as ours I cannot see. In any event one thing is clear: it is seriously misleading to say that autonomist views present an impoverished or thin vision of the self in comparison with a view like this. It is rather such critics who have an impoverished view of the self. They fail to see that the self can sustain and is morally constituted by precisely the tension between serious commitment to its contingent likes, loves, and loyalties and its equally serious commitment to the idea of a comprehensive human community in which no one's projects need be unjust.

Courbet's Metaphysics:
A Reading of 'The Quarry'

MICHAEL FRIED

This essay is mainly concerned with a single work, *The Quarry*, painted by Gustave Courbet in 1856 and exhibited along with several other pictures by the artist in the Salon the following year (Fig. 1).[1] As the first full-dress hunting scene in Courbet's oeuvre, *The Quarry* has a special claim on our attention. It is also one of numerous self-portraits that he painted in the course of his career, the hunter leaning back against a tree in the center of the composition having traditionally been recognized as an image of Courbet himself. And since the implicit narrative of the scene suggests that it is that figure who has killed the *chevreuil*, or roe deer, hanging from a branch to his right (our left), it will be necessary to explore questions of linkage between the theme of hunting and the project of self-representation in Courbet's art, as well as between both of these and Courbet's avowed Realism. Another feature of *The Quarry* that should be mentioned at the outset is that it was composed in stages, by a process that involved joining pieces of canvas to one another. The largest segment, undoubtedly the first to be painted, comprises the roe deer and hunter; to that segment Courbet added another, on which he depicted the young man in a bright red vest blowing a hunting horn and the two dogs in the right foreground; finally, additional strips of canvas were attached at the extreme left and, later, across the upper portion of the picture.[2] *The Quarry* is not unique in Courbet's oeuvre in having been constructed in this fashion, but it is a particularly clear instance of the method and, as we shall see, yields special insight into the forces at work in his art.

My approach to *The Quarry* will be consistent with my other

76

Museum of Fine Arts, Boston, Henry Lillie Pierce Fund. Phot. Museum.
Fig. 1. Courbet, *The Quarry*, 1856.

essays on Courbet, which emphasize the relationship between painting and beholder.[3] Briefly, I interpret Courbet as one of two climactic figures, the other being Manet, in an antitheatrical tradition that arose in France around the middle of the eighteenth century.[4] In its first, Diderotian or Greuzian mode, the aim of works in that tradition was to deploy a set of mutually reinforcing techniques of dramatic closure so as to establish what might be called the meta-

77

illusion of the beholder's absence, or at any rate entire exclusion, from the scene of representation. As time passed, however, each of those techniques and *a fortiori* all of them in concert were increasingly perceived not as walling out the beholder but rather as specifically addressed to an audience of beholders, until by the 1830's and early 1840's (to telescope a long and complex narrative) the dramatic matrix that initially had been the means of achieving antitheatrical effects came to be experienced as signifying theatricality in its starkest, which for certain artists and critics also meant its direst, form.

The radicalness of Courbet's response to this situation can best be brought out through a comparison with his slightly older contemporary, Jean-François Millet, whose revulsion against the overtly theatrical art of his first teacher, Paul Delaroche, is documented by his biographers.[5] In Millet's scenes of peasant life of the 1850's and 1860's, one or more figures are characteristically presented as wholly absorbed in simple, repetitive, often largely mechanical activities and therefore as oblivious to everything else, including the fact of being beheld. The same relation to the beholder is obviously implied by others of those scenes that depict figures immersed in reverie or sunk in mindless exhaustion, as in the notorious *Man with a Hoe*. As will emerge, this aspect of Millet's resort to the ostensible naïveté of the absorptive as an antidote to the worst clichés of the dramatic (i.e., the dramatic become theatrical) nevertheless stopped short of breaking fundamentally with the conventions of visual drama, most importantly the conventions of locating a picture's protagonists at a fixed distance from the beholder within a strongly recessive space, of integrating their actions, poses, and even their contours in a single, narratively coherent, instantaneously legible gestalt, in short of *staging* their absorption and obliviousness in a manner that was likely to be self-contradictory in its effects. And in fact we find a striking division in the critical reception of Millet's work. On the one hand, some critics passionately admired Millet for what they took to be his ability to portray figures immured in their world and thus unaware of being viewed; on the other, a number of critics, including some who had formerly belonged to the first camp, reviled his art for seeking to impose such a fiction by patently theatrical means.[6] This suggests that a less equivocal response to the problem of theatricality in mid-

78

nineteenth-century French painting would have to involve a far more radical rejection of the values and conventions of visual drama, which is one way of describing what took place in Courbet's art virtually from the first.

The principal vehicle of Courbet's early work is the self-portrait, a genre that, by its nature, puts the artist in the picture. Most of the time, of course, this is merely a figure of speech. As said of Courbet, however, it is something more: almost all his self-portraits can be understood as having been produced by an extraordinary effort to translate himself as if bodily into the representation gradually being realized on the canvas before him, an effort that I understand in turn as at least partly motivated by a desire to negate or undo his problematic spectatorship, his identity as beholder—the *first* beholder, or *painter*-beholder—of his own painting. To take just one example, in perhaps the most ambitious self-portrait of the 1840's, the *Man with the Leather Belt* (1845–46; Fig. 2), the apparent proximity of the sitter to the picture surface, especially toward the bottom of the canvas, seems designed to collapse all sense of distance and indeed of separation between representation and painter-beholder and ultimately between painting and painter-beholder. The sitter's oblique posture, somnolent air, and shadowed, averted gaze combine to evoke a relationship between sitter (and painting) and painter-beholder fundamentally different from the one of intense face-to-face confrontation that typifies the self-portrait as a genre. Even more striking, the conspicuously awkward orientation of the sitter's strongly lit right hand and wrist matches what *a priori* we know was the orientation of the painter-beholder's right hand and wrist as he worked on the painting, a congruence of depicted and "real" elements that contributes powerfully to the effect of quasi-corporeal merger of sitter (and representation, and painting) and painter-beholder that I have associated with Courbet's self-portraits as a group. Finally, capping all this, the otherwise inexplicable sense of muscular tension conveyed not only by the sitter's right hand barely touching his jaw but also by his left hand gripping his belt may be seen as evoking the activity of the painter-beholder's right and left hands—the first wielding a brush or knife, the second holding a palette—as they were actually engaged in producing the *Man with the Leather Belt*.

In Courbet's first great Realist painting of 1848–50, the self-

Fig. 2. Courbet, *Man with the Leather Belt*, 1845–46?

portrait format is, to begin with, expanded to include other personages, as in the *After Dinner at Ornans* (1848–49; Fig. 3), and is then ostensibly surpassed in favor of a seemingly objective rendering, on a monumental scale, of chosen scenes from the life of his native region, the Franche-Comté, as in the *Stonebreakers* (1849; Fig. 4), the *Burial at Ornans* (1849–50), and, more folkloristic in character, the *Peasants of Flagey Returning from the Fair* (1850). But the surpassing of the self-portrait in these works is more appar-

80

Fig. 3. Courbet, *After Dinner at Ornans*, 1848–49.

Fig. 4. Courbet, *Stonebreakers*, 1849.

ent than real, or perhaps I should say more literal than metaphorical. Thus I have argued in previous essays that all the personages in the *After Dinner* originate in prior representations of Courbet himself; that the young man carrying a basket of stones and the old man wielding a hammer in the *Stonebreakers* may be seen as personifying the painter-beholder's active (i.e., laboring) left and right hands, respectively, thereby extending the representational strategy of the *Man with the Leather Belt* far beyond the presumed boundaries of the self; and that at work in the *Burial*, traditionally viewed as epitomizing a strictly metonymic pictorial organization, is a highly complex structure of points of view, vectors of attention, and partial identifications—displaced or metaphorical self-representations—by means of which a distinction is asserted between the painter-beholder, who here as elsewhere in Courbet's art cannot simply be equated with the historical Courbet, and the beholder *tout court*, who isn't exactly us. (Both are functions rather than persons, by which I mean that the distinction between them is structural and diacritical rather than empirical or psychological, though naturally any reading of that distinction will bear the stamp of a particular historicity and doubtless of an individual psychology as well.)

The *Peasants of Flagey* marks a tactical retreat from these complexities, but within a few years a new version of the expanded self-portrait turns up in two paintings that, as I interpret them, imply a further reflection on the nature of the enterprise of painting. In the first of these, the *Wheat Sifters* (1853–54; Fig. 5), the central female figure may be regarded as a surrogate for the painter-beholder not only by virtue of her posture (analogous to though not identical with his, seated in a chair before the picture), her orientation (facing into the picture and therefore roughly matching his), and the character of the effort she is putting forth (concentrated, physical, requiring the use of both hands) but also because the particles of grain falling from her sieve are seen to gather, almost to spatter, on the whitish ground cloth, as if on a blank canvas that already embraces the sifter herself. (If this makes the *Wheat Sifters* sound like a prophetic anticipation of the techniques of Jackson Pollock and Morris Louis, perhaps that too should be taken seriously.) Courbet's next ambitious painting, the *Painter's Studio* (1854–55; Fig. 6), makes these concerns all but explicit by depicting at its center the painter-beholder seated before his easel, applying the final strokes

Fig. 5. Courbet, *Wheat Sifters*, 1853–54.

to a river landscape into which he appears virtually to merge, even as the river and waterfall may be seen metaphorically to flow out of the canvas and beyond him, descending to the studio floor in the long folds of the otherwise naked model's white sheet and finally spilling into a heap of pinkish, circular eddies—her discarded dress. In both the *Wheat Sifters* and the *Studio*, moreover, subsidiary characters, notably a woman and child, play significant roles, which I take to indicate that the enterprise of representation required of the artist, at least at this stage in his career, an act of self-division or of self-multiplication—a kind of splitting—that the works in question may be said to allegorize or indeed embody. I also assume that the central group in the *Studio* represents a version of the so-called nuclear family, but that is a topic for another occasion.

I see *The Quarry* as closely related to the *Wheat Sifters* and the *Studio* in its essential concerns but also as going beyond them in ways that I shall try to specify. I will successively consider several closely connected topics: *The Quarry*'s character as a self-portrait; the theme of hunting, with particular emphasis on the treatment of the dead roe deer; the relation of the original or core image of hunter and roe deer to the finished painting; crucial differences between *The Quarry* and later hunting pictures by Courbet; and the implications of all these for our understanding of Courbet's Realism. At issue throughout will be, if not individualism as such, at any rate the structure, situation, and vicissitudes of the self in Courbet's art.

As I remarked earlier, the standing figure in boots and a brimmed hat leaning back against a tree with his arms folded across his chest while smoking a pipe has traditionally been identified as Courbet. There is no reason to doubt that this is correct; there is even a photograph of Courbet in a similar pose that might have served the painter as a model, though whether or not it actually did hardly matters to my argument.[7] What does matter is that the figure of the hunter seems absorbed—lost—in revery or reflection: his gaze appears directed downward, and his expression, what we can tell of it, suggests a prolonged moment of inward recoil after the excitement of the hunt.

Such a mode of self-representation is by no means unique in Courbet's oeuvre. The sitter's expression in the *Man with the Leather Belt* bespeaks a similarly inward mood, and in other self-portraits, notably the famous *Man with the Pipe* (1849?), the sitter's absorptive or reflective state of mind is even more palpable. At the same time, a comparison with the *Man with the Leather Belt* throws into relief the most distinctive feature of the self-portrait in *The Quarry*—the hunter-painter's apparent passivity. Not only is the figure of the hunter not engaged in any action whatsoever (unless we consider smoking a pipe an action, as perhaps we should); his hands have been wholly banished from view, tucked away under his arms, while the slightly concave line of his legs and the backward pressure of his weight against the tree underscore his seeming withdrawal from the events around him. Furthermore, that mood of withdrawal finds expression in the very rendering of the figure—in its shadowiness, its lack of sculptural definition, in short its ideality (a strange term to apply to Courbet but in this instance an appropriate one). We feel this all the more keenly when we compare the hunter, as sooner or later we must, with the young man to his

84

Fig. 6. Courbet, *Painter's Studio*, detail of central group, 1855.

left (our right): traditionally called a *piqueur*—technically, a master of hounds at a hunt—the latter seems to put his whole being into sounding his horn and in fact has been depicted with commensurate painterly vigor, coloristic brilliance, and sculptural force.

These observations lead me to suggest, in keeping with my summary remarks about the *Man with the Leather Belt*, the *Stonebreakers*, and the *Wheat Sifters*, that we are entitled to see in the *piqueur* in *The Quarry* another of Courbet's characteristically displaced and metaphorical representations of the activity, the mental and physical *effort*, of painting. Thus the young man's strange, half-seated pose (with nothing beneath him but his folded jacket) may be taken as evoking the actual posture of the painter-beholder seated before the canvas. The hunting horn, held in his left hand, combines aspects of a paintbrush (I'm thinking of the horn's narrow, tubular neck) and a palette (its rounded shape) though strictly resembling neither, and of course a horn being blown is also a traditional image of the fame Courbet forever aspired to win by his art. The *piqueur*'s right hand, resting on his hip, has been turned back into the picture space so as roughly to match the orientation of the painter-beholder's right hand thrusting toward the surface of the painting, a device we saw at work in the *Man with the Leather Belt*. Finally, the *piqueur*'s bright red vest, coloristically the most vivid element in the picture, associates him with the color Courbet almost always used (and uses here) to sign his canvases as well as with one of the principal signifiers in his art both of carnal presence and of pigment as such.

All this is not to say that the figure of the hunter is only nominally or trivially a self-portrait whereas that of the *piqueur* truly or essentially represents the painter-beholder at work on the painting. In the first place, the implied pressure of the tree against the hunter's back (to reverse the terms in which I put it earlier) may be held to register the pressure of the painter-beholder's chair against his back and rear: as we know from various photographs as well as from the self-portrait at the heart of the *Studio*, Courbet habitually sat as he painted. Thus even as regards bodily position the distinction between hunter and *piqueur* is less acute than at first it seems. (The absence of a seat beneath the *piqueur* I view as acknowledging the need to look elsewhere—to the tree behind the hunter—for the missing support.) Equally important, the apparent contrast between those figures may be seen as only a more emphatic or explicit version of the virtual disjunction within the *Man with the Leather Belt* between the sitter's averted, dreamy head and powerful, active hands, a disjunction that can hardly be taken as opposing nominal and essential modes of self-representation. Eventually I shall want to give a fuller account of the relations between hunter and *piqueur* and in particular of their connection as representations of the painter-beholder, but first it is necessary to consider the significance of other elements in *The Quarry*, starting with the dead roe deer.

In an obvious sense, the prominence in the left-hand portion of *The Quarry* of the roe deer's carcass, awkwardly hanging by its right rear leg from the branch of a tree, identifies the hunter-painter as an agent of pain and death and the enterprise of painting as a kind of killing. What must be stressed, however, is that *The Quarry* makes so little of these identifications, indeed that it suppresses potentially painful or brutal aspects of its subject. In addition to presenting the hunter as tranquil and detached, it shows the roe deer as dead but not bloody; the weapon that killed the roe deer is nowhere in sight; and although the title of the painting refers to a gory procedure, the traditional feeding of the slain animal's entrails to the hounds,[8] not only is that procedure not depicted, one might argue that the looming presence of the two dogs in the right extreme foreground draws attention away from the roe deer's carcass and thereby subtly reinforces the contemplative mood of the scene as a whole.

At the same time, what *The Quarry* elides it also finds means to express, at least indirectly. Thus, for example, blood has fallen on the ground to the right of the roe deer, the dog nearer the carcass straddling an especially bright spill (in fact he appears, from a few telltale strokes of red around his mouth, to have been drinking from it); the vermilion waistcoat of the *piqueur* may also be seen as flashing the color of the roe deer's gore; in place of the missing musket there is the *piqueur*'s hunting horn, previously described as symbolizing the painter's tools (and therefore linking those tools with the absent weapon); and although we aren't shown a disemboweling, I for one am struck by the implied violence of the exposure to the hunter's viewpoint of the dead roe deer's underside, specifically including its genitals.

The last observation may seem excessive. For one thing, I am attaching considerable significance to a "side" of the roe deer we cannot see as well as to a bodily organ that isn't actually depicted. For another, the hunter isn't looking at the roe deer but faces in a different direction. But I would counter that we are led to imagine the roe deer's genitals or at any rate to be aware of their existence by the exposure to our view of the roe deer's anus, a metonymy for the rest. I would also argue that the strategic placement of the anus, by which I mean its visibility (its exposure) *both* to the figure of the hunter within the painting *and* to the beholder (initially the painter-beholder) stationed before the painting, implies an equivalence or translatability between the two points of view. I would further suggest that, precisely because the roe deer's anus stands for so much we cannot see—not simply the roe deer's genitals and wounded underside but an entire virtual face of the painting—such an effect of equivalence or translatability may be taken as indicating that the first, imaginary point of view is more important, and in the end more "real," than the second. As in other pictures by Courbet, a displacement or deprivileging of the second, external point of view is a decisive index of what I have been calling his antitheatricality.

In this connection it is surely relevant that our attention is drawn to the roe deer's anus by the white fur surrounding it, a bright patch that stands out in turn against the dark tree trunk beyond. Further, the significance in *The Quarry* of what in a sense we are shown but cannot see is reinforced by the perspicuous representation of something we cannot hear—the blast of sound produced by the *piqueur* on his hunting horn, which, like the roe deer's underside, is turned away from us toward imaginary depths. Nor is it unimpressive that the exact curve and orientation of the horn are echoed by the tail of the rightmost of the two hunting dogs, whose black patches (the other dog's are reddish brown) suggest a connection with the dark-clad hunter and who gazes pointedly across the extreme foreground toward the slain roe deer.[9] The dog thereby links *piqueur* and hunter even as it redirects—better, activates and relays—the hunter's latent, errant gaze back toward the dead animal, whose wounded underside I have described as wholly exposed to the hunter's point of view. Understood in these terms, the composition of *The Quarry*, always held to be merely additive, a static assemblage of independent elements, emerges on the contrary as a subtly yet intensely mobile circuit of substitutions, displacements, condensations, and recombinations, a circuit in which the painter-beholder is implicated from the first and the beholder *tout court* is tacitly encouraged to take part.[10]

Something of this mobility and complexity is visible even in the original or core image of *The Quarry*, which juxtaposes hunter and roe deer in a rectangle of canvas barely large enough to contain them (Fig. 7). At first, the relations between the two components of this image may seem contrasting, even antithetical. For example, it is impossible not to be struck by the opposition between the slain roe deer's extreme vulnerability, as if to sexual assault, and the hunter's self-containedness, verging on impregnability. In addition a contrast exists between the hunter's shadowiness and recessiveness and the roe deer's comparative definiteness and apparent physical immediacy, a contrast appreciably diminished in the completed painting by the still-greater definiteness of the *piqueur* and hounds. Then too there is the obvious difference in orientation between hunter and roe deer, the first being upright or nearly so and the second pretty much upside down, its hindquarters in the air and its head and forequarters resting on the ground.

But the longer we contemplate these ostensibly simple oppositions, the less simple or clear-cut they are felt to become. To begin with, we gradually become attuned to a rough analogy between the hunter's and the roe deer's respective conditions, as if the hunter's immersion in revery made him dead to the world, or as if the lifeless stare of the roe deer epitomized the extinguishing of outward awareness that marks intensely absorptive states. I shall have more to say about this analogy shortly.

These considerations find support in a further affinity between the hunter's and the roe deer's respective bodily positions, namely in the fact that neither hunter nor roe deer is depicted standing freely on his own legs. Earlier I suggested that the hunter's posture of leaning back against the tree may be taken as indicating a bodily position closer to sitting than to standing, and I related that position to the physical circumstances of the painter-beholder seated before his canvas. Although I don't wish to suggest that the roe deer too is to be seen in these terms, I do want to propose that the relationship between the hunter's and the roe deer's respective situations is more nearly complementary than antithetical. Thus if we imagine the painter-beholder seated before the original or core image of *The Quarry*, the position of the dead roe deer may be read as evoking a quasi-material movement from within the image out to-

Fig. 7. Courbet, *The Quarry*, detail of core image.

ward its maker, much as in the central group in the *Painter's Studio* I have drawn attention to a succession of waterlike representations originating within the river landscape on the easel and flowing toward and beyond the seated figure of the painter. Among those representations, like a minor rapid or cascade, is the white cat playing just to the left of the painter's feet with its rump held high and its tail curving in the air. We might think of that cat as ancestral to the dead roe deer, or at least as expressing a comparable directionality, which in both instances must be seen as reciprocating the painter-beholder's quasi-corporeal absorption in and by the painting before him.

Furthermore, not competing with this structure so much as amplifying it, the opposing vertical orientations of hunter and roe deer—head up versus head down—suggest those of an object (here a subject) and its reflection in water, a motif that occurs frequently in Courbet's oeuvre, where, whatever its justification in nature, it always connotes the primacy of self-representation in his art. In quick succession and almost without comment, here are three examples of reflective motifs in his work: first, a superb and topographically characteristic rendering of a covered stream near Ornans known as *Le Puits noir*, probably dating from the first half of the 1860's (Fig. 8); second, the magnificent *Source* of 1868, a picture that condenses and in effect summarizes the central group in the *Studio* and could be shown to bear an interesting relation to *The Quarry* as well (Fig. 9); and last, a sketchbook page from the early 1840's on which are juxtaposed, at right angles to each other, pencil drawings of a bridge near Ornans reflected in the river flowing beneath it and of a young man in profile reading a book (Fig. 10). I see this page as an early and instructive instance of the mutual articulation of motifs of reflection and absorption that plays a constitutive role in numerous paintings by Courbet, *The Quarry* among them.*

Returning to *The Quarry*'s core image, the mirroring relation-

*In fact both the Baltimore *Le Puits noir* (also called *The Grotto*), with its juxtaposition of "absorptive" cave and gleaming reflections, and the Louvre *Source*, with its absorbed nude seen from the rear reflected up to the calf in the stream in the near foreground, exemplify this mutual articulation as well. It is as though the early drawing implicitly equates absorption in reading with reflection in water, leaving open the question as to how exactly this equation is to be worked out. For example, should we think of the young man as "reflected by" the text in which he has immersed himself? Or would it be more apt to think of the text as "reflected in" his absorbed consciousness? (To phrase these questions in this way is already to simplify the range of possibilities suggested by the juxtaposition of the two sketches.) I am also struck by the silhouettelike shadow on the wall beyond and to the left of

Fig. 8. Courbet, *The Grotto*, ca. 1860–65.

Fig. 9. Courbet, *The Source*, 1868.

Fig. 10. Courbet, early 1840's.

ship between hunter and roe deer seems to imply that the enterprise of self-representation that produced the figure of the hunter
had the immediate consequence of giving rise, as it were naturally,
to the image of the dead roe deer. Or perhaps we should say that the
relationship of something like mirroring that obtained between
the painter-beholder and his depiction as hunter in the original
canvas was displaced onto the plane of the canvas in the relationship between hunter and roe deer. What remains mysterious, taking this figurative reading literally, is the nature of the medium
of that displaced mirroring, that doubled or supplementary self-
representation. That is, in the absence of a body of water or other
reflective surface to "support" that mirroring, the doubling effect
emerges, when at last it is seen, as positively unnatural, all the more
so in that the roe deer's image by no means simply reproduces the

---

the young man reading, a classical trope for the act of representation and one whose
relation to the trope of reflection both in this instance and elsewhere in Courbet's
art requires to be thought through. Shadow and reflection are conflated, or at least
shadows appear in the place of reflections, in the Yale Art Gallery's *Hunter on
Horseback* (1864), a critical work for such an undertaking.

hunter's. In fact the greater vividness of the roe deer suggests that it may be the original and the hunter the reflection, a possibility that makes the medium of their relationship even more unfathomable.[11]

It may be, then, that we have detected in the core image of *The Quarry* an ontological uncertainty or instability that in the end demanded the addition of a third major term, the *piqueur* sounding his horn, as a means of acknowledging the activity of self-representation that produced the core image in the first place. At virtually the same time, the mirroring relationship between painter-beholder and his representation in the core image that I have suggested was displaced onto the place of the canvas in the mutual inversion of hunter and roe deer became displaced in turn, shifted in space and rotated through approximately ninety degrees, in the pairing of not quite identical hunting dogs. This last transformation has the double effect of making the likeness between the two terms far more palpable than ever before and yet of naturalizing it to the point of almost total inconspicuousness. In other respects as well the delicate, uncanny relationship between hunter and roe deer that prevailed in the core image was fundamentally altered by the addition of the *piqueur* and hunting dogs and the enlargement of the painting to its final dimensions. Hence it was only by working our way back to the core image that the internal pressures leading to its supersession could be made manifest.

With this grounding, we can now attempt to interpret *The Quarry* as a whole, by which I mean, first, to specify the conception of selfhood that it represents, and second, to relate that conception to the historically specific enterprise of Courbet's Realism. Our starting point must be the recognition, the gist of everything I have said until now, that all three principals—hunter, roe deer, and *piqueur*—are in different respects figurations of the painter-beholder: the hunter more or less directly (at any rate, the figure of the hunter is a self-portrait); the roe deer through a metaphorics of reflection; and the *piqueur* by virtue of a displaced, condensed, but, within the interpretive framework I have proposed, nonetheless legible thematization of the effort of painting. In addition, I have associated the hunter with the painter-beholder (and by extrapolation with the beholder *tout court*) by means both of a half-visual, half-imaginary relationship to the roe deer's hidden underside and genitals and of a movement into the picture reciprocating the outward movement or directionality of the dead roe deer.

This might be taken to indicate that Courbet in *The Quarry* splits or resolves the self into three distinct components and that the task of interpretation is to identify those components and to construe accurately their connection with one another, perhaps by analogy with classic texts of existential phenomenology. Thus, for example (and I give this as only one of various possible examples), we might find in Courbet's triad of *piqueur*, roe deer, and hunter a close equivalent to Max Scheler's distinction between "lived body," "thing body," and the heightened condition of the ego that he calls "ingatheredness," the last of which he describes as in crucial respects dominant over the others.* But it is here that caution is most required, not so much because of the dangers of anachronism—there is a sense in which efforts at historical understanding are inevitably anachronistic—as because the further gist of my observations has been that all three representations of the painter-beholder in *The Quarry* are so intensively and complexly related to one another that no assertion of fundamental or hierarchical distinctions among them can quite stand up under scrutiny.

For example, my account of the mirroring relation between hunter and roe deer in the core image strongly suggests that any interpretation of *The Quarry* that confers uncontested primacy or even simple centrality upon the figure of the hunter is ignoring certain facts. By the same token, that the figure of the *piqueur* wasn't part of the core image should make us skeptical of the proposition that the *piqueur* somehow outranks the dead roe deer, as in the Schelerian scheme the "lived body" is prior to and of a higher order

*Max Scheler, "Lived Body, Environment, and Ego" (an excerpt from *Der Formalismus in der Ethik und die materiale Wertethik*), trans. Manfred S. Frings, in Stuart F. Spicker, ed., *The Philosophy of the Body: Rejections of Cartesian Dualism* (New York, 1970), pp. 159–83. As defined by Scheler, the "thing body" (*Körper*) is one's body as object of perception by "all external senses by which we perceive the external world" (p. 161). The "lived body" (*Leib*), on the other hand, is something more fundamental—"the underlying form through which all organic sensations [and indeed all perceptions of the "thing body"] are conjoined and through which they are . . . sensations of a *particular* lived body, and not of any other body" (p. 165). In the state of "ingatheredness" (*Sammlung*), Scheler writes, "We are not empty, but inwardly *replete* and fully *imbued* and truly 'with ourselves.' . . . We are 'looking over' our *whole* ego in its total manifold, experiencing it as a totum entering into *one* act, one deed, one action, one work. . . . He who knows about this phenomenon also knows about the unmistakable character of the *givenness of lived body* connected with the phenomenon at this moment. One's own lived bodiliness is given here as 'belonging' to this concentrated totality that may exercise 'power' and sway over it. . . . The respective contents of this bodiliness appear to 'float by' this enduring existence, as it were." (p. 181, his emphasis.)

than the "thing body." It will also be recalled that I have linked the
piqueur's scarlet waistcoat with the roe deer's blood and the spatial
orientation of his hunting horn with that of the dead animal's
underside, thereby further devaluing the apparent opposition between them. Similarly, my earlier contention that the implied pressure of the tree against the hunter's back registers the pressure of
the painter-beholder's chair against his back while he painted *The
Quarry* militates against ascribing all expression of the activity of
painting, and with it the phenomenological value "lived bodiliness,"
to the figure of the *piqueur*. Even the hunting dogs take part in the
process of simultaneously reiterating and counteracting a certain
thematization of difference: each of them may be held to embody
key features of at least two and perhaps all three protagonists, and
moreover to do so in ways that help disseminate those features
across and about the pictorial field. (As I pointed out earlier, the
tail of the rightmost dog echoes the curve of the *piqueur*'s horn,
whereas his black patches are a link to the hunter and his gaze
leads toward the slain roe deer. The brown and white dog to the left
links roe deer and *piqueur* by its color; straddling and lapping the
roe deer's blood, it may also allude to the hunter or at least to his
responsibility for the roe deer's death.)

What must be accounted for, in other words, is not simply the
apparent differentiation of the self into three principal components
but also, more importantly, the double process of producing and undoing differentiation that this reading of *The Quarry* has attempted
to track and that ideally it would in no way arrest.

Earlier I claimed to see an analogy between the respective conditions of hunter and roe deer, as if the immersion in revery of the
one and the lifeless stare of the other could equally be characterized as images of intense absorption. To this I want to add that the
piqueur too appears deeply absorbed in what he is doing—I have
already implied as much by describing him as putting his whole
being into his task—and that, as in the case of the hunter, a shad-
owing of his features not only confirms our sense of his engross-
ment and therefore of his obliviousness to his surroundings but
also hints at a sinking into or merging with those surroundings,
which may perhaps be viewed as absorptive in their own right.
(Bright sunlight strikes the young man's cheek and ear, but his profile, inflected slightly but firmly away from us, is comparatively
dim. Among the features of his environment he seems unaware of is

the absence of a seat beneath him, though precisely the inconspicuousness of that absence testifies to a mutual agreement of figure and
setting that goes far beyond and may even be at odds with traditional
norms of stylistic integration or dramatic appropriateness.)

As in other Realist paintings by Courbet, the outcome of this
subtle concordance among protagonists and between the latter and
their environment is the evocation of what I think of as an absorptive continuum, a single psychophysical mood or condition coextensive with the painting as a whole and seeming almost to ma-
terialize, to find specific expression, in the figures of hunter, roe
deer, and *piqueur*, not to mention in the painter-beholder and beholder *tout court*. What is striking about *The Quarry*, however, is
that more perspicuously than in any previous painting that continuum embraces two extremes, the straining youth and the dead
animal, with a middle term, the abstracted hunter, at once separating those extremes and binding them together. To the extent that
the first extreme demands to be read as representing the effort of
realizing *The Quarry*, of actually producing it, the second extreme
must be understood as representing something "deathly" that nonetheless is continuous with that effort, that shadows or accompanies
or indeed transfuses it, that even perhaps is a condition of its possibility. And *that* can only be a specific body of habits, automatisms,
or, to use their most "deathly" designation, mechanisms, such as
are involved in *all* actions and functions of the living being from
the most primitive, instinctual, and unconscious to the most developed, intentional, and self-reflective.

Seen in this light, the hunter's fantasmatic passivity and *a
fortiori* his ties with the dead roe deer express the fact that the automatisms in question were independent of the painter-beholder's
control; conversely, the manifold affinity between hunter and *piqueur* bears witness to the equally important fact that those automatisms were mostly activated in and by the effort of painting *The
Quarry*, an effort that could not have succeeded—that could not
have begun—except by bringing automatism into play. The difference between Millet's and Courbet's respective treatments of absorption is thus not only a matter of staging, as crucial as I have
claimed such matters are. Taking *The Quarry* as typical of Courbet's
Realist canvases in this regard, an equally crucial difference (actually it is another aspect of the same difference) is that in Courbet
but not in Millet an absorptive thematics comprising a range of

states from the relatively active to the relatively passive is grounded in the painter-beholder's vigorous yet also automatistic engagement in a sustained act of pictorial representation that the painting as a whole—virtually in every feature—can be shown to represent.*

A once-famous but now obscure text by a French philosopher only slightly older than Courbet, Félix Ravaisson's *On Habit*, provides an unexpected gloss on these observations.[12] I can't hope to deal adequately with Ravaisson's little masterpiece in the remainder of this essay, but fortunately there is a brief, useful summary of his principal thesis in a lecture on his life and work by Henri Bergson. As Bergson remarks, *On Habit*

> bears a modest title . . . but it is a whole philosophy of nature that the author sets forth in it. What is nature? How is one to imagine its inner workings? . . . Ravaisson seeks the solution of this very general problem in a very concrete intuition; the one we have of our own particular condition when we contract a habit. For motor habit, once contracted, is a mechanism, a series of movements that determine one another: it is that part of us which is inserted into nature and which coincides with nature; it is nature itself. Now, our inner experience shows us in habit an activity which has passed, by imperceptible degrees, from consciousness to unconsciousness and from will to automatism. Should we not then imagine nature, in this form, as an obscured consciousness and a dormant will? Habit thus gives us the living demonstration of this truth, that mechanism is not sufficient to itself: it is, so to speak, only the fossilized residue of a spiritual activity.[13]

What interests me in Bergson's précis is less the explicit vitalism of the last sentences than the complementary notion that habit and more broadly automatism of every sort is a "part of us which is inserted into nature and which coincides with nature; it is

---

*Thus, for example, in the *After Dinner at Ornans* the active figure of Promayet playing the violin is at the opposite end of the table from the somnolent and perhaps dozing figure of Courbet's father. In the *Wheat Sifters* the kneeling peasant woman in the center foreground appears to exert herself far more energetically (though not much less mechanically) than the seated woman at the left, who seems almost asleep over her less demanding task. And in the *Studio* there is the obvious distinction between the seated Courbet working on his canvas and most of the other personages in the composition, many of whom appear almost stuporous in comparison. In the *Burial at Ornans*, too, a procession of mourners winds somnambulistically toward the open grave, the latter being one of several tokens of effort that I associate with the production of the painting. What distinguishes *The Quarry* from its predecessors is the wider range of absorptive states it depicts and especially the juxtaposition of vigorous *piqueur* and lifeless roe deer, which raises the question of the meaning of the continuity between extremes more pointedly than anything in the earlier pictures.

nature itself." It follows that to represent the self is necessarily to represent nature, just as to represent nature is at the very least to represent something of a piece with the self, something between which and the self no absolute distinction can be drawn. Or, to put this in terms closer to the original, will and nature for Ravaisson are radically, infinitesimally continuous with one another, expressions of a single indemonstrable but fundamental principle to which the concept of habit or automatism holds the key. Thus he argues that "habit is the common limit, or the middle term, between the will and nature; and it is a *mobile* middle term, a limit which ceaselessly displaces itself, and which advances by insensible degrees from one extreme to the other. Habit is therefore so to speak the infinitesimal *differential*, or, again, the dynamic *fluxion* between the Will and Nature. Nature is the *limit* of the movement of diminution [*décroissance*] of habit. Consequently, habit may be considered a method . . . for the approximation of the relationship, real in itself, but incommensurable in the understanding, between Nature and the Will."[14] And in a remarkable passage on what might be called the radical unrepresentability of the absolute continuity of nature, Ravaisson explains that the existence of determinate forms in space—of objects of all kinds—seems to imply discontinuity and limitation. "Nothing, therefore," he writes, "is able to demonstrate between those limits an absolute continuity, and, by virtue of that demonstration, from one extreme of the progression to the other, the unity of a single principle. The continuity of nature is only a possibility, an ideality indemonstrable by nature itself. But this ideality has its archetype in the reality of the progress of habit; it finds there its proof, by the most powerful of analogies."[15] Putting Ravaisson's speculations together with our observations on *The Quarry*, I am moved to suggest that the project of Courbet's Realism—of his metaphysics—was above all to represent that continuity and that unity in the only way they *could* be represented, that is, in figures of ostensible differentiation that ultimately require to be read in terms approximating those developed in these pages: as though the indemonstrable ideality of which Ravaisson speaks found a further archetype in Courbet's Realist paintings, and that there too what is required of the interpreter is a capacity for discerning powerful analogies.

In later hunting pictures by Courbet the depiction of pain and violence becomes increasingly explicit, with disturbing conse-

Musée des Beaux-Arts et d'Archéologie, Besançon. Phot. Museum.
Fig. 11. Courbet, *Death of the Stag*, 1866–67.

quences for his art. This is especially evident in the most ambitious of those pictures, the enormous *Death of the Stag* (1866–67; Fig. 11).[16] In a winter landscape, under an overcast sky, a great stag sprawls on the snowy earth surrounded by more than a dozen hounds. Its magnificently antlered head, profiled against the grayish hills in the distance, arches back in agony as one dog sinks its teeth into its breast and another attacks its right hind leg. To the right of the stag, almost directly in front of it, a bearded hunter cracks a whip in an effort to detach the dogs from their prey and physically restrains another dog, who longs to get at the stag as well. Farther to the right and somewhat nearer to us than either the first hunter or the stag, a second, beardless hunter in a fur jacket and hat, depicted largely from behind, is seated on a rearing horse. Finally, in the lower left-hand corner of the composition, just above the artist's initials, a wounded dog writhes on its back in the snow.

The contrast between this canvas and *The Quarry* could hardly be more extreme. In the first place, neither of the two hunters in the *Death of the Stag* invites being read as standing for the painter-beholder, either directly (neither one is a self-portrait) or indirectly (we aren't initially drawn to regard either figure as embodying the act of painting). Furthermore, *The Quarry's* mood of quiet inwardness, which the silent blast of the *piqueur's* hunting horn seems only to confirm, has given way in the *Death of the Stag* to an almost hallucinatory effect of audial-visual cacophony, both thematically, through images of the bellowing stag, baying dogs, rearing and perhaps whinnying horse, and whip about to be cracked, and formally, by virtue of the too-emphatic silhouetting of irregular, peculiarly spaced, in all respects inharmonious dark shapes (and in the case of the dogs and horse, dark and light shapes) against a bluish white ground. More precisely, the dominant notes of the *Death of the Stag* are, first, a terrible pathos, centered on the unbearable agony of the stag, and, second, an ungovernable excitement, a condition that, originally keyed to the intensities of the chase, now colors the image as a whole, finding explicitly sexual expression in the depiction of the erect penises of three of the more conspicuous dogs and of the wholly exposed and vulnerable genitals of the sprawling stag. To these notes we should probably add a third, the chilling impassiveness of the two hunters. But the crucial difference between the *Death of the Stag* and *The Quarry*, the one that goes a long way toward accounting for all the rest, concerns the issue of self-representation.

I just said that neither of the hunters in the *Death of the Stag* invites being read as an image of the painter-beholder. But if we shift our attention from the human actors to the dying stag, it becomes apparent, at least I claim it does, that Courbet has identified massively and unreservedly with the latter—with its struggles, its exhaustion, its agony, its imminent death. This is to say that the content of the *Death of the Stag* is fundamentally masochistic, the contrast between the sheer intensity of the stag's pain and the thoroughly alienating indifference of the hunters all but compelling us to empathize with the suffering animal even as we observe with detachment the pictorially disruptive consequences of so stark and unmodulated an opposition of expressive registers. From here it is only a step to conclude that the crucial difference between the *Death of the Stag* and *The Quarry* is that between the massiveness and immobility of Courbet's identification with the stricken stag and, in the earlier canvas, the dispersion, mobility, and multivalence of the painter-beholder's plural and partial acts of self-representation. And it requires only a slightly greater step to suggest that the essence, or one essence, of Courbet's Realism, not only in *The Quarry* but in the other post-1848 pictures we have touched on as well, lies in the *resistance* they offer to any massive, immobile, and thus self-transfixing identification with a single protagonist, even when, or especially when, as in the *After Dinner at Ornans* or the *Painter's Studio*, the pictures in question include a portrait of the artist himself. The force of that resistance is perhaps exactly cognate with the strength of the automatisms engaged in the production of a given work, the inherent inertia of automatism—its tendency to continue on its path, to repeat itself endlessly—being in this context naturally opposed to any freezing of imagery and consequent hypostatization of emotional response. And because such resistance involves a refusal to allow painting and painter-beholder simply to confront one another, it serves the aims of the antitheatricality that I have argued was basic to Courbet's enterprise virtually from the first.

I will merely note in closing, far too summarily, that the somewhat frenzied sexuality that glares forth from the *Death of the Stag* may have its origin precisely in the artist's introjection, in the course of painting the picture, of his own representation of the agonized stag. I allude here to the psychic scenario first proposed by Freud in "Instincts and Their Vicissitudes" and recently reformulated by Jean Laplanche and Leo Bersani, according to which an act of primary or nonsexual aggression, when turned back against the self by the introjection of a representation of the effects of that aggression, gives rise to sexual masochism and indeed to sexuality as such.[17] So interpreted, the sexual excitement of the hounds reflects an excitation taking place "within" the painter-beholder, as the extraordinary juxtaposition of writhing dog and Courbet's initials perhaps signals. There is even a sense in which the moment of self-aggression may be seen as delineated in the *Death of the Stag*: the depiction of the mounted horseman largely from the rear may be held to link that figure with typical representations of the painter-beholder in Courbet's art, and the stylized line drawn by the bearded hunter's whip against the sky suggests that the action of cracking that whip may be still another metaphorization of the activity of painting. This would mean that the two hunters are figurations of the painter-beholder after all. But their status as such remains meager and uncompelling, a matter of ideation rather than of incorporation, as if an impulse to declare their connection with the self fell far short of overcoming a prior, massive identification with the agonized stag.

What makes this line of argument especially intriguing is the fact that it isn't just the activity of self-representation that is dispersed, mobilized, and generally disseminated throughout *The Quarry*. In light of what has gone before and specifically of my account of what I have called Courbet's metaphysics, it makes sense to suppose that the theme of hunting that surfaces for the first time in *The Quarry* amounts to an acknowledgment that the painter was able to begin his work of representing the continuity between the self and nature only by shattering that continuity—introducing gaps in it that the ultimate aim of the painting would be to overcome. Put more strongly, *The Quarry* thematizes that shattering of continuity as an act of aggression, not to say of killing.[18] But as we have seen, it also elides, displaces, and disperses the evidence of that act, and moreover goes to great lengths to assert the hunter-painter's passivity, thereby disenabling both any detailed narrative reconstruction of the act itself and any settled, motivated, incipiently masochistic identification with the dead roe deer. In the *Death of the Stag*, by contrast, a narrativizing of aggression underwrites a theatricalizing of pain and suffering that nothing in Courbet's biography at the time suffices to explain. What we witness in the *Death of the Stag* is the breakdown of the metaphysics immanent in Courbet's most characteristic paintings, and what the Freudian scenario suggests is that the acknowledgment of the conditions of representation of that metaphysics in and by the theme of hunting made such a breakdown likely sooner or later.

POSTSCRIPT

In an analysis of late Assyrian sculpture,[19] Leo Bersani and Ulysse Dutoit argue that, at least in Western culture, realism, narrativity, and a fascination with violence are all functionally related. Their argument develops in two principal stages. First, they follow Gombrich in asserting a deep connection between narrative intent and pictorial and literary realism, maintaining, for example, that even the "useless details" said by Roland Barthes to produce "reality-effects" in realistic fiction "serve the narratives which they temporarily suspend; they provide narrative schemes with just the dose of the superfluous, and of the inert, which qualifies, and therefore renders more acceptable (more realistic . . .) the potentially mechanical order and potentially excessive intelligibility of narrative development." Or as they also put it: "It is as if we most easily recognized reality in narrative representations of reality. The dominant mimetic strategy in our culture has been a narrative one." And second, they claim that a narrativizing of violence "produces the ideal conditions for a mimetic relation to violence." Grounding their discussion in an analysis of the Freudian genealogy of sadomasochism, they conclude: "The immobilization of a violent event invites a pleasurable identification with its enactment. A coherent narrative depends on stabilized images: stabilized images stimulate the mimetic impulse. Centrality, the privileged foreground, and the suspenseful expectation of climaxes all contribute, in historical and artistic narratives, to an immobilizing self-displacement—that is, to the type of identificatory representations outlined by Freud in 'Instincts and Their Vicissitudes.' The historian's or the artist's privileging of the subject of violence encourages a mimetic excitement focused on the very scene of violence."

My reading of the *Death of the Stag* would appear to bear out Bersani's and Dutoit's thesis that the narrativizing of violence promotes an identificatory fascination with the resulting scene of violence. Where my reading departs from their larger argument is in my insistence on the anti-Realistic character of the *Death of the Stag*, and more generally in my equation of Courbet's Realism with the denial both of narrative specificity and of identificatory fascination as such. (Significantly, the *Death of the Stag* was criticized by Théophile Gautier in 1869 precisely for its unrealistic and "chimerical" character.[20]) Still more broadly, I would contend—Bersani and Dutoit cite me to this effect—that in the Western pictorial tradition, especially since the seventeenth century, scenes of absorption in which the progress of a narrative has been stilled or suspended function as characteristic matrices for realistic representations. Presumably Bersani and Dutoit would counter that such scenes gain their efficacy as matrices for realism by virtue of a certain tension with the demands of narration, and this may well be true. But the major instance of Courbet's Realism suggests that the required distance from narration may be greater than their position allows.

Just how much stress the theme of hunting exerted on the

counteridentificatory imperatives of Courbet's Realism may be gauged from a painting that amounts to a sadomasochistic reworking of *The Quarry*, the Metropolitan Museum of Art's *After the Hunt* (1863?). But a full account of the relationship between those paintings must await a future occasion.

"Disgregation of the Will": Nietzsche on the Individual and Individuality

WERNER HAMACHER

Individuality: the word is spoken—and not only in the language of philosophy—with a forked tongue.

The concept of individuality, logically determined as mediating between the generality of what it asserts and the specificity of what it means, speaks already of a commonality, of a partaking in the common, that threatens the claim to individuality. The concept of individuality betrays individuality in the very act by which this concept attempts to seize, in mediation, individuality's substance. And the betrayal is double: the concept betrays individuality by sacrificing individuality's claim of immediate singularity to the power of the generalized and generally comprehensible language and language use; and by means of this betrayal, it also indicates the specific structure of individuality both in relation to itself and in relation to generality. The ambiguity of the concept of individuality has left its traces in all systems dedicated to that concept's determination. To enter their history at a relatively arbitrary point: Leibniz insists that each individual is individuated throughout its entire essence ("omne individuum sua tota Entitate individuatur"),[1] and that it therefore comprises an infinity of determinations that correspond to the infinity of the universe even as they escape all finite knowing. He thus characterizes individuality as the representation of a totality with which it nonetheless does not coincide. According to Leibniz, the only entity capable of a complete knowledge of the individual is the one that gathers the totality of necessary determinations unto or into itself and that is therefore not

---

Translated by Jeffrey S. Librett.

subject to the conditions of their representation. The individual is thus a monadic unity of an infinity of determinations, and it can be grasped only by an infinite faculty of knowledge—that of God. Finite individuals are incapable of knowing themselves as individuals. Leibniz grasps individuality with reference to the universality of God; he grasps the representative character of the individual's infinite determination with reference to the presence of an absolutely necessary essence—as with reference to the vanishing point wherein all determinants of the individual are gathered and wherein the individual as such disappears into the universal. Thus conceived, individuality is a fundamentally theological concept destined or determined to redeem finite individuals from their contingency. When Christian Wolff defines the individual, in his *Philosophia prima sive ontologia*, as that "quod omnimode determinatum est,"[2] he expresses in the most simple way the consequence of Leibniz's thought about individuality: the individual is thoroughly determined from or by the totality of its logical, historical, social, and psychic conditions; and it is determined toward or for totality, such that no genuine force of determination can be attributed to the individual by which it might autocratically distance itself from the teleological movement dictated to it. Individuality is hence the not merely theological but also teleological concept of a totality of determinations each of which holds itself in a prestabilized harmony with all the others, a harmony whose stability is impregnable. The *compossibilitas* of all single determinations is the securing and totalizing ground of the individuality they unite into a destiny, and it is the ground of the knowledge of this destiny. The individual is the essence or entity established by its universal determination.

Rejecting the fundamental ontological and epistemological assumptions of the Leibniz-Wolff school, Kant made clear in his reflections on the *prototypon transcendentale* that thorough determination can only be attributed to a thoroughly necessary being, that is, to a highest being, an *ens entium*, which can never be considered an objective being, since it is inaccessible to finite understanding. Rather, this being can always only be considered a general form of representation regulatively underlying our constitution of objects. Individuality thus figures as an unknowable and nonpresentable prototype of objects that, being imitations of it, can never attain to its degree of positive determination. Finite reason constitutes the individual—that is, the infinitely determinate—as finite, changes the particular into the nonspecifically general, detypifies the typical and reduces its being in each representation. Since the original (*Urbild*) is no longer given but rather merely given up or projected, objects hover on the brink of forfeiting at once their imitative character and their determinate form. After Kant, the concept of individuality lacks the assured ground of a determination that could render it an object of knowledge, lacks the nonproblematic theo-teleological destiny by means of which the demand for its internal totality could be fulfilled.

The formula "Individuum est ineffabile" from Goethe's letter to Lavater of September 20, 1780,[3] arises, then, not from a sensualist animosity to conceptual rigor, but rather from an insight delivered by the disintegration of the great seventeenth- and eighteenth-century systems: that the individual must remain inaccessible to a finite faculty of representation, that its particularity cannot be grasped using general linguistic conventions, and that, because it is itself finite, even it does not possess the means to express itself in its totality as individual. In expressing itself as individual, it neither expresses itself as a whole nor expresses itself wholly: the whole has become, for knowledge and for language, a merely finite, temporally as well as structurally limited generality. Henceforth, individuality can stand for the capacity to project oneself onto an indeterminable multiplicity of possible forms, each of which is open to further possibilities of determination and none of which can terminate in a paradigmatic form. Individuality is no longer either the representation of a prior or transcendentally guaranteed presence or the forerunner of a universality in which it could realize its determination. Both Schlegel's thoughts on individuality, formulated in his encounter with Fichte, and Kierkegaard's thoughts on individuality, formulated in his encounter with Hegel and Schlegel, are to be read in this context.

For Nietzsche, the historically individual is first of all a form of past greatness whose attempted representation or repetition must deprive it of precisely its individuality. In *On the Use and Disadvantage of History for Life*, the second of the *Untimely Meditations*, he connects the conditions not only of the writing of history but of history itself and of the making of history to the efficacy of authentic individuality:

In order for [a comparison between the greatness of the past and the greatness of the present] to have a strengthening effect, how much variety must be overlooked, how violently must the individuality of the past be forced into a general form and all its sharp angles and lines smashed to pieces! In principle, that which was once possible could indeed only present itself as possible for the second time if the Pythagoreans were right in believing that, given the same constellation of heavenly bodies, the same would have to repeat itself also on earth, and down to the smallest details. (I, 222.)[4]

The conditions of the representation of the individual demand the generalization—that is to say, the deindividualization, the rape and ruin—of the individual (and even of its possibility) by imposing a universal law. Wherever the individual is repeated, it is already no longer the individual that it is supposed once to have been. The individuality whose images the past holds in store is merely a mythical figure, which can pass as a stereotype through changing times, lending them an aura of lasting glory. The individuality of the historical ideal, whose destiny is to distribute impulses of life in the present, must, by virtue of its character as ideal type, dig life's grave. Such an individuality allows not the individual but only its stiff, typical, and typifying form to be seized. The individual, however, would be precisely that which is consumed in no type, no form, no figure, and no codifiable reference.

Since it is governed by the law of repetition, even the present itself is incapable of offering what the form of representation destroys:

The individual has withdrawn itself into the interior: outside, one can no longer find its slightest trace; apropos of which, one might doubt that there could be causes at all were there not effects. Or do we need to engender a species of eunuchs to serve as attendants in the great historical world-harem? On them, of course, pure objectivity is beautifully becoming. But it almost seems as if the task were to watch over history to make sure that nothing comes of it but stories, and certainly nothing with the remotest resemblance to an event! (I, 239)

Under the pressure of traditional, representative types or models of individuality, the individual has forfeited the ability to differentiate itself effectively from the historical world to which it alludes in knowledge and action. It has become assimilated to the types in distinction from which it was to have borne witness to its own historical, sexual, and semantic difference. It is an equal among equals, castrated, deprived of precisely what made it individual, unequal—it is a eunuch among women. But in the realm of equality—whether historical equality between past and present, epistemological equality between what thinks and what is thought, juridical equality among the citizens of a society, or physiological equality between different genders or different ages—there is no history. History, as Nietzsche conceives of it, depends upon the inequality, indeed, the incommensurability, of the moments that take part in it. In the individual, this incommensurability stands out, becomes a power that deforms and transforms the uniformity of the historical stances and substances of knowledge; only thus can it become a properly historical power.

Individuality is so fully determined as incommensurability that no individual could correspond to its concept if it were at one with and equal to itself, if it were a thoroughly determined, whole form. *Human, All Too Human* proposes, in the interests of knowledge, that one not uniformize oneself into rigidity of bearing and that one not treat oneself "like a stiff, steadfast, *single* individual" (I, 719). Only the individual's nonidentity with itself can constitute its individuality. Measured against itself as concept, bearing, and function, the individual proves to be other, to be more—or less—than itself. Its individuality is always only what reaches out beyond its empirical appearance, its social and psychological identities, and its logical form. Individuality is unaccountable surplus.

Now if individuality is the irreducibly unequal, and if the individuality of past and present life is betrayed in the typological identifications of idealist, positivist, archaeological, and teleological historiographies, then the ground of the possibility of individuality—and so of any discussion, be it affirmative or critical, of individuality—can only lie in the margin of difference between the uniformity of the hitherto historical and a future as yet uninvested with types, meanings, and values. The term "individuality" properly applies only to what transgresses the series of forms and the form of forms (typological knowledge and its objective correlatives), dissociating itself from the rigor mortis of canonical life forms, eluding the subsumptive compulsion of general categories, advancing toward a future that withdraws from every typology and objectification. Individuality is always still to come. Never already given, it is what gives itself up—projects itself—out of the future as a possibility for the present, what has always not quite yet given itself up, and what, in this way, in its giving, withholds itself. In-

deed, there can be no life except where this individuality opens itself onto its future possibility. Hence the importance of the concept
of individuality in Nietzsche's thought. "Even we are not yet persuaded . . . that we truly have life within us," he writes in the second of the *Untimely Meditations*. As a "lifeless and yet uncannily
mobile concept- and word-factory, I may still have the right to say
of myself, 'Cogito, ergo sum,' but never, 'Vivo, ergo cogito.' I am
guaranteed the emptiness of 'being,' not the fullness and greenness
of 'life'; my original feeling ensures only that I am a thinking being,
not that I am a living being; ensures not that I am an *animal*, but
only that I am a *cogital*. 'First grant me life'"—thus cries out every
individual. "Who will grant you this life? No god and no human:
only your own youth." (I, 281.)

No power that transcends the individual—neither another human being nor anything above the human nor even this particular
human being—is the source of historical life; instead, that source
is what, in the individual, reaches out as "youth" beyond the borders of its historical determination into a still-open future. The
proposition with which free individuality grants itself existence—
not expresses or constates its being, since substantial being is not
given to it—reads no longer "Cogito, ergo sum" or, as simple performance, "Ego sum," but rather "Ero sum." With regard to my indetermination by or as totality and my interminable futurity, I
grant myself being. Only my futurity gives me life. This life is
never something present to hand that could be seized in descriptive
speech, never something already there or captured in the statement
of the whole of its readiness, but rather it is always what, in all futures, is still to come and what, in language, is merely announced.
Its discourse involves not predication but rather pre-dication in the
sense of pre-diction and promise, of pro-nunciation.[5] By pro-nouncing
in this manner I grant myself being. Individual being is never established in my speech but is rather announced there as a claim, re-
serving my futurity. Hence never is it stated sufficiently or with
a completeness that could be generalized. If the life of historical
generalities is subject to laws—and the second of Nietzsche's *Untimely Meditations* attempts to describe certain of these laws—
then the futurity of this life and the form of language that corresponds to this futurity in the never-sufficient announcement of its
life comprise the law of these laws.

To this notion of the futurity of the life that the language of free individuality inaugurates, one might object that no language could do without conventional rules of meaning. Nietzsche not only never denied the conventionalism of forms of language and life but devoted a large portion of his analytical labors to demonstrating that even the forms of logic, which don't wear the signs of their historicity on their sleeves, have the character of conventions motivated by cognitive economy. Yet these forms gain meaning only because they collectively relate to a future whose possibilities can be thoroughly determined by none of them, to a future that will decide upon their survival or decay. Thus, even the phenomena of the past and the present must be understood not merely within the frame of such conventional rules but rather in terms of what, as the future, alone sanctions the legitimacy of any given rule or threatens to withdraw this sanction. Nietzsche writes: "The judgment of the past is always an oracular judgment: only as master-builders of the future, as the initiated ones of the present will you comprehend it," and "Only he who builds the future [has] a right . . . to pass judgment on the past." (I, 251.) Even with the images of great historical individuals and individual epochs, individuality stands out only under a gaze out of the future. And even if language and social life are subject to conventional rules, they still gain eloquence and comprehensibility only in the space open to the future, the realm in which their validity, language, and comprehensibility is not assured but suspended. Understanding the evidence is possible only given the suspension of what is understood to be self-evident; language is possible only given the suspension of its traditional forms and living present. Indeed, the most general appears only on the site of what it cannot seize, namely, where it carries the future signature of the individual. Past and present owe their meaning to what, as individual, surpasses their totality, its rules, and its forms. Life springs forth out of its own future; the whole out of a particularity cut off from itself, whose progressive departure incessantly unsettles the borders of the whole and prevents it from closing itself off. Nietzsche's individuality opens to indeterminacy that which was, for Leibniz and his school, the *omnimode determinatum*, the individual. The individual, as the open ground of the thoroughly determinate, is its determinant indetermination.

The emphatic formulations that introduce *Schopenhauer as Educator*, the third of the *Untimely Meditations*, can only be prop-

erly understood when one takes into account the excessive function, in every sense, Nietzsche gives to what is individual and to
the idea of the sovereign individual. He writes:

> At bottom, every human knows quite well that he is only in the world
> one time, uniquely, and that no accident, however strange, will shake
> together for a second time such an oddly bright sundriness into the
> sameness that he is. . . . The artists alone hate this negligent hanging
> about in borrowed mannerisms and drapery of opinions, and they un-
> veil the secret, the bad conscience of everyman, the sentence: Every
> human is a one-time miracle. . . . The human who does not want to
> belong to the mass need only cease to be comfortable with himself: let
> him follow his conscience, which calls out to him: "Be yourself! What
> you're doing, supposing, desiring now—that's not you at all. . . . Each
> one carries a productive uniqueness within himself as the core of his
> being; and when he becomes conscious of this uniqueness, a strange
> radiance appears about him, that of the unusual." (I, 287–88, 306)

To all appearances, the Nietzsche of this text and of countless
others subordinates productive uniqueness—the engenderment
and education of which, despite its debt to chance, is the main concern of *Schopenhauer as Educator*—to an utterly anti-individual
purpose, namely, the metaphysical purpose of assisting nature to enlightenment about itself and of thereby consummating its perfection. This purpose is served by the "engenderment of the philosopher, the artist, and the saint within us and without us" (I, 326).

According to "We Philologists," a note composed about the same
time, "only in three forms of existence [does] a human [remain] an
individual: as philosopher, as saint, and as artist" (III, 326). The
summum of individuality, which nature achieves in the philosopher, the saint, and the artist, touches what is bare of all individuality. Indeed, the highest destiny and determination of individuality, its telos and its sense, is to lead the natural universe—which,
through its spatiotemporal existence, and thus through the effects
of the *principium individuationis*, has become foreign to itself—
back into unity, to reconcile it with itself, and so to become the
organ of its self-knowledge, its self-relation, its self. Individuality is
destined to be extinguished, at its climax, in the undifferentiated—
at the point "where the I is wholly dissolved and its life of suffering is no longer or nearly no longer experienced as an individual
life but as the deepest feeling of the sameness, togetherness, and
oneness of all that is alive" (I, 326). Individuality is here, much as

in Schopenhauer, essentially a function of the self-totalization of totality, of the systematization of the system. And yet, only— as Nietzsche acknowledges in the *correctio* from "no longer" to "nearly no longer"—nearly. Only a most extreme individuality, namely, individuality opposed to the forms of the general consciousness subject to the *principium individuationis*, can suture the gap between the system of nature and the "feeling of the . . . oneness of all that is alive." And this individuality opposed to individuality can only *nearly* sew up the gap between the oneness and the allness of the living, since it too is subject to the principle of (dis)articulation. Such individuality is the disunity of unity and the possible but never-achieved unity of the differentiated. Individuality, and *a fortiori* that of the philosopher, the artist, or the saint, is the moment in which the totality of the living comes to itself, without ever arriving at itself. Its productive uniqueness is productive difference.

Nietzsche treats the problem of individuality similarly in an earlier work, *The Birth of Tragedy*, where he argues that the Apollonian principle of division and differentiation is already at work in the original unity of the Dionysian. Individuation, "dismemberment, the properly Dionysian affliction" (I, 61), torments the "originally unified, the eternally afflicted and self-contradictory" (I, 32), not as a violence from without, but as the accomplishment of its immanent process. And if the Dionysian finds deliverance from the affliction of individuation, it is only in the fleeting forms of interpretation, appearance, and therefore, yet again, individuation. What inflicted the wound is supposed to heal it, but the wound, individuation, is also the life of the original unity of the whole. Thus Nietzsche tries, in this conception of the tragic process, even if not independently of Schopenhauer, to think the Dionysian process of unification and generalization as a process of its immanent Apollo, of the god of individuation—that is, of dismemberment, deception, and the nonsublatably apparent decay into appearance of what truly is. Schopenhauer, on the other hand, to whom Nietzsche's conception alludes, had placed individuality as a fault in direct opposition to the "indestructibility of our essential being in itself. For at bottom each individuality is only a special mistake, a fault, something that it would be better not to have around, from which it is indeed the actual purpose of life to draw us away."[6]

Nietzsche had, then, in *The Birth of Tragedy* already freed himself, by means of the thought of the mutual implication of his two principles, from Schopenhauer's hypostasis of an indestructible life substance, a substance from which individuality represented merely a regrettable, even sinful, deviation. And soon after his homage to Schopenhauer in *Untimely Meditations*, he could also explicitly turn away from the pessimistic philosophy of his teacher, from the condemnation of individuation as the original sin of humanity, a turn that occurs with increasing emphasis in *Human, All Too Human* and *The Gay Science*. A note from the posthumous papers of the 1880's returns critically to Schopenhauer's theory of individuation and attacks in particular the notion that individuation is fault, error, and aberration:

> The pessimistic condemnation of life in Schopenhauer is a moral condemnation. Translation of the herd's criteria into the language of metaphysics. The "individual" is meaningless, so why not give it an origin in the "in-itself" (and give his being meaning as "aberration")? . . . The failure of science to comprehend the individual becomes the object of due revenge: the individual is *the entire previous life in one line* and *not its result.* (III, 545)

The individual is hence not a tangent flying off from the circle of totality, not an error straying into the nothingness of its being from the will's way, the way trodden by only the great individuals, the philosophers, artists, and saints. The individual is also not the result of a process of procreation, for as such it would be a mere example governed by a racial type or lineage. It is the entire life process itself: "Each individual being is in fact *the whole process* in a straight line . . . , and therefore the individual has *monstrously grand significance.*" (III, 558.)

This historicized Leibnizian thesis—that the individual is the whole process and that no foreign instance could stand opposed to its internal universality—is, as it were, crossed out by the further determination that the individual can lay claim to *"monstrously grand significance"* only as a being capable of autonomy. Only in setting new goals for itself, only in tracing the design of a future into which it projects itself, proving itself free of conventions, customs, and morals, free for its own future self, does the individual become the monstrously significant single being in which the whole process of its becoming places itself under the sign of its own futurity. Only in relation to itself as the still-outstanding debt of a future self can it be a single and unique whole, free of any pregiven totality.

Another sketch intimately related in conception reads: "The *excessive* force in *intellectuality*, setting new goals *for itself*; certainly not merely to command and lead the lower world or for the maintenance of the organism, of the 'individual.' We are *more* than the individual: we are the whole chain, as well, with the tasks of all the chain's futures." (III, 561.) This accent upon new goals is reinforced by the following entry, which emphasizes how important the unheard-of is for the theory of exegesis:

> The individual both *is* and *produces* what is wholly *new*; he is absolute, all acts wholly *his own*. The isolated one draws the values that guide his acts ultimately only out of himself: since he must *interpret for himself in a wholly individual manner* even the words he inherits. The *exegesis* of the formula is at least personal; even if he *produces* no formula, as an *exegete* he is still productive. (III, 913)

The innovative character of the individual owes itself, however, to a specific trait of the force that posits values and new interpretations of words. This trait is—beyond the narrow sphere of literary hermeneutics—in every sense decisive for the structures not only of inherited formulas and types of action, but also of individuality.

But the trait would not preserve the organism or its resultant process; it would merely conserve what is already given. Rather, it can be a force for individuation and absolutization only insofar as it is a (self-)excessive force. Only the "feeling of fullness, of power wanting to overflow, . . . the consciousness of a richness wanting to give gifts, deliver up" (II, 731), only this excess of force transgresses the borders of a given inherited context; only this gets beyond the formulas, types, and values of social action, the grammatical rules, words, and codified meanings of a language, undoing their solutions in the act of interpreting them by the new. The individuating force surpasses the individual as determined by the historical totality of his moments. It de-terminates the determined. The individuating force wrests the determined from its determinations and limits, de-limits it and delivers it as a problem or task to a temporal excess that can be contained by no past and no present. The motor of the passage from the conventional formula to its interpretation, from universal type to specific transformation, is neither the individual as an organic unity or a unity of consciousness, nor individuality as an essence of personal identity, but rather individuality as the force that individuates by overabundance and anticipation. Since excess alone individuates, separate beings and their configurations are in debt to this overabundance of waiting. The individual is therefore neither an aspect of the whole, whether the latter be conceived as *totum* or *compositum*, nor the autonomous gestalt of a self-positing, substantial subject. What arises as individuality out of the excess of force structurally outdoes totality and subjectivity, and since there could be neither totality nor subjectivity without this excess, the outdoing of both is one of the conditions of their possibility. Individuality—or, more strictly, singularity—is, as *transcendens*, the transcendental of subjectivity. If there is an autonomy of the individual, it is only by virtue of what exceeds even this autonomy.

The fact that the life of the individual is inscribed in what goes beyond the sphere of its personal or objective givenness renders problematic the concept of life and the concept of individuality and its Being, as well as the language in which these concepts are articulated. In aphorism 262 of *Beyond Good and Evil*, in the chapter "What Is Noble?," Nietzsche pursues this problem, which does not reduce to the problem of the individual forms of discourse on individuality but concerns the articulation of a transcendental language. In accordance with the fictive history of society that he develops here—a history, one might add, of socialization in general—a species or type "becomes fixed, by the long struggle with essentially the same [unfavorable] conditions . . . into rigidity, monotony, and simplicity of form." If in a "fortunate situation . . . the monstrous pressure" to which the type is subject ever subsides, "the fetters and constraints of old training are suddenly [torn] asunder. The variation, whether as deviation [into the higher, freer, or more strange] or as deterioration and monstrosity, suddenly comes on stage in the greatest fullness and splendor; the separated one dares to be separate, dares to remove himself." (II, 735–36.) Deviation and degeneration, atypicality and monstrosity—in short, individuality—arise not simply from a continuous historical process but from the contingency of the lucky break that allows the fetters and traits of training to be broken and the suddenly old morality to be transgressed, so that the "as it were exploding egoisms, wildly turned against one another . . . no longer know how to curb themselves by means of this morality" (II, 735).

Trace, training, and rein rip apart in the fortunate situation in which the type seems to have blossomed into pure autonomy. Their constraint, the force of sociality become excessive, drives the type beyond itself. "It was this morality itself that had accumulated the monstrous force that bent the bow in such a threatening manner—now it is, now it is becoming 'outlived'!" (II, 735.) This morality of the type—of unity, universality, sociability, and form, of the determinant trait or trace and its restraint—has "outlived" itself. The type lives beyond itself, beyond its own life. It outlives its own life, though no longer as itself, no longer as the type and according to the measure of the life it has broken in and holds fixed, but rather as "the greater, more multifarious, more extensive life." The type "outlives" itself as "the individual" (II, 736). Of unity, a structurally illimitable multiplicity remains; of the generality of the communal polis and state, a disorganized anarchy of individuals remains; of logical universality, concepts luxuriating in self-incomprehension remain; of the drawn-out trait that held all within firm, objectifying contours, infinite self-withdrawal remains; and of the life that was coextensive with the reach of form, only "youthful, still undrained, still unexhausted decay" remains (II, 736). For insofar as it "outlives" itself, life becomes—in accordance with a nuance of meaning in the German as well as the English word—obsolete, useless, extinct. Life is "outlived." It no longer lives.

"Outlived" in this manner, life, although now something other than itself, nonetheless lives on out. Nietzsche writes, "Now it is, now it is becoming 'outlived,'" and, playing out the various potential significations of the word "outlived" in this aphorism, in the next sentence he turns to argue that the "dangerous and uncanny point has been reached where the greater, more multifarious, more extensive life lives on *out away* from the old morality"—and from the forms of life contained within it. "The 'individual' stands there, forced into being his own lawgiver, into conceiving his own arts and stratagems for the preservation, exaltation, and deliverance of the self." It is indeed, then, as another phrase puts it, "the genius of the race, overflowing out of all cornucopias of the good and the bad," that "lives on out away" from itself. But it "outlives" itself only as an overflowing, excessive genius that does not contain itself within the race, and it remains alive only as the atypical monstrosity of the individual, who can no longer have the resources of his race or her type at its disposal.

In the individual, this life's form—the life of the society—and its sense "outlive" themselves. But, far from sublating itself, society's life maintains itself in the individual only in delivering itself up to its own decay. In its individual survival, the society does not preserve the essence of its composition but rather essentially decomposes. The individual composes the decomposition of his society. "Outlived"—this means, in "to be outlived," to be wasted, insubstantial, without force; it means also, in "to become outlived," that something not used up, something not exhausted, endures beyond the outlived; and it means—in accordance with a sense of the German word that had itself been outlived but that Nietzsche reenlivened by his metaphorics of luxuriance—to live too excessively, to overlive an oversized, outsized life. In the sentence "The individual outlives," to which Nietzsche's aphorism can be condensed, all of these threads of meaning knot themselves together; the extinct type—of life, of being—has, in the exuberant splendor of the individual, lived out beyond itself in such a manner that now it merely decays there. The individual is nothing other than the unreined, voluptuous self-outliving of life, the ongoing passing away of an excessive being no longer susceptible of being seized in the unity of a historical, social, or logical form. Individuality "is" outliving. Living without living. "Living."

The individual does not live. It outlives. Its being is being out and being over, an insubstantial remainder and excess beyond every determinable form of human life. Instead of being a social or psychic form of human existence, the individual—the self-surpassing of type, or genius—is the announcement of what, generally translated as "superman" or "overman," is best translated in this context as "outman." But the individual is this announcement only in the mode of an uncanny, dangerous, luxuriating monstrosity, in the form of one who, having outlasted the death of its type, has returned to earth in the form of a living corpse. In the individual, Nietzsche diagnoses a "fateful togetherness of spring and fall," which reminds one of the "sign of ascent and descent" that he reads in himself and of which he enigmatically writes in *Ecce Homo*: "I have . . . already died as my father; as my mother I live on and grow old." (II, 1070.) Given the fact that in the form of his own maternity he outlives the form of his own paternity—that he outlives himself

and, thus living on, doubled, is his own *Doppelgänger* (II, 1073)[7]—
Nietzsche sees the good fortune of his existence and its "singularity, perhaps" (II, 1070). The splitting and doubling of the constitutive trait of the type, and not the type's unity, first give rise to
the singularity of a being. Only the dividual is the individual[8]—
"perhaps." This "perhaps" signals, beyond all empirical uncertainty, the impossibility of achieving any unambiguously exact
knowledge of a being whose singularity lies in its very sundrance.

Although the formulation "something becomes or gets outlived" may leave room for the hope that what outlives it is, by contrast, not yet used up or forceless, that what outlives is opposed to
what gets outlived as life is opposed to death, or that the dividing
line between both is as distinct as that which defines the type, the
comment on the "fateful togetherness of spring and fall" in the
epoch of individuality instructs us that there can be an outliving
only by virtue of the alliance—the misalliance—between this outliving and degeneration itself. The individual is the incommensurable, insofar as incommensurability is the site where two irrecon-
cilable magnitudes coincide. In the individual resides no undrained
or unexhausted positive force, but rather there the "still undrained,
still unexhausted decay" lives on and out. The individual is not
merely spring and fall together; it is the springtime of the fall. If the
type or model was the site of force, life, and being that presented
itself within the borders of its form and was supposed to preserve
itself there, then the "excessive force" and the "out(size) life" of the
individual release that which ruptures the form of the being of self-
preserving societal life: the individual's finitude. The being that
"outlives" itself in the individual is delivered up to finitude. The
individual, the "outliving," does not live on.[9]

Nietzsche takes up again at the end of his aphorism the problem and the word "outliving"—thus underlining its determinant
status for this text—and writes about those who alone survive
under the conditions of the general breakdown of a society decom-
posing into individuals: "Only the average ones would have the
prospect of carrying on, of propagating themselves—they are the
people of the future, the only ones to live on and out." (II, 737.) The
criterion of the type, lost to individuality, is reproduced for the purposes of self-maintenance in a quantitatively determined criterion
of the mean. But since the morality of the mean and of average
democratic equality does not serve the intensification but rather
serves the mere conservation of forces under the conditions of their

decline, the mean and its corresponding doctrine of equality are indebted to the excess of individuality against which they attempt to
defend themselves. Sheer living on is an apotropaism against the
finitude of the "outliving" from which it arose. Because the constancy outliving grants is merely appearance, discourse on the outliving of the average as its survival can only be ironic, as Nietzsche
himself implies. But discourse on the "outliving" of the individual,
which only carries itself out in the excess of passing away, is no less
inauthentic.

Nietzsche writes in one of his late notations, under the title
"Renaissance and Reformation":

> What does the Renaissance *prove*? That the reign of the "individual"
> can only be brief. The prodigality is too extreme; it has not even an
> outside chance to collect or to capitalize, and exhaustion follows at its
> heels. There are times when everything is *squandered*, when even the
> force itself with which one collects, converts into capital, and piles
> riches upon riches is squandered. (III, 825)

The realm of the "individual"—Nietzsche places the word again
and again in quotation marks in order to point out its inauthentic
use and its terminological vagueness—is the realm of waste, waste
even of the force that could re-collect, summarize, preserve, and increase what has been so lavishly spent. What wastes itself in the
individual and its "outliving" cannot—not even under the title "individual"—be converted into capital. The individual is just this
wastefulness and incapability to collect and convene itself, either
in the temporal unity of the duration of its outliving, in the unity
of social life, or in the unity of a concept.

If the title "individuality" in Nietzsche's writings says nearly
the exact opposite of what it means in traditional philosophical
texts, the manner in which Nietzsche uses the word "outliving"
corresponds that much more exactly to the event of individuality
his text sketches out. For instead of gathering into one what is not
itself a unit, this word—which thus ceases to be a "word"—disperses, in a grammatically and contextually determined manner, in
at least four different directions of signification: it means at once
longius vivere, supervivere, defungere, and *excedere*—"living-out-
away-from," "outliving," "out-" or "overliving," and "outlived."
The word that is to articulate the over- and out-structure of the
individual is itself over- and out-determined in such a way that
its individual significative moments can no longer be gathered together into a semantic continuum and thus converted into capital.

121

These individual significative moments, like the "egoisms," are individuals and individuals of individuals "side by side and often mutually entangled and ensnared . . . a monstrous ruination and self-ruin, thanks to the as it were exploding egoisms wildly turned against one another" (II, 736).

In "outliving," the individual significative moments outlive their own lexical senses and those of competing semantic tendencies just as the social type, the principle of sociality, and the continuum of sense that sociality guarantees outlive themselves in individuals. Individuality—like every other word in the epoch of "outliving"—takes on meaning only at the price of being ceaselessly irritated by some other meaning, in such a manner that the meaning taken on or assumed, because it is so loosely associated with its word, can be at any time overwhelmed and suppressed by another meaning. For the diversity of these meanings, there is no commonality other than the disparate commonality of "outliving." The construction of internally contradictory principles, excluded from the classical onto-logic that defined the individual by the immanence of its predicates in their subject, becomes, in the case of the structure of "outliving," an event that cannot be brought back under the domination of a semantic or pragmatic type, no matter what means of semiological purification might be employed to this end. The type has "outlived" itself and is "outlived": the individual—"outlived"—does not survive its outliving; the semantic surplus and the equally large semantic deficit of these sentences can be brought into the form of a clear and distinct meaning only by means of an arbitrary reduction.

Nietzsche would not have withheld from such a reduction and its resultant form the attribute of mediocrity. But every semantic restriction depends on the excessive character of "outliving" (the restriction itself having no other sense than that of conservative survival), and, further, every language and every other form of life in society is sketched out in view of the production of a continuum of sense (the continuum being given to this form in neither world nor text). For these reasons, the hyposemic exuberance of the word and thing "outliving" is the abyssal condition for every conventional use of language and for every life that executes itself in the forms of social exchange and communication. The indetermination, the over- and out-determination of "outliving," determines every life. The individual—"outliving"—would hence be the transcendental of the universal. To the same degree as it offers to universality—to society and concept—the ground of its possibility, it lets universality internally decompose. The individual—"outlived"—does not outlive the "over-" of its overlife. It grants neither the permanence that the type had promised nor the constancy that the mean ironically proclaims. Language become individual—the language of "outliving"—speaks no longer with the certainty of a general, communicable sense or of a type uninterruptedly producing new universalities; it speaks, "outlived," in that it breaks down. If its "outliving" is transcendental, it is so only insofar as it detranscendentalizes.

Individuality's structure of dissociation, excess, and remainder affects, further, the central category of Nietzsche's late work—the category of the will. Nietzsche points this out, in aphorism 262 of *Beyond Good and Evil*, with characteristically casual discretion: "Once again, danger is here, the mother of morality, the great danger, this time located in the individual, in what touches one most closely, and in one's friend, in the street, in one's own child, in one's own heart, in all that is most properly and secretly one's desire and will." (II, 736.) Like the individual, the will and even what is most proper to the will are in danger of wasting themselves, of exhausting and ruining themselves. Because the will, which has created the type in order to accumulate its own power, can only be the will to itself and the will to unconditioned autonomy of will insofar as it is already "excessive force," it too must transgress the organizational form of the type and any determined logical, aesthetic, or social structure; it must "outlive" itself in the disintegration of the forms that fix it. The will itself is and is becoming "outlived." It is no longer the center of autonomous operations but rather, disintegrated with itself, it is exposed to a tropical proliferation of its moments become monstrous or unseemly. This inevitable turning of the will against itself is for Nietzsche the signature of modernity. He describes it in the positivist sciences, in the growth of democratic ideals, and in the style of literary and musical decadence, and he analyzes it with the most vehement sarcasm throughout *The Case of Wagner*, in the disintegration of organic forms in Wagner's music.

In a passage that in great part assimilates the convictions of the theoretician of decadence Paul Bourget, Nietzsche writes:

I shall consider here only the problem of *style*. What marks out every *literary décadence*? That life is no longer at home in the whole. The word becomes sovereign and leaps out of the sentence, the sentence invades and obscures the sense of the page, the page takes on life at the expense of the whole—the whole is no longer a whole. But that is a simile for every style of *décadence*: in every case, anarchy of the atoms, disgregation of the will, "freedom of the individual," to put it in moral terms—and when expanded into a political theory, "*equal rights for all.*" (II, 917)

As the word leaps out of the sentence, the moment out of the totality, so the whole leaps away from the whole and becomes its mere suggestion. The whole exists merely as a theatrical play: it is pieced together, calculated, synthetic, an artifact. In contrast, the part is larger than the whole, more lively, organic, and authentic, and the whole merely a part of that part which has become sovereign over it. Thus, with stylistic decomposition, the whole disintegrates not simply into a chaos of parts but rather into, on the one hand, a whole that is essentially appearance, drama, suggestion, rhetoric, hypnosis, and mass-persuasion and, on the other hand, details in which alone life still survives and in which the truth about life can be said: that it is over and can now at most be feigned.

There are two sides of decadence, just as there are two Wagners: "Aside from Wagner the mesmerist and painter of frescoes, there is also a Wagner who leaves little precious objects aside: our most grandly melancholic musician. . . . A lexicon of Wagner's most intimate words, mere little things of five to fifteen beats, mere music, which *no one knows.*" (II, 918.) Unconcealed decadence of style, disarranged by no totalization, shows itself in the "overliveliness [or "outliveliness"] of the most small" (II, 933), shows itself, that is, where the individuated moments "outlive" both style and work and give the lie, through the exuberance of their life, to the mere appearance of life, an appearance engendered by technical management and propagated by the whole. The detail that has emancipated itself from the community of the work does not lie: its mere existence already tells the truth about the lie of the whole, tells the truth that there is no truth aside from the technical production of truth, and tells this truth in such a manner that no one—unless he should be called Nietzsche—apprehends it. The trivialities, the little things in which Wagner's greatness consists, are of the sort that—and Nietzsche underlines this—"*no one knows.*" What no one knows can confront no one under the shining appearance of the whole. But where it is acknowledged, as in Nietzsche, it stands under the sign of melancholy, of the loss of its own fulfilled presence. The "little precious objects," the "most small," the nuances have, scarcely leaving any sheen of appearance, withdrawn. They are left aside without substantial center. With them, both the realm of technics and positivity and the realm of aesthetics and phenomenality are abandoned.

Decadence of style corresponds ontologically to the disgregation of the will. When style as organic form deteriorates, so too does the will: for the will, as will, is nothing other than style. And when style, because of its decomposition, can only be feigned, the will is mere theatricality, rhetoric, and mass hypnosis. The will, "outlived," proves to have been technical management. It degenerates into the play whose movements it no longer dictates, and succumbs to disgregation in a passivity that is its conceptual contrary. "Disgregation" does not mean merely disintegration, dissolution of a whole form closed upon itself; as a term in the then-contemporary physics, with which Nietzsche was well enough acquainted, it also means the separation of the molecules of a body upon increased heat. (It is difficult, in this context, not to think of his remark that Wagner's music sweats.) Beyond this, by etymological connection with *grex* (herd), "disgregation" signifies "unherding," the dissociation of the dull mass Nietzsche again and again denounces as being subject to a will not its own. As his odd discussion of its disgregation implies, the will is itself the herd. The herd—the will's unity and wholeness, its organic totality—comprises the form in which the will ventures upon its overflow of force. Only in the will's degenerescence, when the herd, *will*, scatters apart, do the will's individual moments gain sovereignty and disperse, "outlived" as herding phenomena, into singular molecules of force that no type and no *archē* can gather together.

This emancipation of moments of the will—which can only be called such inauthentically, since they are no longer moments of one will—owes itself to the dissolution of the will itself and of the will's generative and regenerative force. The will's degeneration, its deviation from the form of the species and of the species' homogeneity, frees it of its herd form, of its form *tout court*, and frees it not in order to allow it to realize itself in its unconstrained power but rather in order to open it onto what, always at work within it, withdraws itself from the will's power: the heterogeneity of individuals who do not will, who do not will the will, and who cannot will or want the will; for even the will would still be a form of unification. The disgregation of the will into the singular and smallest sig-

125

nifies—as in the laying by of "little precious objects" in Wagner's melancholy music—a possibility of the will to escape the compulsions of self-relation and form proper to its own figure, to get free of its technical-spectacular style and totalitarian self-presentation. The will experiences this freedom not in itself and not as a will, but in the passivity of a disgregation that, subjectless, succumbs to the laws of the will as little as to those of the concept. That the will experiences disgregation does not mean that it can be sure of or that it can secure this disgregation, for here the will is no longer a subject, and disgregation is the mode of withdrawal from all objectification. It is without closure or determination.

Thus although Nietzsche again and again refers to the degeneration of the will as a descent, he also terms it an "ascent." The will's disgregation does not, however, become the beginning of a new unity, of a realm of freedom, license, and figureless raving. Because of its interminability and incompleteness, it becomes the possible beginning of the new ideologies of the freedom, equality, and destiny of man, indeed of the democratic and communist ideologies Nietzsche never tired of condemning as symptoms of nihilism. These ideologies preach the equality of individuals who, in the disgregation of the whole, have lost all common measure and who as incommensurable singularities can no longer have any social form that would be more than a juridical fiction, that is, a play. But the contextual coherence of those who have forfeited or are about to forfeit all organic context can only be imagined through the fiction of a contextual coherence: for example, through the fiction of the concept "individual," which maintains that these incomparable singularities are all in equal measure individuals.

The economy of this coherence—a coherence that expresses itself in the juridical, moral, and political fictions of the sameness, freedom, and personality of individuals and that is an economy of outliving, as aphorism 268 of *Beyond Good and Evil* displays—operates even for the disgregation of the will, so long as determinations of language and in general of communication are in play. The will does prosecute its own disgregation, and yet, so long as it submits to this disgregation as a will, the image of its objectivity, unity, and possible substantiality remains active in the disgregation (as in the specular subject-object bond of submission). Disgregation takes part in the histrionics of the will, and since disgregation is interminable, its partaking of the play of images or representations has no end. But even in the representations of this play, disgregation has no end; it is not limited by them and is never what they present. Instead of being itself a theatrical play of the will in which the ideas of equality and freedom appear on stage, disgregation discredits these ideas as theatrical play. Its taking part in the play's representations takes away a part of them—their stability, consistency, and technical character—and thus delivers them up to a movement that is restrained by neither political nor moral, neither linguistic nor phenomenological, determinations.

In the epoch of the disgregation of the will—and this epoch is for Nietzsche the epoch of epochs, for it has always already begun—the individual speaks in that it leaves behind linguistic conventions; it shows itself in that it retreats from the scene of generality and includes its own generality in this retreat. This process—this secession—is without destination or destiny not only in the sense that it meets no limit and comes to no end in a new unity but also in the sense that it has no addressee who would not be susceptible to the process itself. Nietzsche expressed this thought long before *The Case of Wagner*, in aphorism 367 of *The Gay Science*, in loose connection with his criticism of Wagner's music and in particular of its histrionics of totality. There he links his distinction between the art of the actor and the strictly individual art of the unseemly with the motif of the death of God:

> Everything that is thought, written, painted, composed, built, or in any way given form belongs either to monological art or to witnessed art. Even all the seemingly monological art that involves the belief in God, all of prayerful lyric poetry, falls within witnessed art: for the pious, there is no solitude—we, the godless, were the first to come up with this invention. I know of no distinction in all the optics of the artist more profound than the following: whether the artist views his work in progress (and "himself") with the eye of the witness or whether he "has forgotten the world." The latter is the essence of all monological art—such art is based on *forgetfulness*; it is the music of forgetfulness. (II, 241)

There can be no distinction in all artistic optics more profound than that between an art intended for a spectator—even if this be a transcendent spectator—and an art without regard for the view of another, even an utterly other, because of the distinction between an art of phenomenality—one which submits to the criteria for perceiving and being perceived—and nonphenomenal art. More precisely, since this distinction has to do not merely with sensual perception but also and more importantly with ideal perception (Nietzsche includes explicitly "everything thought"), it separates an art for another from an art that concerns no one and nothing else: neither a visual spectator nor a listener, neither an earthly public nor a god in whose eyes, according to the doctrine of *The Genealogy of Morals*, human suffering might, as theater, appear justified and fulfilled by meaning.

All art and all philosophy, all thought and all discourse that concern an addressee arise out of the belief in God and unfold as either conscious or involuntary theodicy. In opposition to the social and finally theological art of the dialogue, monological art (including philosophy) is theocidal. It knows no other and recognizes no God who could betoken its determinate destiny. Dialogical thought, action, or life is a form of prayer. The only life capable of monologue is life become godless, no longer in need of an addressee who would bestow sense on it to enable it to bear its own suffering. Only such a life would be able to accept its solitude without the illusion of a transcendental roof over its head and to accept its individuation without need of hope for its generalization. Only the life into whose solitude no God reaches is individual; only the life that gives (itself) up (as) the essential tenor of life is self-reliant. As long as God is not dead, there is no individuality. Individuality exists only as the project of its abandonment.

The solitude of monologue is, however, not the natural form of a discourse that would finally have reflected upon its own truth and self-reliance and rejected all supportive illusions. Even this solitude is, as Nietzsche explicitly states, an invention; even the death of God—as was God himself—is an invention, indeed, an invention made not by an individual in his solitude but by a community in view of its solitude: "We, the godless, were the first to come up with this invention." Even the monologue must bear witness to a community of the we, and even the absence of its addressee, its indeterminacy, takes part in the play of the will's representations. But the indeterminacy of monologue distinguishes its invention as being prior to all other possible inventions in the realms of thought, speech, and action: what is in this manner indeterminate can never become the positive product of the imagination or of the pedagogical force that forms images ("der Einbildungs- oder Bildungskraft"), and it can never be represented as the here and now of an accomplished realization. Indeterminate it remains, despite the most various determinations it may experience, open to all futurity and withdrawn from the constatation of the propositional discourse.

In aphorism 125 of *The Gay Science*, in which Nietzsche lets the madman announce the sentence "God is dead!," one reads: "This monstrous event is still on the way and wanders—it has not yet forced its way to people's ears." (II, 127.) Since it is merely still on the way and wandering, since it has not yet forced its way to people's ears, the speech of the madman changes nothing. It remains uncomprehended. But in his speech, this monstrous event is on the way and wandering and rendering this speech, however dialogically it may have been intended, monological—without referent and without addressee, withdrawn from constative knowledge. The monologue, always still on the way and coming on, never already wholly there and present, is nothing other than the progressive indetermination within the dialectical structures of both language and determination. In this progression God dies. In the monologue, the monstrous enters into the secure space of the conventions of language and thought to turn that space gradually into the unenclosable space of solitude. The monologue of individuality is on the way.

Since it is both outside and inside discourse, the monologue is still not already there ("immer noch nicht schon da"). And since it is the discourse of the departure from the obligatory and communal form of the *logos*, it is "the 'still' of the 'no longer'" ("das Immer-Noch des Nicht-Mehr") of this *logos*, the outliving of individuality in a masklike, posthumous figure foreign to the individuality outlived. The monologue, which is always the discourse of the death of God or his representative—life, the will, the subject—is spoken as posthumous discourse and as the discourse of the posthumous human. Such discourse still has to do with humans; it visits them, but its visitation is that of a ghost. Aphorism 365 in *The Gay Science*, entitled "The Hermit Speaks Again," deals with this matter:

> We too associate with, visit, "humans." We too modestly assume the dress in which (*as* which) one knows, respects, seeks us, and we betake ourselves thus to society—that is, among the disguised who do not want to be considered such—we too act like all smart masks and politely show the way out to each curiosity that does not concern our "dress." But there are also other manners and cunning devices for visiting among humans: for example, as a ghost—which is highly advis-

able if one wants to get rid of them soon, to frighten them away. Test: . . . we come . . . after we have already died. The latter is the cunning device of the *posthumous* humans *par excellence."* (II, 238–39)

Dead during their lifetimes because hidden beneath masks of conventional manners and alive only after their deaths—as script, rumor, remembrance, and delayed aftereffect—posthumous humans announce their individuality only as the living dead, as the survivors of outliving, as ghosts. They present themselves as disarrangement.

This form stands under the sign of withholding and subsequent supplementation; the survivors are not at liberty not to disguise themselves or to present themselves in the *oratio recta* of their authentic and proper being. Their language is, like every language, a mask; they themselves, like those hidden beneath masks, live only as those departed from their masks. The individual is the departed par excellence. Therefore Nietzsche lets the hermit speak as his mask instead of speaking in person, and he lets the hermit speak of his solitude, which is for him a metaphor for death. The individual has departed not only from a life that promises community with others but, by "outliving," from death and from the community of the dead. In the intermediate realm of indeterminacy between life and death, the individual's language is social synthesis only insofar as it is an agent of disgregation, communication only insofar as it preserves a most extreme discretion. Language conceals. It conceals, not a determinate something that might just as well be expressed or caught in a nonlinguistic form of communication, but, as language, what slips away from all determination, the indeterminacy of departedness itself, which can be brought neither to language nor simply to silence since it belongs to no realm of logical distinctions, neither that of life nor that of death.

By concealing yet always presenting the mask of the indeterminate within it, language—as language—announces that it breaks down before the indeterminate, that it changes the indeterminate, through the form of its reference, into one of the departed, and that it itself is departure. Language is departure—from every deep or hidden sense, from the subject that means to express itself in such a sense but takes the fiction of its substantiality only from the linguistic play of masks, and from the addressee toward whose comprehension language turns only in turning away from him as from a possible site of its determination. Individuals partake of one another and begin, under the sign of their nonsynthesis, to communicate exclusively in the moment of departure language marks. The sociality of language fulfills itself when language politely shows the way out to everything that seeks a relation to what it intends, be this a meaning or a person. The site of society as also the site of the individual is this departure, in which the two never cease to part both from each other and from themselves. In this manner, society and individual partake of community with themselves and others without making themselves common or mean. This is the only manner in which there can be any community: as the social visitation (*Umgehen*) of those departed from each other and from their common medium, from life and from death.

As is sufficiently well known but cannot be sufficiently thought out, Nietzsche accords special status to the emblem of the mask in his remarks on language and individuality. In the consideration of this emblem, despite the extent to which it offers itself to controversial interpretations because of its indeterminacy, the relationship of both language and individuality to phenomenality, wholeness, and necessity can be pointed out with particular precision. These problematic concepts—phenomenality, wholeness, and necessity—are in turn bound up with one another in the problem of determination or destiny in all of its dimensions, to which Nietzsche devoted much attention. Beginning at the very latest with "On Truth and Lie in an Extra-Moral Sense," he views language as morphologizing a world that otherwise would be a sheer chaos of infinitely differentiated moments of impression. Even the individual, which Nietzsche invokes in this context primarily against the power of the concept incapable of gaining possession of it, proves to be a morphological, indeed anthropomorphic construction on whose real content no judgment is possible, since the title "reality" is itself taken from and partakes of this morphologizing:

> The overseeing, outseeing, or oversight [*Übersehen*] of the individual and the real gives us the Concept as it gives us also Form, yet nature knows neither forms nor concepts, and therefore no species, but only an X as inaccessible to us as it is indefinable by us. For even our opposition of individual and species is anthropomorphic and does not arise from the essence of things. Although we also do not dare say that

it does not correspond to this essence, for that would be a dogmatic proposition and quite as insusceptible of proof as its contrary. (III, 313–14)

If even the individual is anthropomorphically schematized and if therefore only the overseeing, outseeing, or oversight of the individual gives rise to the "individual," then only the inaccessible, that which differs from whatever is grasped, is individual, whereas what can be caught by the concept of the individual remains a mere figure. Nietzsche later expanded this thought, acquired from his readings of Kant and Schopenhauer, to the question of the self-relation of human individuals and drew from it the consequence for consciousness that "consciousness doesn't actually belong to the individual-existence of humans . . . and it follows that, even with the best of wills, each of us, in the attempt to *understand* himself as individually as possible, to 'know himself,' will always bring only the nonindividual to consciousness, its own meanness" (II, 221). The consciousness of a self that is "incomparably personal, singular, unlimitedly individual," can, as consciousness—that is, as subject to the criterion of communicability—always conceive this self only as "a world of surfaces and signs," hence only in such a manner that it masks this self (II, 221). And the mask can have no point of correspondence with what it hides, for this hidden instance withdraws from all designation and all appearance. The designation phenomenalizes individual difference into something shown. It universalizes its communication in accordance with the measure of an economy of representability that is foreign to the unlimitedly individual. The "phenomenalism and perspectivism" of "communicative signs," of "signs of the herd" (II, 221–22), rests then on the systematic restriction of difference and on a morphologizing of what has neither shape nor self, neither substance nor positive subjectivity. The sign of the herd, consciousness (including even the most individual consciousness), is a mask.

This phenomenalism of consciousness and language is irreducible insofar as what lies hidden beneath the mask of its forms can always only appear yet again masked both in and for consciousness and language. For us, there is nothing behind the mask but masks—ideas, essentialities, meanings—nothing behind the mask but an X. As Kant insists that the barrier before the individual, before the thoroughly determinate *ens entium*, is for finite reason insurmountable, so Nietzsche insists that the unlimitedly individual, which is for him indeterminable, can only be grasped by consciousness and language as a determinate term and thus, beyond all correction, as disfigured. In the phenomenal and morphological determinations to which language and consciousness subject the indeterminable, an original difference from all origin, idea, and substance continues to disfigure the forms of consciousness. Only for this reason is it possible and proper to speak of the indeterminate as the individual and to determine it as the indeterminable.

In the same aphorism of *The Gay Science* in which he analyzes the "signs of the herd" of consciousness, Nietzsche speaks of a "surplus of this force and art of communication," of the surplus of a faculty or of an inheritance the artist and philosopher receive in "expending it wastefully" (II, 220). But this surplus of the capacity of designation and communication, this hypertrophy of form and consciousness—to reformulate Nietzsche's genealogical argument in structural terms—must contribute, always already and as overdetermination, to the determinations of the forms of consciousness and language, indetermining them, making their stiffened distinctions move, and convulsing the opposition between the signs of the herd and the individual-existence insusceptible of designation, between the phenomenalism of consciousness and the unshowing (*Aphanisis*) of its objects.

If the appropriateness or inappropriateness of linguistic signs cannot be measured against what they determine, if, therefore, they lack all transcendental ground of determination, and if their immanent law is subject to unforeseeable alterations, then the universal proposition that all universal propositions are mere appearance denies itself as appearance. By being different from itself, it thus mobilizes, in the economy of universal determinations that work to restrict individual difference, an economy of another sort: the economy of wasteful expenditure, of giving up the determinations themselves, of affirming difference. Since no determination can become an object of a determination in such a manner as to guarantee their strict correspondence, each determination, however general and susceptible of consensus it may appear, is nonetheless an unrepeatable, singular event. Its singularity—the singularity even of the most universal—consists in its destiny of indeterminacy. Singularity is incapable of attaining to a universally valid truth because it has neither a transcendent nor an immanent guarantee of the appropriateness of its forms at its disposal. The indeterminacy of its determinate destiny is its sole law, the law of singularity.

The waste of the "force and art of communication" (II, 220) that art pursues is an articulation of the law of indeterminacy to which every communication, every sign, is subject. Art is never form, shape, or image without at the same time, in its morphological surplus, leaving form behind, disfiguring shape, and surrendering the claim of the image to reproduce or produce a reality. If art wastes the *force and art of communication*, then it does so by partitioning what it imparts in sharing it, partitioning the part it takes both in what it imparts and in the addressee of the imparted. ("Wenn sie die *Kraft und Kunst der Mitteilung* verschwendet, so durch die Teilung jenes Mit, in dem sie ihre Gemeinsamkeit mit der von ihr gemeinten Sache und den von ihr angesprochenen Adressaten hat.") The phenomenalism of the sign opens itself in art onto the unseemly. If anything there still gets shown, presented, lit up, then it is the extinction of phenomenality, of the *eidos*, and of meaning itself; Wagner composed this extinction in the "secrecies of dying light" (II, 918). In art, communication (*Mitteilung*) denies both its claim to be able to operate in the space of appearances and forms as in the homogeneous sphere of the given and its claim to be able to belong immediately to this sphere itself. Art is nothing but the wasting of its appearance, and the expenditure of its communicative riches is also the internal communication of its moments. It is not a whole, but the whole that reveals itself as mask. Its form—which is not the form of a particular genus or genre but that of art insofar as it is art, of philosophy insofar as it is philosophy—is the form of the *aphorism* in its broadest sense: what is cut off, differentiated, and singled out. The site of art and of philosophy—the inexplicit site of every communication and of consciousness—is departure, for the organic totality that these discourses attempt to project in each of their acts begins where it is cut off from every foundation of determination, even if this foundation should be the definitive absence of foundation. The whole and each of its moments carry the trace of this severance, which makes each into a *singulare tantum*. Nietzsche plays out their associative possibilities in his books of aphorisms. Indeed, one could designate these aphorisms *metaphorisms*, if the word existed: particles that extend their particularity out beyond themselves and therein, *metaphorice*, impart themselves to one another as the im-parted.

If communication denies its claim to totality, then it also simultaneously denies its claim to the necessity of its forms. As an example of this, Nietzsche again and again chooses causality as the figure of explanation. Against the teleological assumption that all appearances have to be thought with reference to a common purpose, Nietzsche had already called up, in his early notes "Teleology since Kant," the "coordinated possibility" of chance to maintain the rights of the incalculably individual against the universal law of a final destiny.[10] In contrast to the necessity that every totality of representation requires, the individuality of the individual—which only stands out more clearly in art than in other communicative forms—is contingent and is the affirmation of contingency. Only contingency can accomplish what is denied to any rule, any decision of the will, and any act of consciousness as such; as the groundless, contingency can ground the singularity of the individual. Whereas the logical determinism and the determinist ideology of religious systems place the individual immediately before God, the thought of indetermination leaves it alone before the impossibility of deciding the existence or nonexistence of God, alone before the undecidability of its own substantial subjectivity. Exposed to the contingencies of randomness, the individual is never destined for wholeness either in itself, or in a nonproblematically accessible other, or in the history it would dominate. Randomness is not the other of the self, but rather the indeterminacy that governs the self—which has no power to determine it in turn—and that can be represented in forms of thought and life only as disfigured, incomprehensible, broken off. Not merely the appearance of the individual, rendered indeterminate by randomness, but its being is a mask.

Indeed the mask is for Nietzsche never arbitrarily selected and worn by one who could also choose to wear none. The mask—much like the desert—grows. "Every deep spirit needs a mask: further still, about every deep spirit there grows incessantly a mask, thanks to the permanently false, that is, *flat*, interpretation of every word, every step, every sign of life such a spirit gives." (II, 603–4.) But the mask grows on the individual and on each of the individual's words not only because of the leveling interpretation others give it and not only because they are incapable of keeping their eyes on the face or the backgrounds and the grounds of the mask—rather, each word is already a mask for the one who speaks

it and for the word that it is denied him to speak. "Every philosophy also *conceals* a philosophy, every opinion is also a hiding place,
every word also a mask." (II, 752.) The mask stands before no face
that would not itself be a mask; the word conceals—or designates—no sense that would not itself be a mask; the grounds of the
mask can be followed back to no ultimate ground that would not be
an abyss.

Nietzsche lets the hermit speak one more time: "The hermit
doesn't believe that a philosopher *could* ever have—assuming that
a philosopher has always been a hermit first . . . 'final and authentic' opinions at all, if for him behind every cave there were not another, would not have to be another, deeper cave . . . an abyss beneath every ground, beneath every 'grounding.'" (II, 751.) The mask
is a structural end for all knowledge and self-knowledge, for every
word and every communication, because all forms of knowledge
and representation must run aground in the attempt to secure the
ground of their determination. Determinate types of representation
in philosophy, art, and practical life may be historically, sociologically, or psychologically reducible to determinate motifs, but their
own relation to the possibility of their groundlessness and indeterminacy remains indeterminable and irreducible. The mask, and
therefore the entire realm of signs of phenomenality and forms of
consciousness, lies over an abyss whose cavity can be filled by no
form and no thought. Thanks to the mask, the illusion of a face can
take form, that of a subject thoroughly in control of itself yet hidden by the mask it has put on to protect its grounds and itself as
ground. The possibility of such a ground is an effect of the mask,
and this effect is always accompanied and suspended by the effect—
equally powerful yet incomparably more difficult to seize—of this
ground's impossibility. The mask shows itself, Janus-faced, to be
the opening of both of these possibilities, of grounding and groundlessness. It shows no determinate something and hides no showing,
but shows instead its hiding. In opposition to image and simile,
which still nourish the referential, semantic illusion that they
show something determinate or at least determinable, "all that is
deep loves the mask; indeed, the deepest of things hate images and
similes" (II, 603).

Form of appearance and thought though it be, the mask offers
in its self-denials a space for the suspension of appearance and
thought. If each language is structured like a mask, then each

speaks out of its incapacity to be, to hide, or to reveal its own foundation; it speaks out of the impossibility of determining definitively either itself or what it means. The determination by indeterminacy precedes in each language any possibility of determination. The deep ambiguity of language—its nihilism, if one wishes—is that it finds with each of its traits its determination, which it nonetheless cannot secure with a second trait as its own.

The mask, then, takes itself off. In that the universality of its form offers itself as detachable from every individual difference, in that it offers itself as universality, it leaves room for the possibility that it is without ground and background. In that it sets itself off from itself, the mask makes space for the individual in its difference from its presentational function. The site of the individual is neither before nor beyond the mask, but only in its differential self-relation. The individual is only what is exposed to the possibility of its groundlessness. It speaks in the gap between determination and the absence of determination, out of the "pathos of distance," out of the pathos of the progressive "expansion of distance within the soul itself" and its signs of life (II, 727). It speaks not as the substance of indivisible subjectivity but rather out of the distance and interminable expansion of distance that divides substantial subjectivity as the form of universality from itself.[11]

The individual shows itself only in the breach of its sign— where its showing gives itself up. If it can still be said, this can be only in a saying that unsays ("in einem Aussagen, das versagt"). Individuality unsays itself. It is, in a formula for the sublime that Nietzsche applies to the "free spirit," "what remains hidden beneath the cloaks of light," and—in a less biblical turn of phrase— at once "night owl" and "scarecrow" (II, 607): the Hegelian bird of absolute knowledge and what holds this bird at a distance (auto-apotropaism, the process of the self's taking self-distance, of conceptual withdrawal, of estrangement). Individuality unsays itself in the differential self-relation of saying; it is unsaid in all constatations, hence it says only in the mode of the not, the no longer, or the not yet. Because it is still to come, individuality is always only promised. It is not, but comes. Since it remains, however, without determination or addressee, hence also without goal and direction, it never comes as that which is destined for me, as my due, my own; rather it remains still to come, comes without end—it is the open distance out of which a substantial self never results. As promise, the monologue of my singularity must itself renounce me; other than as thus promised yet self-withholding, it cannot be. The future of this monologue is not the programed one into which I prolong my present self in order to sustain it and retain it as my own, but chance that strikes me without being destined for me and without being able to become mine. It is not I who speak the monologue of my futurity, but rather what in it, unarriving, indefinite, withdraws itself from my will: fate as a law that owes itself to no subjective positing act but to the speech of an instance, of a distance, of a disgregation that cannot be controlled by a subject—be it immanent or transcendent, conscious or unconscious—and that is never sufficiently spoken, never spoken as whole and as law itself, but that can only be perceived fragmentarily, in pieces.

"The individual is a piece of fate from the front and from the back, one more law, one more necessity for all that is coming and shall be." (II, 969.) But if this law of the individual, the law of its individuality, is fate "from the front and from the back," fate out of the past and out of the future, then the individual is individual and a law for all only after the entire future has been exhausted and the circle of recurrence has closed an infinite number of times. Even then, it is not the whole but a piece of fate that has become law for all. The individual is a fragment of the decree of fate that only in its entirety could ground the individual's autonomy; for only that entirety would allow the individual to be exclusively determined by what it determines. But as this fragment it becomes the law "for all that is coming and shall be," and for all that has been. The individual, a broken piece, is a law for the totality that alone could determine the piece as piece and fit it together into a whole—into the whole the individual itself would be. But a whole that is, even as a whole, a mere piece, a whole that stands, in its moral and social coherence and in its temporal extension, beneath the law of the piece, hence beneath a law in pieces—such a whole can offer to the individual as consolation neither the internal determination of an identical self that would have itself at its disposal, nor social totalization in the historical process. For the individual, there remains, without consolation, the freedom: to assume himself, under the law of disgregation, as indeterminate.

In contrast to the individualism that can be reconstructed by historiography—but within the frame of what concepts of the individual?—as a social and political movement or as an ideology, individuality allows neither reconstruction nor construction. For every such construction would need a principle that, as principle, would already mean the exclusion of individuality. What individuality is can only be experienced in the attempt to unfold the logic of indetermination that makes all constructions finally fail. The individual is the incessant undoing of the modes of identification it attracts. As the success of this undoing can never be guaranteed, the individual is in each of its experiences in danger. One of the dangers to which individuality is exposed is the danger of totalitarianism connected with all types of construction that make the individual their subject. Nietzsche indicates this attentively, but not without a slightly paranoiac and thus itself dangerous tone, when he writes in *Daybreak*: "They want nothing less—whether they admit it to themselves or not—than a fundamental transformation, indeed a weakening and cancellation of the individual; they do not tire of enumerating and accusing the evil and malignance, the wastefulness, the costliness, the extravagance of the previous form of individual being; they hope to administer more cheaply, less dangerously, more homogeneously, and more uniformly, when only large bodies and their limbs remain" (I, 1104).

On Ethnographic Self-Fashioning: Conrad and Malinowski

JAMES CLIFFORD

> . . . the age in which we are camped, like bewildered
> travellers in a garish, unrestful hotel.
>
> Conrad, *Victory*
>
> My whole ethics is based on the fundamental instinct
> of unified personality.
>
> Malinowski, Trobriand field diary

To say that the individual is culturally constituted has become a truism. We are accustomed to hear that the person in Bali,
or among the Hopi, or in medieval society, is different—with different experiences of time, space, kinship, bodily identity—from the
individual in bourgeois Europe or in modern America. We assume,
almost without question, that a self belongs to a specific cultural
world much as it speaks a native language: one self, one culture,
one language. I do not wish to dispute the considerable truth contained in even so bald a formula; the idea that individuality is
articulated within worlds of signification that are collective and
limited is not in question. I want, however, to historicize the statement that the self is culturally constituted by examining a moment, around 1900, when this idea began to make the sense it does
today.

In the mid-nineteenth century, to say that the individual was
bound up in culture meant something quite different from what it
does now. "Culture" referred to a single evolutionary process. The
European bourgeois ideal of autonomous individuality was widely
believed to be the natural outcome of a long development, a process
that, although threatened by various disruptions, was assumed to
be the basic, progressive movement of humanity. By the turn of
the century, however, evolutionist confidence began to falter, and
a new, ethnographic conception of culture became possible. The
word began to be used in the plural, suggesting a world of separate,
distinctive, and diversely meaningful ways of life. The ideal of an
autonomous, cultivated subject could now appear as a local project,
not a telos for all humankind.[1]

The underlying causes of this ideological shift are beyond my present scope.* I want only to call attention to the development, in the early twentieth century, of a distinctive ethnographic subjectivity. Modern anthropology—a Science of Man linked closely to cultural description—presupposed the ironic stance of participant observation. By professionalizing fieldwork, anthropology transformed a widespread predicament into a scientific method. Ethnographic knowledge could not be the property of any one discourse or discipline: the condition of off-centeredness in a world of distinct meaning systems, a state of being in culture while looking at culture, permeates twentieth-century art and writing. Nietzsche had clearly announced the new stance in his famous fragment "On Truth and Lie in an Extra-Moral Sense," asking: "What, then, is truth? A mobile army of metaphors, metonyms, and anthropomorphisms—in short, a sum of human relations, which have been enhanced rhetorically, and which after long use seem firm, canonical, and obligatory to a people."[2] Nietzsche, perhaps more than Tylor, was the main inventor of the relativist idea of culture. And my essay could well have been called "On Truth and Lie in a *Cultural* Sense."

I have instead taken my title from Stephen Greenblatt's *Renaissance Self-Fashioning*, a work that traces an emerging, bourgeois, mobile, cosmopolitan sense of the self.[3] The ethnographic subjectivity I am concerned with may be seen as its late variant. The sixteenth-century figures of More, Spenser, Marlowe, Tyndale, Wyatt, and Shakespeare exemplify for Greenblatt "an increased self-consciousness about the fashioning of human identity as a manipulable, artful process" (p. 2). I cannot do justice to the book's subtle and persuasive individual analyses, but I want to note Greenblatt's own ethnographic standpoint, the complex attitude he maintains toward fashioned selves, including his own. He recognizes the extent to which recent questions about freedom, identity, and language have shaped the version he constructs of sixteenth-century culture. He imports a modern critical approach to his material. Yet he writes, too, as someone caught up with and loyal to a tradition.

---

*A full analysis of changes in the "culture" response presupposes those forces taken by Raymond Williams as determinants: industrialism, social conflict, the rise of mass culture (*Culture and Society*, New York, 1966). To this would be added the needs of high colonial societies to understand the increasingly accessible diversities of the planet as a dispersed totality. The mapping of the world's human arrangements as distinct cultures asserts that things hold together, separately.

He expresses in a moving epilogue his stubborn commitment to the possibility of shaping one's own identity, even if this means only to "selfhood conceived as a fiction" (p. 257). He is led to what Conrad approvingly called a "deliberate belief."

Greenblatt is a participant analyst, constructing and engaging a cultural formation that is both distanced in the sixteenth century and dialectically continuous with the present. His "late," reflexive version of Renaissance self-fashioning relies on a sharply articulated ethnographic viewpoint. The fashioned, fictional, self is always located with reference to its *culture* and coded modes of expression, its *language*. Greenblatt's study concludes that Renaissance self-fashioning was anything but the unconstrained emergence of a new individualist autonomy. The subjectivity he finds is "not an epiphany of identity freely chosen but a cultural artifact" (p. 256), for the self maneuvers within constraints and possibilities given by an institutionalized set of collective practices and codes. Greenblatt invokes recent symbolic-interpretive anthropology, particularly the work of Geertz (also Boon, Douglas, Duvignaud, Rabinow, and Turner). And he knows, moreover, that cultural symbols and performances take shape in situations of power and dominance. One hears echoes of Foucault in Greenblatt's warning: "The power to impose a shape upon oneself is an aspect of the more general power to control identity—that of others at least as much as one's own" (p. 1). It follows that ethnographic discourse, including Greenblatt's literary variant, works in this double manner. Though it portrays other selves as culturally constituted, it also fashions an identity authorized to represent, interpret, even to believe—but always with some irony—the truths of discrepant worlds.

Ethnographic subjectivity is composed of participant observation in a world of "cultural artifacts," linked (and this is the originality of Nietzsche's formulation) to a new conception of language or, better, languages, seen as discrete systems of signs. The thinkers who stake out my area of exploration are, with Nietzsche, Boas, Durkheim, and Malinowski (inventors and popularizers of the ethnographic-culture idea), and Saussure. They inaugurate an interconnected set of assumptions that are just now, in the last quarter of the twentieth century, becoming visible. An intellectual historian of the year 2010, if such a person is imaginable, may even look back on the first two-thirds of our century and observe that this was a time when Western intellectuals became preoccupied with grounds of meaning and identity they called "culture" and "language" (much as we now look at the nineteenth century and perceive there a problematic concern with evolutionary "history" and "progress"). I think we are seeing signs that the privilege given to natural languages and, as it were, natural cultures is dissolving. These objects and epistemological grounds are now appearing as constructs, achieved fictions, containing and domesticating heteroglossia. In a world with too many voices speaking all at once, a world where syncretism and parodic invention are becoming the rule, not the exception, an urban, multinational world of institutionalized transience—where American clothes made in Korea are worn by young people in Russia; where everyone's "roots" are in some degree cut—in such a world it becomes increasingly difficult to attach human identity and meaning to a coherent "culture" or "language."

I evoke this syncretic, "postcultural" situation only to gesture toward the standpoint (though it cannot be so easily spatialized), the condition of uncertainty, from which I'm writing. But my concern is not with the possible dissolution of a subjectivity anchored in culture and language. Rather, I want to explore two powerful articulations of this subjectivity in the works of Conrad and Malinowski, two displaced persons, both of whom struggled in the early twentieth century with cosmopolitanism and composed their own versions of "On Truth and Lie in a Cultural Sense." Conrad may have seen more deeply into the matter, for he built into his work a vision of the constructed nature of culture and language, a serious fictionality he deliberately, almost absurdly, embraced. But a comparable grappling with culture and language may be seen in Malinowski's work, particularly in the difficult experience and literary representation of his famous Trobriand fieldwork. (This fieldwork has served as a kind of charter for the twentieth-century discipline of anthropology.)[4] Conrad accomplished the almost impossible feat of becoming a great writer (his model was Flaubert) in English—a third language he began to acquire at twenty years of age. It's not surprising to find throughout his work a sense of the simultaneous artifice and necessity of cultural, linguistic conventions. His life of writing, of constantly becoming an English writer, offers a paradigm for ethnographic subjectivity; it enacts a structure of feel-

ing continuously involved in translation among languages, a consciousness deeply aware of the arbitrariness of conventions, a new
secular relativism.

Malinowski remarked, "[W. H. R.] Rivers is the Rider Haggard
of Anthropology: I shall be the Conrad!"[5] He probably had in mind
the difference between Rivers's multicultural survey methodology
(collecting traits and genealogies) and his own intensive study of
a single group. For Malinowski, Conrad was a symbol of depth,
complexity, subtlety. (He invokes him in this sense in the field diary.) But Malinowski was not the Conrad of anthropology. He was
more like its Zola, a naturalist presenting facts plus heightened
"atmosphere," his scientific cultural descriptions yielding morally
charged humanist allegories. His most direct literary model was,
certainly, Frazer. Anthropology is still awaiting its Conrad.

My comparison of Malinowski and Conrad focuses on their difficult accession to innovative professional expression. *Heart of
Darkness* is Conrad's most profound meditation on the difficult
process of giving himself to England and English.[6] It was written in
1898–99, just as he definitely adopted the landlocked life of writing, and it looked back to the beginning of the process, his last,
most audacious voyage out—to his "farthest point of navigation."
On the journey up the Congo a decade earlier, Konrad Korzeniowski
carried with him the initial chapters of his first novel, *Almayer's
Folly*, written in awkward but powerful English. My reading of
Heart of Darkness embraces a complex decade of choice, the 1890's,
beginning with the African voyage and ending with its narration.
The choice involved career, language, and cultural attachment.
Malinowski's parallel experience is marked off by two works, which
may be treated as a single expanded text: *A Diary in the Strict Sense
of the Term*, his intimate Trobriand journal (1914–18), and the clas-
sic ethnography that emerged from the fieldwork, *Argonauts of the
Western Pacific* (1922).[7]

A word of methodological caution is needed at the outset. To
treat the *Diary* and *Argonauts* together need not imply that the former is a true revelation of Malinowski's fieldwork. (This is how the
Diary was widely understood on its publication in 1967.) The
Trobriand field experience is not exhausted by *Argonauts* or the
Diary or by their combination. The two texts are partial refrac-
tions, specific experiments with writing. Recorded largely in Polish
and clearly not intended for publication, the *Diary* caused a minor

scandal over the public image of anthropology—although field-workers recognized much in it that was familiar. One of the discipline's founders was seen to have felt considerable anger toward his native informants. A field experience that had set the standard for scientific cultural description was fraught with ambivalence. The authoritative anthropologist, in his intimate journal, appeared a self-absorbed hypochondriac, frequently depressed, prey to constant fantasies about European or Trobriand women, trapped in an endless struggle to maintain his morale, to pull himself together. He was mercurial, trying out different voices, personae. The anguish, confusion, elation, and anger of the *Diary* seemed to leave little room for the stable, comprehending posture of relativist ethnography. Moreover, in its rawness and vulnerability, its unquestionable sincerity and inconclusiveness, the *Diary* seemed to deliver unvarnished reality. But it is only one, crucial, version of a complex, intersubjective situation (which also produced *Argonauts* and other ethnographic and popular accounts). The *Diary* is itself an inventive, polyphonic text. And it is a crucial document for the history of anthropology, not because it reveals the reality of ethnographic experience, but because it forces us to grapple with the complexities of such encounters and to treat all textual accounts based on fieldwork as partial constructions.*

Malinowski and Conrad knew each other, and there is evidence from Malinowski's comments on the older, already well-known writer that he sensed a deep affinity in their predicaments. With reason: both were Poles condemned by historical contingency to a cosmopolitan, European identity; both pursued ambitious

*I juxtapose *Argonauts* and the *Diary* to highlight a critical discrepancy—historically important in the changing public constitution of ethnographic authority—between the best-known accounts of Malinowski's research process. At times I oversimplify the course of Malinowski's research and writing; the *Diary* actually covers work done in both the Trobriands and Mailu. By concentrating on two texts I ignore other, complicating ones, most notably, unpublished and presently unavailable diaries; Malinowski's "The Natives of Mailu" (1915); and his "Baloma: The Spirits of the Dead in the Trobriand Islands" (1916). In these last two studies he can be seen working out the personal and scientific ethnographic style that achieves full expression in *Argonauts*. A biographical account, or a thorough portrayal of Malinowski's fieldwork, or a depiction of Melanesian culture and history would select a different corpus. By stopping at 1922, I neglect Malinowski's ongoing rewriting of the dialogue with the Trobriands. In important ways, his last major monograph, *Coral Gardens*, experimentally and self-critically questions the rhetorical stance constructed in *Argonauts*.

145

writing careers in England. Drawing on Zdzislaw Najder's excellent studies of Conrad, one can speculate that the two exiles shared a peculiar Polish cultural distance, having been born into a nation that had since the eighteenth century existed only as a fiction— but an intensely believed, serious fiction—of collective identity.[8] Moreover, Poland's peculiar social structure, with its broadly based small nobility, made aristocratic values unusually evident at all levels of society. Poland's cultivated exiles were not likely to be charmed by Europe's reigning bourgeois values; they would keep a certain remove. This viewpoint outside bourgeois society (but maintained with a degree of artifice—rather like Balzac's standpoint in France of the 1830's), is perhaps a peculiarly advantageous "ethnographic" position. Be that as it may, there is no doubt about Malinowski's strong affinity for Conrad. (Just before the war, he presented the older man with a copy of his first book, *The Family among the Australian Aborigines*, with a Polish inscription; what Conrad made of Arunta notions of paternity remains, perhaps fortunately, unknown.) Although their acquaintance was brief, Malinowski often represented his life in Conradian terms, and in his diary he seemed at times to be rewriting themes from *Heart of Darkness*.

Nearly every commentator on the *Diary* has plausibly compared it with Conrad's African tale.[9] Both *Heart of Darkness* and the *Diary* appear to portray the crisis of an identity—a struggle, at the limits of Western civilization, against the threat of moral dissolution. But this struggle, and the need for personal restraint, is a commonplace of colonial literature. Thus, the parallel is not particularly revealing, beyond showing life (the *Diary*) imitating literature (*Heart of Darkness*). In addition to Kurtz's moral disintegration, however, Conrad introduces a more profound, subversive theme: the famous "lie"—indeed, series of lies—that in *Heart of Darkness* both undermines and somehow empowers the truth of the tale, the complex truth of Marlow's narration. The most prominent of these lies is, of course, Marlow's refusal to tell Kurtz's Intended his last words, "The horror," substituting instead words she can accept. This lie is then juxtaposed with the truth—also highly circumstantial—told to a restricted group of Englishmen on the deck of the cruising yawl *Nellie*. Malinowski's unsettled *Diary* does seem to enact the theme of disintegration. But what of the lie? The all-too-believable account? Malinowski's saving fiction, I will

argue, is the classic ethnography *Argonauts of the Western Pacific.*
Heart of Darkness is notoriously interpretable. But one of its
inescapable themes is the problem of truth-speaking, the *interplay*
of truth and lie in Marlow's discourse. The lie to Kurtz's Intended
has been exhaustively debated. Very schematically, my own position is as follows. The lie is a saving lie. In sparing the Intended
Kurtz's last words, Marlow recognizes and constitutes different domains of truth—male and female, as well as the truths of the metro-
pole and of the frontier. These truths reflect elementary structures
in the constitution of ordered meanings—knowledge divided by
gender and by cultural center and periphery. The lie to the Intended
is juxtaposed with a different truth (and it too is limited, contextual, and problematic) told on the deck of the *Nellie* to Englishmen identified only as social types—the Lawyer, the Accountant,
the Director of Companies. If Marlow succeeds in communicating,
it is within this limited domain. As readers, however, we identify
with the unidentified person who watches Marlow's dark truths
and white lies enacted on the stage of the yawl's deck. This second
narrator's story is not itself undermined or limited. It represents, I
propose, the ethnographic standpoint, a subjective position and a
historical site of narrative authority that truthfully juxtaposes different truths. Marlow initially "abhors a lie." But he learns to lie,
that is, to communicate within the collective, partial fictions of
cultural life. He tells limited stories. The second narrator salvages,
compares, and (ironically) believes these staged truths. This is the
achieved perspective of the serious interpreter of cultures, of local,
partial, knowledge. But the voice of Conrad's outermost narrator is
a stabilizing voice, whose words are not meant to be mistrusted.*

---

*For a reading close to my own but significantly different, see J. Hillis Miller,
"Conrad's Darkness," in *Poets of Reality* (New York, 1969), pp. 13–38. Here we find
strong arguments for seeing *Heart of Darkness* not as a positive choice for the "lie of
culture," but as undermining all truth, a more tragic, dark, ultimately nihilistic
text. Undoubtedly both in form and content the tale grapples with nihilism. Nonetheless, it does dramatize the successful construction of a fiction, a contingent,
undermined, but finally potent story, a meaningful economy of truths and lies. Biographical evidence reinforces my suggestion that *Heart of Darkness* is a story of
qualified but distinct success in truth-telling. I have already noted that the tale was
written just when Conrad finally decided to stake everything on his career of writing in English. In the autumn of 1898 he left Essex and the estuary (the place between land and sea) for Kent, to reside near other writers—H. G. Wells, Stephen
Crane, Ford Madox Ford, Henry James. This move, immediately following his last
recorded search for a maritime post, inaugurated his most productive years of literary work. A serious writing block was broken; *Heart of Darkness* emerged in an

Heart of Darkness offers, then, a paradigm for ethnographic subjectivity. In what follows I will be exploring specific echoes and analogies linking Conrad's situation of cultural liminality in the Congo with Malinowski's in the Trobriands. But the correspondence is not exact, and perhaps the most important textual difference is that Conrad expresses an ironic position with respect to representational truth, a stance only implicit in Malinowski's writing. The author of *Argonauts* devotes himself to constructing realistic cultural fictions, whereas Conrad, though similarly committed, represents the activity as a contextually limited practice of storytelling.*

In comparing the experiences of Malinowski and Conrad, one is struck by their linguistic overdetermination. In each case three languages are at work, producing constant translation and interference. Conrad's predicament is extremely complex. During the summer and fall before he left for Africa he had unaccountably begun writing what would become *Almayer's Folly*. After composing the opening chapters, he ran into obstacles. Around this time he came to know a cousin-by-marriage, Marguerite Poradowska, with whom he became in some significant way amorously involved. She was married and a well-known French author; it was largely a literary entanglement. Conrad wrote her rather passionate and self-

---

uncharacteristic rush. From this standpoint of decision, the tale reaches back a decade to the beginning of Korzeniowski's turn to writing, when, in the Congo, his luggage contained the first chapters of *Almayer's Folly*. In the reading I'm sketching out, *Heart of Darkness* is centrally about writing, about telling the truth in its most alienated, nondialogical form. Conrad does succeed in becoming an English writer, a limited truth-teller. It is not surprising, then, that in the blurred cacophony of the jungle Marlow yearns for English words. Kurtz was partly educated in Britain, and his mother, we recall, was half English. From the beginning, Marlow searches for Kurtz's intimate and elemental voice. And in the end, "this initiated wraith from the back of Nowhere honoured me with its amazing confidence before it vanished altogether. This was because it could speak English to me." (p. 50.) I cannot here discuss the many complexities in the staging and valuing of different languages in *Heart of Darkness*.

*Peter Brooks nicely observes that *Heart of Darkness* presents its truth as a "narrative transaction" rather than a "summing up" (i.e., Kurtz's last words). Meaning in the narration is not a revealed kernel but exists outside, dialogically, in specific transmissions; it is "located in the interstices of story and frame, born of the relationship between tellers and listeners." (*Reading for the Plot: Design and Intention in Narrative* [New York, 1984], pp. 259–60.) But in stressing the tale's "interminable analysis," Brooks minimizes the first narrator's stabilizing function as a special listener (reader), not named or given any such limited cultural function as are the others on the deck. This listener's invisibility guarantees an ironic authority, the possibility of seeing and not being seen, of speaking without contradiction about relative truths, of deciding their undecidability.

revelatory letters—in French. Poradowska, who lived in Brussels, was instrumental in arranging her kinsman's Congo employment. Then, in the months just before he left for Africa, Conrad returned to Poland for the first time since he had run away to sea fifteen years before. This renewed his Polish, which had remained good, and revived its association with childhood places and ambivalent feelings. From Poland (actually, the Russian Ukraine) he rushed almost directly to take up his post in the Congo. There he spoke French, his most fluent acquired tongue, but kept a diary in English and may have worked on the chapters of *Almayer*. (He claims as much in his "Biographical Note" of 1900.) In Africa Conrad established a friendship with the Irishman Roger Casement and generally maintained the pose of an English nautical gentleman. His intense letters to Poradowska continued, as always in French. His mother tongue had just been revived. The Congo experience was a time of maximal linguistic complexity. In what language was Conrad consistently thinking? It is not surprising that words and things often seem disjoined in *Heart of Darkness* as Marlow searches in the dark for meaning and interlocution.

As for Malinowski, in the field he kept his private diary in Polish and corresponded in that language with his mother, who was behind enemy lines in Austria. He wrote in English on anthropological topics to his professor, Seligman, in London. To his fiancée, E.R.M., in Australia, he wrote frequently, also in English. There are, however, at least two other women, old flames, on his mind, at least one of them associated with Poland. His most intimate Polish friend, Stanislas Witkiewicz ("Staś" in the *Diary*), soon to become a major avant-garde artist and writer, also haunts his consciousness. The two had traveled together to the Pacific and had fallen out just before Malinowski's Trobriand sojourns. He yearns to set things right, but his friend is now in Russia. These powerful English and Polish associations are interrupted by a third linguistically coded world, the Trobriand universe, in which he must live and work productively. Malinowski's daily transactions with Trobrianders were conducted in Kiriwinian, and in time his fieldnotes were largely recorded in the vernacular.*

*The "Polish" diary is extraordinarily heteroglot. Mario Bick, whose task was to compile a glossary and generally to "sort out this linguistic melange," specifies that Malinowski wrote "in Polish with frequent use of English, words and phrases in German, French, Greek, Spanish, and Latin, and of course terms from the native languages." (There were four: Motu, Mailu, Kiriwinian, and Pidgin; *Diary*, p. 299.)

We can suggest a tentative structure for the three languages active during Conrad's and Malinowski's exotic experiences. Between Polish, the mother tongue, and English, the language of future career and marriage, a third intervenes, associated with eroticism and violence. Conrad's French is linked with Poradowska, a problematic love object (both too intimidating and too intimate); French is also linked with Conrad's reckless youth in Marseilles and with the Imperial Congo, which Conrad would abhor for its violence and rapacity. Malinowski's interfering language was Kiriwinian, associated with a certain exuberance and ludic excess (which Malinowski enjoyed and portrayed sympathetically in his accounts of Kula rituals and sexual customs) and also with the erotic temptations of Trobriand women. The *Diary* struggles repeatedly with this Kiriwinian realm of desire.

So it is possible to distinguish in each case a mother tongue, a language of excess, and a language of restraint (of marriage and authorship). This is surely too neat. The languages would have interpenetrated and interfered in highly contingent ways. But enough has been said, perhaps, to make the main point. Both Conrad in the Congo and Malinowski in the Trobriands were enmeshed in complex, contradictory subjective situations, articulated at the levels of language, desire, and cultural affiliation.

In both *Heart of Darkness* and the *Diary* we see the crisis of a self at some "farthest point of navigation." Both render an experience of loneliness, but one that is filled with others and with other accents and does not permit a feeling of centeredness, of coherent dialogue or authentic communion. In Conrad's Congo, his fellow whites are duplicitous and uncontrolled. The jungle is cacophonous, filled with too many voices—therefore mute, incoherent. Malinowski was not, of course, isolated in the Trobriands, either from natives or from local whites. But the *Diary* is an unstable confusion of other voices and worlds: mother, lovers, fiancée, best friend, Trobrianders, local missionaries, traders, plus the escapist universes, the novels he can never resist. Most fieldworkers will recognize this multivocal predicament. But Malinowski experiences (or at least his *Diary* portrays) something like a real spiritual and emotional crisis: each of the voices represents a temptation; he is pulled too many ways. And thus, like Marlow in *Heart of Darkness*, Malinowski clings to his work routines, his exercises,

and his diary—where confusedly, barely, he brings his divergent
worlds and desires together.

A passage from the *Diary* will illustrate his predicament:

7.18.18 . . . *On the theory of religion.* My ethical position in relation
to Mother, Staś, E.R.M. Twinges of conscience result from lack of integrated feelings and truth in relation to individuals. My whole ethics
is based on the fundamental instinct of unified personality. From this
follows the need to be the same in different situations (truth in relation to oneself) and the need, indispensability, of sincerity: the whole
value of friendship is based on the possibility of expressing oneself,
of being oneself with complete frankness. Alternative between a lie
and spoiling a relationship. (My attitude to Mother, Staś, and all my
friends was strained.) Love does not flow from ethics, but ethics from
love. There is no way of deducing Christian ethics from my theory. But
that ethics has never expressed the actual truth—love your neighbor—
to the degree actually possible. The real problem is: why must you always behave as if God were watching you? (pp. 296–97)

The passage is confused. But we can extract, perhaps, the central
issue on which it turns: the impossibility of being sincere and thus
of having an ethical center. Malinowski feels the requirement of
personal coherence. A punitive God is watching his every, inconsistent move. He is thus not free to adopt different personae in different situations. But he suffers from the fact that this rule of sincerity, an ethics of unified personality, means that he will have to be
unpleasantly truthful to various friends and lovers. And this will
mean—has already meant—losing friends: "Alternative between a
lie and spoiling a relationship."

There is no way out. There must be a way out. Too much truth-
telling undermines the compromises of collective life. Malinowski's
solution consists in constructing two related fictions—of a self
and of a culture. Although my task here is neither psychological
nor biographical, let me simply suggest that the personal style—
extravagant, operatic—that both charmed and irritated Malinowski's contemporaries was a response to this dilemma. He indulged
in "Slavic" extremism; he liked to shock people. His revelations
about himself and his work were exaggerated and ambiguously
parodic. He would strike poses (he claimed to have singlehandedly
invented "The Functional Method"), challenging the literal-minded
to see that these personal truths were in some degree fictions. His
character was staged but also truthful, a pose but nonetheless
authentic.

One of the ways Malinowski pulled himself together was by writing ethnography. Here the fashioned wholeness of a self and of a culture seem to be mutually reinforcing allegories of identity. An essay by Harry Payne, "Malinowski's Style," suggestively traces the complex combination of authority and fictionality that the narrative form of *Argonauts* enacts: "Within the immense latitude of [its] structure Malinowski can determine shifts in focus, tone, and objects; the cyclical thread will always provide a place of return. Functional therapy acts only heuristically. Since everything adheres to everything, one can wander without ever getting fully disconnected."[10] The literary problem of an authorial point of view, the Jamesian requirement that every novel reflect a controlling intelligence, was a painful personal problem for the Trobriand diarist. The ample, multiperspectival, meandering structure of *Argonauts* resolves this crisis of sincerity. In effect, as the scientific, persuasive author of this fiction, Malinowski can be like Flaubert's God, omnipresent in the text, arranging enthusiastic descriptions, scientific explanations, enactments of events from different standpoints, personal confessions, and so forth.

Cultural descriptions in Malinowski's style of functionalism strove for a kind of unified personality, but a convincing totalization always escaped them. Malinowski never did pull together Trobriand culture; he produced no synthetic portrait, only densely contextualized monographs on important institutions. Moreover, his obsessive inclusion of data, "imponderabilia," and vernacular texts may be seen as a desire to unmake as well as to make a whole; such additive, metonymic empiricism undermines the construction of functional, synecdochic representations. Malinowski's ethnographies—unlike Radcliffe-Brown's spare, analytic functional portraits—were multifarious, loose, but rhetorically successful narrative forms.[11] Fictional expressions of a culture and of a subjectivity, they provided a way out of the bind of sincerity and wholeness, the Conradian problematic of the lie at issue in the *Diary*.

There are more specific echoes of *Heart of Darkness* in Malinowski's intimate Polish text. Speaking of informants who will not cooperate with his research, he damns them in Kurtz's terms: "At moments I was furious at them, particularly because after I gave them their portions of tobacco they all went away. On the whole my feelings toward the natives are decidedly tending to 'Exterminate the brutes.'" (p. 69.) Malinowski flirted with various colonial white roles—Kurtz-like excess included. Here the ironic invocation provides him with a fictional grasp on the stresses of fieldwork and on the violence of his feelings. In the *Diary*, like Marlow in his ambivalent doubling with Kurtz, Malinowski often faces the inseparability of discourse and power. He must struggle for control in the ethnographic encounter.

Another, non-ironic echo of *Heart of Darkness* is heard in his grief-stricken response to the news of his mother's death, which shatters the *Diary*'s last pages: "The terrible mystery that surrounds the death of someone dear, close to you. The unspoken last word—something that was to cast light is buried, the rest of life lies half hidden in darkness." (p. 293.) Malinowski feels he has been denied Marlow's rescued talisman, an ambiguously illuminating, potent last word, breathed in the moment of death.

But beyond the more or less direct citations in the *Diary*, one notes also more general, thematic and structural parallels with *Heart of Darkness*. Both books are records of white *men* at the frontier, at points of danger and disintegration. In both, sexuality is at issue: both portray an other that is conventionally feminized, at once a danger and a temptation. Feminine figures in the two texts fall into either spiritual (soft) or sensual (hard) categories. There is a common thematization of the pull of desire, or excess, barely checked by some crucial restraint. For Malinowski, the restraint is embodied by his fiancée, E.R.M., linked in his mind to an English academic career, to an elevated love, and to marriage. "Thought of E.R.M. . . ." is the *Diary*'s censor for lascivious thoughts about native or white women: "I must not betray E.R.M. mentally, i.e., recall my previous relations with women, or think about future ones. . . . Preserve the essential inner personality through all difficulties and vicissitudes: I must never sacrifice moral principles or essential work to 'posing,' to convivial *Stimmung*, etc. My main task must be work. Ergo: work!" (p. 268.)

Like Conrad's protagonist, the ethnographer struggles constantly to maintain an essential, inner self-reliance—his "own true stuff," as Marlow puts it. The pull of dangerous others, the disintegrating frontier, is resisted by methodical, disciplined work. For Marlow, obsessive attention to his steamboat and its navigation provide the "surface wisdom" needed to hold his personality in place. As invoked in the *Diary*, Malinowski's scientific labors serve a similar purpose. Restrained, ethical personality is relentlessly achieved through work. This structure of feeling can be located with some precision in the historical predicament of late Victorian, high colonial society. And it is closely related to the emergence of the idea of ethnographic culture.

Victorian social critics discerned a pervasive crisis for which Matthew Arnold's title *Culture and Anarchy* provided the basic diagnosis: against the fragmentation of modern life stood the order and wholeness of culture. Raymond Williams has offered a subtle account of these humanist responses to the unprecedented technological and ideological transformations in the mid-nineteenth century. George Eliot's strange affirmation is characteristic: of the three words "God," "immortality," and "duty," she pronounced, "with terrible earnestness, how inconceivable was the *first,* how unbelievable was the *second,* and yet how peremptory and absolute the *third!*"[12] Duty had become a deliberate belief, a willed fidelity to aspects of convention, and to *work* (Carlyle's solution). Ian Watt has persuasively tied Conrad to this response.[13] Marlow, in the midst of Africa, clings for dear life to his steamboat, to the routine duties of its maintenance and navigation. And the structure persists in Malinowski's *Diary,* with its constant self-exhortations to avoid loose distractions and get down to work. In the culture and anarchy problematic (which persists in those plural, anthropological concepts of culture that privilege order and system over disorder and conflict), personal and collective essences must continuously be *maintained.* The ethnographic standpoint that concerns us here stands half outside these processes, observing their local, arbitrary, but indispensable workings.

Culture, a collective fiction, is the ground for individual identity and freedom. The self, Marlow's "own true stuff," is a product of work, an ideological construction that is nonetheless essential, the foundation of ethics. But once culture becomes visible as an object and ground, a system of meaning among others, the ethnographic self can no longer take root in unmediated identity. Edward Said has remarked that Conrad's principal struggle, reflected in his writing, was "the achievement of character."[14] Indeed he reconstructed himself quite carefully in the persona of an English author, the character who speaks in the "Author's Note" he would later add to each of his works. This construction of a self was both artificial and deadly serious. (We can see the process parodied by the accountant in *Heart of Darkness,* who seems literally to be held together by his ridiculously formal but somehow admirable getup.) All of this gives special poignancy to the sentence that ends the published *Diary:* "Truly I lack real character."

Malinowski did, however, rescue a self from the disintegration and depression. And that self was to be tied, like Conrad's, to the process of writing. In this context it is worth exploring another region of similarity between the *Diary* and *Heart of Darkness,* the role of incongruous written texts. The fragmented subjectivity manifested in both works is that of a writer, and the pull of different desires and languages is manifested in a number of discrepant inscriptions. The most famous example in *Heart of Darkness* is Kurtz's strident essay on the suppression of savage customs, abruptly canceled by his own scrawled comment: "Exterminate all the brutes." But another, equally significant text loose in Conrad's jungle is a strange book Marlow discovers on one of only two perilous departures from his steamboat (on the other he wrestles Kurtz back from the wilderness). In a shack by the riverbank, he falls into an almost mystical reverie:

> There remained a rude table—a plank on two posts; a heap of rubbish reposed in a dark corner, and by the door I picked up a book. It had lost its covers, and the pages had been thumbed into a state of extremely dirty softness; but the back had been lovingly stitched afresh with white cotton thread, which looked clean yet. It was an extraordinary find. Its title was, *An Inquiry into some Points of Seamanship,* by a man Towser, Towson—some such name—Master in His Majesty's Navy. The matter looked dreary reading enough, with illustrative diagrams and repulsive tables of figures, and the copy was sixty years old. I handled this amazing antiquity with the greatest possible tenderness, lest it should dissolve in my hands. Within, Towson or Towser was inquiring earnestly into breaking strain of ships' chains and tackle, and other such matters. Not a very enthralling book; but at the first glance you could see there a singleness of intention, an honest concern for the humble pages, thought out so many years ago, luminous with another than a professional light. The simple old sailor, with his talk of chains and purchases, made me forget the jungle and the pilgrims in a delicious sensation of having come upon something unmistakably real. Such a book being there was wonderful enough; but still more astounding were the notes pencilled in the margin, and plainly referring to the text. I couldn't believe my eyes! They were in cipher! Yes, it looked like cipher. Fancy a man lugging with him a book of that de-

scription into this nowhere and studying it—and making notes—in cipher at that! It was an extravagant mystery. (pp. 38–39)

The passage has religious overtones—a miraculous relic, an abrupt movement in imagery from dirt and decay to transcendence and light and thence into mystery, the naive witnessing of a moment of faith. We must be careful not to interpret the *Inquiry*'s appeal to Marlow simply as nostalgia for the sea, though that is part of its charm. The Russian "harlequin," who turns out to be the book's owner, seems to read the treatise primarily in this way; for he takes careful notes, presumably on the book's content, as if he were studying seamanship. The inspiration of the book for Marlow, however, proceeds in some way directly out of the writing itself, which, transcending the chains and ships and tackle, is "luminous with another than a professional light." Marlow heeds not the content but the language; he is interested in the old sailor's painstaking craft; his way of making the book and his "talk" seem concrete—even to the abstract, numerical tables.

What charms Marlow is not primarily the possibility of sincere authorship. The old salt, "Towser, Towson—some such name—Master in His Majesty's Navy," is personally elusive; it is not his being that counts, but his language. The man seems to dissolve into vague typicality; what matters is his plain English. But, significantly, the text fails to unite its two equally devout readers. For when they finally meet, the Russian is overjoyed to greet a fellow seaman, whereas Marlow is disappointed not to find an Englishman. Readership is in question. The same physical book provokes different, equally reverent reactions. I cannot explore here the biographical significance of the disjuncture: Conrad had just shed his official Russian citizenship for British nationality, and arguably the harlequin is connected with the young wanderer Korzeniowski, who was becoming Conrad. It is enough to notice the radical relativity, the distance between the two readings. The "cipher" makes the point graphically. And if the marginalia turn out later to be in a European language, that in no way diminishes the graphic image of a separateness. (It is reminiscent of the unease one experiences upon finding strange markings in a book and then recognizing having made them oneself—another person—in a previous reading.)

What persists is the text itself, barely. Worn by readerly thumbing and cut loose from its covers—which may symbolize the context of its original publication—the written text must resist decay as it travels through space and time. After sixty years—a human lifetime—the moment of disintegration has come. The author's creation faces oblivion—but a reader lovingly stitches the pages back together. Then, abandoned to its death in the midst of a strange continent, its nautical content run aground in the absence of context, once more a reader comes to the rescue. Rescue is one of Conrad's key images for his work, and the act of writing always reaches toward rescue in an imagined act of reading. Significantly, the text that means most in *Heart of Darkness* is the one with least reference to the situation near at hand.

Malinowski's fieldwork experience is filled with discrepant inscriptions: his detailed fieldnotes, written in English and Kiriwinian; vernacular texts, often recorded on the back of letters from abroad; his Polish (actually heteroglot) diary; the multilingual correspondence; finally, a corpus worth lingering on for a moment— the novels he cannot resist. These are whole, narrated worlds that seem at times more real (in any case, more desirable) than the day-to-day business of research with its many incomplete, contradictory notes, impressions, data that must be made to cohere. Malinowski catches himself "escaping from [Trobriand actuality] to the company of Thackeray's London snobs, following them eagerly around the streets of the big city." (The escapist reading of ethnographers in the field perhaps requires an essay of its own.)

Malinowski's novels suggest a revealing though imperfect parallel with Towser's *Inquiry*—another wonderfully compelling fiction in the midst of confusing experience. Towser's book shows the possibility of personally and authentically speaking the truth, and it points toward writing (a miraculous presence-in-absence) as salvation. But Towser is also a temptation, like Malinowski's novels, drawing Marlow away from his work, his steamboat, into a kind of vertiginous reverie. Such readings are desired communions, places where a coherent subjectivity can be recovered in fictional identification with a whole voice or world. But Towser and the novels do suggest a viable path beyond fragmentation, not for the charmed reader but for the hard-working, constructive writer. For Malinowski rescue lies in creating realist cultural fictions, of which *Argonauts* is his first fully realized success. In both novels and ethnographies the self as author stages the diverse discourses and scenes of a believable world.

The loose texts in *Heart of Darkness* and the *Diary* are scraps of worlds; like fieldnotes, they are incongruent. They must be *made* into a probable portrait. To unify a messy scene of writing, it is necessary to select, combine, rewrite (and thus efface) these raw texts. The resulting true fictions for Malinowski are *Argonauts* and the whole series of Trobriand ethnographies; for Conrad, *Almayer's Folly* and the long process of learning to write English books, culminating in his first masterpiece, *Heart of Darkness*. Obviously these are different writing experiences. Ethnographies are both like and unlike novels. But in an important general way, the two experiences enact the process of fictional self-fashioning, in relative systems of culture and language, that I am calling "ethnographic." *Heart of Darkness* enacts and ironically calls attention to the process. *Argonauts* is less reflexive, but it does both produce a cultural fiction and announce the emergence of an authoritative persona: Bronislaw Malinowski, New-Style Anthropologist. This persona, endowed with what Malinowski called "the ethnographer's magic," a new kind of insight and experience, was not, properly speaking, constructed in the field. The persona does not represent, but rationalizes, an experience. The *Diary* shows this clearly: for the fieldwork, like most similar research, was ambivalent and unruly. The confused subjectivity it records is sharply different from that staged and recounted in *Argonauts*. When the *Diary* was first published, in 1967, the discrepancy was shocking. The authoritative participant-observer, a locus of sympathetic understanding of the other, is simply not visible in the *Diary*. Conversely, the pronounced ambivalence toward the Trobrianders, empathy mixed with desire and aversion, is nowhere in *Argonauts*, where comprehension, scrupulousness, and generosity reign.

One is tempted to propose that ethnographic comprehension (a coherent position of sympathy and hermeneutic engagement) is better seen as a creation of ethnographic *writing* than as a consistent quality of ethnographic *experience*. In any event, what Malinowski achieved in writing was simultaneously (1) the fictional invention of the Trobrianders from a mass of fieldnotes, documents, memories, and so forth, and (2) the construction of a new public figure, the anthropologist as fieldworker, a persona that would be further elaborated by Margaret Mead and others. It is worth noting that the persona of the participant-observer anthropologist was not the professional image about which Malinowski fantasized in the *Diary* (where it was a matter of knighthoods, Royal Societies, New Humanisms, and the like). Rather it was an artifact of the version he constructed retrospectively in *Argonauts*. In fusing anthropology with fieldwork Malinowski made the most, the best story, of what circumstance had obliged him to attempt.

Such considerations lead us to a problem in discussing Malinowski's—and indeed, nearly all—ethnographic production. Thanks to a flurry of recent confessional and analytic accounts, we know more and more about fieldwork experiences and their constraints. But the actual writing of ethnographies remains obscure and unanalyzed. We know something about Malinowski's Trobriand research between 1914 and 1918, but virtually nothing of what he was doing on the Canary Islands during 1920 and 1921. (He was writing *Argonauts of the Western Pacific*.)

The *Diary* leaves us hanging. There is a sudden gap in the writing that—we learn from small revelations as the text struggles to resume—signals the arrival of word that his mother has died. And then the desperate envoi: "Truly I lack real character." Silence. Three years later, Malinowski reappears as the author of *Argonauts*, charter of the new fieldworker-anthropologist. What has intervened? Like Conrad, in the period between the rout of his African adventure and the success of *Heart of Darkness*, he accepts three major commitments: (1) to writing, (2) to marriage, (3) to a limited audience, language, and culture.

The Canary Islands are an intriguing scene for Malinowski's writing cure. He goes there for his health, but the choice is overdetermined. One is tempted to see this place as a liminal site at Europe's outer edge, propitious for a displaced Pole writing Pacific ethnography. But much more important is the fact that he had vacationed in the Canaries with his mother. Now he was there again, with his new wife, writing, producing his first major work. He is fully in the realm of substitution, a series of compromises and replacements. I've suggested that for Malinowski, as for Conrad, three are crucial: (1) marriage, with mother replaced by wife; (2) language, with the mother tongue abandoned for English; (3) writing, with inscriptions, texts, substituted for immediate, oral experience. The arbitrary code of one language, English, is finally given precedence. The mother tongue recedes, and (here the personal and

the political coincide) English dominates—represents and interprets—Kiriwinian.* Cultural attachment is enacted as marriage.
The yearning for sincere, interlocutory speech gives way to the play
of written substitutes. Some of this was surely at stake in the successful writing on the Canary Islands. Malinowski's *Diary* ends
with the death of a mother; *Argonauts* is the rescue, the inscription of a culture.

A few final reflections on the present status of the ethnographic author. When Malinowski's *Diary* was first published, it
seemed scandalous. The quintessential anthropologist of *Argonauts* did not, in fact, always maintain an understanding, benevolent attitude toward his informants; his state of mind in the field
was often anything but coolly objective; the story of ethnographic
research included in the finished monograph was stylized and selective. These facts, once entered into the public record of anthropological science, shook the fiction of cultural relativism as a
stable subjectivity, a standpoint for a self understanding and representing a cultural other. In the wake of the *Diary*, cross-cultural
comprehension appeared a rhetorical construct, its balanced comprehension traversed by ambivalence and power.

We recall the fate of Kurtz's violent scrawl in *Heart of Darkness*, "Exterminate all the brutes." Marlow tears off the damning,
truthful supplement when he gives Kurtz's disquisition on savage
customs to the Belgian press. It is a telling gesture, and it suggests a
troubling question about Malinowski and anthropology. What is always, as it were, torn off to construct a public, believable discourse?
In *Argonauts*, the *Diary* was excluded, written over, in the process
of giving wholeness to a culture (Trobriand) and a self (the scientific ethnographer). The discipline of fieldwork-based anthropology,
in constituting its authority, constructs and reconstructs coherent
cultural others and interpreting selves. If this ethnographic self-

*It would be interesting to analyze systematically how, out of the heteroglot
encounters of fieldwork, ethnographers construct texts whose prevailing language
comes to override, represent, or translate other languages. Here Talal Asad's conception of a persistent, structured inequality of languages gives political, historical content to the apparently neutral process of cultural translation. See Asad, "The Concept of Cultural Translation in British Social Anthropology" in James Clifford and
George Marcus, eds., *Writing Culture: The Poetics and Politics of Ethnography*
[Berkeley, Calif., 1986], pp. 141–64.

fashioning presupposes lies of omission and of rhetoric, it also makes possible the telling of powerful truths. But like Marlow's account aboard the *Nellie*, the truths of cultural description are meaningful to specific interpretive communities, in limiting historical circumstances. The "tearing off" (Nietzsche reminds us) is simultaneously an act of censorship *and* of meaning-creation, a suppression of incoherence and contradiction. The best ethnographic fictions, like Malinowski's, are intricately truthful. But their facts, like all facts in the human sciences, are classified, contextualized, narrated, and intensified. The omissions and commissions of ethnographies, their particular shadings of "subjective" and "objective," their paradigms of cultural coherence and temporal process, their modes of authority, irony, allegory, and belief— all these have changed and are changing.

In recent years new forms of ethnographic realism have emerged, more dialogical and open-ended in narrative style. Self and other, culture and its interpreters, appear as less confident identities. Among those who have revised ethnographic authority and rhetoric from within the discipline I'll mention just three, whom Clifford Geertz recently marked off for critique in a series of provocative lectures on the writing of ethnography: Paul Rabinow, Kevin Dwyer, and Vincent Crapanzano.[15] (For their sins of self-display Geertz calls them "Malinowski's children.") But they stand for many others who are presently engaged in a complex field of textual experiments at the limits of academic ethnography.[16] I've said that anthropology still awaits its Conrad. In various ways the recent experimentalists are filling that role. They teeter productively, as Conrad did—and as, more ambivalently, Geertz himself balances—between realism and modernism. The experimentalists reveal in their writings an acute sense of the fashioned, contingent status of all cultural descriptions (and of all cultural describers).

These self-reflexive writers occupy ironic positions within the general project of ethnographic subjectivity and cultural description. And they stand, as we all do, on an uncertain historical ground, a place from which we can begin to analyze the ideological matrix that produced ethnography, the plural definition of culture, and a self positioned to mediate discrepant worlds of meaning. (To say that this historical ground is, for example, postcolonial or postmodern is not to say much—except what one hopes no longer to have to be.) In fact, most of the self-conscious, dialogical, hermeneutic ethnographers writing today get about as far as Conrad did in *Heart of Darkness*, at least in their presentation of narrative authority. For they now gesture toward the problematic other narrator on the deck of the *Nellie*—as they say with Marlow: "Of course in this you fellows see more than I did then. You see me, whom you know."

The Beautiful Lie:
Heroic Individuality and Fascism

PAOLO VALESIO

To P. de M. *in memoriam*

A few lines before the beginning . . .

No academic communication, obviously, could exist without
the standard-format learned paper. But if this form becomes exclusive, the very existence of variant and varied thought within institutions will be threatened.

What follows is in the tradition of the essay. If I dare borrow a
leaf from that scintillating English stylist Thomas De Quincey, I
can speak of this as a narrative paper.

The word that inevitably stands out in such a narrative is
"Fascism." Its root—as is well known—is the Latin fascis, 'bundle, bunch,' specifically the bundle of rods with an axe protruding
from the middle that in ancient Rome was carried in front of the
consuls, symbolizing their power of punishing unto death. Fascis
is also one possible etymology of another Latin word, fascinus; according to this etymon, fascinus designates a magical operation
by "virtue" of which the victim is magically bound.[1]

A fascination with Fascism is thus something more than a
pun: it evokes obscure ob-ligations (rather than explicit political
litigations), it points to a knot that slows down the natural flow of
blood in what the macroscopic optimism of the humanists would
still like to conceive as a unitary body politic—the body of culture
and human communication.

"Now, imagine," exclaims at a certain point a character in a
great modern tragedy:

> Now, imagine: someone, unaware, drinks a poison, a potion, some-
> thing impure that stains his blood, that contaminates his thought. . .

163

a clouded thought against which your whole being shudders with disgust... In vain! In vain! The thought persists, its strength grows, it becomes a monster, it looms tyrannically... Oh, is this possible? ... It possesses you, it inhabits your blood, it invades all your senses. And you're its prey, its miserable, trembling prey; and your whole soul, your pure soul, is infested, and everything inside you is a stain, a contamination... Oh, is this believable? [2]

This desperate young man is talking about his temptation to incest—but I would like these words to resonate in our ears as we try to understand Fascism. The danger is that of contamination . . . and yet we must brave that danger, for we have no choice but to try to understand.*

> Il pensiere ha per cima la follia.
> (The culmination of thought is madness.)
> Gabriele D'Annunzio

T he first scene is actually one-in-two: two tableaux linked by the *repetitio* that is one of the features of literary writing (beyond the clumsy *repetitio* of private letters etcetera and the haphazard *variatio* of public journalism or scholarship).

First, we see a coarse peasant father surprise his frail, intellectual son in the flagrant crime of reading a book, while he is supposed to be minding the family sawmill:

> A violent blow sent Julien's book flying into the stream; a second cuff, just as heavy, fell on his head and caused him to lose his balance. He was about to fall a distance of ten or fifteen feet into the middle of the machinery, which would have ground him up, but his father caught him, with his left hand, just as he was falling. . . . His eyes were full of tears, less from physical pain than for the loss of his book, which he worshipped. . . . As they passed the stream into which his book had fallen, he glanced sadly aside; it had been his favorite book, the *Mémorial de Sainte-Hélène*.

---

*We can take comfort from a courageous essay written in the troubled year 1939 by an American critic apropos of Hitler's *Mein Kampf*, in which we read, among other thoughts: "Hitler's 'Battle' is exasperating, even nauseating; yet the fact remains: If the reviewer but knocks off a few adverse attitudinizings and calls it a day, with a guaranty in advance that his article will have a favorable reception among the decent members of our population, he is contributing more to our gratification than to our enlightenment." (Kenneth Burke, "The Rhetoric of Hitler's 'Battle,'" in *The Philosophy of Literary Form: Studies in Symbolic Action* [Baton Rouge, 1941], pp. 191–220; later anthologized in *Terms for Order*, ed. Stanley E. Hyman with Barbara Karmiller [Bloomington, Indiana, 1964], pp. 95–119.)

Second, our hero Julien is afraid that a portrait he has hidden in his mattress may be discovered. Having recovered it just in time (rather, after having forced his mistress to recover it—which she does sorrowfully, believing it to be the portrait of another woman), he mentally surveys the danger just past:

> The portrait of Napoleon, he said to himself, shaking his head; and found on a man who professes such hatred for the usurper! Found by M. de Rênal, a black reactionary and in bad humour! And to top it all, on the cardboard mounting of the portrait, phrases written in my hand which leave no doubt of the depth of my admiration! Each one of these transports was dated, too, and the last one just yesterday![3]

Why this scene? It shows an individual who is frantically trying to individualize himself—that is, to become a hero—deriving courage for the enterprise by contemplating another individual, a famous one whose individuality has been institutionalized. A paradoxical process? Certainly, and as such particularly apt to illuminate the basically contradictory nature of the notion "individualism."

But again, why this scene? Because it shows individualism as a poetic concern, a concern with linguistic intensification and shaping. The quotes describe acts of reading—whether a book or a portrait—which in the second tableau culminate in the intensification of reading that is writing, specifically, in writing as a loving act of inscription.

As in every intensification of reading, not only the link with the process of writing emerges (this being by now a commonplace in the rhetoric of literary criticism), but the link of both processes with solitary and self-sufficient love—with the softly existential grounding of solipsism, masturbation.

Think of Rilke's beautiful description of reading in the *Notebooks of Malte Laurids Brigge*; think of Freud's sketchy notes, whose plodding English title ("Contributions to a Discussion on Masturbation") hides the more suggestive and theological-sounding German phrase "Zur Onanie-Diskussion."[4] Onanism—on the one hand, a small-scale, cozy secrecy, therefore an experience of decrease or shrinkage (akin to what certain cultural anthropologists call "Gulliverization"),[5] of gliding under a surface (the book drowned in the waters of the stream), or of boxes within boxes (the bedroom, in it the bed, in it the mattress, in it the little box, and in it the portrait).

165

But on the other hand, the practice of Onan evokes broad land-scapes. An ancient cosmological myth tells us that the world was created out of the sperm ejaculated by a masturbating god. It is a crazily noble vision, of which we in the land of the setting sun inherited only the demonic shadow—the voyeuristic pleasure of the masturbator (masturbatrix) who (like that arch-individualist, Juliette) feels in control of a scene of violence.

In this French provincial scene, then, we confront two extreme forms of individuality: on the one hand, individualism as a retreat into the smallest part of the self (etymologically the *in-divisible* part, too small to be parceled up any further), and, on the other hand, individualism as the growing development of one individual at the expense of others, projecting a dominant shadow over smaller individuals. ("He waxed like a sea," as Shakespeare described Coriolanus.)

The erotics of these rhetorics are, at least at first sight, different: if that of the former is (as has already been seen) an onanistic eros, that of the latter obviously (perhaps too obviously) is a vigorously coital eros. Such a characterization should not be pushed too far: if erotic phenomenology can demystify ideology, it runs the risk of itself mystifying rhetorical strategies.

Better get back, then, to these strategies, which are—in the long run—the decisive ones. A text a little less than a century younger than the quoted "Chronique du 1830," although bizarrely a "Thèse de Médecine" (presented in Paris in 1924), hides like the mattress of young Julien a small, shining portrait of Napoleon:

> In the course of those monstrous years when blood flows, when life gushes forth and dissolves itself from a thousand breasts at one time, when mens' loins are threshed and crushed like grapes in a wine-press—in those years a male is needed.
> At the first lightning flashes of that immense storm Napoleon took Europe and, by fair means or foul, kept it for fifteen years.
> For the duration of his genius the fury of peoples seemed to become organized—the storm itself obeyed his commands.
> Slowly, people began to believe in the good times again, to believe in peace.[6]

One of the crucial genealogies of the broad scene that Céline feels he must paint in order to introduce his medical hero Semmel-weis is the sequence of Napoleonic cameos in *Red and Black*. Genealogical indeed, this relationship—not simply a question of sources: for what matters is the tone of the discourse.

166

But Napoleon, the Great Individual—how could one talk about him? Stendhal's tone is that of a cold nostalgia (all the more desperate because of its coldness), which poetically historicizes Romanticism, making us feel what it is that we come after. The discourse of Céline, by contrast, brings us into a territory of mind for which Romanticism is irrelevant—rather than telling us that Romanticism is past, Céline suggests that it never existed.

But this contrast is already something broader than a point of literary history. The tone of these literary discourses is not some optional ornament but a form of philosophy, a poetic philosophy.

Céline's description of Napoleon is a fitting emblem of individualism: both in its grandeur and in its conative, pathetically strained, aspect.

For a time, let us leave scenes behind—close readings are no substitute for thinking. But only after anchoring ourselves to such scenes can we start thinking (anew).

Work on the individual is one thing, individualism quite a different thing. Work on the individual is, primarily, a person's growth and struggle toward a definition of the self, a search for what Jung would call the *principium individuationis*. Secondary work on the individual is the analysis of such growth and struggle as developed by traditional disciplines (theology, metaphysics, jurisprudence, etc.) as well as by more modern ones (logic, psychology, sociology, and so forth). Individualism, on the other hand, is a modern (post-Romantic) hybrid, occupying the twilight zone where the bright rocks of the sciences and the arts shade into the foggy marshes of ideology.

Literary criticism is particularly well suited to deal with the notion of individualism because as a poetic philosophy it is, like individualism, a hybrid. Individualism is a complex or constellation of concepts whose nature is essentially political, that is, essentially concerns the symbolic and compulsive (hence also the sensuous and aesthetic) side of human action. As a hybrid formation, an asystematic, nay, contradictory, approximation to philosophy, it is peculiarly modern, for modernity thrives on such mixtures. Now literary analysis, as a hybrid, is really the most appropriate way of dealing with political formations. Pure philosophical and sociological approaches are too heavy: their excessive solemnity, when applied to the soft and soiled body politic, creates a mock-heroic irrelevance. Literary criticism, on the other hand, has just the right balance of effusion and irreverence.

The domain toward which we are moving can be called the literature of politics—not in the superficial senses of a kind of literature connected with a given party or sect, or of a writer's effect on political life,[7] but in the sense of a sustained reflection on the close links between political and poetic practices.[8]

In reflecting upon all this, poetic philosophy does not proceed by slow gradations and transitions. It tries to survey the landscape in all its breadth, while leaping rapidly to vividly picture salient points. Of course it risks making mistakes, but its procedure is not loose or ungoverned in comparison with the more cautious style of political science. Instead, it works in this way because of a sense of responsibility toward its own peculiar subject. It uses juxtaposition as analysis, as a mode of arguing and of thereby making a claim on texts. Rather than indulge itself, it soberly refuses a privilege: it cannot afford the luxury of marching slowly, by way of stately transitions. This is why, as soon as I have touched on the complicated issue of individualism as a modern formation, I must rush to an allegedly monstrous deformation of such individualism, a thing whose very name is reified as an infamous exhibit in the museum of political criminology through which academics sometimes parade their flocks: Fascism.

A magic word—merely pronounced, it creates a turbulence, an agitation. This quick movement of emotions and ideas brings another scene to the fore.

A French writer is sitting in a jail cell, waiting to be tried for collaboration with the occupying forces. He is writing a very long letter—"Letter to a Soldier of the Class of 1960"—a letter in which he is trying to explain. Explain what, exactly?

To explain himself, and yet not only himself—not a biographical, but a politically transcendent self. Such a transcendence is not an escape into the etiolating space of ideology, however. For he is trying to situate himself at the crossroads of history and existence, of ethical and aesthetic concerns—in short, he is doing the literature of politics. And he is doing this a few weeks before what he must already have felt would be his death sentence. (He writes the letter between November and December 1944; on February 6, 1945, he is shot.) His imminent death should be more than sufficient to convince us that the literature of politics is a very serious enterprise indeed.

The political prisoner Robert Brasillach (who at 35 is already a very distinguished intellectual in France) writes to his four-year-old nephew.[9] This letter to a future reader would seem to realize very neatly the jump from the microscopic diachrony of biography to the panchronicity of general literature's address to what the rhetoricians call the "universal audience." It is too neat a jump, indeed. In several contemporary letters addressed to small posterities, the grandly solemn manner of the epistolary essay (be it in prose or poetry) in the tradition of Dante and Petrarch twisted itself into something very close to coyness. Those modern letters reflect a too-narrow rhetoric of self-righteousness (their authors are so good, so reasonable). This text, instead, is tortured and not beyond embarrassment. It is not, thank God, fully convincing.

Most important, Brasillach's epistle is one of those texts in which a knot causes a wrinkle or ripple (a place where a Zarathustrian tight-rope walker might stumble) in the excessively taut and smooth line stretching from biographic particularity to solemn generality. This knot ties life and history, perceived diachronically in the middle range that is the central domain of the literature of politics.

I mean—this letter is addressed to all the people of my generation who, in France and Italy and Greece and elsewhere have experienced as children the deep wounds of occupation:

> At each line I wrote, I kept seeing the face of a four-year-old child, who had been born when German troops disembarked in Norway, as a prelude to the great offensive of 1940. Until now, he has not known what peace is. He has spent his days first under the German occupation, then under the American occupation. He went down into the cellar during the air-raid alarms; he has come to know bombardments, and the landscapes of wrecked railway stations, and the crackling of airplane machine guns. Until a few months ago he thought that the French flag was the white flag, because that was the sign he saw fluttering on the food trucks, which hoped in this way to escape American bombs. He has learned the songs of the German soldiers. But he does not know what a banana is, or an orange, or a chocolate pastry.

The knot I am talking about ties the large history together with the small, binding lives to politics and to the diachrony of important events. This sensuous, imaginative extension is the only way of really feeling history—and, once again, it is nothing but the literature of politics. (Brasillach's work illustrates another, related category I have explored, that of semio-history, which holds, among other things, that historical figures "use their actions, their own life, as extended strings of citations.")[10]

But can this knot of life and history be made even more vividly present to the mind—and not only to the mind? That requires direct confrontation with concrete, specific objects.

In the museum of the military academy at West Point are several trophies of war—spoils of vanquished armies. In one glass case, for instance, one sees a fez—the small hat shaped like a truncated cone that became one of the distinctive features of the Fascist militia—which once belonged to Benito Mussolini. Indeed (if memory does not play too many tricks) that fez is a particularly elegant one: blackly gleaming and perhaps gold-tasseled. Seeing this trophy, one Italian observer felt himself blush violently. Later he asked himself: Why such a reaction?

First, he thought he had blushed with shame at this symbol and reminder of tyranny—shame before the democratic society of which he was now more or less a part. But this conceit was too pat—surely it was not the reason for that brief but hot onrush of uneasiness.

The Italian onlooker then tried to convince himself that his reaction had been a slight revulsion at an object that was not yet historical—that had not had time to acquire a full symbolic charge. The fez then would be, so to speak, premature as a historical symbol: it had not been "made up"; it had not yet "put on" its historical implications like (echoing its own original function) a suit of ceremonial clothes.

According to this interpretation, that strange hat stood in a bare cheapness that made it somewhat obscene, with the defenseless, pathetic obscenity that hovers around certain tools displayed in the windows of porn shops.

This second explanation is certainly more satisfactory. It sheds some light on the mystery of history, bringing to the fore the Nietzschean motto (in the *Genealogy of Morals*) about the *pudenda origo*, the shameful origin, at the root of every historical tradition, no matter how illustrious.

Yet not even this interpretation is the full explanation for the blush. The basic reason is brutally simple and at the same time of historical interest: what made the cheeks burn was, quite simply, the humiliation of defeat, a sentiment that, if followed frankly and straightforwardly, leads to a sense (however bitter) of national solidarity. The sorrow, the anger, the confused but deepened awareness that revealed themselves in front of that glass case concern a whole generation of Italians. In fact, the process of going deeper and deeper into these feelings is probably the only historical possibility left for forging a link between the men of the class of 1960 and their fathers. But this sentiment of solidarity runs over every ideological caesura and every act of censorship. (In Italian, *cesura* and *censura* are very similar words.)

One cannot choose his own genealogies, and when such genealogies are (to be euphemistic) occasionally unpleasant, every reinscription involves a vindication. Thus the Italian citizen today can find his integrated individuality only in the wake of a total vindication of the past. If he derides that easily vanquished (but long-lived) dictatorship, if he laughs at that slightly pompous black cap—if he stoops to that, in an homage to the victorious empire that surrounds him, then it is at himself, at his historical self, that he is laughing, it is himself he degrades into a caricature.

At a salient point in that letter to a future soldier, Brasillach (after a few not very enlightening comments on Italian Fascism) comes to grip with the broader problem:

Fascism—we did not wait until today to think that it was a form of poetry, indeed, *the* poetry of the twentieth century (together with Communism, to be sure). What I keep telling myself is that all this cannot die. The little boys on their way to become young men of twenty will learn, with a sort of sad wonder, about the existence of this exaltation of millions of men, about the youth camps and the glory of the past, the parades and the cathedrals full of light, the heroes struck down in the fight and the bonds of friendship between the young people of all awakening nations, about José Antonio—about red, boundless Fascism. And I am well aware that Communism also has its greatness.

Maybe a thousand years from now—who knows?—they will confuse these two revolutions of the twentieth century. It will be conceded, I hope, that within the Fascist revolution the nation found its most violent, its most strongly distinctive, place. The nation—isn't it a form of poetry, too? All this can be temporarily vanquished by the trappings of liberalism, by Anglo-Saxon capitalism, but it will not die, no more than the revolution of 1789 died, notwithstanding the comeback of the kings. And I myself, who in these last months have become hesitant before the many errors made by Italian Fascism, German nationalism, Spanish phalangism—I don't believe that I will ever

171

forget the marvelous shining forth of the universal Fascism of my youth, Fascism, the melancholia of our century [notre mal du siècle.][11]

It would be easy to smile at these lines or to avert one's eyes in embarrassment, for this mythology of youth seems implausible and until now Fascism and Communism have come together, not in a marriage of poetic appreciation, but only as targets of a common opprobrium. They are both dirty words, labeling the twin monstrosities of the century.

And yet in that youthful myth there is a vitality that should not be discounted. The attempt to reclaim a measure of happiness out of the wreckage of war makes a kind of crazy sense, although it is not a "common" sense. (But then, what real sense is ever really common?) Brasillach's parallel between Fascism and the French Revolution is not altogether outrageous. Like certain pages in Jean Genêt's *The Thief's Journal*, or the savagely resistant merriment among the ruins in the latest novels by Céline, or the prophetic insight zigzagging through the war writings of Gabriele D'Annunzio twenty years before, it identifies a subterranean history linking back to the years of the other Great War and beyond.

In Brasillach, what counts is the hermeneutic move (the literature of politics has its own way of criss-crossing institutional history): he gives proof of the persistent vitality (the historical continuity) of the para-Napoleonic strategy by which Julien Sorel lives. Elsewhere, he explicitly re-writes himself into history as André Chénier, the French poet executed by the Terrorists of the Revolution. He does so not so much by the relatively easy moves of using "Chénier" as a pen name or comparing himself directly to the poet, but by writing a critical assessment of Chénier, his fore-brother who died at 32—writing the essay in his jail cell at Fresnes and completing it five days before his execution. In semio-historical terms, Brasillach re-writes himself as a (politically) literary character: he in-scribes himself in the history of French politics as an actual descendent of the actual man of letters André Chénier, and he in-scribes himself in the history of French letters as the actual descendent of the phantasmatic political man Julien Sorel.[12]

There is a moving faith, a courage and love of life, in this man about to die who writes, "Je ne puis dire, que je pourrais jamais oublier"—as if he still had the time of forgetting. He is not merely posing for future journalistic historiography. His informal tone ("Peut-être même dans mille ans, confondra-t-on les deux Révolutions du XXe siècle, je ne sais pas") should not fool us. By tying himself to history he writes as if from one shore to another, distant one—the only way in which one can write something that counts.

(Remarkably, we have not had to wait a thousand years for the two revolutions to be confused. I was bemused a few years ago when an American college student, mentioning a well-known Partisan song that he had learned about in an Italian class, referred to it as one of "those Fascist or Communist" songs. In the voice that proceeded to correct him, history spoke in its rational—and rather shallow—dimension; what was not shallow in that voice was piety rather than philology, the sense that such a confusion was, in a way, a blasphemy against the past. Yet through that con-fusion history spoke in its deeper and more savage voice—so that it became a question of listening rather than didactically and professorially speaking.)

Time (historical times) has marched fast—it is now time (in the small-scale time marked by this discourse) to move beyond specific images and develop some general reflections.

Strip the attribute "poetic" of several layers of aesthetic nicety; strip it also (and this is harder) of many strata of narrow ethical evaluation, and you are left with the designation of a turbulent force that reshapes . . . what, is not clear—reality, or our perceptions of reality? The distinctive feature of major poetic ideas is precisely that of making such a choice meaningless. And distinctively such ideas operate in the communal flow of events, in the politics that "makes history."

Thus Fascism and Communism are the two great and sinister poetic ideas, the two *maux du siècle*. Communism is clearly the more sophisticated and coherent, because it is an *ancilla philosophiae*. For all its insistence on radical action, it sits meditatively at the feet of Marxism enthroned in state. Fascism, on the contrary, is nobody's *ancilla*; it is not beholden to any specific philosophy, which is both its weakness and its strength.

Any asystematic and heterogeneous ideology accommodates better—just because of its inner disorder—an appreciation of the role of the individual. There is an essential contradiction in individualism (this is why it is always a beautiful lie), a contradiction implicit in the morphology of its designation. The stem, "individual," points to the deepest nucleus of originality, what cannot be duplicated or repeated; the suffix, "-ism," labels collectivity. Individualism, then, is *a collective ideology of the unique*. The oxymoronic quality of such a project is clear.

What is in this suffix, this label for collectivity, "-ism"? Let us enter another, earlier scene:

> . . . pamphlets about Antinomianism and Evangelicalism, whatever they may be. I can't think what the fellow means by sending such things to me. I've written to him to desire that from henceforth he will send me no book or pamphlet on anything that ends in *ism*.

Thus speaks a young country gentleman, on a June morning of 1799.[13] But his interlocutor, a reverend with several ecclesiastical titles, replies in a more prudent vein: "Well, I don't know that I am very fond of isms myself; but I may as well look at the pamphlets; they let one see what is going on."

This brief exchange, which its author, George Eliot, surely did not mean for heavy pondering, is a handy synthesis of attitudes. It marks the historical transition whereby, through the medium of pamphlets and periodical literature, specialized language (here, the terminology of theological disputation) became a matter of public domain, that is, a political matter. Also, it shows us the labyrinthine prison of the modern intellectual, who—however strongly he may yearn for free modes of expression—cannot afford to ignore "ismic" writings: "they let one see what is going on."

But such sociological generalizations do not lead us very far. To walk the genealogical path, we must take these theological "isms" seriously, for in their precursors—certain late, radicalized movements of the Reformation—we see anticipated formally the modern, secular paradox of individualism. Take these Hegelian-sounding lines from an analysis of certain relatively obscure theological disputations in seventeenth-century Holland:

> Emerging, as far as its psychological sources are concerned, in opposition to the Church apparatuses, this individualism could attack such systems only insofar as it was a collective movement; therefore, it was able to realize itself only by negating itself. Insofar as it remained a matter of individual religious conscience, it could without difficulty adapt itself to the very organism against which it was born as a rebellion. On the other hand, insofar as this individualism was not able to adjust, thus insofar as it realized the principles which had given it birth, individualism was in fact the contrary of what it was in the specific content which had determined its appearance.

174

. . . From this point of view, religious individualism has become, in the course of its history, an example of the incurable inner antinomy of all social movements that would like to preserve both their efficacy and a character of absolute freedom.[14]

In its early-modern (Romantic) phase, individualism was reborn as a polarized concept—as I tried to suggest in my extrapolations from *Red and Black*. That polarization radically reshaped the structures of the world. Now, every reshaping is not only a reformation but also inevitably a deformation. Individualism, as we have seen, alternates between the Lilliputian and the Gargantuan, between gnome and Titan. It focuses either on the small inner chamber of man or on his shadow, which, broadly projected against the wall of history, constitutes a fleeting but powerful monument.

Late-modern ideologies—those of the winners in the latest European conflict—have misunderstood this powerful aesthetic (and ethic) re- or de-formation, reducing it to a tautology: individualism, in this pale liberal reading, is nothing more than a way of taking care of each individual. Individuals in this banalized sense are simply a reflex of the masses, a product of their rebellion (already analyzed by Ortega y Gasset), yet individualism is often presented as a passionate revolt against the masses.

Individualism, then, was (re)born as a revolt against the mass rebellion that erupted into history as the French Revolution. I do not believe that this deeply serious response, or revolt, or revulsion, should be simply labeled "reactionary."

One of the most effective scenes in European literature as it turns the cape of the century is the speech put in the playwright Stelio Èffrena's mouth in Gabriele D'Annunzio's *The Flame of Life* (*Il Fuoco*, 1900). This text-within-the-text deserves detailed analysis, but I will confine myself to a salient point: what is crucially important in this speech by a great aesthete and agitator is not so much the address itself (a piece of brilliant symbolist eloquence that belongs to the nineteenth century, yet whose genealogy reaches backward toward the great orations of the Italian Renaissance), but rather the writer's descriptions interspersed through it, which segment it critically.

The interaction between the oration and the comments (the contextualization of the oration within the larger text of the novel) determines its major significance—in a genealogy that leads, for instance, to Joyce and Mann. What it effectively shows are the two poles of individualism. On the one hand, the orator bodies forth individualism as a heroic or titanic idea (or form of life—an *idea vivente*, to use D'Annunzio's own image in the tragedy *Parisina*). His audience, on the other hand, is skillfully individualized by the author (in the concrete making-of-individuals that is the distinctive procedure of the literature of politics, as opposed to abstractive ideologies): the group of Stelio's disciples and admirers is thus differentiated from the generic mass around them—a mass that, unlike them, does not recognize, acknowledge, and respond to Stelio as its opposite. These admirers represent the other pole of individualism—the crepuscular, intimately reflexive pole. The tone of the description makes clear (even too clear, with a touch of naïveté) that the sympathies of the author lie with titanic individualization, but that is less important than the vivid delineation of the two poles.

In any case, only at this level of dynamic imagination and commitment can we see what is at stake in all its poetic or political importance. Fascism and individualism are not, of course, coextensive concepts: Fascism is but a part of that larger whole. Moreover, the two are heterogeneous quantities: Fascism is a poetic idea, individualism a strategy that runs (with different intensities, in diverse ways) through several different, and divergent, poetic ideas.

The emphasis must be on "different." For in the literature of politics our theme, individualism, lies at the intersection of several diverse antitheses or polarizations, which cannot be fitted into one master antithesis. Thus, D'Annunzio's opposition between a heroically shaped individual in the role of a master and a relatively small group of reclusive, crepuscular individuals as his disciples does not represent the same relationship as the opposition between politically and socially dominant men and their underlings.

Thus no nice schema opposes *Übermensch*, or Overman, to *Untermensch*, or Underman. Like Stelio with his disciples, the Overman's dialectical antithesis is not a mass but an elite—the elite of crepuscular, sophisticated, modern men and women. In this sense *The Flame of Life* as a whole (not only in the oratorial scene I mentioned) is a brilliant critique of *Thus Spake Zarathustra*. As for the Underman, his antithesis does not exist—at least it does not exist as a single, clearly defined entity. Hence the rage, the inchoate frustration, of the Underman.

Overman, Underman . . . what—who—is missing? The pat answer is: man is missing. The golden mean, the reasonable balance—such a middle ground does not exist. "Man," the construct of humanism, is a much flimsier abstraction than any overman or underman. Hence the drama of the human sciences, which do not really have an object.

Overman, Underman, man . . . who else? Who else but the Godman?

> If one inclines to regard the archetype of the self as the real agent and hence takes Christ as a symbol of the self, one must bear in mind that there is considerable difference between *perfection* and *completeness*. The Christ-image is as good as perfect (at least it is meant to be so), while the archetype (so far as is known) denotes completeness but is far from being perfect. It is a paradox, a statement about something indescribable and transcendental. Accordingly the realization of the self, which would logically follow from a recognition of its supremacy, leads to a fundamental conflict, to a real suspension between opposites (reminiscent of the crucified Christ hanging between two thieves), and to an approximate state of wholeness that lacks perfection.[15]

Jung's reflections not only underscore the peculiar tension—the dramatic play of antitheses—out of which individualization is born, they introduce a general hypothesis.

The Western history of individualization is primarily a struggle on the blind side of the story of Jesus. By this I mean the side opposite (and complementary) to that of the *allegoria Christi* or the *imitatio Christi*, the edifying side (in the etymological sense, the side on which confessions of faith are built). It is a very peculiar blindness—a blindness that does not by any means exclude hermeneutic penetration. On this side of the story, in fact, a double process of reinterpretation is at work.

On the one hand, the modern history of individualism (and of its portion that is my particular topic, Fascism) brings to the fore the darker aspect of the Nazarene—his necromantic element, the one closer to his putative elder brother, Satan.[16] (Jung writes: "The Antichrist develops in legend as a perverse imitator of Christ's life. He is a true *antimimòn pneûma*, an imitating spirit of evil who follows in Christ's footsteps like a shadow following the body.") On the other hand there emerges the religious nucleus that is active (no matter how degraded, fragmented, or repressed—no matter, ultimately, whether more demonic than angelic)[17] in every heroic defense of individual assertion, even in the most militantly atheistic ones.*

In enacting this play of antithesis, the modern process of individuation gives the lie to humanism—that noble ideological conation born in late-fifteenth-century Italy. Since then the human sciences have tried to be scientific, that is, to systematize a secular approach; but their ship has been wrecked on the hidden rock of what lies beyond (behind, or even below) the human. For no deep problem in human life can really be posited, let alone solved, in human terms. This is something that literary texts have always told us, in their stubborn resistance to every structuralist colonization.

The dilemma that has emerged can be introduced by Nietzsche's contrast, for instance in section 39 of his *Antichrist*, of the German word *Christ* ("Christian") with the other German term *Christus* ("Christ"): "It is false to the point of nonsense to find the mark of the Christian [*des Christen*] in a 'faith,' for instance, in the faith of redemption through Christ [*durch Christus*]." This alternation or altercation of terms is interesting: to interpret the title—and not only the title—carefully, this little book is as much *The Antichristian* as *The Antichrist*.

But the issue I am pointing out is not philological so much as philosophical. What is evoked right from the beginning is not the specific person to whom Jung refers (Christ's devilish alter ego), but the abstract concept of Christianity.† Whatever the linguistic solutions available, this uneasy coupling is not simply a nuance of the

---

*I speak here of the primary presence of the *numinosum* in creative texts, not of the secondary interventions of theological metalanguage in the texts of commentators. But even at this secondary level the theological element points in the right direction, where the deeper energies run. This evaluation is the opposite of Nietzsche's attack on the theologians at the beginning of his *Antichrist*—or is it? For it seems clear to me (in what could be a Jungian, but not a Freudian, reading) that there the language of furious assault against the omnipresence of theology is at the same time a hurriedly whispered declaration of jealous love.

† Insofar as Nietzsche aims his attacks at Christianity rather than at Christ, his apparently so alien and blasphemous essay falls into the line of an ancient Christian genealogy (no matter how heterodox, or even heretical): the topos of the vindication of the true Christ against the misunderstandings of the Christians. This tortured sense of a response to tradition is lost in a certain political interpretation. This was concretely brought home to me when I checked the German text (in the temporary absence of a recent edition) in an edition published in Berlin, n.d., and presented by Wilhelm Matthiessen, who dates his Introduction (pp. 7–16) in 1941. In his ideological update, he straightforwardly vindicates the book as an all-out attack on every-

German language but an apt symbol for the block on which modern individualism stumbles.

Modern individualism is by and large anti-Christian in the wishful sense of being ante-Christian: it wants to function as a *novus ordo* in which the ancient pagan figure of the hero is resurrected.[18] It seeks a mixture of Socrates and Herakles, to finally lay to rest the ghost of the Crucified. This reconstruction of heroes is in itself close to the heroic (in its daring, its imaginative commitment), but it almost never succeeds in reaching a full serenity of persuasion.

In the modern saga, philosophical heroes, like Zarathustra, tend to be too pale and bloodless. They are not sufficiently animated by the erotic energy that pervades the heroes of the classical world. Poetic heroes, like Stelio, on the contrary (but this is always a relative distinction), although erotically strong, miss the peculiar ethical qualities of the ancient. Thus their eros tends to be morbid and gloomy. Rather than being Antichristians in the sense of "beyond Christianity," these poetic heroes are—in the impossibility of being fully Antechristians—little Antichrists.

The "anti" here evokes tragic caricature, mime (the *antimimòn pneûma*), or, at the most, the other panel in a diptych—it is not an overcoming, a total rehauling or revolution. When the invisible choir of Spirits refers to Faust as a *Halbgott* (l. 1612), the historically primary translation is "demigod," with its classical Greek connotation of divinized heroism. But we could translate (or traduce) the term with the less flattering "half-god." The last two emblems of Nietzsche's disappearing lucidity, in January 1889, are poignant symbols of this dilemma: he signs his January 4 note to Gast "The Crucified" and his note of January 6 to Overbeck "Dionysus." The tragedy of this (beyond Nietzsche's case) is that no Dionysus had—or has—emerged.

What, for instance, makes the weakness of *Thus Spake Zarathustra* is not its most melodramatic, purple passages but its basic structure: this, the book in which Nietzsche comes closest to philosophical fiction, is too an-erotic and too vague in its staging. Zarathustra is a Saint John the Baptist without the erotic background of

---

thing Christian, collapsing Christ and Christians together in a metonymic block of Christ(ians). Such a coarsening of the fine texture is no worse than the opposite ideological piety that has been imposed on Nietzsche of late.

a destructive Salome, and he announces a Jesus figure who does not have the counterpart of a Mary Magdalene.

Nietzsche's most threatening precursor, Kierkegaard, understood well that poetic philosophers must—as all poets do—plunder life without making exceptions. His Don Juan is more of a hero (more, also, of a philosophical hero) than Zarathustra because he dares to draft the shadow of the author's fiancée into the service of his army of inventions, whereas Zarathustra forbids himself to play with the allusive presence of his contemporary Salomé (Lou). The result is that this Zarathustra full of genius does not show his living, tormented face with the immediacy of the ancient John the Baptist in Flaubert's novella *Hérodias* (1877).

And yet Nietzsche himself vividly expressed the great staging process in Christianity:

> To make *love* possible, God must be a person; to permit the lowest instincts to participate, God must be young. To excite the ardor of the females, a beautiful saint must be placed in the foreground, and to excite that of the men, a Mary—presupposing all along that Christianity wants to become master on soil where some Aphrodisiac or Adonis cult has already established the general conception of a cult.

These (in section 23 of *The Antichrist*) are very ironic lines—but on whom does the irony ultimately fall? The images seem, indeed, to come back to haunt their author; for they objectively define, in contrast to the tone in which they are written, the imaginative power of the Christian scene—the scene against which all modern secular writing must compete.

Contrary to conventional statements, it is not with the weapons of morality that Christianity haunts every secular attempt to construct heroic figures, but rather with the instruments of aesthetic creation. It reveals their tragic weakness—the weakness of, say, Sorel's Napoleon.

> Faith was at all times . . . only a cloak, a pretext, a *screen* behind which the instincts played their game—a shrewd *blindness* about the dominance of *certain* instincts. "Faith"—I have already called it the characteristic Christian *shrewdness*—one always *spoke* of faith, but one always *acted* from instinct alone.

Even if we grant that this (from section 39 of the *Antichrist*, with all original emphases faithfully maintained) is an adequate account, the imaginative writer asks: "So what?" If faith is but a screen, the question is what to do with that screen—how to use it in order to reshape and reunderstand life. Without work on sensuous data, philosophy—especially the kind of philosophy of which Nietzsche is a modern master (although second to Kierkegaard)—remains ineffective.

The scene delineated above—the fascinating young god, the alluring Mary—is too deeply rooted to be shaken by any such irony; it can be challenged (and even so, to a very small extent) only by the brutality of violent parody. Indeed the much more powerful scene that lies behind Nietzsche's sketch (which then turns out to be a prudent screen), marking its sinister eighteenth-century genealogy, is that of the poor wretches—convinced of being God, Mary, and Jesus Christ—who are sexually tormented and murdered in the insane asylum near Salerno where Juliette and her friends are fêted by Vespoli, the libertine who manages the place on behalf of King Ferdinand of Naples.[19]

The retreat from the sensuous gives *Zarathustra* an anemic quality that brings it much closer than might seem to the traditional philosophical discourses it attacks. In *The Flame of Life* the erotic is fully acknowledged; the dynamism and disorder that eros brings end up by giving some order—as ironic distance, as a sense of proportion—to excessively inflated individualistic assertions. This presence of eros makes the novel a penetrating critique of Nietzschean ideology.*

If further proofs are needed of the gap between philosophy and eros that literary strategies must fill, it is enough to recall Maurice Maeterlinck's drama in three acts, *Marie-Magdeleine*.[20] That the play is far from an aesthetic success (unlike the D'Annunzio novel) is not very important; what matters is that Maeterlinck, too, understands (as is clear from the very title) that the exceptional individual can only come alive as a silhouette, under a ray of light behind the screen provided by a scene of tension where Eros, too, makes an appearance.

We have come back, by a necessarily tortuous route, to onanism (but not to a Freudian gloss). Onanism in an extended sense is defined in an Italian dictionary as: "Every personal or cultural ac-

---

*Stelio Èffrena introjects, or telescopes within himself, both the figures of the Baptist (some of whose elements are transferred to the pale aesthete Daniele Glauro) and the Nazarene (some of whose features are astutely shifted to the dying Wagner); the great actress Foscarina is a sumptuous Mary Magdalene.

tivity devoid of real ends, foundations, and results, and fancifully brought into being for self-pleasure or for the artificial gratification of one's ideological needs or emotional impulses."[21] This sounds like an unsympathetic and malicious, but not completely off-target, definition of literary writing.

As with the two poles of individualism—the crepuscular and private versus the heroic and expansive—one is tempted to oppose an onanistic eros in *Zarathustra* to a triumphantly phallic eros in *The Flame of Life*. But such a move would be wrong. If Nietzsche's book is about anything in this vein, it is about chastity. (The section devoted to chastity in the First Part plays a strategic role.) Zarathustra is as chaste as snow; and Stelio Èffrena? The attribute "phallic" does not make serious sense for him, as it does not for any really important literary characterization—or for significant political figures.

Political Progressives' sarcasm about the supposed phallic emphasis in figures like Mussolini is more shallow than its target ever was (even when it comes from the pen of a novelist who should know better, as in Carlo Emilio Gadda's facile *Eros and Priapus: From Wrath to Ashes*).[22] Writing as an intensification of reading (we saw at the beginning) has much to do with Onan, and little or nothing with Priapus.

We have come back to Fascism, and we are thus at the (provisional) conclusion of this essay. Fascism is one of the most important stages in the history of modern individualism (in and out of the literature of politics) because it shows up—albeit in a degraded and desperately entangled form—the polarity in the story of the Passion. The whole history of the Nazarene as it unfolds toward the Passion brings together—in an illogical but convincing marriage— a feverish quickening of life and an exaltation of death. The black of Fascism has a strong pulsation—it is an orgiastic black. (I speak of a Dionysiac, not of a suburban, orgy.) Or let us interchange the colors, in order to go beyond the tired clichés. Let us think of Fascism (following Brasillach's suggestion) as red, and Communism as black. Fascism is a desperate *imitatio* of the Passion: as Gabriele D'Annunzio—the first, and a very penetrating, critic of Italian Fascism—felt and expressed even before Fascism got really started.

And finally. I indicated that the real interlocutor of the Overman is a crepuscular elite, not the masses. Fascism leapt to political success when it brutally cut this delicate but essential elite mediation, characteristic of its precursor, mystic nationalism (which is what D'Annunzio is really about). Cutting this balance or mediation means instituting a direct but conative dialogue between some sort of Overman and the masses—but with this move the Overman is degraded to the role of an overseer.

The Overman comes into being as the "antimime" of the ancient *antimimòn pneûma* of the Godman. The Fascist leader then is (in a kind of ironically Platonic vindication) the antimime of an antimime of an antimime. It is a lowly place on the ladder, but, before we feel too complacent in our bright world, let us ask ourselves: What is the place of the democratic leaders who have succeeded, in the wake of the victorious armies, the individualists entangled in those monstrous poetic ideas?

The answer, alas, is not difficult. They limp along, miming the antimime of an antimime of an antimime. Such is the tragico-ironic genealogy of our modern security.

A certain kind of political science fiction asks of us an effort of the imagination, depicting a world in which the Axis has won the Second World War.[23] I ask now a greater, though subtler, effort of the historical imagination: really imagine (think, feel) that the Allies *have* won World War II; give this scene a long, hard, detached look; and ask what all this really means. Reconstructing history within ourselves inevitably means also recreating it—thus is the old continually made new, with the constant disquiet of discovery.

The Dissolution of Character in the Novel

CHRISTINE BROOKE-ROSE

I would like to start with a quotation from "Life-Story," a chapter of *Lost in the Funhouse* by John Barth: "D comes to suspect that the world is a novel, himself a fictional personage . . . since D is writing a fictional account of this conviction. . . . Moreover E, hero of D's account, is said to be writing a similar account. . . . If I'm going to be a fictional character G declared to himself. . . . If he can only get K through his story I reflected grimly. . . . Why could he not begin his story afresh et cetera? Y's wife came into the study."[1]

Barth is doing several things here. For one thing, he is representing the disappearance of character from the modern novel—the character has become mere letters, even if one of them is I, who may also be Y, whose wife comes into the study. (The briefest epigram of metaphysical anguish could be said to be "I—Why?") And there is a *mise en abîme*, E being the hero of D's novel and so on, all being in fact versions of I.

Barth is also representing the creative process in this new, denuded situation. Gone is the trepidation of a Henry James stepping warily around his complex creations. Gone too are the Jamesian ecstasies of the notebooks as the author pictures his creations, deftly adding stroke to stroke. Instead, we have a raging despair at the emptiness of D or E, mere supports for their own self-reflections and quickly replaced by G or K. They express all frustrated attempts at character making and all versions of the author's various selves, lasting but a few seconds and presumably torn up and thrown into the wastepaper basket. The process perhaps reached its peak in Brautigan's *Trout Fishing in America*, where the title phrase is used in every function from title via adjective to character: "trout fishing in America terrorists," "Dear Trout Fishing in America," and the reply signed, "Your friend, Trout Fishing in America," or again, "This is the autopsy of Trout Fishing in America as if Trout Fishing in America had been Lord Byron and had died in Missolonghi, Greece, and afterwards never saw the shores of Idaho again, never saw Carrie Creek, Worsewick Hot Springs, Paradise Creek, Salt Creek and Duck Lake again."[2]

But Barth is simultaneously parodying a technique typical of the late realistic novel, namely, defocalization of the hero. This technique had two main functions: first, to avoid, precisely, the heroic or "novelistic" (*le romanesque*), which ensured the reader's identification by a sustained focalization on the main character;[3] second, and more especially, to build up a portrait of society, however small or large, by focalizing on one character at a time, introducing A, then B, then C, then A again, then D, and so on. The climax of this technique was reached in the 1930's, in Huxley's *Point Counter-Point*, for example, and it has become the most familiar cliché of the current traditional novel and the main technique of films. In its extreme mechanical form, TV soap, we pass from couple to couple, hardly able to distinguish one drama from another or one serial from the next in the subsequent half-hour or, for that matter, from the interjected commercials: two intense actresses in a kitchen discussing either detergents or infidelity.

Defocalization is parodied in Pynchon's *V*, where we are never allowed to identify for long with any one of the innumerable characters or to grasp the real nature of their complicated quests. As Mas'ud Zavarzadeh has said of postmodernism's parody of the traditional novel and its totalizing attempts to impose an interpretation and synthesis of life:

> "Metafiction" is ultimately a narrational metatheorem whose subject matter is fictional systems themselves and the molds through which reality is patterned by narrative conventions. . . . The main counter-techniques of metafiction are two-dimensional, flat characterization, consciously contrived plots, and paralogical, noncausal, and antilinear sequences of events, all of which are carried out in a highly foregrounded language embedded in a counterhumor that is nondidactic, distancing, and not [here he quotes Scholes] "concerned with what to do about life but how to take it."[4]

Already in Barth's *Lost in the Funhouse*, in the chapter called "Title," we see the blatant naming of a technique comically replacing the use of it: "'Why do you suppose it is,' she asked, long participial phrase of breathless variety characteristic of dialogue attributions in nineteenth-century fiction, 'that literature people such as we talk like characters in a story?'"[5] In fact, however, the process is not, except perhaps in some of its extreme forms, peculiar to postmodernism. There it is the final outcome of something that had begun much earlier—with Kafka's K, for example. Although still a character complex and puzzling enough to elicit the countless reinterpretations of our trade, K (divested of even a proper name) merely supports an emotional state and an asocial situation, as Nathalie Sarraute pointed out thirty years ago in *The Age of Suspicion*. The surrealists twisted mimetic description into zanier language-games than anything found in postmodernism, and Djuna Barnes parodied every style from *Tristram Shandy* to the surrealists, describing a character (to take but one instance) by what she was not.[6] As for the dazzling and better-known parodies in *Ulysses*, it is surely moot whether they partake in or dismantle the mimetic illusion.

Valéry's scornful sentence "La marquise sortit à cinq heures" ("The marquise went out at five o'clock"), admired by the surrealists, epitomized the detailed social trivia of a typical character's activities and consciousness in the novel. In the 1950's and 1960's it became a joke phrase for the writers of the *nouveau roman* and of the *nouvelle critique*, which both had turned against the novel of minute psychological and social analysis, against "the old myths of depth" (*les vieux mythes de la profondeur*), as Robbe-Grillet called them.[7] Some think the character died then; some date its death much farther back, to Freud on dreams and the case histories so much more convincing than any subsequent ghosts of fiction.

For two centuries characters had reigned supreme in our imagination. Ostensibly we valued the way they were created, but above all we received them and talked of them—Emma (Woodhouse or Bovary), Becky Sharp, Jean Valjean, Little Dorrit, Fabrice, Rastignac, Marcel, Leopold Bloom, or even the Man Without Qualities—as if we knew them better than we knew our friends and kin. This has been revealed to be a wholly fantasmatic process: characters are verbal structures; they are like our real-life relationships but have no semblance of a referent. More and more swollen with words, like stray phalluses they wander our minds, cut off from the body of the text—hence the endless character analysis of a certain type of traditional criticism; hence also our disappointment when we see these characters incarnated by flesh and blood actors.

Nevertheless, for many critics the ultimate value of a novel depends on the author's ability to create characters as complex and convincing as real people. But the way this illusion was created and then, curiously, uncreated, so that it now lies in pieces at our feet like a disassembled toy, together with the novel as we commonly understand that term, surely deserves serious consideration. We certainly do not feel we know, as we feel we know the characters of earlier novels, the mostly unnamed personages of Sarraute, Butor, Barthelme, or Barth—or even those named but ambiguously existing creatures of the Beckett novels, or those great paranoiacs Pirate Prentice and Tyrone Slothrop of Pynchon's *Gravity's Rainbow*. We do not, and we are not meant to. The one postmodern character I do feel I know is Borges's briefly textualized Pierre Menard—and he was writing Don Quixote in the twentieth century, word for word the same as the sixteenth-century text.[8] The postmodern novel is at best a desperate self-parody of a dying genre, though some, like Barth, believe in regeneration through genre parody.[9] The reasons are many, and they have been much discussed in a dispersed way, so I'll gather up a few here.

One is of course the dead hand of history. Heidegger proposed to counter this with his *Destruktion* of the history of ontology; Susan Sontag wrote about it in "The Aesthetics of Silence" when she said that secular, historical consciousness, the crowning achievement of European thought, had transformed itself in little more than two centuries into "an almost insupportable burden of self-consciousness." "It's scarcely possible," she went on, "for the artist to write a word, or render an image or make a gesture, that doesn't remind him of something already achieved." Moreover, even history has become as inaccessible to us as the ontological it purports to relate; all our realities have been revealed to be products of our many systems of representation and, in particular, of our tropes, as Hayden White has suggested in his *Metahistory* and *Tropics of Discourse*.[10]

This long epistemological crisis, with its inevitable advances and retreats, denials and desires, has in addition taken the very specific form of technical self-consciousness, and this not only at the level of high philosophy. As in all decadent periods, the rhetoricians, from the schools of creative writing to the formalists, have moved in with a vengeance. If every scriptwriter knows the few deft touches needed to make a character convincing in one shot, so does the structuralist. The character, Roland Barthes told us, by then in his poststructuralist period, is the convergence of selected semes upon a proper name,[11] and Philippe Hamon, who has remained closer to structuralism, goes farther toward reductionism in "Toward a Semiotic Law of Character." Hamon compares characters to signs, of which he finds three main types:

1. Referential signs, which refer to an exterior reality coded in institutionalized knowledge: we also have referential characters (historical, allegorical, mythical, social, psychological) immobilized by a culture.

2. Deictics (the egocentric circumstantials of Russell or the shifters of Jakobson, which refer back to the situation of utterance): thus we have deictic characters, marking the presence of the author, the reader, and their substitutes in the text.

3. Anaphoric signs, which refer back to other disjoined signs in the spoken or written chain: so we have anaphoric characters recognizable only within the system of the work and forming a network of reminders and interpreters.[12]

In this rhetoric or semiotic superconsciousness, it would seem that postmodernism has eliminated all but the egocentric circumstantials.

But not only self-consciousness has made techniques overfamiliar and helped to explode the mimetic illusion; misunderstanding and misuse through overfamiliarity have also done their share. One interesting example is the various modes novelists have invented to represent what goes on, either consciously or unconsciously, inside characters. These conventional literary modes do not exist outside of fiction: in real life we do not have access to people's minds, nor is this access verbally possible on the stage except through soliloquy. To the novel's immense credit, by the end of the eighteenth century, notably in Jane Austen, it had invented, among others, the mode of representation traditionally called "free indirect style." (Now usually called "free indirect discourse," the same mode was labeled "narrated monologue" by Dorrit Cohn in her remarkable *Transparent Minds* and "represented speech and thought" by Ann Banfield, who analyzed it linguistically in her equally remarkable *Unspeakable Sentences*.)[13]

For decades this mode of representation was treated in the haziest of confusions by critics; it is only now receiving adequate attention. But I shall not enter here into its controversies. I merely want to add what no one else has said, namely, that if the critics did not grasp its full effect, the writers certainly did. This fascinating sleight of hand—using present deictics in past-tense sentences— had by Flaubert's time become the mark of his individual style (so much so that the French as usual assumed he had invented it). But during the twentieth century it was so blindly imitated and abused that it became meaningless. Invented to represent a character's words, thoughts, or unconscious attitudes, it came to be used to filter all narrative information through the character in the name of the elimination of the author. Thus the narrator/character ambiguity of a sentence like Jane Austen's "He was more in love with her than Emma had supposed" would be lost in the average modern novel.[14] At first reading we can take it as narrator's information— Frank Churchill was in love with Emma—but at second reading we know it must be Emma's semiconscious thought, which could be, and is, mistaken. It cannot therefore come from an omniscient voice, which by convention (at least in Austen's time) cannot lie.

The use of this subtle device for narrative information thoroughly blurs and weakens it, exposing it as a "mere" device. Though no one noticed, the *nouveau roman* dropped it, instinctively, without the flourish with which Robbe-Grillet disowned the past tense as *the* mark of traditional narrative. In fact, free indirect discourse much more specifically marks traditional narrative. Its disappearance in Robbe-Grillet via the present tense is not surprising, since he also refused "the old myths of depth." Nathalie Sarraute, who by contrast explores depth, or what she calls "subconversations," also turned instinctively away from free indirect discourse and uses, as does Beckett, mostly either direct discourse or what Bakhtin calls "free direct." Yet some postmodernists, especially in their longer novels, still use free indirect of the most fatigued kind.

Besides an increased technical consciousness, we have an increased technical knowledge, provided by psychoanalysis, of what the novel's modes of representation are assumed to convey. Perhaps this too helped tire the novel's manner, partly for the second reason I shall now give for the character's collapse. This is the bourgeois origin of the novel, which Ian Watt was the first to show.[15] The society that the novel was developed to study and depict has lost all solid basis, stability, and belief in itself; our vision of it has broken up into fragments. On the one hand, the individual has lost any central role and has been replaced by a collectivist mode of thought, as has often been said. On the other hand, the philosophers and critics of the deconstructionist movement have, since 1966–67, steadily subverted what was left of the mimetic and expressive theories of literature, killing the referent in favor of the floating signifier, the author in favor of the reader, and the work in favor of textuality as an activity, an endless dissemination or even, for the Barthes of the 1973 *The Pleasure of the Text (Le plaisir du texte)*, a *jouissance* of infinite codes. Above all, they deconstructed the self into a disintegrating play of selves.[16]

People still behave, and writers still write, as if the old, mimetic belief in a referential language still existed. Novelists portray and satirize, but the society they refer to is no longer there, in the sense that there is no fixed or certain belief in it. Serious writers have lost their material. Or rather, this material has gone elsewhere: back to the novelist's original sources in documentary, journalism, chronicles, letter writing—but in their modern forms, such as the media and the human sciences, which supposedly "do it better." Nonfiction has taken back all the sociology, the psychology, and the philosophy—moral or epistemological—while the poetry, the myth, and the dream have also moved elsewhere, to pop and rock, for example, with their flashing laser lights and surrealistic video clips. Even dialogue, which the novel had learned from sophisticated seventeenth- and eighteenth-century comedy, has long returned to the stage and screen, as has storytelling. In 1966 George Steiner could speak already of a new nonfiction genre that would replace the novel, including works ranging from the high journalism of documentaries like Oscar Lewis's *The Children of Sanchez* to far more fundamentally changed forms, perceptible in Blake and including Nietzsche, Kierkegaard, or, today, Bloch's *Das Prinzip Hoffnung*. Steiner even included Wittgenstein's *Tractatus* as a borderline case.[17]

The third reason is what Walter J. Ong, perhaps simplistically, has called "secondary orality." In primary orality, he says, narratives are episodic and characters are what E. M. Forster called "flat" as opposed to "round." Round characters, like Aristotle's well-made plot, could not occur before the advent of writing (in the non-Derridean sense). We meet them first in the Greek tragedies, which their actors' written parts rendered more analyzable and linear than the earlier, stereotyped oral-formulaic epics. A second technological revolution, of print, widened and deepened our ability to analyze and present complex characters, first on stage and later in the novel. And now, of course, through the electronic media we have entered a secondary orality. It is quite unlike the first, since writing and print have profoundly altered our minds, but it may re-alter us no less profoundly.[18]

Prior and opposed to writing, primary orality belongs to what Derrida, in his understanding of *écriture* as the ability to differentiate and defer, deconstructs as the "logocentric and phonocentric tradition," based on a metaphysics of presence and responsible for all our systems and mental structures. I shall return to this. But on a simpler and more superficial level, and whether or not we agree with Father Ong and his predecessors and contemporaries (McLuhan, Havelock, and Lord, for example), flat characters *are* coming back. They have been coming back for some time, through the comic strips and the media, and they seem more real to the young than all the rounded, complex characters of our classic loves. It is Superman and Wonder Woman, the Smurfs, or even the new heroes of the computer games, that the young identify with.[19]

Round characters seem to have vanished back into fact, into the news clips and the documentaries, retaining all their real-life opacity. The realistic novel's window into their souls seems to have closed again; the reader got bored, perhaps, and for a long time now has preferred nonfiction or pure fantasy to fiction. A real terrorist or an Iranian fanatic is far more mysterious and convincing than all our acutely observed and literate bourgeois tizzies.

Moreover—and this would be the fourth reason—the human need for fictions has been channeled into the "popular" genres, which have been making a big comeback for over thirty years, not only in popularity but in respectability. University courses are given and theses are written on science fiction, on the thriller and the detective story, on comic strips. As Northrop Frye showed in *The Secular Scripture*, there is always, in any culture, a "secular" tradition on the fringe of the "central myth" tradition (in our case the Greco-Judeo-Christian). The central tradition despises the secular tradition, except when it is itself exhausted. Then it turns to the secular or popular genres to find new vigor.[20]

Of course, the characters of these popular genres are flat characters. It was easy for Propp to show that the action, not the actor, makes up a folktale's basic structure. The medieval romance moved for a while into the central tradition, but basically its characters were still flat, supports for this or that strength, weakness, passion, or, in their most profound interpretation, seasonal (or some other) archetypes. Similarly, in science fiction, which many agree is in some ways a modern equivalent of romance, the characters were for a long time flat. Only in the 1950's, when science fiction wanted its respectable pedigree, did it try to imitate the realistic novel, adopting all of realism's narrative clichés and introducing some psychology and social background—badly, on the whole, since rounded characters don't belong to the genre. Even now, when science fiction has at its best developed into a highly serious, even poetic, literary form (or "structural fabulation," as Scholes puts it), the best sci-fi critics still maintain that realistic characterization is not its job: landscape as hero, said Mark Rose, and Kingsley Amis long ago went one better—idea as hero.[21]

The latter notion has taken a good while to spread, but I am convinced that a proper examination of characters in both the postmodern novel and the best science fiction (which rejoins postmodernism) would show that they exist in any complexity only insofar as they represent ideas rather than individuals with a civic status and subtle social and psychological history. Or, if such a history is given, it is not what interests the reader, which amounts to the same thing: rounded individuation has become an addition, like the ornaments of traditional rhetoric. At best the characters are poems in themselves, as in Joseph McElroy's *Plus*, where the central consciousness is a brain orbiting the earth in an experimental capsule, a brain that starts growing limbs as it absorbs the sun's energy and relearns cognition and memory.[22]

The fifth and last reason I shall discuss lies in Frye's historical and cyclical theory of modes, based on the hero's power of action. Frye identified five modes: myth, where the hero is a god; romance, where he is man with magical powers; high mimetic, where he is a leader, who in the tragic version falls; low mimetic, where he is a man like us; and irony, where his power of action is less than ours, so that we watch his mistakes or, by Kafka's time, his torments. But when existence outbids fiction in the savagery of this ironic mode, fictions escape and return to myth—as happened, for instance, in the modernist period of Pound, Eliot, and Joyce.[23] Or, as George Steiner put it for a later time, fiction is silent before the horrors of the mid-twentieth century.[24]

I am not sure that this last is wholly true. I would say that the mimetic tradition is silent before these horrors and cannot cope with them, but that poetry, being essentially nonmimetic, can, like various types of modern fantastic, cope with everything from the sublime to the horrific and the ridiculous.

Not only the horror of violence but the clamor of sexuality has killed the mimetically realized character, then gone detumescent. Steiner says in *Language and Silence*: "The novels being produced under the new code of total statement shout at their personages: strip, fornicate, perform this or that act of sexual perversion. So did the S.S. guards at rows of living men and women."[25] Yet French critics like Kristeva and Sollers have called this "the experience of limits," with reference to Bataille and others; and Barthes, in *The Pleasure of the Text*, has written ecstatically on the erotics of textuality. Surely the merely mimetic fails here, because there is referentially not only a limit but also a severe limitation to this type of activity. I for one do not consider the merely said orgies of sodomy and shit swallowing and pee drinking in Burroughs or in a few scenes of *Gravity's Rainbow* to be high literary achievements. It is of course fashionable not to show oneself shocked, but one is oddly enough not allowed to be bored either, on pain of being accused of some abnormal syndrome thoroughly repressed. With a few notable exceptions, some by women, both the postmodern novel and science fiction, like the utopias of Scholes's structural fabulation, are surprisingly phallocratic. It is as if the return to popular forms or the parody of them, even via the intellectual cognition of utopian models, necessarily entailed the circulation of women as objects, which we find both in those models and in folktales and early cultures.

Be that as it may, Frye's theory of modes seems so far to be right, though we see it operating in an accelerated way. We are obviously now in an age of romance after a brief flirtation with myth. Are we going toward tragedy in the high mimetic mode again? It seems to me that any mimetic, high or low, is philosophically impossible at the moment. Steiner thinks that though conflict will persist, tragedy without a god is self-contradictory; it would be indistinguishable from serious comedy, an acting out of argument—like Brecht, for instance.[26]

So where do we go from here? Fictional character has died, or become flat, as had *deus ex machina*. We're left, perhaps, with the faint hope of a ghost in the machine.

"La marquise revint à minuit." (The marquise returned at midnight.) This was the title of an article by Philippe Muray in *L'Infini*, the review that replaced *Tel Quel*.[27] Character, Muray noted, may well be coming back but, precisely, as a *revenant*, a ghost; and we must know it for what it is. Yet surely this knowing it for a ghost, for a verbal construct, and the consequent loss of our innocence and our passionate identifications, has created the situation. Fragmented ectoplasms, pale copies of case histories or of ancient mythic archetypes, our characters are either documented records artificially animated or fictional ghosts.

We are in transition, no doubt, like the unemployed waiting for the newly structured technological society. Realistic novels continue to get written, but fewer and fewer people buy them or believe in them, except for the best-sellers with the right admixture of voluptuousness and violence, sentimentality and sex, familiarity and fantasy. Serious writers have joined the poets as elitist outcasts, and have retreated into self-reflexive, self-mocking forms—from the fabulated scholarship of Borges to the cosmicomics of Calvino, from Beckett's despairing hollow men to the choreography of mere pronouns in the *nouveau nouveau roman*, from Barthelme's mysterious stylizations to Brautigan's and Ishmael Reed's light funny ones, from Barth's anguished Menippean satires to Pynchon's disorienting symbolic quests for nothing at all—which use all the techniques of the realistic novel to show that they can no longer be used for the same purposes. The dissolution of character is a conscious gambit of postmodernism as it rejoins the techniques of science fiction. The move was, however, already inherent in modernism.

Here, perhaps, lies our hope: a starting again, *ex* almost *nihilo*, so that narrative can again, as it once did, aspire to the condition of poetry. The impetus comes from two apparently contradictory sources, the technological revolution and the feminist revolution.

And they are indeed contradictory sources. On the one hand, computer science seems to root our thought structures—either again (i.e., despite the apparent escape of deconstruction) or even more deeply—in the absolute limitation imposed by logical operations based on binary oppositions, whose positive and negative values, since they are mere electric impulses, are of course completely neutral and unprivileged. On the other hand, the more interesting feminists have been attracted by and are contributing to the deconstructionist movement in both its radical and its less radical variations. Deconstruction is ultimately also based on guiding polarities—such as voice/writing, sound/silence, being/nonbeing, presence/absence, man/woman, conscious/unconscious—yet it has shown how in the logo-phonocentric metaphysics of presence that has ruled us for over two thousand years the first term is always somehow privileged, even when equilibrium is supposed. Inverting the polarities (writing/voice, nonbeing/being, etc.) produces dizziness and fear (and resistance). But could the ultimate effect not be reequilibration, which should produce (and has produced) flights of creativity and word-game processes as enriching and magical as those produced by the incredibly complex flow-charts and numerical logical operators of computer science?

To come back to earth, just as the flat characters of romance eventually, through print and the far-reaching social developments connected with it, became rounded and complex, so, if we survive at all, perhaps the computer, after first ushering in (apart from superefficiency) the games and preprogrammed oversimplifications of popular culture, will alter our minds and powers of analysis once again, and enable us to create new dimensions in the deep-down logic of characters. I do not mean computers with human emotions or humanoids with computer brains. As the relevant article in the *Science Fiction Encyclopedia* says, science fiction has so far been disappointingly unimaginative in its treatment of computer science. I mean a completely different development arising from computer logic but as unimaginable to us now as a Shakespearean character would have been to an oral-epic culture, and a different way of thinking about and rendering the human character, of thinking about and rendering all worldly phenomena, as revolutionary as the scientific spirit that slowly emerged out of the Renaissance and the Gutenberg galaxy.

The second source, feminism, is more problematic, but we should remember that it is in the novel that the feminine contribution was most allowed and most able to flourish, for all the reasons analyzed in Virginia Woolf's *A Room of One's Own* and since. Moreover, I believe that it is the feminine element in humankind that creates art, as was long represented by the Muse. Lacan, for example, argues that totalization, or the construction of a whole, is always based on exclusions and therefore is always on the masculine side in his division *tout/pas tout* (whole/nonwhole); the *pas tout* is quite evidently on the feminine side. The desiring subject on the masculine side desires the *objet petit "a" (l'autre)* (the object with a small "o"; the other), located on the feminine side— desiring it via the phallus as psychic construct and with a phallic enjoyment. But the desiring subject on the *pas tout*, feminine side has two directions of desire: toward the phallus and toward *l'Autre* with a capital "A," the Unconscious, the Symbolic, the Infinite, God—the cause of the feminine element in anyone. But each must pass through the other.[28]

As Jean-Claude Milner argues, this scheme can apply to any totalizing, excluding system, such as science and, in particular, linguistics. Thus the language of the linguists (*la langue*) totalizes and excludes, whereas *lalangue* (in one word) is nontotalizing and feminine: in it all substitutions and arborescences are possible. The linguist's desire for this *lalangue* operates via *la langue*, the linguistic system, just as in the psychic model the desiring subject passes through the phallus. By contrast, on the *pas tout*, feminine side, *lalangue*, having access to language as Symbolic, can cause surplus pleasure and produce language as substance, or what is closest to the real, the poem.[29]

In this new psychology both women and men artists who have rejected the totalization, the *tout*, of traditional and even modernist art and chosen the underdetermination and opaqueness of the *pas tout* may clash in an enriching and strengthening way with the binary, superlogical, and by definition exclusive structures of the electronic revolution. But this must be a mating, not merely a clash; the *pas tout* and *tout* must absorb and quicken each other, not merely refuse each other.

When women have passed the stage of what I call "mere" feminism, however radically necessary, when they have ceased to feel obliged to pounce on phallocratic instances and to claim or sometimes shriek their equality with or superiority to men in both ability and sexuality, perhaps they will turn their attention, as they did in the past and as mostly men are doing now, to the deep-down regeneration of the novel and, therefore, as *sine qua non*, of character in the novel. This may take a long time, or it may be stopped by a holocaust, but it may also happen with incredible speed, like the technological revolution. It might even be instrumental in avoiding that holocaust. Meanwhile, perhaps we will have to be satisfied with self-conscious parody or documentaries on the one hand, and, on the other, with Superman, Wonder Woman, Smurfs, and the dwarfs, giants, monsters, and magic monarchs of pseudoscientific romance.

Toward a Relational Individualism: The Mediation of Self Through Psychoanalysis

NANCY JULIA CHODOROW

Psychoanalysis begins with a radical challenge to traditional notions of the individual self. As Freud, with characteristic modesty, puts it:

> In the course of centuries the *naive* self-love of men has had to submit to two major blows at the hands of science. The first was when they learnt that our earth was not the centre of the universe but only a tiny fragment of a cosmic system of scarcely imaginable vastness. This is associated in our minds with the name of Copernicus, though something similar had already been asserted by Alexandrian science. The second blow fell when biological research destroyed man's supposedly privileged place in creation and proved his descent from the animal kingdom and his ineradicable animal nature. This revaluation has been accomplished in our own days by Darwin, Wallace and their predecessors, though not without the most violent contemporary opposition. But human megalomania will have suffered its third and most wounding blow from the psychological research of the present time which seeks to prove to the ego that it is not even master in its own house, but must content itself with scanty information of what is going on unconsciously in its mind.[1]

According to Freud, then, we are not who or what we think we are: we do not know our own centers; in fact, we probably do not have a center at all. Psychoanalysis radically undermines notions about autonomy, individual choice, will, responsibility, and rationality, showing that we do not control our own lives in the most fundamental sense. It makes it impossible to think about the self in any simple way, to talk blithely about the individual.

At the same time, however, psychoanalysis gives us an extraordinarily rich, deep, and complex understanding of whatever it is that is not the simple self we once thought we were, and it explains how whatever this is develops. "What is going on unconsciously in its mind" are forces and structures beyond conscious control or even knowledge: sexual and aggressive drives within the id; primary-process thinking with no respect for time, logic, reality, or consistency; powerful ideas and wishes that anxiety and repression have removed from consciousness and that defenses like resistance, isolation, and denial work to ensure will not reappear there; conflict, as these wishes and ideas seek recognition and meet with resistances and defenses; superego pressures that once were felt to come from recognized external forces but now operate relatively independently, fed by aggressive drives turned inward. This fragmentation of structure, function, and process that the psychoanalytic metapsychology describes affects the everyday subjective experience of self, lending what Freud recognized as a certain unease to expressed certainties about autonomous individuality and sparking a fierce opposition to his theories.

Even though Freud radically undermined notions of the unitary and autonomous individual, we can also see psychoanalysis, in its endless, reflexive involvement with self-investigation, as a particularly intense scrutiny of the individual, the apogee of the development of individualism in Western culture.[2] From the earliest days of psychoanalysis until the present, cultural thinkers, artists, and writers have celebrated the fragmented self that psychoanalysis portrays, denigrating character in literature, romanticizing the lack of agency, meaning, morality, and authorship.

Freud, however, wanted to resolve the paradox he created, to use the scrutiny of individual and self not to celebrate fragmentation but to restore wholeness. He could not accept that the self is the outcome of messy unconscious processes and a warring structure, that it disallows individual morality, autonomy, and responsibility; he wanted to reconstitute the individual and the self he had dissected. That metapsychological dissection shows who we are, but the clinical project of psychoanalysis is to develop individual autonomy and control in the self. As Freud put it, "Where id was, there shall ego be. It is a work of culture—not unlike the draining of the Zuider Zee."[3] And where an overwhelming, punitive superego was, there shall a conscious ego be. These goals, I think, have to be made very clear. Freud, and later psychoanalysts, did not just give up in despair; that is, although he did despair that the dikes could keep back the Zuider Zee entirely, he certainly wanted to give it a good try. All analysts probably want to restore a certain wholeness and agency to the self.

In this paper, I discuss two psychoanalytic solutions to the dilemma posed by Freud's challenge to individualism and the self, two different conceptions of wholeness and agency. These solutions are not mutually exclusive: they overlap each other in psychoanalytic thought and in theory and therapy. One solution is, in essence, to reconstitute, or resuscitate, the traditional autonomous self of the pristine individual; the other is to reconstruct a self that is in its very structure fundamentally implicated in relations with others. Because the mediation of self through psychoanalysis happens within the psychoanalytic process, we must examine this mediation in clinical practice as well as in theory.[4]

In the traditional model, based on Freud's drive theory along with his late structural theory, "where id was, there shall ego be," maturation and psychic health consist in rational ego control over the insistent drives, reducing the tyranny of the superego in order to harmonize conscience and wish, ego-ideal and ego-actuality. Internal conflict, then, is between different aspects of the psychical personality; reduction of this conflict will presumably lead to fulfillment in the external world, although traditional psychoanalysis does not specify how that will happen. The developmental model here is the oedipal struggle between self and father, where the Oedipus complex—the relational complex itself—is "smashed to pieces" and leaves in its wake a superego "so inexorable, so impersonal, so independent of its emotional origins."[5] Autonomy is key: although the superego is originally formed in response to parental prohibitions and the relationship to parents, this relational history ceases to be actively part of one's psychic makeup. The focus on individual autonomy is extended in Heinz Hartmann's work on ego psychology, which contributes to psychoanalytic metapsychology the notion of autonomous, conflict-free ego spheres; it is also reflected in the work of Heinz Kohut, who assesses the psychic functioning of the bipolar self in terms of ambitions and ideals.*

*Kohut is somewhat paradoxical in terms of the antinomy I am trying to develop here. On the one hand, he is seen as an object-relations theorist par excellence, who locates disorders of the self squarely in early failures of the mirroring and idealizing relationship to mother and father. He is contrasted (and contrasts himself) with the classical theorists in his focus on the self and the self's disorders, as opposed to the classical concern with conflict. Yet on the other hand, his goals for the self—ambitions and ideals mediated by skills and talents—could not be more individualist. In his version, the object-relations route is to lead to individual fulfill-

An alternative psychoanalytic view of the individual and the self emerges, not from Freud's structural discussions or from the exhortation that "where id was, there shall ego be," but from his essay "On Narcissism." Here, Freud notes how libido can be directed alternately toward objects (other people) or toward the self. He calls these forms "object libido" and "ego libido," and he locates psychic wholeness in a delicate balance between them. In Freud's view here, exclusive investment in the self with no connection to the other creates the narcissistic neuroses and psychoses; relatedness is the sine qua non of mental health. At the same time, he warns against the opposite danger, complete investment in the object—as in slavish unrequited love, which debases the self and deprives it of energy. As he puts it, "A strong egoism is a protection against falling ill, but in the last resort we must begin to love in order not to fall ill, and we are bound to fall ill if, in consequence of frustration, we are unable to love."*

The developmental theory Freud begins to describe in the same essay points toward a maturation of belongingness or connectedness (such as Carol Gilligan outlines)[6] instead of ego autonomy and control. He proposes that in its original libidinal state the infant has two love objects, "itself and the woman who tends it," and conceptualizes development in terms of what happens to these two libidinal attachments: in the best case, unproblematic self-regard and lack of self-punitiveness on the one hand, and "true object love," loving a person as a complement to and not an extension of the self, on the other.

Just as Hartmann and others picked up from Freud's metapsy-

---

ment of individual goals. Where Freud, Hartmann, and others assume that harmonizing internal conflict will somehow harmonize relations with the external world, Kohut seeks to harmonize external relations to enable internal resolution. See his *Analysis of the Self* (New York, 1971) and *Restoration of the Self* (New York, 1977).

*"On Narcissism: An Introduction" (1914), *The Standard Edition of the Complete Psychological Works of Sigmund Freud*, ed. James Strachey (London, 1953–66), XIV, p. 85. Freud in this essay still makes object-relatedness residual. Thus he assumes that libido proceeds onto the object as a spillover from narcissism: "What makes it necessary at all for our mental life to pass on beyond the limits of narcissism and to attach the libido to objects? The answer which would follow from our line of thought would once more be that this necessity arises when the cathexis of the ego with libido exceeds a certain amount." And although he notes the *two* original love objects of the infant (mother and self), he and his followers go on as if primary narcissism precedes any object-directedness and is the exclusive original state of the infant.

chology and developmental theory an emphasis on the autonomous ego and rational superego, so other post-Freudian psychoanalysts have expanded upon the theory of narcissism. Object-relations theorists conceptualize the infant in terms of its cognitive narcissism and primary libidinal relatedness—that is, its inability to distinguish itself conceptually from its primary caretaker and other objects in the world, even while it feels itself in, and gets gratification from, a relationship to an other.[7] As cognitive narcissism gives way to a sense of bounded self, internality and externality come to have both a simple cognitive and a complex affective reality.* On the physical level, the infant comes to be unproblematically aware of its own boundaries and separateness. On the affective level, as the infant defines a self out of the mother-child matrix, the early flux of projections and introjections ensures that some aspects of that self are likely to have originally been perceived or experienced as aspects of the primary other or others, and aspects of the other may have originally been felt as aspects of the self.[8] On a psychological level, then, even the apparent boundaries of the individual do not separate in any simple way the pristine individual from the rest of the world.

The core of the self, or self-feeling, is also constructed relationally. Michael Balint locates the primary feeling of self in terms of the sense of fit or lack of fit with the primary caretaker; Winnicott characterizes as "the capacity to be alone" a sense of individuality and autonomy that includes the internalization of the benign but uninvolved presence of the mother. The development of psychic structure begins with this basic self-feeling and self-structure, which includes relatedness to and aspects of the other, and it continues through internalizations and splittings-off of internalized self-other representations to create an inner world consisting of different aspects of an "I" in relation to different aspects of the other. Psychological disorders, the problem of the fragmented individual, are seen here not so much in terms of conflict and defenses but

---

*Recent infancy research claims that the infant's cognitive sense of separateness is innate, rather than developed in the manner described by Mahler and others. Such a revision of our understanding of the infant's mental capacities does not undermine the understanding of the affective and object-relational components of sense of separateness and relatedness that I discuss here. See Daniel N. Stern, "The Early Development of Schemas of Self, Other, and 'Self with Other,'" in Joseph D. Lichtenberg and Samuel Kaplan, eds., *Reflections on Self Psychology* (Hillsdale, N.J., 1983).

rather in terms of problematic self-other relationships, which themselves internally constitute low self-esteem, self-punitiveness, lack of control, and so forth.* Thus, the object-relations perspective gives us a very different notion of the construction of individuality than does the classical analytic account. In the classical account, the inner world is conceived in terms of different aspects of the psychical personality, and the goal is reduction of conflict among these. The classical account accords some recognition to the implicit relatedness of the individual: Freud claims that "the superego continues to play the part of an external world for the ego, although it has become a portion of the internal world," and he also mentions the role of identifications in the formation of the ego-ideal.⁹ But these origins are not stressed in accounts of psychic functioning or models of the psychic constitution; instead, autonomy and the resolution of conflict are seen in terms of modes of ego functioning.

By contrast, the object-relations model, although it recognizes the role of defenses in ego functioning (understanding these defenses as operating in terms of an internal sense of self in relationship and of internal objects) and acknowledges the desirability of conflict-free ego spheres, conceptualizes the self as inexorably social and intrinsically connected. Thus, both views challenge the traditional notion of the pristine individual, but one does so without fundamental recourse to the "outside world." In neither view is the self unitary, but in object-relations theory it is also not apart from the other. Joan Riviere—an associate of Melanie Klein, who first made projection, introjection, and the role of internal objects central in psychoanalytic theory—puts the position as follows:

> We tend to think of any one individual in isolation; it is a convenient fiction. We may isolate him physically, as in the analytic room; in two minutes we find he has brought his world in with him, and that, even before he set eyes on the analyst, he had developed inside himself an elaborate relation with him. There is no such thing as a single human being, pure and simple, unmixed with other human beings. Each personality is a world in himself, a company of many. That self, that life of one's own, which is in fact so precious though so casually taken for granted, is a composite structure which has been and is being formed

*In the course of this development, what were originally unstructured and unorganized drive potentials come to be differentiated into aggressive and libidinal components, given affective meaning and organized by attachment to aspects of the inner world. See Edith Jacobson, *The Self and the Object World* (New York, 1964).

and built up since the day of our birth out of countless never-ending influences and exchanges between ourselves and others. . . . These other persons are in fact therefore parts of ourselves, not indeed the whole of them but such parts or aspects of them as we had our relation with, and as have thus become parts of us. And we ourselves similarly have and have had effects and influences, intended or not, on all others who have an emotional relation to us, have loved or hated us. We are members one of another.[10]

Riviere, like Freud, points to the threat that this conception of the individual poses:

The "inner world," like other psychoanalytical concepts, meets with a twofold resistance; on the one hand, the incapacity to understand it, and on the other a direct emotional rejection of it . . . an acute reaction which arises, as experience teaches, from an acute anxiety. . . . When this proposition meets with an intense emotional rejection there is clearly a direct association in the hearer's mind of this idea with danger, as though anything inside one which is not "oneself" pure and simple is and must be dangerous—or pathological.[11]

Object-relations theory does not need to idealize a hyperindividualism; it assumes a fundamental internal as well as external relatedness to the other. The question is then what kind of relation this can or should be. The relational individual is not reconstructed in terms of his or her drives and defenses but in terms of the greater or lesser fragmentation of his or her inner world and the extent to which the core self feels spontaneous and whole within, rather than driven by, this world. Even the sense of agency and autonomy remain relational in the object-relations model, because agency develops in the context of the early relationship with the mother and bears the meaning of her collaboration in and response to it. Separation and autonomy are not so crucial to development, because the model assumes the permeability of boundaries and focuses instead on the nature of the inner world and the inner core of self, whose implicit relatedness is acknowledged in its very structure. Paraphrasing Freud, we might say that the goal in the object-relational reconstruction of the individual is: where fragmented internal objects were, there shall harmoniously related objects be; and where false, reactive self was, there shall true, agentic self be, with its relationally based capacity both to be alone and to participate in the transitional space between self and other self that creates play, intimacy, and culture.

Object-relations psychoanalysis, in reformulating the psycho-analytic conception of self, also reformulates a self for social theory and analysis.[12] This self is intrinsically social, and, because it is con-structed in a relational matrix and includes aspects of the other, it can better recognize the other as a self and, ultimately, attain the intersubjectivity that creates society. This self's full historical grounding contrasts with that of the drive-determined individual. The grounding of the object-relational self derives from an appro-priation and interpretation of experienced relationships and accord-ingly varies by individual, culture, period, gender, and so forth. By contrast, the self of the drive-determined individual is originally constructed not through historically grounded experience but from universal and unchanging drives; this leads to a more abstract and universalist view of the self. (Insofar as this latter self has historical grounding, that grounding also derives from its object-relational history, the "precipitate of abandoned object-cathexes"[13] that it contains.) We might speculate that a fully social and historical con-ception of self provides an alternative to the autonomous ego and responsible, nonpunitive superego as a solution to the problems of morality, responsibility, and so forth posed by the psychoanalytic dissolution of the individual.

Psychoanalytic knowledge of the individual and the self is developed in theoretical and in metapsychological writings, but this knowledge is originally derived from the clinical setting, the analytic situation. Thus, an investigation of this setting can give further insight into the differentiated or relational self and help us decide between classical and object-relations models.

It would seem that the epistemological setting provided by the analytic situation requires that the knowledge of self emerging within it be relational, because this situation is a reflexively con-structed collaboration in which analyst and analysand, through their interaction, create a history, or story, of the analysand's life.[14] Engagement with others as subjects (an engagement moderated by objectivity) is central to clinical practice, as opposed to meta-psychology. In fact, this practical activity, empathetically involved with and taking account of another's interests, while objectively as-sessing the other and the self, in some ways illustrates a desirable sociality in general. A clinically derived view of the self also seems to require a historical as well as a social view of the self because of this concretely based engagement. Thus, a clinical perspective on the self seems to require engagement with the other, no matter what your theory.

Nevertheless, psychoanalysts have developed two clinical approaches, which reflect—though less starkly than the theory, for reasons I have suggested—the two approaches to the individual I have discussed. The first approach is popularly caricatured in the silent, uninvolved, blank-wall analyst, the object of a transference brought entirely from past experiences and relationships, who says little except, "What comes to mind?" or "umhmm," and occasionally offers brief nuggets of interpretation.* Analytic technique here consists in analyzing resistances and defenses that prevent the analysand from acknowledging transference feelings. The relentless analysis of all the analysand says in terms of these resistances will eventually lead to an acknowledged transference relationship, which can then be analyzed to bring out and resolve early developmental material. This assumes that what is going on in the analysis has nothing to do with any actual relationship to the analyst or with the reality of the person of the analyst, that this relationship is entirely transference and as such is entirely one-way. There is also a "therapeutic" or "working" alliance between analyst and analysand,[15] but this is merely an agreement made with the unneurotic parts of the analysand's ego to work on change, in tandem as it were, and does not involve any reciprocity or acknowledged connection.[16]

In this view, what the analyst does is to help the analysand reorganize a psychic organization and mental processes conceived as drives, superego, ego defenses, and resistances. In Freud's original view, countertransference—strong feelings about the analysand or about particular moments in the analysis, feelings perhaps evoked by the analysand—was always an unwelcome intrusion and a sign of the analyst's own inadequate analysis. The later classical model recognizes countertransference but prescribes that it should count for little in the analysis.

---

*As we know from Freud and others, this is hardly the stance that Freud himself took. He took walks with patients, talked to their relatives, gave and got cigars, and in the case of Dora was quite happy to attempt to browbeat her into submitting to his definition of the intrapsychic and interpersonal situation. Yet officially his interpretive stance was closer to the classic model of interpretation of resistances. In addition, as I mention below, he felt that countertransference signified inadequacy on the part of the analyst. See on this Samuel Lipton, "The Advantages of Freud's Technique as Shown in His Analysis of the Rat Man," *International Journal of Psycho-Analysis*, 58 (1977), 255–73.

This view of the analytic process corresponds with and nicely reinforces a metapsychology that posits a pristine individual who is all ego and id, and whose autonomous ego must take more and more spheres of control from id, unconscious ego defenses, and superego. Nonetheless, in spite of formal intention the clinical situation almost requires some recognition of the interpersonal construction (and reconstruction) of a self. Various residual concepts in the classical account of technique (none formally acknowledged in theory and all requiring justification and scrutiny in the individual case), much like the Ptolemaic epicycles, point to an alternative formulation of the analytic process and the selves involved in it. The relentless interpretation of resistances is sometimes avoided for considerations of "tact" and "timing"—if pointing them out might lead to the creation of even more ego defenses by the analysand. Deviations from technique (in revealing information about yourself, in allowing the analysand to sit up, in responding to questions) are occasionally allowed if these will help the analytic work by making the analysand more secure. Similarly, building a therapeutic alliance may depend partly on the analysand's trust in the analyst's good intent and may therefore require the analyst to indicate such intent.

All of these, of course, are ways to acknowledge that the actual relationship between analyst and analysand matters, that change in the analysand depends at least partly on the nature and meaning of that relationship. An alternative clinical position makes this engagement and its consequences more explicit. Formulated variously by Michael Balint, Heinz Kohut, Frieda Fromm-Reichman, Margaret Little, Leo Stone, Harold Searles, D. W. Winnicott, and others, this position proposes, not that the analyst should participate equally in a real relationship (always answering questions about her or himself, always being supportive and responsive), but that what is central to an analysis and must be constantly kept at the forefront of the analyst's awareness is an affective and cognitive exchange between two people.[17] Choices in technique accordingly have the aim of enhancing this relationship so that the analytic work can progress; analysis focuses primarily on experiences of the self in both internal and external relationship rather than on the analysis of resistances and defenses.

In this model the analyst's attentiveness to and investigation of countertransference is a crucial part of every analysis, not a holdover to be avoided. Moreover, countertransference involves all feelings evoked in the analyst, and these feelings are not seen as purely neurotic. As Elizabeth Zetzel puts it: "Many analysts to-day believe that the classical conception of analytic objectivity and anonymity cannot be maintained. Instead, thorough analysis of reality aspects of the analyst's personality and point of view is advocated as an essential feature of transference analysis and an indispensable prerequisite for the dynamic changes."[18] These "many analysts" would claim that a focus on the analyst's own reactions will provide the best clue to what is going on with the patient (and with the analyst's self as well). Thus, they would explicitly recognize that the analysand's self is reconstructed in and through both conscious and unconscious interaction with the analyst.

The focus on countertransference points to a final, important part of the first psychoanalytic formulations of the self: psychoanalytic knowledge of the self originally concerned the self of the analyst as well as the self of the patient. Thus, Freud first learned about the unconscious, resistance, and repression from his hysterical patients, but he learned about dreams and the Oedipus complex from self-analysis.[19] And in the countertransference, perhaps not only the self of the analysand is reconstructed or reconstituted; the analyst's self may be changed, or at least better understood, as well.[20] Thus, knowledge of the other and knowledge of the self, construction of the self and construction of the other, are intimately related.

Psychoanalytic theory radically challenges our understanding of ourselves as whole, autonomous individuals, then seeks to reconstruct that wholeness and autonomy. It poses two solutions to this goal in its metapsychology and attempts them in its therapeutic technique and understanding. But the therapeutic setting can, finally, produce knowledge and self-knowledge only of a relational self. And psychoanalysis can only know the self in the analytic situation; anything else is ungrounded speculation. Thus, when we investigate psychoanalytic theory and practice, we see a historical progression from a view favoring a pure, differentiated individuality based on rigid notions of autonomous separateness toward a relational individualism.

Myths of Socialization and of Personality

JOHN W. MEYER

Individualism, along with the rest of the Western ideological system, has undergone a long process of expansion and institutionalization. In recent decades it has become worldwide one of the constitutive doctrines of modern society. I will focus on two of its established notions: first, that human actors, who constitute small systems incorporating biological, personal, and social elements, can and must be systematically socialized; second, that this socialization is largely effected by institutionalized mass education. A concern to construct individuals in a way appropriate to society's needs is as intrinsic a component of the modern social structure as are large-scale economies and bureaucratic states.

Some preliminary background may be useful. First, individualism is a highly institutional, historical construction; it is not centrally the product of human persons organizing their experience for themselves, but of various bodies of professional officials—religious ideologues, their secular counterparts (e.g., psychologists, teachers, lawyers, and administrators)—and by other institutions of the modern state.

Second, individualism, like other central elements of Western doctrine, is continually being "reconstructed." The incessant talk of crises in individualism indicates, not some real decline of the individualist theme, but only changes in its still-central importance. We must not take at face value all the talk about the crisis of the rootless individual, or the view that individualism is a derivative and fragile element of Western history perpetually threatened by such Leviathans as the economic market and the bureaucratic state. It is not so: individualism is part and parcel of the system of

208

the market and state. Some, following Weber, would see it as a main driving force behind them;[1] historically, as market and state have expanded, so has individualism. For instance, it is impossible not to notice the chronological and functional links among modern notions of the individual personality, its social construction by education, and the late-nineteenth-century expansion of the state and the economy in the centers of the modern world.

Third, individualism is growing. Since World War II, the whole Western ideological system has spread, both as a doctrine and as a social structure, with astonishing rapidity all over the globe. Everywhere societies have been reorganized as nation-states and immersed in modern economic life, often at the price of considerable material and cultural impoverishment.

Individualism, it is not always noticed, is a social doctrine. It is a public, not a private, view of the person, which others are bound to respect and to which a person is obliged to conform. It should be unnecessary in America, especially in California, to note that persons (even children) are supposed to behave, and to be treated, as responsible individuals. Society is rationalized as rooted in the behavior and choices of individuals and as functioning for their benefit; it is, as it were, not quite sacred itself but rather the product of its sacred individual members. It is justified, not by its history, but by the extent to which it benefits the individuals who are both its ultimate producers and its ultimate consumers.

Both the moral and the natural universes are supposed to exist for individuals, not society. The dualism of God and nature has often been seen as a central, driving theme in Western history, which is traced back to Augustine, or, earlier, to Rome or Greece or Jerusalem.[2] Indeed, Western history can be seen as a kind of "cargo cult"—a ritual project for the recovery of a lost political or cultural vision that is quite common in the debris or on the periphery of large empires. The idea is to carry out rituals and conduct ceremonies so that the lost resources (the cargo) return. At the center of this vision is the individual suspended between God and nature, organizing a morally unified society before the former and a socially and economically efficient one within the latter. At the natural pole, modern societies subject individuals' actions to detailed rationalistic analysis, summing up these actions and judging them by a single set of values: together they make up the Gross National

Product (GNP) of each society, with a future integrated World Product clearly in the offing. This GNP spans an enormous range of human activity. Speaking and listening at an intellectual conference such as the present one, enter it in various ways; so do the writing, printing, and reading of the associated book. Increasingly the activities of every human on earth are analyzed for their long-run cost or benefit to the GNP.

At the other, divine pole, the individual confronts an integrated moral universe in which he is defined, increasingly, as a sacred equal to all the other members of society. The lists of personal rights expand, and with them the political organizations (prominently states) in which these rights inhere. Human beings are now counted at the world level, and statistical details of their quality of life are recorded ever more fully: here the total GNP is less important than GNP per capita. The underlying idea is that society fulfills the will of God, not directly but by maximizing the welfare of each individual. This modern convention requires little elaboration; it implies the general assumption that every individual human has the right and the obligation, not only to develop himself as fully as possible, but to produce and consume as much as he can.

All modern societies are individualistic in a broad sense: they locate the value of life in the social action of individual persons. All define progress as socially achieved benefits for those individual persons. These notions, however, take a number of different forms, which imply different conceptions of human political organization.

At one extreme is American individualism, routinely celebrated by Europeans and Americans alike at least since Tocqueville's classic observations of the 1830's.[3] In the popular view, this individualism is thought to reach its apogee in California; some would even specify Southern California. There all of society, both in its productive relations to nature and in its organization of the sacred individual's consumption, is rationalized around individual ends. History and tradition have no standing, and the community is simply the negotiated product of individuals who choose to "get it on" together. The ground for thinking of Southern Californian individualism as the culmination of the Western form is that there a person's relation to the moral and the natural universes is unmediated by the surrounding social community. Both in cultural theory and in the empirical reality of survey research, this individual is unmatched in an enhanced conception of personal efficacy in the real

world and in the assumption of his ability to hold and express opinions in all matters of general moral purpose.[4] Tocqueville noted the
extraordinary opportunities for personal expansion in the American polity, but he also described the extraordinarily tight control
within which Americans function—the relentless pressure to conform for which the American system was then, and still is, re-
nowned. The individual, in this context, achieves freedom and
power only under the condition that he become isomorphic, or
similar in form, to all the other individuals in the society. This
similarity is not mediated by the individual's peers, organized as a
community; the American individual feels, rather, that he is responsible to the moral universe itself, and to the same moral universe as everyone else. He must also deal rationally with the real
world—the same practical world as everyone else. So in its American variant, individualism is required to be in tune with a highly
standardized and universalistic vision of both practical reality and
moral purpose. The individual is free, but not to adopt idiosyncratic or parochial purposes, or a unique notion of practical reality.
He is free to expand as a standardized individual, but not to withdraw to another plane; such a withdrawal, from either pole of the
standardized universe, invites censure. A host of legal and social
rules, for instance, make forming a community or a binding commitment (in a marriage, to a residential locale, or in a work organization) difficult and unrewarding.

Overall, then, the notion that the American individual has an
unmediated relation to the moral and the natural environments is
deceptive. In this cultural context the enforcement of a disciplined
cosmology—a standardized and scientized view of nature and a
universalized notion of the moral universe—performs that mediation. The American individual is free and empowered only within
this constraining scheme, and within it freedom is compulsory.

Even from the perspective of American individualism, much
European social organization looks equally individualistic. There
the individual's relation to the moral and the natural universes is
also mediated, but not by a society organized as a rationalized system for the purpose. In Europe aspects of social organization that
are, or are treated as, natural—family and gender relationships, local traditions, ethnic and regional patterns, and so on—perform the
mediation. But society as a rational project is still seen, ultimately,
as the product of individual action legitimized by its putative bene-

fits for the individual human beings in the group. In Europe, however, the individual is disciplined, not by the moral and technological rationales of American individualism, but by the natural and traditional laws of communal social structure (which sometimes take rather ugly forms, as in the recent German conception of the *Volk*). There is, in short, less display of individual efficacy and choice than in America, yet every individual has very real rights and obligations.

All modern systems are rooted in individualism; its form merely varies. Even the socialist world resolutely and overtly roots its theory of value and its political doctrine in individual action, in the benefits that the individuals in its present or future population will attain. The mediation itself, of course, takes place through some communal vision—a party here, a picture of the future community there—nevertheless the difference between this and the liberal European or American forms of individualism should be seen as one of degree rather than of kind.

This view may be difficult to accept in a predominantly liberal epoch; perhaps it is easier to understand the ideology of the American form in a university like Stanford. Here one finds the technological side of the American individualist vision—the dedicated scientific and technical search for prosthetic devices to improve individual human life (by engineering, medicine, or psychology). At Stanford one also finds a dedication to individualist moral universalism: for instance, in the use of National Science Foundation funds to attempt to communicate with potential intelligence nearer the center of the galaxy. Consider the cosmic assumptions implied in such an effort.

Only in individualist societies is it so important to control what individuals are and how they behave and think. There it is understood that the society's success or failure, its integration or breakdown, is ultimately determined by the competence and conformity of the individual. As a result much of the effort of modern society goes into constructing appropriate individuals.

In the eighteenth and nineteenth centuries, ideologies and institutions arose to deal with this problem. On the ideological side, one finds the progressive discovery of human personality—the notion that each person carries a whole system of motives and perceptions reflecting biological and social forces and distinctively integrated around an individuated self. And one finds the further doctrine that the natural development of this personality can and should be rationally managed by society for individual and social ends: a theory of socialization on a mass scale. The two doctrines match. If individuals are idiosyncratic, each reflecting completely distinct forces, then patterned socialization makes no sense. Nor does it make sense if individual action is seen as continuously and directly managed by social forces. Further, if individual personality has no inherent consistency over time, socializing children would not be a likely way to achieve progress. Hence an ideological faith in the coherence, continuity, and value of personality, operating under scientifically comprehensible general laws, is necessary for a general doctrine of socialization.[5]

On the institutional side, there has been a rapid, unprecedented development of both mass and elite systems of education. Universal schooling institutionally embodies the doctrines of socialization and personality for a society that sees itself and its betterment as products of the individuals within it. By the late nineteenth century, there was a shift toward more highly organized conceptions of society. The state organization expanded, and more highly bureaucratized structures arose to manage small elements of society. This required an elaboration of the idea of citizenship and of the notion that the state rested for its legitimacy and success on the solidarity, competence, and commitment of its individual members. Economic organization also became more bureaucratic; the large-scale modern economy arose, along with a social policy that supported it as the height of rational planning. Both developments required fuller incorporation and management of the individual. Economic change pressed for a more rationalized account of the individual's action; political change demanded a more complete account of the individual's identity.

In the late nineteenth century and early in the twentieth, education everywhere became more organized, more standardized, and more directly and centrally controlled.[6] The first generally used measure of human personality was created—the intelligence quotient, or I.Q., designed to indicate individual competence. Later, education became an important part of state ideology; almost all independent countries of the time built educational principles into their constitutions.[7]

As one might expect, the general trend toward greater educational organization hit hardest in America. Here psychology developed very rapidly, with an unusual concentration on human development and socialization; concepts of personality, development, and socialization were central for almost all the great early American psychologists. Similarly, educational expansion was especially important in America, since American individualism did not rely on human embeddedness in a supposedly natural community. Secondary and higher education grew faster in America than in any other country.

Education in America is used for ever more numerous social ends: whatever the social problem, more education is always the answer. Sex education will reduce the number of adolescent pregnancies; driver-training courses will result in fewer automobile accidents; job training and "career education" will lessen youth unemployment; special kinds of education must be found to address the difficulties of the handicapped. There is a parallel reaction to national needs. Sputnik prompted more training in engineering and science; Watergate, more instruction in ethics, especially in law schools. This is the historical American pattern, a lineal descendant of the earlier American emphasis on collective responsibility for salvation. The psychologies have also developed farther and more rapidly in the United States; every newspaper is filled with accounts of new problems of personality and their assorted new therapies. A noted psychologist at Stanford has both "discovered" the psychological problem of shyness and devised treatments for it. It is a fair guess that this country has a higher number of psychologists per capita than any other, and that the subdisciplines most important to individualist ideology (personality, socialization, and human development, say, in contrast to narrowly educational psychology) are more dominant in American psychology than elsewhere. The ratio of psychologists to other social scientists is undoubtedly higher; on the Stanford faculty, for instance, psychologists outnumber sociologists two to one.

In the rest of the world, the state system—rooted in the doctrine of individual citizenship—and with it the cultural theory of the individual have spread throughout the twentieth century. In a study of the evolution of national constitutions, Boli-Bennett, for example, notes how standard lists of the individual's political and economic rights and obligations grow.[8] New elements—for instance, many tenets of socialist doctrine—arise and spread rapidly as general principles. As they are added to the officially legitimated individualist ideology, the scope of psychology also widens, and its emphasis on socialization increases.

With the establishment of American political hegemony after World War II, American educational goals were even more rapidly adopted throughout the world. From 1950 to 1970, the proportion of primary-school-aged children enrolled in schools in poor countries jumped from 37 percent to 72 percent. Enrollment in secondary schools and universities increased at even greater rates—in what Coombs calls a world educational revolution. And the great bulk of this expansion occurred in institutions operated by nation-states.[9]

The rationale for these developments is a broad doctrine of human socialization. Lanford and Fiala have coded UNESCO educational reports, in which national officials describe the formal purposes of their educational systems; they found that the twin themes of national development (mentioned by 52 percent of the reports) and individual development (mentioned generally by 39 percent, in particular aspects by many more) were the most prominent. This fact reveals the general notion that individuals have a right to grow as individuals and that the nation benefits from their doing so. Strikingly, a new theme was initiated, especially by American academics, from 1955 to 1965. In 1955 only 16 percent of the UNESCO reports mentioned economic development as a goal of the national educational system. By 1965, 57 percent of the reports' writers had learned to give this answer; they reflected a new economic doctrine of human capital, whose value can be enhanced by education.[10]

These changes of attitude can be seen most dramatically on the world's political and economic periphery. Countries that only recently became independent create and enlarge their educational systems with astonishing speed, and on the most advanced ideological grounds. They are even more likely than the richer and older countries to make education a central national institution; for example, they build it into national constitutions as a citizen's right and duty.[11] Almost all new states do this, specifying the appropriate ideological rationales and officially subscribing to the most advanced notions of the individual's rights to and obligations in society. This network has now become established at a suprastate level. A good many treaties and administrative charters in the

United Nations system spell out in detail the individual's educational rights.

But of course the rules and the rhetoric far outweigh the achievements. The proliferation of statements about human rights in United Nations treaties or in national constitutions does not guarantee any improvement in the condition of actual human beings. The expansion of formal systems of education may also mean very little for effective education or social opportunity. But the data show the extent to which modern individualism is a central institutional and ideological thrust in its own right. Even if nation-states or the weak world government are simply lying, clearly individualism is important enough to lie about.

Many kinds of evidence suggest that individualism is central to modern consciousness—a main ingredient, not an accidental by-product. First, in the modern period education has become a major state (and world) institution. It is seen as directly linked to progress and justice, and it is thus a matter for major constitutional doctrine. Second, as I have noted, when peripheral areas of the world adopt the modern individualist system, education appears at the center of their vision. They adopt the rules and build the appropriate institutions much more quickly than educational theories deriving from other political, economic, or practical requirements might dictate. Third, and most important, the form of educational institution-alization everywhere suggests that education is a matter of high and highly ritualized importance.

In every country education is organized in public categories: first grade, second grade, and so on, followed by secondary school and university. These categories correspond poorly to an individual's actual knowledge or competence. For one thing, there are enormous variations within and between nation-states in what a student in the third grade, or the third year of university, may know. Further, educational researchers have found that they cannot use educational categories to predict how competent a pupil will be as an adult.[12] Public educational categories, we must conclude, matter because they are made to matter by the modern belief in credentials, and the associated doctrines of individualism and socialization matter more as ideology than in practice. They cannot have been justified by any demonstrable success.

The cultural need, then, to standardize and manage individuals has generated a worldwide system of graded categories, exhibiting a broad formal equality (mass education) and a carefully rationalized inequality (elite education). This system's priority over practical concerns is evident in recent research by Benavot. He shows that, despite the practical economic need in many parts of the world for young people trained to fit specialized roles in society, work-oriented, vocational education has declined regularly in secondary education, to be replaced by general education—a system of categories in which everyone is graded on the same general scale, as if there were an all-purpose virtue, which some people demonstrate more and others less. This, of course, is a radical departure from societies not based on an underlying conception of individuals within a homogeneous scheme of assessment. Benavot suggests, revealingly, that more differentiated systems of secondary education with diverse tracks are now seen as undemocratic in many countries.[13]

Individualism's ritualized character, and thus its fundamental importance, is revealed in what is reported about individuals in the modern large-scale counting systems. We count individuals on both national and world scales, recording data on age, sex, and other matters. Among these data is education, defined in terms of ritual categories, not actual competence; thus in UNESCO data literacy is much more poorly measured than educational status.[14] Apparently it seems important to modern man to be able to count up the number of people in different educational categories, and so we have a statistical system that permits one, for instance, to make a fair assessment of the number of third graders in the world.

The importance of education as a modern ceremony is further indicated by how quickly nation-states bring their educational systems into line with the world classification and organize them in much the same way. Thus each country can count its secondary-school students, though the evidence on what these students know shows astonishing—but in an important sense concealed—cross-national variation. Students in the poorer countries have a kind of formal equality in categorical status with those in richer ones, although they perform much more poorly on the hidden matter of measured competence and achievement.[15]

The centrality, legitimacy, and institutionalization of individualist doctrine have a great effect on how people behave. On the one hand, both national and world ideologies encourage the adoption of the social postures of individualism on intrinsic grounds; on the other hand, political and economic incentives to organize the self in this way are overwhelming. Anyone who wishes to succeed had best become an educated self.

Modern persons do obviously organize themselves in this way. The main available measures of attitudinal and behavioral individualism are, first, conceptions of the self and its legitimacy, and, second, notions of the self's efficacy as an actor in the world around it. Both of these increase as nations become modernized and make available a higher level of education.[16] Inkeles and Smith provide a list of indicators for these changes: an emphasis on action rather than fate, a conviction that the world is orderly enough to warrant rational action, a deemphasis of traditional or primordial identities, a belief in inherent rights, and so on.

The inner structure of family life also changes drastically in modern society; it, too, becomes a vehicle for constructing the individual. Children are not passive objects to be managed, but active ones to be turned into individuals, and a great many professionals and organizations offer to help. In modern social settings, families develop radically changed patterns of childrearing, which considerably affect the child's self-esteem and sense of his own intelligence. Such trends are stronger in more-educated and higher-status families. Heyneman and Loxley showed two effects of these changes: first, even very young children in most modernized countries are much more effective as individuals in school; second, as the higher social classes learn to rear children to be modern individuals, large class-related differences in children's intelligence appear. In less modern countries these differences do not appear.[17]

In research on the implicit values of educational systems, four main themes describe the contemporary picture of the individual. Strikingly, these themes recapitulate the core principles of the whole history of Western individualism. First, descended from Augustine's City of God and medieval conceptions of the ultimate equality of all souls, is the virtue of the self that is both well bounded and in tune with others. It is celebrated in psychological doctrines of self-esteem and the internal locus of control. Paralleling it is the educational aim of training young persons to feel competent and to have a sense of mastery, and the glorification of a maximal development of inner human potential. All this is much more explicitly rationalized than in the past and is more securely rooted in educational and childrearing principles. It is a rationalized version of the secular celebration of the moral sovereignty of the individual.

Second, descending from Augustine's City of Man and its celebration of an orderly Nature, is the idea that the individual is to be a competent actor. All of modern society operates on the belief that competent individuals with high I.Q.'s build the good society—their action in the world around them is the crucial variable.

The third theme (developed in the modern period) is the continuing discovery of new and more abstract elements of personhood: new dimensions of development, new and subjective motives and perceptions, new rights and qualities, new individual capabilities. The reasons for this are clear. The senses of internal mastery and of competence as an actor are so closely tied to educational and other institutions that the individual may fear he is disappearing into the masses of a new Leviathan. But the ideologies of modern societies clearly rest on the contributions of the individual; to see the individual as entirely under social control would undercut the grounding principle of the modern individualist ideology. So reconstructing individualism—finding and legitimating the true, hidden individual behind the masks of social rationalization—has been a continuing and active process. New dimensions of self-consciousness and ever more abstract and subjective ideas of the person are continually being created and legitimized. This process goes on, as always, under the guidance of the professional elites of individualism—intellectuals, theologians, psychologists—but the lawyers are also at work constantly giving the individual new rights, such as privacy, personal space, environmental purity, and welfare.

The fourth theme, the continual reconstruction of a myth of the primordial individual, is also a continuing part of the Western dialectic. As the scale and complexity of society expand, so does the idea of the individual person. He, too, must be given a new look. If we ignore this theme of the primordial individual self or treat it as an irrational or perverse reaction, accusing it of being narcissistic or the explosion of an overburdened unconscious, we fail to understand that it is a legitimated and authorized myth of the Western system as a whole.

The continuing expansion of the Western system must, then, be seen as a flow in the meaning of specific aspects of human life and action from private to public. Food choices, for instance, are no longer private matters; they must now be managed by medical and economic professionals. The most extreme example of this flow from private to public is sexual. In early Western history sexuality seems to have been a defining characteristic of the sacred or quintessential aspect of the individual—a mystery of solidarity and procreation (as Stephen Greenblatt suggests in this volume). But now it has been rationalized. As a result, individual sexual satisfaction is becoming a kind of social entitlement. Welfare systems and insurance companies, by and large, do not yet consider it a matter of right, but it is at least a point of academic instruction and medical therapy. Also, rational goals are prescribed for sexual activity. It becomes an obligation of the properly matured individual in tune with others, a part of his responsibility to contribute to society. In the course of this long transformation, of course, sexuality's unique and personal quality is, or seems to have been, lost; the sexual individual is now under social control and is expected to look and act and enjoy in standard ways. But this migration of sexuality from the private to the public is also accompanied by various definitions of the legitimate self as beyond sex and gender: there appears a new and in some respects sexless figure for whom sexuality is a technique of proper linkage to the world, not an intrinsic element. The modern self is in some respects an abstraction or a stick-figure, but the individualist notion remains, and can still be celebrated on abstract grounds of effectiveness and of fulfillment.

We have seen individualism as a complement to the expansion of modern Western society. At present, individualism in essence represents a continuation, not a transformation, of the process of historical change. As the human actor enters an expanding and rationalized society, new elements of the individual are created or discovered: new rights and obligations, new motives and perceptions. Western cultural ideology requires individualism at its base, and it also requires that its conception of this individualism be constantly changing. Thus reconstructing individualism is a continuing process.

Throughout Western history, changes in individualism have been seen as threatening crisis and disorder. We fear alternately that the individual will be overwhelmed by rationalization or that the social order will be exploded by an expression of the untamed aspects of the individual. Both these fears can be calmed by observing that they merely redefine the individual, who subsists through them all. Worries about the explosive individual call for more disciplined socialization and a more controlled, more useful personality; the fear of the totalitarian or one-dimensional tendency of society results in new conceptions of the self. Threats to individualism are no more than calls for its continuing reconstruction.

Making Up People

IAN HACKING

Were there any perverts before the latter part of the nineteenth century? According to Arnold Davidson, "The answer is NO. . . . Perversion was not a disease that lurked about in nature, waiting for a psychiatrist with especially acute powers of observation to discover it hiding everywhere. It was a disease created by a new (functional) understanding of disease."[1] Davidson is not denying that there have been odd people at all times. He is asserting that perversion, as a disease, and the pervert, as a diseased person, were created in the late nineteenth century. Davidson's claim, one of many now in circulation, illustrates what I call making up people.

I have three aims: I want a better understanding of claims as curious as Davidson's; I would like to know if there could be a general theory of making up people, or whether each example is so peculiar that it demands its own nongeneralizable story; and I want to know how this idea "making up people" affects our very idea of what it is to be an individual. I should warn that my concern is philosophical and abstract; I look more at what people might be than at what we are. I imagine a philosophical notion I call dynamic nominalism, and reflect too little on the ordinary dynamics of human interaction.

First we need more examples. I study the dullest of subjects, the official statistics of the nineteenth century. They range, of course, over agriculture, education, trade, births, and military might, but there is one especially striking feature of the avalanche of numbers that begins around 1820. It is obsessed with *analyse morale*, namely, the statistics of deviance. It is the numerical analysis of suicide, prostitution, drunkenness, vagrancy, madness, crime, *les*

miserables. Counting generated its own subdivisions and rearrange-
ments. We find classifications of over 4,000 different crisscrossing
motives for murder and requests that the police classify each individual suicide in 21 different ways. I do not believe that motives of
these sorts or suicides of these kinds existed until the practice of
counting them came into being.[2]

New slots were created in which to fit and enumerate people.
Even national and provincial censuses amazingly show that the
categories into which people fall change every ten years. Social
change creates new categories of people, but the counting is no
mere report of developments. It elaborately, often philanthropically,
creates new ways for people to be.

People spontaneously come to fit their categories. When fac-
tory inspectors in England and Wales went to the mills, they found
various kinds of people there, loosely sorted according to tasks and
wages. But when they had finished their reports, millhands had precise ways in which to work, and the owner had a clear set of concepts about how to employ workers according to the ways in which
he was obliged to classify them.

I am more familiar with the creation of kinds among the masses
than with interventions that act upon individuals, though I did
look into one rare kind of insanity. I claim that multiple personality
as an idea and as a clinical phenomenon was invented around 1875:
only one or two possible cases per generation had been recorded before that time, but a whole flock of them came after. I also found
that the clinical history of split personality parodies itself—the
one clear case of classic symptoms was long recorded as two, quite
distinct, human beings, each of which was multiple. There was
"the lady of MacNish," so called after a report in *The Philosophy of
Sleep,* written by the Edinburgh physician Robert MacNish in
1832, and there was one Mary R. The two would be reported in successive paragraphs as two different cases, although in fact Mary
Reynolds was the very split-personality lady reported by MacNish.[3]

Mary Reynolds died long before 1875, but she was not taken up
as a case of multiple personality until then. Not she but one Félida
X got the split-personality industry under way. As the great French
psychiatrist Pierre Janet remarked at Harvard in 1906, Félida's history "was the great argument of which the positivist psychologists
made use at the time of the heroic struggles against the dogmatism
of Cousin's school. But for Félida, it is not certain that there would

be a professorship of psychology at the Collège de France."⁴ Janet held precisely that chair. The "heroic struggles" were important for our passing conceptions of the self, and for individuality, because the split Félida was held to refute the dogmatic transcendental unity of apperception that made the self prior to all knowledge.

After Félida came a rush of multiples. The syndrome bloomed in France and later flourished in America, which is still its home. Do I mean that there were no multiples before Félida? Yes. Except for a very few earlier examples, which after 1875 were reinterpreted as classic multiples, there was no such syndrome for a disturbed person to display or to adopt.

I do not deny that there are other behaviors in other cultures that resemble multiple personality. Possession is our most familiar example—a common form of Renaissance behavior that died long ago, though it was curiously hardy in isolated German villages even late in the nineteenth century. Possession was not split personality, but if you balk at my implication that a few people (in committee with their medical or moral advisers) almost choose to become splits, recall that tormented souls in the past have often been said to have in some way chosen to be possessed, to have been seeking attention, exorcism, and tranquility.

I should give one all-too-tidy example of how a new person can be made up. Once again I quote from Janet, whom I find the most open and honorable of the psychiatrists. He is speaking to Lucie, who had the once-fashionable but now-forgotten habit of automatic writing. Lucie replies to Janet in writing without her normal self's awareness:

Janet. Do you understand me?
Lucie (writes). No.
J. But to reply you must understand me!
L. Oh yes, absolutely.
J. Then what are you doing?
L. Don't know.
J. It is certain that someone is understanding me.
L. Yes.
J. Who is that?
L. Somebody besides Lucie.
J. Aha! Another person. Would you like to give her a name?
L. No.
J. Yes. It would be far easier that way.
L. Oh well. If you want: Adrienne.

J. Then, Adrienne, do you understand me?
L. Yes.[5]

If you think this is what people used to do in the bad old days, consider poor Charles, who was given a whole page of *Time* magazine on October 25, 1982 (p. 70). He was picked up wandering aimlessly and was placed in the care of Dr. Malcolm Graham of Daytona Beach, who in turn consulted with Dr. William Rothstein, a notable student of multiple personality at the University Hospital in Columbia, South Carolina. Here is what is said to have happened:

> After listening to a tape recording made in June of the character Mark, Graham became convinced he was dealing with a multiple personality. Graham began consulting with Rothstein, who recommended hypnosis. Under the spell, Eric began calling his characters. Most of the personalities have been purged, although there are three or four being treated, officials say. It was the real personality that signed a consent form that allowed Graham to comment on the case.[6]

Hypnosis elicited Charles, Eric, Mark, and some 24 other personalities. When I read of such present-day manipulations of character, I pine a little for Mollie Fancher, who gloried in the personalities of Sunbeam, Idol, Rosebud, Pearl, and Ruby. She became somewhat split after being dragged a mile by a horse car. She was not regarded as especially deranged, nor in much need of "cure." She was much loved by her friends, who memorialized her in 1894 in a book with the title *Mollie Fancher, The Brooklyn Enigma: An Authentic Statement of Facts in the Life of Mollie J. Fancher, The Psychological Marvel of the Nineteenth Century.*[7] The idea of making up people has, I said, become quite widespread. *The Making of the Modern Homosexual* is a good example; "Making" in this title is close to my "making up."[8] The contributors by and large accept that the homosexual and the heterosexual as kinds of persons (as ways to be persons, or as conditions of personhood), came into being only toward the end of the nineteenth century. There has been plenty of same-sex activity in all ages, but not, *Making* argues, same-sex people and different-sex people. I do not wish to enter the complexities of that idea, but will quote a typical passage from this anthology to show what is intended: "One difficulty in transcending the theme of gender inversion as the basis of the specialized homosexual identity was the rather late historical development of more precise conceptions of components of sexual identity.

[fn:] It is not suggested that these components are 'real' entities, which awaited scientific 'discovery.' However once the distinctions were made, new realities effectively came into being."[9]

Note how the language here resembles my opening quotation: "not a disease . . . in nature, waiting for . . . observation to discover it" versus "not . . . 'real' entities, which awaited scientific 'discovery.'" Moreover, this author too suggests that "once the distinctions were made, new realities effectively came into being."

This theme, the homosexual as a kind of person, is often traced to a paper by Mary MacIntosh, "The Homosexual Role," which she published in 1968 in *Social Problems*.[10] That journal was much devoted to "labeling theory," which asserts that social reality is conditioned, stabilized, or even created by the labels we apply to people, actions, and communities. Already in 1963 "A Note on the Uses of Official Statistics" in the same journal anticipated my own inferences about counting.[11] But there is a currently more fashionable source of the idea of making up people, namely, Michel Foucault, to whom both Davidson and I are indebted. A quotation from Foucault provides the epigraph—following one from Nietzsche—for *The Making of the Modern Homosexual*; and although its authors cite some 450 sources, they refer to Foucault more than anyone else. Since I shall be primarily concerned with labeling, let me state at once that for all his famous fascination with discourse, naming is only one element in what Foucault calls the "constitution of subjects" (in context a pun, but in one sense the making up of the subject): "We should try to discover how it is that subjects are gradually, progressively, really and materially constituted through a multiplicity of organisms, forces, energies, materials, desires, thoughts etc."[12]

Since so many of us have been influenced by Foucault, our choice of topic and time may be biased. My examples dwell in the nineteenth century and are obsessed with deviation and control. Thus among the questions on a complete agenda, we should include these two: Is making up people intimately linked to control? Is making up people itself of recent origin? The answer to both questions might conceivably be yes. We may be observing a particular medico-forensic-political language of individual and social control. Likewise, the sheer proliferation of labels in that domain during the nineteenth century may have engendered vastly more kinds of people than the world had ever known before.

Partly in order to distance myself for a moment from issues of repression, and partly for intrinsic interest, I would like to abstract from my examples. If there were some truth in the descriptions I and others have furnished, then making up people would bear on one of the great traditional questions of philosophy, namely, the debate between nominalists and realists.[13] The author I quoted who rejects the idea that the components of the homosexual identity are real entities, has taken a time-worn nominalist suggestion and made it interesting by the thought that "once the distinctions were made, new realities effectively came into being."

You will recall that a traditional nominalist says that stars (or algae, or justice) have nothing in common except our names ("stars," "algae," "justice"). The traditional realist in contrast finds it amazing that the world could so kindly sort itself into our categories. He protests that there are definite sorts of objects in it, at least stars and algae, which we have painstakingly come to recognize and classify correctly. The robust realist does not have to argue very hard that people also come sorted. Some are thick, some thin, some dead, some alive. It may be a fact about human beings that we notice who is fat and who is dead, but the fact itself that some of our fellows are fat and others are dead has nothing to do with our schemes of classification.

The realist continues: consumption was not only a sickness but also a moral failing, caused by defects of character. That is an important nineteenth-century social fact about TB. We discovered in due course, however, that the disease is transmitted by bacilli that divide very slowly and that we can kill. It is a fact about us that we were first moralistic and later made this discovery, but it is a brute fact about tuberculosis that it is a specific disease transmitted by microbes. The nominalist is left rather weakly contending that even though a particular kind of person, the consumptive, may have been an artifact of the nineteenth century, the disease itself is an entity in its own right, independently of how we classify.

It would be foolhardy, at this conference, to have an opinion about one of the more stable human dichotomies, male and female. But very roughly, the robust realist will agree that there may be what really are physiological borderline cases, once called "hermaphrodites." The existence of vague boundaries is normal: most of us are neither tall nor short, fat nor thin. Sexual physiology is unusually abrupt in its divisions. The realist will take the occasional com-

227

pulsive fascination with transvestitism, or horror about hermaphrodites (so well described by Stephen Greenblatt in this volume), as human (nominalist) resistance to nature's putative aberrations. Likewise the realist will assert that even though our attitudes to gender are almost entirely nonobjective and culturally ordained, gender itself is a real distinction.

I do not know if there were thoroughgoing, consistent, hardline nominalists who held that every classification is of our own making. I might pick that great British nominalist Hobbes out of context: "How can any man imagine that the names of things were imposed by their natures?"[14] Or I might pick Nelson Goodman.*

Let me take even the vibrant Hobbes, Goodman, and their scholastic predecessors as pale reflections of a perhaps nonexistent static nominalist, who thinks that all categories, classes, and taxonomies are given by human beings rather than by nature and that these categories are essentially fixed throughout the several eras of humankind. I believe that static nominalism is doubly wrong: I think that many categories come from nature, not from the human mind, and I think our categories are not static. A different kind of nominalism—I call it dynamic nominalism—attracts my realist self, spurred on by theories about the making of the homosexual and the heterosexual as kinds of persons or by my observations about official statistics. The claim of dynamic nominalism is not that there was a kind of person who came increasingly to be recognized by bureaucrats or by students of human nature but rather that a kind of person came into being at the same time as the kind itself was being invented. In some cases, that is, our classifications and our classes conspire to emerge hand in hand, each egging the other on.

Take four categories: horse, planet, glove, and multiple personality. It would be preposterous to suggest that the only thing horses

---

*Trendy, self-styled modern nominalists might refer to his *Ways of Worldmaking* (Indianapolis, Ind., 1978), but the real hard line is in his *Fact, Fiction, and Forecast* (Cambridge, Mass., 1955)—a line so hard that few philosophers who write about the "new riddle of induction" of that book appear even to see the point. Goodman is saying that the only reason to project the hypothesis that all emeralds are green rather than grue—the latter implying that those emeralds, which are in the future examined for the first time, will prove to be blue—is that the word "green" is entrenched, i.e., it is a word and a classification that we have been using. Where the inductive skeptic Hume allowed that there is a real quality, greenness, that we project out of habit, for Goodman there is only our practice of using the word "green" (*Fact*, chap. 4).

have in common is that we call them horses. We may draw the boundaries to admit or to exclude Shetland ponies, but the similarities and difference are real enough. The planets furnish one of T. S. Kuhn's examples of conceptual change.[15] Arguably the heavens looked different after we grouped Earth with the other planets and excluded Moon and Sun, but I am sure that acute thinkers had discovered a real difference. I hold (most of the time) that strict nominalism is unintelligible for horses and the planets. How could horses and planets be so obedient to our minds? Gloves are something else: we manufacture them. I know not which came first, the thought or the mitten, but they have evolved hand in hand. That the concept "glove" fits gloves so well is no surprise; we made them that way. My claim about making up people is that in a few interesting respects multiple personalities (and much else) are more like gloves than like horses. The category and the people in it emerged hand in hand.

How might a dynamic nominalism affect the concept of the individual person? One answer has to do with possibility. Who we are is not only what we did, do, and will do but also what we might have done and may do. Making up people changes the space of possibilities for personhood. Even the dead are more than their deeds, for we make sense of a finished life only within its sphere of former possibilities. But our possibilities, although inexhaustible, are also bounded. If the nominalist thesis about sexuality were correct, it simply wasn't possible to be a heterosexual kind of person before the nineteenth century, for that kind of person was not there to choose. What could that mean? What could it mean in general to say that possible ways to be a person can from time to time come into being or disappear? Such queries force us to be careful about the idea of possibility itself.

We have a folk picture of the gradations of possibility. Some things, for example, are easy to do, some hard, and some plain impossible. What is impossible for one person is possible for another. At the limit we have the statement: "With men it is impossible, but not with God: for with God, all things are possible" (Mark 10:27). (Christ had been saying that it is easier for a camel to pass through the eye of a needle than for a rich man to enter the kingdom of heaven.) Degrees of possibility are degrees in the ability of some agent to do or make something. The more ability, the more possibility, and omnipotence makes anything possible. At that point, logicians have stumbled, worrying about what were once called "the eternal truths" and are now called "logical necessities." Even God cannot make a five-sided square, or so mathematicians say, except for a few such eminent dissenters as Descartes. Often this limitation on omnipotence is explained linguistically, being said to reflect our unwillingness to call anything a five-sided square.

There is something more interesting that God can't do. Suppose that Arnold Davidson, in my opening quotation about perversion, is literally correct. Then it was not possible for God to make George Washington a pervert. God could have delayed Washington's birth by over a century, but would that have been the same man? God could have moved the medical discourse back 100-odd years. But God could not have simply made him a pervert, the way He could have made him freckled or had him captured and hung for treachery. This may seem all the more surprising since Washington was but eight years older than the Marquis de Sade—and Krafft-Ebing has sadomasochism among the four chief categories of perversion. But it follows from Davidson's doctrine that de Sade was not afflicted by the disease of perversion, nor even the disease of sadomasochism either.

Such strange claims are more trivial than they seem; they result from a contrast between people and things. Except when we interfere, what things are doing, and indeed what camels are doing, does not depend on how we describe them. But some of the things that we ourselves do are intimately connected to our descriptions. Many philosophers follow Elizabeth Anscombe and say that intentional human actions must be "actions under a description."[16] This is not mere lingualism, for descriptions are embedded in our practices and lives. But if a description is not there, then intentional actions under that description cannot be there either: that, apparently, is a fact of logic.

Elaborating on this difference between people and things: what camels, mountains, and microbes are doing does not depend on our words. What happens to tuberculosis bacilli depends on whether or not we poison them with BCG vaccine, but it does not depend upon how we describe them. Of course we poison them with a certain vaccine in part because we describe them in certain ways, but it is the vaccine that kills, not our words. Human action is more closely linked to human description than bacterial action is. A century ago I would have said that consumption is caused by bad air and sent the patient to the alps. Today, I may say that TB is caused by microbes and prescribe a two-year course of injections. But what is happening to the microbes and the patient is entirely independent of my correct or incorrect description, even though it is not independent of the medication prescribed. The microbes' possibilities are delimited by nature, not by words. What is curious about human action is that by and large what I am deliberately doing depends on the possibilities of description. To repeat, this is a tautological inference from what is now a philosopher's commonplace, that all intentional acts are acts under a description. Hence if new modes of description come into being, new possibilities for action come into being in consequence.

Let us now add an example to our repertoire; let it have nothing to do with deviancy, let it be rich in connotations of human practices, and let it help furnish the end of a spectrum of making up people opposite from the multiple personality. I take it from Jean-Paul Sartre, partly for the well-deserved fame of his description, partly for its excellence as description, partly because Sartre is our premium philosopher of choice, and partly because recalling Sartre will recall an example that returns me to my origin. Let us first look at Sartre's magnificent humdrum example. Many among us might have chosen to be a waiter or waitress and several have been one for a time. A few men might have chosen to be something more specific, a Parisian *garçon de café*, about whom Sartre writes in his immortal discussion of bad faith: "His movement is quick and forward, a little too precise, a little too rapid. He comes toward the patrons with a step a little too quick. He bends forward a little too eagerly, his eyes express an interest too solicitous for the order of the customer."[17] Psychiatrists and medical people in general try to be extremely specific in describing, but no description of the several classical kinds of split personality is as precise (or as recognizable) as this. Imagine for a moment that we are reading not the words of a philosopher who writes his books in cafés but those of a doctor who writes them in a clinic. Has the *garçon de café* a chance of escaping treatment by experts? Was Sartre knowing or merely anticipating when he concluded this very paragraph with the words: "There are indeed many precautions to imprison a man in what he is, as if we lived in perpetual fear that he might escape from it, that he might break away and suddenly elude his condition." That is a good reminder of Sartre's teaching: possibility, project, and prison are one of a piece.

Sartre's antihero chose to be a waiter. Evidently that was not a possible choice in other places, other times. There are servile people in most societies, and servants in many, but a waiter is something specific, and a *garçon de café* more specific. Sartre remarks that the waiter is doing something different when he pretends to play at being a sailor or a diplomat than when he plays at being a waiter in order to be a waiter. I think that in most parts of, let us say, Saskatchewan (or in a McDonald's anywhere), a waiter playing at being a *garçon de café* would miss the mark as surely as if he were playing at being a diplomat while passing over the french fries. As with almost every way in which it is possible to be a person, it is possible to be a *garçon de café* only at a certain time, in a certain place, in a certain social setting. The feudal serf putting food on my lady's table can no more choose to be a *garçon de café* than he can choose to be lord of the manor. But the impossibility is evidently different in kind.

It is not a technical impossibility. Serfs may once have dreamed of travel to the moon; certainly their lettered betters wrote or read adventures of moon travel. But moon travel was impossible for them, whereas it is not quite impossible for today's young waiter. One young waiter will, in a few years, be serving steaks in a satellite. Sartre is at pains to say that even technical limitations do not mean that you have fewer possibilities. For every person, in every era, the world is a plenitude of possibilities. "Of course," Sartre writes, "a contemporary of Duns Scotus is ignorant of the use of the automobile or the aeroplane. . . . For the one who has no relation of any kind to these objects and the techniques that refer to them, there is a kind of absolute, unthinkable and undecipherable nothingness. Such a nothing can in no way limit the For-itself that is choosing itself; it cannot be apprehended as a lack, no matter how we consider it." Passing to a different example, he continues, "The feudal world offered to the vassal lord of Raymond VI infinite possibilities of choice; we do not possess more."[18]

"Absolute, unthinkable and undecipherable nothingness" is a great phrase. That is exactly what being a multiple personality, or being a *garçon de café*, was to Raymond's vassal. Many of you could, in truth, be neither a Parisian waiter nor a split, but both are thinkable, decipherable somethingnesses. It would be possible for God to have made you one or the other or both, leaving the rest of the world more or less intact. That means, to me, that the outer reaches of your space as an individual are essentially different from what they would have been had these possibilities not come into being.

Thus the idea of making up people is enriched; it applies not to the unfortunate elect but to all of us. It is not just the making up of people of a kind that did not exist before: not only are the split and the waiter made up, but each of us is made up. We are not only what we are but what we might have been, and the possibilities for what we might have been are transformed.

Hence anyone who thinks about the individual, the person, must reflect on this strange idea, of making up people. Do my stories tell a uniform tale? Manifestly not. The multiple personality, the homosexual or heterosexual person, and the waiter form one spectrum among many that may color our perception here.

Suppose there is some truth in the labeling theory of the modern homosexual. It cannot be the whole truth, and this for several reasons, including one that is future-directed and one that is past-directed. The future-directed fact is that after the institutionalization of the homosexual person in law and official morality, the people involved had a life of their own, individually and collectively. As gay liberation has amply proved, that life was no simple product of the labeling.

The past-directed fact is that the labeling did not occur in a social vacuum, in which those identified as homosexual people passively accepted the format. There was a complex social life that is only now revealing itself in the annals of academic social history. It is quite clear that the internal life of innumerable clubs and associations interacted with the medico-forensic-journalistic labeling. At the risk of giving offense, I suggest that the quickest way to see the contrast between making up homosexuals and making up multiple personalities is to try to imagine split-personality bars. Splits, insofar as they are declared, are under care, and the syndrome, the form of behavior, is orchestrated by a team of experts. Whatever the medico-forensic experts tried to do with their categories, the homosexual person became autonomous of the labeling, but the split is not.

The *garçon de café* is at the opposite extreme. There is of course a social history of waiters in Paris. Some of this will be as anecdotal as the fact that croissants originated in the cafés of Vienna after the Turkish siege was lifted in 1683: the pastries in the shape of a crescent were a mockery of Islam. Other parts of the story will be structurally connected with numerous French institutions. But the class of waiters is autonomous of any act of labeling. At most the name *garçon de café* can continue to ensure both the inferior position of the waiter and the fact that he is male. Sartre's precise description does not fit the *fille de salle*; that is a different role.

I do not believe there is a general story to be told about making up people. Each category has its own history. If we wish to present a partial framework in which to describe such events, we might think of two vectors. One is the vector of labeling from above, from a community of experts who create a "reality" that some people make their own. Different from this is the vector of the autonomous behavior of the person so labeled, which presses from below, creating a reality every expert must face. The second vector is negligible for the split but powerful for the homosexual person. People who write about the history of homosexuality seem to disagree about the relative importance of the two vectors. My scheme at best highlights what the dispute is about. It provides no answers.

The scheme is also too narrow. I began by mentioning my own dusty studies in official statistics and asserted that these also, in a less melodramatic way, contribute to making up people. There is a story to tell here, even about Parisian waiters, who surface in the official statistics of Paris surprisingly late, in 1881. However, I shall conclude with yet another way of making up people and human acts, one of notorious interest to the existentialist culture of a couple of generations past. I mean suicide, the option that Sartre always left open to the For-itself. Suicide sounds like a timeless option. It is not. Indeed it might be better described as a French obsession.

There have been cultures, including some in recent European history, that knew no suicide. It is said that there were no suicides in Venice when it was the noblest city of Europe. But can I seriously propose that suicide is a concept that has been made up? Oddly, that is exactly what is said by the deeply influential Esquirol in his 1823 medical-encyclopedia article on suicide.[19] He mistakenly asserts that the very word was devised by his predecessor Sauvages. What is true is this: suicide was made the property of medics only at the beginning of the nineteenth century, and a major fight it was too.[20] It was generally allowed that there was the noble suicide, the suicide of honor or of state, but all the rest had to be regarded as part of the new medicine of insanity. By mid-century it would be contended that there was no case of suicide that was not preceded by symptoms of insanity.[21]

This literature concerns the doctors and their patients. It exactly parallels a statistical story. Foucault suggests we think in terms of "two poles of development linked together by a whole cluster of intermediary relations."[22] One pole centers on the individual as a speaking, working, procreating entity he calls an "anatomo-politics of the human body." The second pole, "focused on the species body," serves as the "basis of the biological processes: propagation, births, and mortality, the level of health, life expectancy and longevity." He calls this polarity a "biopolitics of the population." Suicide aptly illustrates patterns of connection between both poles. The medical men comment on the bodies and their past, which led to self-destruction; the statisticians count and classify the bodies. Every fact about the suicide becomes fascinating. The statisticians compose forms to be completed by doctors and police, recording everything from the time of death to the objects found in the pockets of the corpse. The various ways of killing oneself are abruptly characterized and become symbols of national character. The French favor carbon monoxide and drowning; the English hang or shoot themselves.

By the end of the nineteenth century there was so much information about French suicides that Durkheim could use suicide to measure social pathology. Earlier, a rapid increase in the rate of suicide in all European countries had caused great concern. More recently authors have suggested that the growth may have been largely apparent, a consequence of improved systems of reporting.[23] It was thought that there were more suicides because more care was taken to report them. But such a remark is unwittingly ambiguous: reporting brought about more suicides. I do not refer to suicide epidemics that follow a sensational case, like that of von Kleist, who shot his lover and then himself on the Wannsee in 1811—an event vigorously reported in every European capital. I mean instead that the systems of reporting positively created an entire ethos of suicide, right down to the suicide note, an art form that previously was virtually unknown apart from the rare noble suicide of state. Suicide has of course attracted attention in all times and has invited such distinguished essayists as Cicero and Hume. But the distinctively European and American pattern of suicide is a historical artifact. Even the unmaking of people has been made up.

Naturally my kinds of making up people are far from exhaustive. Individuals serve as role models and sometimes thereby create

235

new roles. We have only to think of James Clifford's contribution to this volume, "On Ethnographic Self-Fashioning: Conrad and Malinowski." Malinowski's book largely created the participant-observer cultural-relativist ethnographer, even if Malinowski himself did not truly conform to that role in the field. He did something more important—he made up a kind of scholar. The advertising industry relies on our susceptibilities to role models and is largely engaged in trying to make up people. But here nominalism, even of a dynamic kind, is not the key. Often we have no name for the very role a model entices us to adopt.

Dynamic nominalism remains an intriguing doctrine, arguing that numerous kinds of human beings and human acts come into being hand in hand with our invention of the categories labeling them. It is for me the only intelligible species of nominalism, the only one that can even gesture at an account of how common names and the named could so tidily fit together. It is of more human interest than the arid and scholastic forms of nominalism because it contends that our spheres of possibility, and hence our selves, are to some extent made up by our naming and what that entails. But let us not be overly optimistic about the future of dynamic nominalism. It has the merit of bypassing abstract hand-waving and inviting us to do serious philosophy, namely, to examine the intricate origin of our ideas of multiple personality or of suicide. It is, we might say, putting some flesh on that wizened figure, John Locke, who wrote about the origin of ideas while introspecting at his desk. But just because it invites us to examine the intricacies of real life, it has little chance of being a general philosophical theory. Although we may find it useful to arrange influences according to Foucault's poles and my vectors, such metaphors are mere suggestions of what to look for next. I see no reason to suppose that we shall ever tell two identical stories of two different instances of making up people.

Remapping the Moral Domain:
New Images of the Self in Relationship

CAROL GILLIGAN

In Book 6 of the *Aeneid*, when Aeneas goes to the underworld he is startled to discover that Dido is dead. He did not believe the story that had reached him: "I could not believe," he tells her, "that I would hurt you so terribly by going."[1] Seeing her wound, he weeps, asking, "Was I the cause?"[2] Yet, explaining that he did not willingly leave her, he describes himself as a man set apart, bound by his responsibility to his destiny. Caught between two images of himself—as implicated and as innocent, as responsible and as tossed about by fate—he exemplifies the dilemma of how to think about the individual as at once separate and connected to others in a fabric of human relationship.

The representation of the self as separate and bounded has a long history in the Western tradition. Consonant with, rather than opposed to, this image of individual autonomy is a notion of social responsibility, conceived as duty or obligation. Yet as Virgil tells this story in the *Aeneid*—of a man apart, devoted to his mission of founding a city and bringing home his gods to Latium—he shadows the story with others that resist expression, of "a sorrow too deep to tell" and "a love beyond all telling,"[3] Aeneas's story of the fall of Troy and Dido's of her passion. These stories of sorrow and love have generally been kept apart from discussions of morality and the individual; as in the *Aeneid*, they are considered *infandum*, told in private, known but unspeakable. Interspersing these stories with the account of Aeneas's heroic and arduous journey, Virgil, however, suggests a connection. The uncertainty created by this conjunction emerges in the underworld meeting of Aeneas and Dido. In this scene, described by T. S. Eliot as one of the most poignant and

237

civilized passages in poetry,[4] an acute psychological wisdom leads to a profound sense of moral ambiguity.

Was Aeneas responsible for Dido's self-inflicted wound? Why couldn't he believe that he would hurt her so terribly by leaving? These questions reflect in their essential tension two ways of thinking about the self in relationship. A psychology of love that can explicate the connection between Aeneas's departure and Dido's action, as well as her subsequent anger and silence, vies with the categories of moral judgment that presuppose a separate and autonomous individual. The two images of self anchored by these two conceptual frameworks imply two ways of thinking about responsibility that are fundamentally incompatible. When Aeneas encounters consequences of his action that he had neither believed nor intended and Dido, once generous and responsive, is rendered by grief cold and impassive, this disjunction momentarily surfaces. The detachment of Aeneas's *pietas* becomes the condition for his ignorance of her feelings; yet his adherence to his mission does not imply the indifference that she in her responsiveness imagined. Thus the simple judgment that would condemn Aeneas for turning away from Dido or Dido for breaking her vow of chastity yields to a more complex assessment that encompasses the capacity for sustained commitment and the capacity for responsiveness in relationships and recognizes their tragic conflict.

The two meanings of the word "responsibility"—commitment to obligations and responsiveness in relationships—are central to the mapping of the moral domain put forth in this paper.[5] Since moral judgments reflect a logic of social understanding and form a standard of self-evaluation, a conception of morality is key to the construction of the individual. By asking how we come to hold moral values and by tracing the ontogenesis of values to the experience of human relationships, I will claim that two moral predispositions inhere in the structure of human connection. These predispositions—toward justice and toward care—arise from the experience of inequality and of attachment embedded in the relationship between child and parent. Since everyone has been vulnerable to oppression and to abandonment, two stories about morality recur in human experience.

The different parameters of the parent-child relationship—its inequality and its interdependence or attachment—also ground a distinction between the dimensions of inequality/equality and attachment/detachment that characterize all forms of human connection. In contrast to a unitary moral vision and to the assumption that the opposite of the one is the many, these dimensions of relationship provide coordinates for reconstructing the individual and for remapping development. The two conceptions of responsibility, reflecting different images of the self in relationship, correct an individualism that has been centered within a single interpretive framework. At the same time, the identification of attachment or interdependence as a primary dimension of human experience ties the psychology of love to the representation of moral growth and to identity formation.

The haunting simile that Virgil suspends over the scene of the underworld encounter, comparing Aeneas seeing Dido wounded to "one who sees, / Early in the month, or thinks to have seen, the moon / Rising through cloud, all dim,"[6] catches the uncertainty surrounding the perception of a reality that has been obscured or diminished. As the dim moon recalls the ideals of stoic detachment and heroic individualism, it also conveys the fragility of love and its vulnerability to loss and separation. Thus two stories in their shifting configuration create a fundamental confusion; yet one story tends to get lost, buried in an underworld region.

In recent years, two classical scholars, W. R. Johnson and Marilyn Skinner, have noted the continuing tendency of critics to reduce the complexity of Virgil's poetic statement, to override ambiguity in an effort to resolve the central problem of competing loyalties.[7] The same tendency to reduce complexity is evident in contemporary psychology as well, where the ideal of individual autonomy has rendered the reality of love evanescent. In this sense, the current readings of the *Aeneid* by Johnson and Skinner, which focus the significance of the underworld meeting, correspond to efforts within psychology to recover a story about love that is known but dimly apprehended. In both instances, this retrieval reveals an inherent complication by drawing attention to "the ethical dilemma, now perceived, in what formerly had been thought of as a right and proper, albeit painful, course of action."[8] As the perception of this dilemma "requires of Virgil that he shape a new formulation of heroism,"[9] it currently implies a change in our psychological theories about development and about the individual.

The individualism defined by the ideal of the autonomous self reflects the value that has been placed on detachment—in moral thinking, in self-development, in dealing with loss, and in the psychology of adolescence. By reconstituting the tension between attachment and detachment, which is dissolved by this representation, I will describe two conceptions of morality and of the self that lead to different ways of understanding loss and thinking about the conflicts of loyalty that arise in the course of human life. The close tie between detachment and dispassion reveals the problem I wish to address by showing how the recovery of a lost story about love changes the image of the self in relationship.

The definition of the self and morality in terms of individual autonomy and social responsibility—of an internalized conscience enacted by will and guided by duty or obligation—presupposes a notion of reciprocity, expressed as a "categorical imperative" or a "golden rule." But the ability to put oneself in another's position, when construed in these terms, implies not only a capacity for abstraction and generalization but also a conception of moral knowledge that in the end always refers back to the self. Despite the transit to the place of the other, the self oddly seems to stay constant. If the process of coming to know others is imagined instead as a joining of stories, it implies the possibility of generating new knowledge and transforming the self in the experience of relationship. The reference for judgment then becomes the relationship between the other and the self. Although the capacity for engagement with others—for compassion and for response to another's pleasure and distress—has been observed in early childhood and even in infancy, this capacity is not well represented in accounts of human development, in part because it is at odds with the image of relationships embedded in the prevailing concept of the self.

From George Herbert Mead's description of the self as known through others' reflection and Cooley's conception of the "looking-glass self," to Erikson's emphasis on the discovery of self in others' recognition and the current psychoanalytic fascination with the process of "mirroring," the relational context of identity formation has repeatedly been conveyed. But the recurrent image of the mirror calls attention to the lifelessness in this portrayal of relationships. When others are described as objects for self-reflection or as the means to self-discovery and self-recognition, the language of relationships is drained of attachment, intimacy, and engagement. The self, although placed in a context of relationships, is defined in terms of separation. Others disappear, and love becomes cast in the depersonalized language of "object relations."[10]

240

A different way of describing the self, generally confused with a failure of self-definition, has been clarified in recent years by attention to the experience of women.[11] In this construction, the self is known in the experience of connection, defined not by reflection but by interaction, the responsiveness of human engagement. The close tie I have observed between self-description and moral judgment illuminates the significance of this distinction by indicating how different images of the self give rise to different visions of moral agency, which in turn are reflected in different ways of defining responsibility.

When asked "What does responsibility mean to you?" a high school student replied: "Responsibility means making a commitment and then sticking to it." This response confirms the common understanding of responsibility as personal commitment and contractual obligation. A different conception of the self and of morality appears, however, in another student's reply: "Responsibility is when you are aware of others and you are aware of their feelings. . . . Responsibility is taking charge of yourself by looking at others around you and seeing what they need and seeing what you need . . . and taking the initiative."[12] In this construction, responsibility means acting responsively in relationships, and the self—as a moral agent—takes the initiative to gain awareness and respond to the perception of need. The premise of separation yields to the depiction of the self in connection, and the concept of autonomy is changed. The seeming paradox "taking charge of yourself by looking at others around you" conveys the relational dimension of this self-initiated action.

These two conceptions of responsibility, illustrated here by the definitions of two young women, were focused initially in my research by a dissonance between women's voices and psychological theories.[13] Exploring this dissonance, I defined new categories of moral judgment and self-description to capture the experience of attachment or interdependence, which overrides the traditional contrast between egoism and altruism. This enlarged conceptual framework provided a new way of listening to differences not only between but also within the thinking of women and men. In a series of studies designed to investigate the relationship between conceptions of the self and morality and to test their association with gender and age, two moral voices could reliably be distinguished in the way people framed and resolved moral problems and in their evaluations of the choices they made: one that speaks of connection, not hurting, care, and response; and one that speaks of equality, reciprocity, justice, and rights. Although both voices regularly appeared in conjunction, the tension between them was evident in the confusion that marked their intersection and in the tendency for one voice to predominate. The pattern of predominance, although not gender specific, appeared to be gender related, suggesting that the gender differences recurrently observed in moral reasoning signify differences in moral orientation, which in turn are tied to different ways of imagining the self in relationship.[14]

The values of justice and autonomy, presupposed in current theories of human growth and incorporated into definitions of morality and of the self, imply a view of the individual as separate and of relationships as either hierarchical or contractual, bound by the alternatives of constraint and cooperation. In contrast, the values of care and connection, salient in women's thinking, imply a view of the self and the other as interdependent and of relationships as networks created and sustained by attention and response. The two moral voices that articulate these visions thus denote different ways of viewing the world. Within each perspective, the key terms of social understanding take on different meanings, reflecting a change in the imagery of relationship and signifying a shift in orientation. As the illustration of the ambiguous figure is perceived alternately as vase or faces, so there appear to be two ways of perceiving the self in relation to others, both grounded in reality but each imposing on that reality a different organization. But, as with the perception of the ambiguous figure, when one configuration emerges, the other temporarily vanishes.

The nature and implications of these differences are clarified by the example of two four-year-old children who were playing together and wanted to play different games.[15] In this particular version of a common dilemma, the girl said, "Let's play next-door neighbors." "I want to play pirates," the boy replied. "Okay," said the girl, "then you can be the pirate that lives next door." By comparing this inclusive solution of combining the games with the fair solution of taking turns and playing each game for an equal period, one can see not only how the two approaches yield different ways of solving a problem in relationships but also how each solution affects the identity of the game and the experience of the relationship.

The fair solution, taking turns, leaves the identity of each game intact. It provides an opportunity for each child to experience the other's imaginative world and regulates the exchange by imposing a rule based on the premise of equal respect. The inclusive solution, in contrast, transforms both games: the neighbor game is changed by the presence of a pirate living next door; the pirate game is changed by bringing the pirate into a neighborhood. Each child not only enters the other's imaginative world but also transforms that world by his or her presence. The identity of each separate game yields to a new combination, since the relationship between the children gives rise to a game that neither had separately imagined. Whereas the fair solution protects identity and ensures equality within the context of a relationship, the inclusive solution transforms identity through the experience of a relationship. Thus different strategies for resolving conflict convey different ways of imagining the self, and these different forms of self-definition suggest different ways of perceiving connection with others.

In 1935 the British psychiatrist Ian Suttie called attention to the representation of love in modern psychology, asking, "In our anxiety to avoid the intrusion of sentiment into our scientific formulations, have we not gone to the length of excluding it altogether from our field of observation?"[16] Noting that science, as generally conceived, "is at a particular disadvantage in dealing with the topic of human 'attachments,'" Suttie observed that love is either reduced to appetite or dismissed as an illusion.[17] Thus he set out to reconstitute love within psychology, defining love as a "state of active, harmonious interplay" and tracing its origins to a "pleasure in *responsive* companionship and a correlative discomfort in loneliness and isolation" that are present in infancy.[18]

This understanding of love was substantially extended by the British psychoanalyst John Bowlby.[19] As Freud found in dreams and free associations a window into men's souls, Bowlby discovered in children's responses to loss a way of observing relationship. From this angle of vision, he came to see in the sorrow of children's mourning a capacity for love that previously was unimagined. The knowledge that this capacity is present in early childhood required a transformation in the account of human development. Tracing the formation of attachment to care giving and responsiveness in relationships, Bowlby rendered the process of connection visible as a process of mutual engagement. On this basis, he challenged the value psychologists have placed on separation in describing normal or healthy development, arguing instead that in separation lies a pathogenic potential for detachment and disengagement. Thus he asked how the capacity for love can be sustained in the face of loss and across the reality of separation.

Bowlby's method was essentially the same as the one Freud set forth in his *New Introductory Lectures on Psychoanalysis*. Relying on the magnification of pathology to reveal what otherwise was invisible, Bowlby viewed loss as a fracture that exposes the underlying structure of connection. As Freud observed the psyche fractured in neurotic symptom formation, Bowlby observed in traumatic separation the breaking apart of a relationship. Quoting Goethe's statement that "we see only what we know" and William James's observation that "the great source of terror in infancy is solitude,"[20] he set out to describe the phenomena of human attachment and sorrow, to separate the account of loss, mourning, comfort, and love from orthodox psychoanalytic interpretations and to anchor it instead in direct observation. The unit of his analysis was the relationship rather than the individual.

In his essay "Mourning and Melancholia,"[21] Freud describes with a clarity that remains unequaled the symptomatology of depression, attributing it to a failure of mourning, conceived as a failure of detachment. Rather than withdrawing libido from a lost and irretrievable object, the depressed person as it were takes his stand against reality, digging his heels into the argument that the object in fact cannot be lost. The mechanism of this denial, Freud says, is identification, complicated by anger and consequently leading to self-denigration. In an effort to ward off a seemingly unbearable sorrow, the depressed person becomes the lost object of his affections. Rather than abandon the other, he chooses to become the other and abandon himself. Thus, in Freud's exquisite statement, "the shadow of the object fell upon the ego";[22] the self undergoes eclipse.

In charting the natural history of mourning from his observations of children dealing with loss and separation, Bowlby demarcates a three-stage sequence of protest, despair, and detachment.[23] Seeing denial and anger as inevitable responses to loss—the concomitants of normal grieving—he reinterprets detachment as the sign of a pathogenic repression rather than as a signal of mourning completed. Although both Freud and Bowlby stress the importance of remembering, Freud emphasizes remembering the loss and coming to terms with its reality, whereas Bowlby focuses on remembering the love and finding a means for its representation. This divergence leads to opposing predictions about the capacity for love following loss. Freud implies that only when the last shreds of hope and memory have been relinquished will the libido be free to attach again.[24] Bowlby, proceeding from a different conception of relationships and a different model of psychic energy, describes the process of mourning in terms of a separation or tear that must be mended, tying the renewal of the capacity for love to weaving together the broken narrative. The story of love must be told not so that it can be forgotten but so that it can be continued into the present. Although "object-finding" may be "object-refinding," in Freud's famous phrase,[25] attachments—located in time and arising from mutual engagement—are by definition irreplaceable.

Thus Bowlby introduces a new language of relationships into psychology and recasts the process of development as one of elaboration rather than of replacement. Pointing to the visible signs of human engagement, he records the interplay of attachment seeking and care giving by which human bonds are formed and sustained. Yet in drawing the underpinnings of his revised theoretical conception from ethology and the study of information processing, he moves away from the human world of love he set out to describe. Using animal analogies and machine images, he aligns his work with the prevailing metaphors of science; the cost of this assimilation is a reduction in the portrayal of relationships. The mother, cast as "attachment-figure," is seen primarily through the eyes of the child, and the mutuality of relationships, although stated, is lost in the way they are presented.

In directing attention to the observable signs of human connection, Bowlby's work recasts the distinction between mourning and melancholia in terms of a distinction between real and fabricated relationships. Seen in this light, mourning signifies grief over the loss of an attachment whose felt reality can be sustained in memory; melancholia signifies the isolation felt when an attachment is found to be fragmentary. If separation exposes the nature of connection, then the melancholia of depression, with its endless argument of self-accusation, may be seen as a response to a failure of attachment rather than as a failure of separation. This interpretation offers a new way of reading the stories about sorrow and love in the *Aeneid*.

Dido, discovering that Aeneas is secretly planning to leave her,

245

suddenly sees the love between them to have been imagined. Correcting for distance in light of this perception, she replaces the term "husband" first with "guest" and then with "deserter."[26] Yet, driven by a wavering memory, searching wildly for support and finding only disconfirmation, she turns in the end to enact the destruction of the relationship upon herself. Aeneas's surprise at seeing her dead confirms the reality of his separation. Yet his belated expressions of sorrow reveal the love which he had previously kept hidden. In Book 4, two uses of the word "husband" convey a central misapprehension: Aeneas, saying "I never held the torches of a bridegroom, / Never entered upon the pact of marriage," refers to the absence of contract; Dido, "humbling her pride before her love," refers to the fact of conjugation.[27] In Book 6, these two perspectives begin to cross and intermingle.

By verbal echoes and situational reversals, Virgil spins a skein of ironic allusion that serves, as Skinner observes, "to recall prior tragedy and examine it from an altered perspective."[28] The compelling poignancy and ultimate futility of Aeneas's and Dido's last meeting arise from the recognition that Aeneas's stoic detachment has lost its heroic quality, "becoming instead pathetically defensive," and that Dido's death has come to appear less tragically necessary, seeming "a wretched, preventable accident."[29] Thus the costs of detachment—whether undertaken out of a mistaken notion of *pietas* or arising from traumatic separation—become increasingly clear. Dido flees while Aeneas stands pleading, demonstrating her unwillingness now to respond and recognizing that again he will leave her. Aeneas, his "once kindly ears"[30] having been blocked by divinely ordained duty, continues his mission of founding a city. At the end of the epic, he appears "fierce under arms" and "terrible in his anger"; driven by anguish and fury, he enacts a senseless retribution on Turnus in the name of keeping a promise.[31]

The image of a civilization built on detachment returns in Freud's description of adolescent development, where he identifies as "one of the most significant but also one of the most painful psychical accomplishments of the pubertal period . . . detachment from parental authority, a process which alone makes possible the opposition, which is so important for the progress of civilization, between the old generation and the new."[32] This view of detachment as a necessary, although painful, step in the course of normal development casts problems in adolescence as problems of separation. Observing that "as at every stage in the course of normal development through which all human beings ought by rights to pass, a certain number are held back, so there are some who have never gotten over their parents' authority and have withdrawn their affection from them either very incompletely or not at all," Freud concludes that this failure of development occurs mostly in girls.[33]

Seen from a different perspective, however, the resistance of girls to detachment calls attention to the ethical dilemma that the orthodox account of development obscures. Rather than signifying a failure of individuation, the reluctance to withdraw from attachment may indicate a struggle to find an inclusive solution to the problem of conflicting loyalties. Adolescent girls resisting detachment generally have appeared in the literature on adolescence to illustrate the problems that arise when childhood forms of relationship are not changed. But by drawing attention to the problem of loyalty and to a transformation of attachment that resists the move toward disengagement, the experience of girls in adolescence may help to define an image of the self in relationship that leads to a different vision of progress and civilization.

Psychological development is usually traced along a single line of progression from inequality to equality, following the incremental steps of the child's physical growth. Attachment is associated with inequality, and development linked to separation. Thus the story of love becomes assimilated to a story about authority and power. This is the assimilation I wish to unravel in remapping development across two dimensions of relationship to distinguish inequality from attachment. Starting from the child's position of inequality and attachment, one can trace the straight line that leads toward equality and increased authority. But one can also trace the elaborating line that follows the development of attachment, depicting changes in the nature and configuration of relationships and marking the growth of the capacity for love. This two-dimensional framework of interpretation clarifies the problems created by oppression and by detachment. But the interweaving of the two lines of development reveals a psychological ambiguity and ethical tension, which is most sharply focused by two opposites of the word "dependence."

Since dependence connotes connection, it can be extended along both dimensions of relationship, leading in one direction to

247

independence and in the other to isolation. These contrasting opposites of dependence—independence and isolation—illuminate the shift in the valence of relationships that occurs when connection with others is experienced as impeding autonomy and when it is experienced as protecting against isolation. When dependence is opposed simply to independence, this complexity disappears. Progress becomes equated with detachment, seen as a sign of objectivity and strength; ambiguity vanishes and attachments appear as an obstacle to the growth of the autonomous self.

The opposition of dependence to isolation, retrieving the ethical problem and the psychological tension, was highlighted by adolescent girls' responses to a question about the meaning of dependence. The girls were participants in a study designed to map the terrain of female development that remains largely uncharted in the literature on normal adolescence.[34] In an interview that included questions about past experience, self-description, moral conflicts, and future expectations, the question about dependence was asked at the end of a section about relationships. The study served to underscore the contrast between the view of relationships conveyed by the opposition between dependence and autonomy, which has structured the discussion of adolescent development and appears on most scales of psychological assessment, and the view of relationships conveyed by the opposition of dependence to isolation, implied in the following examples:

What does dependence mean to you?

> I think it is just when you can be dependent on or you can depend on someone, and if you depend on someone, you can depend on them to do certain things, like to be there when you need them, and you can depend on people to understand your problems, and on the other hand, people can depend on you to do the same thing.

> When you know that someone is there when you are upset, and if you need someone to talk to, they are there, and you can depend on them to understand.

> Well, sometimes it bothers me, the word, because it means that you are depending on somebody to make things happen. But also that you are depending on someone else to help you, you know, either to make things happen for you that are good or just to be there when you need them to talk to and not feel that you are cutting into their time or that they don't want you there.

> I wouldn't say total dependence but if we ever needed each other for anything, we could totally be dependent on the person and it would be

no problem. For me, it means that if I have a problem, I can depend on her to help me or anything I need help with, she will be there to help, whether she can help me or not, she will try, and the same goes for me.

Caring. Knowing that the person will always be there. I think there is a word like "painstaking care." You know that the other person would go through all the pain . . . it is so rare, you are really lucky if someone is like that.

That I know if I go to her with a problem or something like that or not a problem but just to see her, even if she has changed and even if I have changed, that we will be able to talk to each other.

Dependence, well, in this case it would be just like I really depend on him to listen to me when I have something to say or when I have something I want to talk about, I really want him to be there and to listen to me.

Here, dependence is assumed to be part of the human condition, and the recurrent phrases—"to be there," "to help," "to talk to," "to listen"—convey the perception that people rely on one another for understanding, comfort, and love. In contrast to the use of the word "dependence" to connote hanging from someone like a ball on a string, an object governed by the laws of physics, these responses convey the perception that attachments arise from the human capacity to move others and to be moved by them. Being dependent, then, no longer means being helpless, powerless and without control; rather, it signifies a conviction that one is able to have an effect on others, as well as the recognition that the interdependence of attachment empowers both the self and the other, not one at the other's expense. The activities of care—being there, listening, the willingness to help, and the ability to understand—take on a moral dimension, reflecting the injunction to pay attention and not to turn away from need. As the knowledge that others are capable of care renders them lovable rather than merely reliable, so the willingness and the ability to care become a standard of self-evaluation. In this active construction, dependence, rather than signifying a failure of individuation, denotes a decision on the part of the individual to enact a vision of love.

I would say we depend on each other in a way that we are both independent, and I would say we are very independent but as far as our friendship goes, we are dependent on each other because we know that both of us realize that whenever we need something, the other person will always be there.

> I depend on her for understanding a lot and for love and she depends on me for the same things, understanding and just to be there for each other, we know that we are there for each other.

These portraits of love reveal its cognitive as well as its affective dimensions, its foundation in an ability to perceive people in their own terms and to respond to need. Because such knowledge generates power both to help and to hurt, the uses of this power become the standard of responsibility and care in relationships. In adolescence, when both wanting and knowing take on new meanings, conflicts of responsibility assume new dimensions, creating conflicts of loyalty that are not easily resolved. Seeking to perceive and respond to their own as well as to others' needs, adolescent girls ask if they can be responsive to themselves without losing connection with others and whether they can respond to others without abandoning themselves. This search for an inclusive solution to dilemmas of conflicting loyalties vies with the tendency toward exclusion, manifest in the moral opposition of selfish and selfless choice—an opposition in which selfishness connotes the exclusion of others and selflessness the exclusion of self. Thus the themes of inclusion and exclusion, prominent in the childhood games girls play and manifest in their strategies for resolving conflicts, come to be addressed consciously in adolescence, in a line of development that leads through changes in the experience and understanding of attachment.

Within this framework of interpretation, the central metaphor for identity formation becomes dialogue rather than mirroring; the self is defined by gaining perspective and known by experiencing engagement with others. The moral passion that surrounds this quest for self-definition was evident when adolescent girls were asked to describe a situation in which someone was not being listened to. The acuity of their perceptions of not listening, their awareness of the signs of inattention, extended across examples that ranged from a problem in international politics to conflicts in personal relationships, making the public as well as the private dimensions of attachment or interdependence clear. The themes of silence and voice that emerge so centrally in female narratives convey the moral dimensions of listening, but also the struggle to claim a voice and the knowledge of how readily this endeavor is foiled. When someone refuses to listen—interpreted as a failure to care—adolescent girls speak of themselves as coming up against a wall. Silence can be a way of maintaining integrity in the face of such disconfirmation, a way to avoid further invalidation. But the willingness to speak and to risk disagreement is central to the process of adolescent development, making it possible to reweave attachment, and informing the distinction between true and false relationships.

"I just wish to become better in my relationship with my mother, to be able more easily to disagree with her." This adolescent's wish to engage with others rather than "making myself in their image" signifies both her temptation to yield to others' perceptions—to become, as it were, the mirror—and the recognition that the exclusion of the self, like the exclusion of others, renders relationships lifeless by dissolving the fabric of connection. With this dissolution, attachment becomes impossible. Given the failure of interpretive schemes to reflect female experience and given the celebration of selflessness as the feminine virtue, girls' resistance to detachment challenges two long-standing equations: the equation of human with male and the equation of care with self-sacrifice. At the base of this challenge lies a story about love that joins opposition and progress to attachment as well as a view of the self as an individual within the context of continuing relationship.

Jane Austen structures the plot of her novel *Persuasion* to reveal a transformation in the understanding of love and duty—a transformation that hinges on a change in self-perception.[35] Anne Elliot, the heroine, yields to the persuasion of her "excellent friend," Lady Russell, and breaks off her engagement to Captain Wentworth in the name of duty and prudence. The suffering brought on by this detachment is chronicled in the course of the novel. The resolution, however, takes an interesting turn: Anne Elliot reconstructs her understanding of relationships in light of her recognition that "she and her excellent friend could sometimes think differently";[36] Captain Wentworth comes to see the impediment created by "my own self." He explains, "I was too proud, too proud to ask again. I did not understand you. I shut my eyes."[37] Two ways of defining the self—by submission and by detachment—have created an obstacle to attachment that begins to give way when dialogue replaces reflection and blind commitment yields to response. Like searchlights crossing, these transformations intersect to form a bright spot of illumination, making it possible to join the self with the other and the other with the self. In this novel, where the engagement of divergent perspectives defines happy marriage, new images of the self in relationship convey a new understanding of morality and love.

Love and the Individual: Romantic Rightness and Platonic Aspiration

MARTHA C. NUSSBAUM

> *Veritas*
> motto, Harvard University
> *In Deo Speramus*
> motto, Brown University

Last month, while I was worrying about how to write a paper on this impossible topic, I was moving all my books and papers from Harvard down to Brown. The movers carried my files and boxes of papers into the Philosophy Department building, storing them in a closet under the stairs where I had been given permission to leave my things for the year. There in this closet, on the floor, I noticed a strange document: a manuscript of some 38 pages, typewritten. Its title was "Love and the Individual: Romantic Rightness and Platonic Aspiration. A Story." Now, this was a remarkable coincidence; for I had just chosen this title for my presentation at Stanford. I sat down right there in the closet and read it through. It was an odd document indeed, a strange hybrid of fiction and philosophy. But it was on my topic, a topic on which I myself had found nothing at all to say. I began to consider taking it and reading parts of it at Stanford. But I could not figure out who its author was. I strongly suspected that it was a woman, and a philosopher. The setting is a real place, a philosopher's house; I've even been there. I thought immediately of my one female colleague in philosophy; but, I reasoned, she works on completely different topics. This author is clearly familiar with Plato and Aristotle, Proust and Henry James. Her interests, in fact, lie very close to mine. What's odder still, she introduces as a sentence allegedly written by one of her characters (the one called "she") a sentence that I wrote and published in an article on Plato's *Symposium*.[1] Her other character (the one called "I") claims to have written my article on Henry James.[2] Well, I thought, sitting on the closet floor, whoever she is, if she can lift my words, I can lift hers. So I have decided to do that here.

A STORY

> Or incomincian le dolenti note
> a farmisi sentire; or son venuto
> là dove molto pianto mi percuote.
>
> Now the sounds of misery have begun
> to reach my ears. Now I come to a place
> where many cries of anguish beat against me.
>
> Dante, Inferno V.25–27

Late one January night, in that winter of 1982, when it snowed all over Florida, blighting the orange crop, she found herself wide awake in Tallahassee, thinking about love. And, not surprisingly, about an individual who was the object of hers. Her guest room looked out over a white-blanketed golf course whose genteel contours, enduring with Protestant dignity the region's prospective loss of millions, offered a polite reproof to her more disorderly experience of loss. The insouciant smile of the country club moon, floating above natural disaster as clear and round and single-natured and unaffected as a Platonic form—or a resurrected orange—seemed to her to express the Platonic thought that loved individuals, like orange crops or even like oranges themselves, always came along one following the other in due succession, essentially undistinguishable from one another in their health-bringing and energizing properties. A loss of one could be compensated fully and directly by the coming-into-being of the homogeneous next. One had only, therefore, to endure a brief interstitial period of whiteness, snow, and clear light.

Finding this hygienic Diotiman optimism impossibly at odds with her messier ruminations, finding it, indeed, not to speak genteelly, absurd as a consolation addressed to real personal loss (for it was in those days a point of honor with her to accept no replacements, to insist that any willingness to be so consoled was a falling off from grace), she rejected it and considered other possibilities. As she leaned out the window, feeling the preternaturally calm starry air on her eyelids, she saw that the appropriate next step would be to break up that calm; to demonstrate somehow her complicity with Diotima's opponent Alcibiades and his more accurate view of love. Perhaps by going out and smashing several sacred statues; or by doing violence to the seventeenth green. But the truth was that she was a gentle character, for whom the consolation of violence was a constitutional impossibility. And besides, wasn't her own real view the view she had found and described in writing about the *Phaedrus*, namely, that personal love was not necessarily linked with disorder, but was actually constitutive of the best sort of orderly life, a life dedicated to understanding of value and goodness? That madness and sanity, personal passion and rational aspiration, were, in their highest forms, actually in harmony with or even fused with one another? That we do not really need to choose between Socrates and Alcibiades? It was just this, indeed, that she saw as her problem; for if only disorder were gone one might even contrive to be pleased.

That afternoon when she first saw him, years before, he was walking down the sun-streaked hallway, laughing and talking, his whole body fiercely illuminated from behind by the light from the door, so that he looked to her like Turner's Angel Standing in the Sun. Or, better, like some counterpart good angel, equally radiant but entirely beneficent in power. Like what the *Phaedrus* calls a "form truly expressing beauty and nobility." It is not necessary to choose between Socrates and Alcibiades. Under the right circumstances.

At odds, then, with both Diotima's order and Alcibiades' violence; feeling not like Turner's fishermen, irradiated by that angel's light; or even like the lover of the *Phaedrus*, awestruck by the splendor of some beautiful boy; feeling more like Plato's Stesichorus, blinded by the gods, groping for the verses that would restore his sight, she turned for help and light to the only help that occurred to her. Nothing dramatic, or even Platonic. Aristotelian rather. She turned into the room and began looking through the books.

There are too many individuals, and all of them are married. This is the only piece of general wisdom I have to offer on this topic about which I so rashly agreed to write. Socrates said in the *Symposium*, "I understand nothing—with the exception of love." This preposterous statement tips us off, of course, that something funny is going on. For, sure enough, it turns out that the claim to have grasped and understood the nature of love is part and parcel of an enterprise that is busy converting loved persons into instantiations of a universal, and so into proper objects of (scientific) understanding, all in order to repudiate and transcend the phenomenon of love as ordinary mortals experience it. The sight of the knowing intellect is incompatible, Diotima tells us, with the sight of the human body. Uttered about ordinary passion by an ordinary mortal, the claim to have a general understanding of love is as good an example of the self-refuting proposition as anything philosophy has to offer. More: like Socrates' claim, it is also some sort of denial or refusal of love's dangers. As Alcibiades, telling his love story, shows. ("Oh love. I know all about that." I'd say that in the same tone of voice I used for my opening "general truth." For similar reasons.) The question, then, becomes how to write about love of the individual, if one does not wish, even tacitly, to make the Socratic claim to general understanding. How to limit and undercut one's claims, making it clear that they are not guilty of Socratic "overweening." How, at the same time, to authenticate such limited statements as are made, showing where they come from and what gives them any claim to be telling human truth. Thinking of what I had written about Alcibiades, about Henry James, above all about Proust, I could not avoid the conclusion that I would only be entitled to speak about love in the form of a narrative.

This will, to be sure, be a conspicuously philosophical narrative. Most of its "plot" will be a story of thought and work. Its title sounds like the title of an article. Part of it will be an article, or a sketch for one. It will tell you at length about this lady's general reflections; how she thought and even wrote; how she interpreted the *Phaedrus*; how she marshaled objections and counterexamples. For thought is one of the things that occupies space in a life, especially this one. It is also a major device by which this life tries to keep itself in line. A love story should not fail to show this.

And her story is philosophical in yet another way—in the way in which Aristotle said poetry was philosophical and history was not. For it is, like Alcibiades' narrative, like Proust's, not simply the record of some idiosyncratic things that in fact happened. (You should doubt whether any of it happened as told.) It is, rather, a record, addressed to the reader, of "the sort of thing that might happen" in a human life. And if the reader is not determined to conceive of himself or herself as radically individual, sharing with this lady no relevant responses and possibilities, the reader can take it to be, *mutatis mutandis*, his or her own love story.

But it will be, this philosophical story, quite unlike a philosophical treatise or article on the same topic. For it will show her thoughts arising from pain, from hope, from ambition, from desperation—in short, from the confusion in which thought is born, more often than not. It will present them, these offspring, all wrinkled and naked and bloody, not washed and dressed up for the nursery photographer. You will be in no doubt as to their provenance, and also their fragility. And you will be encouraged to ask how their characteristics are explained by the particular desires and needs that engendered them. This should by no means make you dismiss the question of truth or treat them as mere subjective reportings. But when you entertain them as candidates for truth, you will be able to ask hard, suspicious questions about background conditions that might have biased the inquiry, questions about what bias is in such an inquiry, and what objectivity. While you are made suspicious, however, you are to feel in another way reassured. For seeing the blood and hearing the cries, you are to know that these babies did come out of somewhere real, that they are live, ordinary children of human life and action, not some philosophical changelings simply masquerading as children. For changelings never go so far as to masquerade the pain of being born.

I shall embark, then, on this rather confused lady's philosophical love story. I am not certain that I am entitled now to write it. It is not 1982 now. Though once again it is cold and white and silent, and oranges (grapefruits, I believe, as well) are dying all over Florida. It is not 1982; and I am not, like her, mourning. In fact, I have been happily sitting in my kitchen this afternoon drinking tea and reading Dante. Just now I was in the middle of writing a love letter to somebody else. The title "Love and the Individual" is, I now see, ambiguous. I took it as a question about the individuality of the object of love. But it also forces me to raise questions about my own individuality and continuity from one love to the next. As Wittgenstein said, the world of the happy man is different from the world of the unhappy man. Can the inhabitants of two such different worlds really be the same person?

My discontinuity from her is not, however, total. For the radio's mournful announcement, last night, of the demise of fruit, the solemnly intoned tale of moribund grapefruit and of orange juice cut off before its prime, pulled me oddly back inside her old tale of the demise of a love. And today the newspaper photograph of a young orange wrapped in a sheath of ice reminded me of a sentence she once wrote: "When the light of Socrates 'appears all at once' for Alcibiades, it is the sort of light that, radiantly poured round the aspiring body, may seal or freeze it in, like a coat of ice. That is its beauty." I don't altogether approve of that, but it moves me. Now, in

spite of my lack of sympathy with her more apocalyptic and self-
indulgent responses, despite my desire to treat the topic playfully
and not to weep over it at all, I find myself once again in her presence, seeing her and seeing the image of him that she then saw, that
image more like a lightning bolt than a sun (as Alcibiades knew) in
its power to strike, even as it brings illumination.

You shall have her story, then—but as I tell it. And you must,
therefore, be on your guard. For you can see by now what an interest
I have in making it come out one way rather than another. So that it
will be both true and morally acceptable that I survived and am
here cheerfully replacing. That, loving a different individual, I am
myself the same one, and not too bad either. For I have an interest
in being her heir and continuant, rather than a mere two-year-old.
And if I shall say, further, that to survive the death of love is not just
logically possible but also morally best, if I even contend that the
best conception of love is one that permits some sort of replacement of individuals, you must remember that these arguments,
though placed in her mouth, may be shaped by the fact that I have
just been writing a love letter to somebody else. It is not only in the
context of war that survivor guilt is a useful explanatory concept.

Now, guarding against her and yet pulled by the power of her
love, half toughly warding her off, half longing to know her passion,
in the manner of cautious Dante before the spirit of Francesca, I
approach her. What can I do but what he did: call her "by the love
that leads" her? And like some mad, disorderly dove, through the
dark air of that malignant winter, she comes before me, "directed
by desire," quite gentle in her grief. I'm not like that.

I said that her search through the books was Aristotelian. This
was inexact. Augustine's *Tolle lege* was, far more, the motivating
hope. She wanted to have, right then, a text that would change the
course of her life from damnation to salvation, a text that would set
her on the path to beatitude, lifting her above the winds of longing
onto a promontory from which she could survey all the world and
her own place in it. She was not quite but almost *nel mezzo dal
cammin*, as they liked to conceive of it in those unhealthy times,
so it seemed about right that some salvation should come her way.

But there are no sacred books in Tallahassee. So what could she
do but see what was in fact in the guest room, taking a book at ran-
dom and reading her fate in its pages? (And how clear it was in any
case that she desired the salvation not of religion but of love.)

Her hosts had filled this particular guest room with books by and about members of the Bloomsbury group. This did not seem promising. She would have preferred Proust. She knew little about the people of Bloomsbury, but she thought they were probably well suited to their Diotiman surroundings. She knew enough, at any rate, to suspect them of excessive gentility of feeling and a strong interest in the replacement of one person by the next. It was, then, with no very high expectations that she selected from the shelf nearest the windows a large volume of Dora Carrington's letters and diaries and turned (hoping against hope, I suspect, for something tragic enough to suit her) to the end, though ignorant, as yet, of the nature of Carrington's.

There she came upon the following entry. (She memorized much of it at once involuntarily and carried it about with her for some months as a ready source of tears, but I have had to get hold of it from the library. And when I read it I find that very little of it is even familiar. This makes me wonder.)

No one will ever know the special perfectness of Lytton. The jokes when he was gay. "The queen of the East has vanished." I believe you eat my nail scissors and then at lunch pretending to play a grand fugue before we got up. And the jokes about the coffee never coming because I stayed so long eating cheese. Sometimes I thought how wasteful to let these jokes fly like swallows across the sky. But one couldn't write them down. We couldn't have been happier together. For every mood of his instantly made me feel in the same mood. All gone. . . . And now there is nobody, darling Lytton, to make jokes with about Tiber and the horse of the ocean, no one to read me Pope in the evenings, no one to walk on the terrace. No one to write letters to, oh my very darling Lytton.

. . . What point is there now in what I see every day, in conversations, jokes, beautiful visions, pains, even nightmares? Who can I tell them to, who will understand? One cannot find such another character as Lytton and curious as it may seem to G. B. these friends that he talks of as consolers and substitutes for Lytton cannot be the same, and it is *exactly* what Lytton meant to me that matters.

One cannot live on memories when the point of one's whole life was the interchange of love, ideas, and conversation.

She felt that she had written this entry, so directly did it express her own mourning. She sat there, somewhat absurdly weeping into the book, and the phrase "special perfectness" conjured up an image so concrete that she shuddered at its nearness and wept again. (I find it difficult to describe this.)

Here, she thought, was something worth reading about love.

Call it the view of Alcibiades. Call it (right now) her own. For she too knew those consolers and their games. She knew, and all too well, that what she loved and did not have was, as this woman said, a special perfectness, an exact, nonrepeatable thing that could not be found again. There was a value and a knowledge that were inseparable from this particular relation. To try to recapture or replace them would be as futile as to go hunting for a joke after it has gone by. And she thought of their jokes.

Well, what was this individuality? In what did it consist, according to Carrington? (You now begin to see how this lady is: she goes on thinking at all times. She won't simply cry, she will ask what crying consists in. One tear, one argument: that's how her life goes on.) Carrington had, in this passage, several distinct, though related, quarrels with her consolers. Three, to be exact. First, the friends do not seem to grasp the fact that unique, nonrepeatable properties are essential to love. They talk of others who could be substitutes. This implies that they believe that there are certain general features of Lytton that could be instantiated in someone else—perhaps in someone with similar values and character. But Carrington knows that, in the sense that counts for loving, there is not such another character as Lytton. That nobody else makes those wonderful jokes or has the power to transform the ordinary by that precise sort of magic. Sameness of species might be good enough for Aristotle; it is not what she wants. It is that exact thing, unique and (as she too well knows) transient. ("Death," she writes on the same page, "is unfortunately *not* incomprehensible. It is all too easy to understand." The end of an affair brings similar epistemic problems, with less dignity.)

Beyond this, second, she knows that some of the things she most loves in Lytton are not in him at all; they are properties of his relation to her. There was a special affinity of mood, a rightness of humor, a mutuality of understanding, that are themselves nonrepeatable values, not to be searched for by any rational method, but just found—as when one of Aristophanes' jagged people suddenly comes upon the jagged other half that perfectly fits his or her own odd shape. Surely, surely, part of what so moved her in Carrington's diary was that so much of it was private and unintelligible to her; it gestured toward a density of intimate communication that no person outside the relation could altogether grasp. For she knew, like Carrington, the dreadful isolation that comes with the knowledge that nobody will laugh with her in just that way or respond with that special rightness to her responses. It occurred to her to remember many things. These thoughts took some time. She did not find it possible to include them in a numbered list of any kind.

And beyond all this, she thought—pulling herself back to the list, for she had said there were three items, and in her stubbornness of character she was not going to let anything stop her before she reached three—beyond all this, there is their history. Even if there might have been in the first place more than one person who could have aroused the same dimension of love in Carrington (a fact that in her own case she very much doubted), such another person could not possibly step in as a substitute now. For now the relationship had been enriched by years of intimacy, of conversation, of letters written and received. One could say that the love is in large measure constituted out of this history, out of the habit, for example, of telling every experience and of finding a fresh joy from each experience in the telling. Their relational rightness may have been in part a matter of initial fit, but history and its intimacy is a large part of what constitutes it as this deep, this irreplaceable.

Nobody else will ever know his special perfectness. One cannot find such another character. And if I chose to describe the images that filled her as, her list of three points exhausted, she reached Carrington's uncompromising conclusion, you would perhaps understand her better, and the love that was so great a part of what she then was. I do not so choose. I plan that you shall know nothing of the concrete individuality of her beloved, of their relation, their history, the immediate reasons for her grief. There are many reasons for this. Some I won't mention; some are connected with the Aristotelian point about what makes a story philosophical. But not least among the reasons is the thought that if I allowed myself to become the full companion of her wanderings through memory and pain and wonder, if I allowed the power of that individuality to overwhelm me as it then intermittently overwhelmed her, I would not, perhaps, go on with the letter I am writing. And, equally clearly, I would not continue writing this paper or story, whichever it is. There is a price, I think, for writing about love's fragility; this is a certain refusal of a certain sort of knowledge or recognition of that fragility. Could it be that to write about love, even to write humbly and responsively, is itself a device to control the topic, to trap and bind it like an animal—so, of necessity, an unloving act? And if I could set him down in writing, every move-ment and look and virtue translated into words, if I could do this without in fact ceasing to write, would I not have most perfectly, most finally controlled him and so banished the power of that love? Seen this way, my inability to do so looks like an accidental grace.

What I am after, it seems, is a noncontrolling art of writing that will leave the writer more receptive to love than before. That will not be guilty of writing's usual ruthlessness toward life. For the fashionable idea that writing is a form of creative play, and that everything is, after all, writing, seems to me to ignore the plain fact that much of human life is not playful at all, or even creative. And writing's relation to that nonplayful side of life is deeply ambigu-ous. Writing records it, to be sure. But even as it does so it goes to work fixing, simplifying, shaping. So it seems difficult for it not to be the enemy and denier of mystery and of love. Overwhelmed by the beauty of some landscape, the power of some emotion, I run for my pad of paper; and if I can put it into words, set it down, I breathe a sigh of relief. A kind of humble passivity has been banished. Writ-ing, then, seems not to be everything, but to be opposed to some-thing—say, waiting. Beckett tries to find a way to use language to undo, unravel the simplifications and refusals of language, under-mining stories with a story, words with words. If I were not so de-termined to survive, I'd try to write like that.

These are thoughts she might have had. They don't entirely suit me. She probably reads Heidegger too, heaven help her. I'm get-ting too close to her, like Dante. But for me, there's only one angel in the picture, and the only salvation might be to be as thoroughly damned as possible. Now, as I watch her weeping, uncontrollably at this point, into the pillow on which she has placed her book, I feel with her what it is to love an individual and to be loved, as well, by one. And for fear of saying something individual of my own—for it would describe him and thus violate the canons I have laid down— I simply say:

> Oh lasso,
> quanti dolci pensier, quanto disio
> meno costoro al doloroso passo!

> Alas,
> how many sweet thoughts, how much desire
> led them to this miserable condition.

But even as she wept, she began to wonder whether Carrington had really had the last word against her consolers. It was a terrible last word; she had read far enough to see to what conclusion it led. She wanted to know, so did it frighten her, whether Carrington had been altogether fair. (For fairness in argument seemed a possible way of evading that conclusion.) It was clear as one read on that one of the consolers' arguments did precisely address the conception of individuality relevant to her love and blamed her for in effect misunderstanding the very thing on which she herself laid most stress. She seems to find all of Lytton's individuality, all of what he really is, in the unique, the evanescent, the relational. And yet, they argue, Lytton was a person with a definite moral and intellectual character and a definite set of values, commitments, and aspirations. How could she claim to love Lytton if she did not love and see the central importance of these elements, which are a far deeper part of him than the fact that on a particular day he talked about cheese? All of this had promising implications for mourning and the continuation of life. But for now, what began to impress her was this idea that the extreme romantic view of love (or Aristophanic, since we can trace it back at least to those unique jagged other halves), this view that holds that love is above all a matter of contingent particular fit, may not contain a deep enough conception of the individual, precisely because it slights these repeatable elements.

These elements are, of course, really at the heart of Carrington's love. (So, clearly, at the heart of her own.) For consider her talk of the exchange of ideas and conversation. Or consider even her sentence "One cannot find such another character as Lytton." One does not, she thought, use such a sentence of someone whom one does not admire, and admire on account of certain virtues and values. What one means in saying it (what she herself meant when she thought it especially apt for her case) is that this person is exceptionally good in ways in which one believes it important to be good. Alcibiades said it of Socrates, not confining his love to the (repeatable) virtues, but insisting that they were a very central and essential part of what he loved when he loved Socrates. In loving he was aspiring; he was not simply seeking his other half. He could not have said the same thing of Agathon, except as a joke. How could Carrington claim to love Lytton without understanding how central it was to his being Lytton that he had and lived by certain values, that indeed he built his life around a certain picture of value?

But now something intriguing seemed to follow. For in that case, as the consolers correctly argue, there is something that has survived his death, something that she can continue to love and cherish although it is no longer realized in that particular life. Listen to how she answers them. "They say one must keep your standards and values of life alive. But how can I, when I only kept them for you? Everything was for you. I loved life, because you made it so perfect, and now there is no one left to make jokes with, or to talk about Racine and Molière and talk of plans and work and people." They ought to reply, she thought, excited, that this utterance reveals a deep confusion about love and about Lytton. For it is crucial to his being him that he is a person who does have values and standards, who loves valuable things for their own sake. How can she claim it is Lytton that she loves, if she has not tried to share the sense of what Racine means for him, if she makes of Racine just a jagged idiosyncrasy, a piece of contingent fit? These consolers, she began to think, had a point. For, clearly, she herself did not love the man she loved just as someone who was in arbitrary ways right for her, but more because he was an angel. This is to say, radiantly good and fine in ways in which it was important to her also to be good and fine. That is to say, uncompromised in his pursuit of standards to which she also aspired, loving them for their own sake. (You think you don't know anything about him. Knowing that, you could pick him out from ten million.)

She was by now not weeping but pacing about the room, excited. For it seemed to her that it would be an excellent result for her grief if a richer love of the individual, a love that was most truly a love of the individual, her love let us say, turned out to be based upon an acknowledgment that certain things have intrinsic value which, being repeatable and not idiosyncratic, will survive the death or departure of the individual. That the better one loved this individual the more one would see that there was, in fact, something to live for beyond that person, something connected with the commitments and aspirations on which the love is itself based. And this something could be sought in someone else, even pursued on its own, apart from love. (For like many a recalcitrant pupil of Diotima, this lady, who thought of herself as a hopeless romantic, and was so on Mondays, Wednesdays, and Fridays, also liked to look about for the morally acceptable ways to satisfy her longing for stability. The way of Diotima was not acceptable. But if the truest value of the unique and uniquely loved could turn out also to impart stability to the life that loved it—this would be the best conjuring trick of all. As I warned you, I'm trying a variant of that trick now: trying, by doing justice in writing to love's fragility, to make that very fragility a source of stability for myself.)

The hope of bringing off this argument against Carrington excited her beyond tears. It would require a lot of probing, of debating back and forth—since the powerful appeal of that implacable grief made her deeply suspicious of any such *consolatio philosophiae*. And to be convincing it would have to be done in writing, for she was never convinced by her own thoughts until she saw them fixed.

Where would she begin this assault on Carrington (also, as you see, an assault on the moral superiority of her own death)? She envisaged a statement of the view about value and the superiority of a love based upon repeatable features of commitment and aspiration, followed by a series of objections by Carrington and replies to those objections. For the initial statement she might have thought only of her own love, but so much was she a lover of the general that she could not even try to understand something so particular without holding it up against some philosophical account that would illuminate it, and be illuminated by it. The text that had always seemed to her to describe better than any her own views about love, the text that seemed to her to argue effectively both against Diotima's banishment of individual passion and against Aristophanes' extreme emphasis on other halves was, of course, Plato's *Phaedrus*. She got out a pen and a pad of yellow paper (with which she was always equipped, even in despair), sat down at the desk, and began to write, for herself, the following.

I feel no pity for her now. For she is a very tough lady, as she sits there writing objections and arguments. No longer a timorous dove, but a self-assured, agile professional. Far more like me.

"*A la guerre comme à la guerre*, then," I say to her, as James's Prince, so ambiguously, to Charlotte Stant. "But I am charmed by your courage and almost surprised by my own."

Loving an Individual: Romantic Rightness
and Platonic Aspiration

I. The 'Phaedrus': the best view of love bases it on a view of the individ-
ual as essentially constituted by values and aspirations.

This is not a description of what passionate love in general is like. It is
a description of the best type of passion. Socrates argues that this sort of
"mad" passion for another individual is an essential part of the best human
life and the way that passion best figures in a good life. This is also supposed to be the best way in which love loves an individual. Against Lysias,
who argues that the person in love never gets to know who the beloved
really is, Socrates argues that it is in passion (not all sorts, but this high
sort) that one person is most truly able to know and to love another—to
love what the other most truly is.

It begins with the recognition of values. Souls are individuated by
what they most deeply care about. For example, the Zeus-like type cares
most about philosophy and moral value and pursues these two together. To
care about these values is the essence of such a soul. We could imagine
these people losing their money, their reputation, their youthfulness—and
still being essentially the same. We couldn't in the same way imagine them
ceasing to care about knowledge or justice. Aristotle says this succinctly:
the character and value commitments (as opposed to superficial pleas-
antness or advantageousness) are what each person is *kath' hauto*, in virtue of himself or herself. To love a person himself or herself, and not the
accidental features of a person, is to love that.

The values are recognized in a way that truly involves, even requires,
passion. And being passive. The first thing that happens is that the lover is
simply, mysteriously, struck by the splendor of the other, the "form truly
expressing beauty and nobility." He is dazzled, aroused, illuminated. His
soul is compared, in its arousal, to the gums of a teething child. He is also
compared to a plant, watered and nourished by the presence of the other's
beauty and excellence. What he experiences is nothing like cold respect or
mere admiration. And yet, it is crucial that in the beauty that arouses him
he sees a sign of the values that he cherishes and pursues. What he is always doing is "following the trace of his god." The beauty of the other is
not, even in the beginning, seen as mere superficial attractiveness but as
the radiance of a committed soul. Awe and wonder are essential components of his love.

The point is, he wouldn't be in love really if the other didn't answer to
his aspirations. Love and sexuality (at least in good people) are themselves
selective and aspiring. What excites the passion, makes him shudder and
tremble, is the perception of something that answers to the desires of his
soul. Passion loves *that*: it demands an object that is radiant with value.
What it wants from the person, ultimately, is a mutual exchange of love
and ideas that will be a seamless part of each one's pursuit of their central
aspiration.

Aspiration, on the other hand, becomes in this account something not

266

detached and self-sufficient, but needy, vulnerable, bound up with motion and receptivity. They cannot pursue their values without the inspiration and nourishment of love. In order to be moved toward value, each soul must, first of all, be open and receptive. The crucial first step toward truth and knowledge comes when the stream of beauty that enters in at the eyes is allowed to moisten and melt the solid dry elements of the soul. Only then does the soul begin to have insight into itself and its aims. And as time goes on, with "unfeigned passion," both touching and conversing, they "follow up the trace," each in the other, of their own god, coming to know one another, themselves, and true value at the same time.

And where, in all this, is the individual? The essential individuality of each is to be found in the fineness of soul, the character and commitments that make each the follower of a certain god. Since these patterns of commitment are repeatable and not idiosyncratic, the account implies that there might have been, at least at the beginning, more than one person of the appropriate soul type who might have answered to the lover's inner needs. It is also plausible that a single life might (in the wake of a death or a departure) come to contain a plurality of similar loves. And yet there are limits. First, such people will not be easily found. Then, the person must also have a more mysterious attractiveness that compels and overwhelms. Next, there is, too, the evident importance of history: the deepening of the relationship over time is clearly one of the sources of its value as a source of knowledge, self-knowledge, and motivation. The accidents in this way draw close to the core. Finally, against Carrington's consolers we must notice that Plato's account does not allow the bereaved person to go on pursuing the loved one's values alone, in the total absence of love; at least, they cannot be pursued nearly as well. The bereaved person has to wait to be struck again.

Still, there is room both for personal survival and for replacement. The lover will not feel that he is nothing at all without the love, has nothing to live for, can't go on being the same person. For his love was based on things that endure—that are, we might say, "bigger than both of us." To have a new love is crucial to the continued pursuit of philosophy, or whatever, and if what the lost love loved was that, it is natural that the bereaved person should try to perpetuate and further the goals of the relationship.

She paused, relatively satisfied. Here was a challenge to Carrington subtle enough that even that hopeless romantic ought to take it seriously. But she was not really convinced, as she reread what she had written, that it did justice to the things that had moved her in Carrington's account of Lytton. For didn't this view imply, after all, that one could in principle advertise for a lover, say, in the *New York Review of Books?* (Zeus-type soul, committed to philosophical and ethical values, seeks excellent man with similar aspirations . . .) And if the list could be complete enough, and if there were in addition some reliable way of making sure that the applicant really had the virtues he purported to have, then didn't the view imply that the successful applicant would be her passionate lover? And wasn't this absurd? Plato is less crude than the advertisement on the epistemological issue, for he insists that real knowledge of habits and ways requires a context of intimacy. You cannot tell beforehand: you go by that trace; you allow yourself, in considerable ignorance, to be melted. But it looked as if the real presence of these general traits was, in his view, sufficient for passionate love and sufficiently defined love's object. And this seemed bad or absurd enough. It was not only epistemology, surely, that prevented her from taking out such an advertisement.

I tend to agree with her here. When I first said that I would write on this topic, I tried to draw up a list of the repeatable properties I admired and aspired to; I rated against this list of properties men I had loved, and also men that I plausibly might have but hadn't. Not surprisingly, the men I had seriously loved came out with the highest rating. But I knew that I had made up the list by thinking about them. Like Aristotle's flexible ruler, this list looked posterior to the perception of concrete particulars. Though it might summarize these, it "bent to the shape of the stone, and was not fixed." It was quite clear that a new lover who lacked some of the properties on this list and had others would not, just on that account, be rejected. If I loved him I'd change the list. The question then would be, was I discovering something about myself that had been true all along (a kind of Platonic inner list), or was I really changing the list? I saw no clear reason to prefer the first alternative.

Her sketch, she saw, had not gone far enough. She was left still feeling the absurdity of Platonism, the dignity and truth of Carrington's repudiation. She would have to go on with the second part of her plan: a real debate between Carrington and the *Phaedrus*. She would imagine the romantic objections one by one, giving Plato in each case the strongest possible reply. The scholastic and numerical look of what she then wrote testifies to the violence of her confusion.

(When, much later, I first felt desire for another man, she became violent in a different way. I hadn't realized she was still there; or I thought that she had by now become me. She, or the he that she carried around inside her, the internal person who had, like Proust's Albertine, walked down into her heart and taken up residence there, a jealous and disturbing guest, kept me awake all night for several days with what felt like a series of kicks to the head and stomach. It was later diagnosed as viral labyrinthitis. But I knew.)

II. Romantic objections and Platonic replies.

The romantic opponent has several different types of objections to make to Plato. Some are objections to the particular contents of a Platonic list of valuable properties; some pertain to his use or construal of that list; some, finally, are objections to the entire idea of basing love on a list of properties.

A. *Objections to the content of Plato's list.*

Objection 1. The Platonic list enumerates the individual's commitments and aspirations. But a lot of the valuable properties of an individual are not values. Intelligence, a sense of humor, warmth: these are not commitments and aspirations, and yet they are very valuable, arguably central, to the individuality of the person who has them.

Objection 2. Furthermore, the properties on the list are all high-minded moral and intellectual properties. But some of the repeatable features that will be pertinent to my loves will not be of this sort. They may be morally (aspirationally) irrelevant, such as a certain coloring, or height, or ethnic background. They may even have a negative relation to aspiration. Carrington's persistent choice of men who belittled her artistic ambitions and treated her like a child surely worked against her aspirations, and yet it is a salient pattern in her loves and an important part of the individuality of those she loves.

Objection 3. The Platonic list stresses shared aspiration and similarity of commitment. But some of the properties that will be most valued in a beloved person are properties that are not shared; often they are valued precisely because the lover lacks them. Carrington, not well educated in literary matters, values Lytton's eloquence and knowledge. A shy and nervous person, she values someone who has the ability to tell marvelous fantastic jokes.

Objection 4. There are far too few properties on Plato's list. He says that there are twelve types of souls, correlated with twelve forms of aspiration. But in fact the properties that are relevant to aspiration are much more subtly demarcated, more numerous, and susceptible of more varied combination.

Reply to Objection 1. It is indeed striking how many valuable properties do have to do with a person's values and commitments. We don't value a person's kindness, or courage, unless we believe that the person is in some sense committed to behaving in that way, values that way of behaving. If it's just accidental or sporadic, it won't be valued in the same way, and it won't enter in the same way into an account of what that person really is.

Reply to Objection 2. Plato does not want to insist that all loves fit his account. This is a normative, not a descriptive, view of human love. Of course there are people who are repeatedly attracted to some arbitrary property, or even to evil. Aristotle points out that the first is characteristic of immature people, of whatever age; the second is clearly an illness, though the Greeks have little to say about it. Furthermore, if we find a repeated feature in our loves that seems aspirationally irrelevant but is ubiquitous and rather deep, it may turn out that its deep meaning for us is, after all, not unconnected with our aspirations and values.

Reply to Objection 3. These diversities, if we press them, are rooted in a similarity. Their different careers are complementary ways of pursuing a commitment to artistic creation. Bloomsbury is nothing if not a community of aspiration based upon shared values. It would have been a different matter had the commitments been altogether unrelated, or even antithetical. Then, however, we would feel that the difference was a disadvantage to the love; we would doubt whether they could fully love one another for what each one really was. Plato's soul types are very general forms of aspiration. He nowhere rules out complementary differences of this sort, and the differences in age and experience between the lover and beloved make some such differences inevitable.

Reply to Objection 4. Here Carrington seems to have a point. Being a philosopher is, for example, far too coarse a property to explain the shape of my aspiration and therefore my aspiring love. It all depends on what kind of philosopher, and what the view of philosophy is. Furthermore, the combination of values that I will go for in making up a plan for a good life will almost surely be heterogeneous enough not to correspond to any one of Plato's types. But we should be wary of pressing this specificity too far, for one thing Plato's approach does permit is an informative account of the unity among the loves of a single person.

So far, she saw, Plato had not had to give very much ground before the objections. His essential conception remained untouched. Carrington, however, had barely begun to state her case.

.   B. *Objections to the use or construal of the list.*

Objection 5. The list, insofar as it suggests that I can go out into the world looking (or advertise in the *New York Review*) for someone with, for example, justice or wisdom, fails to capture the most characteristic ways in which the deeper aspiration-properties present themselves to our awareness. They do not march up to us wearing placards; they make themselves known through other related and more obvious properties, through images, masks, and disguises. Often I will know only that this person is beautiful and exhilarating in some way I cannot yet describe.

Reply to Objection 5. This point was not ignored by Plato. Indeed, he insists on it. It is in fact one of his main reasons for thinking that you can't understand values like justice or wisdom in yourself or in the world without personal love. For only personal love draws a person into the exchange of choices and thoughts that will suffice to reveal, over time, the nature of these values. Love itself begins not so much with these values, which are hard to discern, as with the experience of being struck by a mysterious kind of beauty. (She tried not to think of the way the sunlight from the doorway flamed at the edges of his shoulders and ringed his head.) Even if the values are apprehended through these indirect traces, they are still what is loved. A more serious point lurks here, however, a point about how beloved properties are really individuated and which the really relevant ones are. What's to say that looking a certain way in the sunlight is merely a mode in which brilliance and beneficence make themselves visible?

Objection 6. A list of value properties is something fixed, fixed in advance of the discovery of the loved one. I am a Zeus-like soul, and what I want is to match up with another similar soul. I may as yet not know what type I am, but according to Plato I am already one type or another. It is there for me to discover, partly by following up the traces of my god in the soul of the person I love. But in real life my aspirations and values are not this fixed. I operate with an open-ended, revisable list, and I frequently must decide to commit myself to one thing or another, to pursue one value rather than another. When I love in the aspiring way, it is as much a matter of decision as of discovery. The choice between one potential love and another can feel, and be, like a choice of a way of life, a decision to dedicate oneself to these values rather than these. The choice to devote myself to that love is a choice to love and cultivate those elements in myself.

Reply to Objection 6. This objection has force, but it is not an objection to the list per se, or even to the idea of regarding the list of value properties as normative for particular choices of lovers. It just points out that not all my norms and values are set; some are still evolving. If we think about how this evolution works, we find that it has very much the same shape as rational deliberation elsewhere in life. In neither case does the deliberation proceed in a vacuum. When I think about what, for me, will count as living well, I hold certain commitments firm in order to deliberate on others, or I hold the general conception of one element firm while I ask, more concretely, what will count as realizing that. Even so, in making choices in love I recognize and hold firm some general values while deliberating about others. So the objection does not even show that an antecedent list is a bad guide; it just warns us about holding too fixedly to it. We have, then, a friendly amendment.

She paused. Plato was enormously strong. She was surprised at the strength of the replies she was finding on his behalf.

And here she noticed, all at once, that this well-ordered scholastic questioning, this probing scrutiny of love with its numbered objections and replies, could not claim to constitute an external and neutral investigation of the phenomenon that resided in her heart (and in the obscure connections between that organ and other portions of the world distant, perhaps, in space, but dwelling in close proximity). For as she investigated, the investigation was effecting a change in her heart, was calming its grief and loosening its connections. It was opening a clear, high space over and around her ribs, a space that, being empty of the internal presence of the loved person, was filled with air and light. She thought of Proust's narrator, trembling before the equanimity of his own heart as be-

271

fore a deadly snake; for he knew that a life in which his love and his suffering for Albertine no longer existed would be a life in which he no longer existed. She too felt panic. Am I really myself right now? she asked herself, hoping that some tears would come to prove it.

How clear it is to me that there is no neutral posture of reflection from which one can survey and catalogue the intuitions of one's heart on the subject of love, holding up the rival views to see how well they fit the intuitions—no activity of philosophizing that does not stand in some determinate relation to the love. The relations can be of many kinds; they are not always, as here, inhibitory and consoling. For the *Phaedrus* shows, precisely, that a certain high type of philosophical activity may be called into being by, and in turn express and nourish, the energy and beneficence and subtle insight of happy love. And the insights gained in passion can best be pursued collaboratively, in the context of the love. (As in Phaedrus's fantasy, in the *Symposium*, of an army composed of pairs of lovers, a fantasy made reality in the Sacred Band. We might by analogy imagine a philosophy department similarly constructed, dedicated to the understanding of love. I wonder what the Thebans did when they broke up.) On the other hand, as in her case, the philosophy might, as here, emerge from and reinforce the desire for distancing and safety; it might effect and express a transformation of the perceptions and intuitions of love, and even of the lover, inasmuch as the relation seems to her to be partly constitutive of her identity. The object of my scrutiny, Heraclitean (or rather Cratylan even) is never the same the minute you begin to step into it, even once.

In addition to the question who shall write about love, we have still on hand our old question how. I gave you some reasons for thinking that a narrative might be truer than a treatise or article on the subject. I can add to these now the argument that narrative writing, more than standard philosophical writing, seems to express the author's own acknowledgment of the power and importance of particular love and to elicit from the reader a similar response. (My experience right now is different from hers; as she is moving further from her love through scholastic argument, I risk being quite immersed. I can't write this story, however abstract it is and however much concerned with thought and argument, without launching myself into those currents.)

But the point is not simple, as I see it. For stories too impose their own simplifications. They demand that something happen, that there be a plot with a beginning and a middle and an end. They demand singleness where in life there is multiplicity, statement where there is indeterminacy, description where there are indescribable, undepictable things. So they do not escape the general suspicions I have expressed about writing. In some ways philosophy might fare better; for it follows the inquiry wherever it leads, without insisting on drama, or interest, or endings. Proust's idea was that only through the focusing and sharpening power of narrative art could the messy matter of life assume a shape, become really real and true. I feel the force of that. But I see even more clearly the other side, and here I turn to Beckett: art, especially narrative art, forces life to assume a shape rather than letting it be in its formlessness; forces it to demand an ending where one way of loving might be to forbear to do that. This forces us to ask, not just who should write about love, not just how, but also whether.

As she took note of her own forgetfulness, her heart shivered. And as it shivered, it cracked like the ice on top of a stream, and the currents of her feeling, like the liquid in one of Plato's melted souls, welled up. Outside, oranges were dying, wrapped in their coats of ice. Inside, she could not find ice enough to halt her own demise. For she knew, and with certainty, that Carrington was right. There was no life for her without that love, no continuation of its meanings without that particular person, radiant and separate. Carrington's diary goes on: "Human beings seem to me divided into those who can say 'I live for myself alone' and those who know that 'without this person or thing I could not live.'" Once Plato's souls were melted, how could they help dying of a loss? She knew, and with certainty, that she was not one of the self-sufficient ones.

What do I mean by writing "She knew, and with certainty"? Not that she had come up with new and clever arguments destined to refute the skeptic on the plane of intellect. Argument, indeed, had led her to the opposite conclusion. I mean that she felt her stomach rising up into her mouth. That she felt like one of those Greek tragic unfortunates to whom someone has given a poisoned cloak that causes the wearer to sweat blood. The half of her had gone out, the next minute, into the empty space where he was and was floating around with him in the still moonlight above the golf course, lightly carried on the wind. For she saw how beautiful he was, and she did not want to be apart from him. All this is knowledge of love. And all this is happening now to me.

"Amor ch'al cor gentil ratto s'apprende," love that quickly takes hold in the gentle heart, is taking hold in mine as I watch, showing it to be more gentle than hard. I am, I tell you, the visitor and watcher of her grief, and yet as I record her knowledge I begin to have it. Francesca says:

> Amor, ch'a nullo amato amar perdona,
> mi prese del costui piacer si forte,
> che, come vedi, ancor non m'abbandona.
>
> Love, who absolves no beloved one from loving,
> seized me with such a strong desire for him
> that, as you see, it has not left me yet.

I want only to watch. But she is seeing him. Her watcher sees him too. I can hardly distinguish the spectator I am from the one she is. She wants Carrington to win the debate now. She wants to get all the way to that conclusion, so she won't be happier than love is.

I'm very tired, and I'm shaken by all this. I haven't finished my letter. What's strangest is that I'm more worn out than she is. I'll tell you what's going to happen now. She's going to write some more. Can you believe it? She will go all the way back to her original list of three objections, calling them, now, Objections 7, 8, and 9; she writes them out, putting Carrington's case with new force. She adds two more she has just thought up to help her. One charges the Platonist list with making love seem more determinate and reason-based, less mysterious, than it is; the other with making it too active and will-governed. I don't feel like reproducing them; you know the sort of thing she will say. And I suppose you expect that now she will get exhausted and go to sleep despairing. Not this lady. Her father died putting his papers into his briefcase; shriveled by cancer to half his former weight, he never lay down once. Her father's father once served on a jury. After ten days of deliberation he came home: the jury couldn't agree; they had ordered a new trial. He walked into the house and said to his wife, "Those were eleven of the stubbornest men I have ever seen." Now you know what you're dealing with. Do you think a lady from that background— and a philosopher on top of it all—is going to give up the argument just because it is 3:00 A.M. and most of the oranges are dead? Do you suppose, furthermore, she is going to let Carrington, and death, have the last word? No, she's going to fight it out to the end, fighting against that love with Platonist replies about value, pen in her hand and a stubborn foot in his face.

This is love she's dealing with. Can't she ever stop writing?

I won't reproduce it all. I'll give you the last paragraphs. Then I'll go to sleep, or faint like Dante.

I propose, then, a new construction of the individual as object of love. We can, I think, combine the best elements of the *Phaedrus* with several concessions to the strongest romantic objections. We begin by insisting with Plato that the best kind of love, the kind that loves the individual for what he or she really is, is a love of character and values. But we make some alterations in the way the *Phaedrus* presents the search for character. To the first six objections we make the concessions already noted, concerning variety of properties and flexibility of choice. The final five require us to make a more substantial modification. We say something like this: in any love that is based upon character, the lovers will also see in one another, and truly love, many relational and nonrepeatable properties. They will not love these in a merely incidental way; they will come to see one another as wholes, not as composites of essence and accident, so that the nonrepeatable will be just as intrinsic to the love as the repeatable. The history, too, will come to have more than an enabling and extrinsic value; they will love it for its own sake too, rejecting even a substitution that could (*per impossibile*) preserve the same trust and knowledge. Carrington will love Lytton's character and standards; she will also love his jokes, their letters, their years of intimacy.

We can still maintain, however, that the *Phaedrus* elements take priority, in the following way. We know that to be a good object of love, a person must have these repeatable character traits and not these—for example, be committed to justice and not injustice. We don't in the same way care which lovable accidents the person has. There have to be some; but insofar as they are morally neutral, it seems not to matter what they are (whether he makes jokes about cheese or some other jokes).

This construction permits of real mourning; for there has been a real loss of an intrinsic value that will never come again. But it also entails that not everything is lost when a particular love is lost. The *Phaedrus* elements will sustain the person and provide continuity from one love to the next. Because both lovers love the values for themselves, it will not be disloyal to engage in such a search.

This proposal has not made things altogether easier for the bereaved person. In one way, it has made them harder—by insisting on the felicitous combination of two elements that are hard enough to find singly. A few people are really good; a few are truly pleasing and 'right'; very few indeed are both. The romantic can take comfort from the thought that Platonism, so modified, has actually made things worse.

Now she's going to sleep at last, feeling victorious. She's not going to die, not her. Me? As Dante says, and Virgil's Dido before him, "Conosco i segni de l'antica fiamma." "Agnosco veteris vestigia flammae." I recognize those traces.

It's morning now. When morning came in Florida, she went running on the golf course. For even when she had been thinking of death it never occurred to her not to be healthy. The cover of snow was thawing under a cheerful Florida sun. She ran, as often, to the tune of the March to the Scaffold from Berlioz's *Symphonie Fantastique*, which she could conjure up in her head when she wished to go on, but in a tragic way. She ran from one fairway to the next, aware that she did not know the way back to her hosts' house but convinced that the numbers would bring her back in safety. She noticed the opulent ugliness of the bordering houses and remembered true beauty. She did not want to go on. She went on. And as the frozen ground began to thaw beneath her feet, the Berlioz march paused briefly. A head, flaming in the doorway. The unhappy lover heard once more from a distant place, tender and absent, the music of his only beloved. It came and hovered over the guillotine. The angel standing. And then the rapid cymbal clashes came to end it. She went on, as she thought she might. Someone went on; she thought that it was her.

When I first saw him, he was walking down the sun-streaked hallway, laughing and talking, his whole body fiercely lit up from behind by the light from the door. He looked to me like Turner's Angel Standing in the Sun, or like a counterpart good angel, victorious but tender, beneficent in power. And was there, within that remarkable and dangerous radiance, a division to be found between repeatable value properties and idiosyncratic accidents? Or was it all one seamless "perfectness"? In spite of all her constructing, there still seems to me to be no clear answer to this question. So much depends on the use you intend to make of it. And now I don't want to use it to forget. I would like to want that, but I don't. "Amor, ch'a nullo amato amar perdona,"—love who lets no loved one off the hook—"mi prese del costui piacer sì forte, che, come vedi, ancor non m'abbandona." I'm in the story now, floating around. "Amor condusse noi ad una morte. Caina attende chi a vita ci spense." Love brought us to one death; Caina waits for the one who took our life.

Who am I, then, truly? Am I Francesca, the dead one, carried on the winds, dead of her love and loving on in death? Or am I, as seems more likely, the one who was responsible for her death and the death of her love, for whose callousness, for whose happiness, the icy pit of traitors is the just reward? I used to be able to distinguish myself from her, my narrative voice from hers. I was the bright, wary, slightly tough, optimistic one, the one who made jokes, who was happy, who was writing a love letter, who had survived to love again through her Platonic commitment to general values. She was the fragile one, in mourning for her loss, tossed on the currents of confused desire. Then I, sympathizing, came like Dante close to her, and the intensity of her devotion put my salvation to shame. And now: haven't we changed places? There she goes, running along the melted fairway, listening to heaven knows what romantic music. But she goes quite toughly on, thinking and running. She has survived. She is well on her way to being me. I, now, am mourning, now I feel the force of the past upon me, I am no different from her; I will not finish a love letter to somebody else; I'll be the individual constituted by her love.

I refuse to be happier than love is.

I didn't expect the story to end like this. My writing didn't have the same result for me as hers did for her, clearly. Perhaps because it was a different kind of writing. There is much more to be said about the connection between these experiences and ethical objectivity. But I am too immersed to say it. I'm seeing a "form truly expressing beauty and nobility." It's like being one of those fishermen in their light-drowned boat.

Did I find what I wanted, then, the noncontrolling art of writing?

I write only what occurs to me now. It won't look this way tomorrow. Tomorrow I'll see my current lover. Who is an individual. With many repeatable (and even repeated) properties, and some that are unique. We'll have dinner in a good restaurant, and I'll tell jokes about this paper and its strange effect upon my mood. I'll say how happy I am. It will be true.

"Caina attende chi a vita ci spense."

What ending did you expect? Did you think I would collapse, or die? Remember, I'm the one who wrote this down. Remember, this is writing you're reading.

"Love, and be silent."

Being Odd, Getting Even: Threats to Individuality

STANLEY CAVELL

In the lobby of William James Hall at Harvard, across the story-tall expanse of concrete above the bank of elevators facing you as you enter, brass letters spell out the following pair of sentences, attributed by further such letters to William James:

THE COMMUNITY STAGNATES WITHOUT THE IMPULSE OF THE INDIVIDUAL

THE IMPULSE DIES AWAY WITHOUT THE SYMPATHY OF THE COMMUNITY

The message may be taken as empirically directed to whoever stands beneath and reads it, and thence either as a warning, or an exhortation, or a description of a state of current affairs—or else it may be taken as claiming a transcendental relation among the concepts of community and individual as they have so far shown themselves. Does this multiplicity produce what certain literary theorists now speak of as the undecidable? Or is the brass indifference of this writing on the wall an apt expression of our avoidance of decision, a refusal to apply our words to ourselves, to take them on?

This essay is a kind of progress report on my philosophical journey to locate an inheritance of Wittgenstein and Heidegger, and of Emerson and Thoreau before them, for all of whom there seems to be some question whether the individual or the community as yet, or any longer, exists. This question (or, you may say, this fantasy) gives ground equally for despair and for hope in the human as it stands. It is also the question or fantasy in which I have been seeking instruction from certain Hollywood comedies of remarriage and, before them, from Shakespearean romance and tragedy. In this mood I do not wish to propose a solution to the riddle of whether

278

society is the bane or the blessing of the individual, or to offer advice about whether a better state of the world must begin with a reformation of institutions or of persons, advice that would of course require me to define institutions and individuals and their modes of interpenetration. So I will pick up the twist in the story of the discovery of the individual where Descartes placed it in his *Meditations*—before, so to speak, either individual or institutional differences come into play. This twist is Descartes's discovery that my existence requires, hence permits, proof (you might say authentication)—more particularly, requires that if I am to exist I must name my existence, acknowledge it. This imperative entails that I am a thing with two foci, or, in Emerson's image, two magnetic poles—say a positive and a negative, or an active and a passive.

Such a depiction may not seem to you right off to capture Descartes's cogito argument. But that something like it does capture that argument is what I understand the drift of Emerson's perhaps inaudibly famous essay "Self-Reliance" to claim. My first task here will be to establish this about Emerson's essay; my second will be to say why I think Emerson is right, as right in his interpretation and inheritance of Descartes as any other philosophical descendant I know of. Following that, as a third principal task, I will take up a pair of tales by Edgar Allan Poe, primarily "The Imp of the Perverse" and subordinately "The Black Cat." These stories, I find, engage with the same imperative of human existence: that it must prove or declare itself. And since Poe's "The Imp of the Perverse" alludes more than once to *Hamlet*, it will bring us to my title, the idea of thinking about individuality (or the loss of it) under the spell of revenge, of getting even for oddness.

Emerson's incorporation of Descartes into "Self-Reliance" is anything but veiled. At the center of the essay is a paragraph that begins: "Man is timid and apologetic; he is no longer upright; he dares not say 'I think,' 'I am,' but quotes some saint or sage." It is my impression that readers of Emerson have not been impressed by this allusion, or repetition, perhaps because they have fallen into an old habit of condescending to Emerson (as if to pay for a love of his writing by conceding that he was hardly capable of consecutive thought, let alone capable of taking on Descartes), perhaps because they remember or assume the cogito always to be expressed in words that translate as "I think, *therefore* I am." But in Descartes's

Second Meditation, where I suppose it is most often actually encountered, the insight is expressed: "*I am, I exist,* is necessarily true every time that I pronounce it or conceive it in my mind." Emerson's emphasis on the *saying* of "I" is precisely faithful to this expression of Descartes's insight.

It is this feature of the cogito that is emphasized in some of the most productive thinking about Descartes in recent analytical philosophy, where the issue, associated with the names of Jaakko Hintikka and Bernard Williams, is phrased as the question whether the certainty of existence required and claimed by the cogito results from taking the claim "I think" as the basis (i.e., premise) for an inference, or is the expression of some kind of performance. Williams does not quite rest with saying, with Hintikka, that the cogito just is not an inference, and just is a performance of some kind, but Williams does insist that it is not an ordinary, or syllogistic, inference, as he insists, at the end of his intricate discussion, that the performance in play is no less peculiar of its kind, demanding further reflection.[1] The cogito's peculiarity can be summarized as follows, according to Williams. On the one hand, the force of the first person pronoun is that it cannot fail to refer to the one using it, hence one who says "I exist" must exist; or, put negatively, "I exist" is undeniable, which is to say, "I do not exist" cannot coherently be said. On the other hand, to be said sensibly, "I" must distinguish the one saying it, to whom it cannot fail to refer, from others to whom it does not, at that saying, refer. But Descartes's use of it arises exactly in a context in which there are no others to distinguish himself (so to speak) from. So the force of the pronoun is in apparent conflict with its sense.

Compared with such considerations Emerson's remark about our not daring to say "I think," "I am," seems somewhat literary. But why? Emerson is picking up a question, or a side of the question, that succeeds the inferential or performance aspect of the cogito—namely, the question of what happens if I do *not* say (and of course do not say the negation of) "I am, I exist" or "conceive it in my mind." An analytical philosopher will hardly take much interest in this side of the question, since it will hardly seem worth arguing for or against the inference that if I do not say or perform the words "I am" or their equivalent (aloud or silently) that therefore I perhaps do not exist. Surely the saying or thinking of some words may be taken to bear on whether the sayer or thinker of them exists at most in the sense of determining whether he or she *knows* of his or her existence, but surely not in the sense that the saying or thinking may create that existence.

But this assurance seems contrary to Descartes's findings. He speculates a few paragraphs after announcing the cogito: "I am, I exist—that is certain; but for how long do I exist? For as long as I think; for it might perhaps happen, if I totally ceased thinking, that I would at the same time completely cease to be." This does not quite say that my ceasing to think would cause, or would be, my ceasing to exist. It may amount to saying so if I must think of myself as having a creator (hence, according to Descartes, a preserver) and if all candidates for this role other than myself dropped out. These assumptions seem faithful to Descartes's text, so that I am prepared to take it that the cogito is only half the battle concerning the relation of my thinking to my existing, or perhaps "I think, therefore I am" expresses only half the battle of the cogito: Descartes establishes to his satisfaction that I exist only while, or if *and only if*, I think. It is this, it seems, that leads him to claim that the mind always thinks, an idea Nietzsche and Freud will put to further use.

Emerson goes the whole way with Descartes's insight—that I exist only if I think—but he thereupon denies that I (mostly) do think, that the "I" mostly gets into my thinking, as it were. From this it follows that the skeptical possibility is realized—that I do not exist, that I as it were haunt the world, a realization perhaps expressed by saying that the life I live is the life of skepticism. Just before the end of the Second Meditation, Descartes observes that "if I judge that [anything, say the external world] exists because I see it, certainly it follows much more evidently that I exist myself because I see it." Since the existence of the world is more doubtful than my own existence, if I do not know that I exist I so to speak even more evidently do not know that the things of the world exist. If, accordingly, Emerson is to be understood as describing the life left to me under skepticism—implying that I do not exist among the things of the world, that I haunt the world—and if for this reason he is to be called literary and not philosophical, we might well conclude: so much the worse for philosophy. Philosophy shrinks before a description of the very possibility it undertakes to refute, so it can never know of itself whether it has turned its nemesis aside.

But it seems to me that one can see how Emerson arrives at his conclusion by a continuing faithfulness to Descartes's own procedures, to the fact, as one might put it, that Descartes's procedures are as essentially literary as they are philosophical (and that it may even have become essential to philosophy to show as much). After arriving at the cogito, Descartes immediately raises the question of his metaphysical identity: "But I do not yet know sufficiently clearly what I am, I who am sure that I exist." He raises this question six or seven times over the ensuing seven or eight paragraphs, rejecting along the way such answers as that he is a rational animal, or that he is a body, or that his soul is "something very rarefied and subtle, such as a wind, a flame, or a very much expanded air . . . infused throughout my grosser components," before he settles on the answer that he is essentially a thing that thinks. There is nothing in these considerations to call argument or inference; indeed, the most obvious description of these passages is to say that they constitute an autobiographical narrative of some kind.[2] If Descartes is philosophizing, and if these passages are essential to his philosophizing, it follows that philosophy is not exhausted in argumentation. And if the power of these passages is literary, then the literary is essential to the power of philosophy; at some stage the philosophical becomes, or turns into, the literary.

Now I think one can describe Emerson's progress as his having posed Descartes's question for himself and provided a fresh line of answer, one you might call a grammatical answer: I am a being who to exist must say I exist, or must acknowledge my existence—claim it, stake it, enact it.

The beauty of the answer lies in its weakness (you may say its emptiness), indeed, in two weaknesses. First, it does not prejudge what the I or self or mind or soul may turn out to be, but only specifies a condition that whatever it is must meet. Second, the proof only works in the moment of its giving, for what I prove is the existence only of a creature who *can* enact its existence, as exemplified in actually giving the proof, not one who at all times does in fact enact it. The transience of the existence it proves and the transience of its manner of proof seem in the spirit of the *Meditations*, including Descartes's proofs for God; this transience would be the moral of Descartes's insistence on the presence of clear and distinct ideas as essential to, let me say, philosophical knowledge. Only in the vanishing presence of the state of such ideas does proof take effect—as if there were nothing to rely on but reliance itself. This is perhaps why Emerson will say, "To talk of reliance is a poor external way of speaking."

That what I am is one who to exist enacts his existence is an answer Descartes might almost have given himself, since it is scarcely more than a literal transcript of what I set up as the further half of the cogito's battle. It is a way of envisioning roughly the view of so-called human existence taken by Heidegger in *Being and Time*: that Dasein's being is such that its being is an issue for it. But for Descartes to have given such an answer would have threatened the first declared purpose of his *Meditations*, which was to offer proof of God's existence. If I am one who can enact my existence, God's role in the enactment is compromised. Descartes's word for what I call "enacting"—or "claiming" or "staking" or "acknowledging"—is "authoring." In the Third Meditation:

> I wish to pass on now to consider whether I myself, who have the idea of God, could exist if there had been no God. And I ask, from what source would I have derived my existence? Possibly from myself, or from my parents. . . . But if I were . . . the author of my own being, I would doubt nothing, I would experience no desires, and finally I would lack no perfection . . . I would be God (himself). . . . Even if I could suppose that possibly I have always been as I am now . . . it would not follow that no author of my existence need then be sought and I would still have to recognize that it is necessary that God is the author of my existence.[3]

Apparently it is the very sense of my need for a human proof of my human existence—some authentication—that is the source of the idea that I need an author. ("Need for proof" will be what becomes of my intuition of my transience, or dependence, or incompleteness, or unfinishedness, or unsponsoredness—of the intuition that I am unauthorized.)

But surely the idea of self-authorizing is merely metaphorical, the merest exploitation of the coincidence that the Latin word for author is also the word for creating, nothing more than the by now fully discredited romantic picture of the author or artist as incomprehensibly original, as a world-creating and self-creating genius. It is true that the problematic of enacting one's existence skirts the edge of metaphysical nonsense. It asks us, in effect, to move from the consideration that we may sensibly disclaim certain actions as ours (ones done, as we may say, against our wills), and hence from the consideration that we may disclaim certain of our thoughts as ours (ones, it may be, we would not dream of acting on, though the terrain here gets philosophically and psychologically more dangerous), to the possibility that none of my actions and thoughts are mine—as if, if I am not a ghost, I am, I would like to say, *worked*, from inside or outside. This move to the metaphysical is like saying that since it makes sense to suppose that I might lack any or all of my limbs I might lack a body altogether, or that since I never see all of any object and hence may not know that a given object exists I may not know that the external world as such exists. Ordinary-language philosophy, most notably in the teaching of J. L. Austin and of Wittgenstein, has discredited such moves to the metaphysical, as a way of discrediting the conclusions of skepticism. But in my interpretation of Wittgenstein, what is discredited is not the appeal or the threat of skepticism as such, but only skepticism's own pictures of its accomplishments. Similarly, what is discredited in the romantic's knowledge about self-authoring is only a partial picture of authoring and of creation, a picture of human creation as a literalized anthropomorphism of God's creation—as if to create myself I were required to begin with the dust of the ground and magic breath, rather than with, say, an uncreated human being and the power of thinking.

That human clay and the human capacity for thought are enough to inspire the authoring of myself is, at any rate, what I take Emerson's "Self-Reliance," as a reading of Descartes's cogito argument, to claim. I take his underlying turning of Descartes to be something like this: there is a sense of being the author of oneself that does not require me to imagine myself God (that may just be the name of the particular picture of the self as a self-present substance), a sense in which the absence of doubt and desire of which Descartes speaks in proving that God, not he, is the author of himself is a continuing task, not a property, a task in which the goal, or the product of the process, is not a state of being but a moment of change, say of becoming—a transience of being, a being of transience. (Emerson notes: "This one fact the world hates; that the soul *becomes.*") To make sense of this turn, Emerson needs a view of the world, a perspective on its fallenness, in which the *uncreatedness* of the individual manifests itself, in which human life appears as the individual's failure at self-creation, as a continuous loss of individual possibility in the face of some overpowering competitor.

This is to say that, if my gloss of Emerson's reading of Descartes is right, the cogito's need arises at a particular historical moment in the life of the individual and in the life of the culture.

Emerson calls the mode of uncreated life "conformity." But each of the modern prophets seems to have been driven to find some way of characterizing the threat to individual existence, to individuality, posed by the life to which their society is bringing itself. John Stuart Mill called it the despotism of opinion, and he characterized being human in his period in terms of deformity; he speaks of us as withered and starved, and as dwarfs. Nietzsche called the threat the world of the last man, of the murderers of God. Marx thinks of it rather as the preexistence of the human. Freud's discovery of the uncomprehended meaningfulness of human expression belongs in the line of such prophecy. Emerson's philosophical distinction here lies in his diagnosis of this stage and in his recommended therapy.

It is as a diagnosis of this state of the world that Emerson announced that Descartes's proof of self-existence (the foundation, Descartes named it, of the edifice of his former opinions, the fixed and immovable fulcrum on which to reposition the earth) cannot, or can no longer, be given; he asks us to conclude (such is the nature of this peculiar proof) that man, the human, does not, or does no longer, exist. Here is Emerson's sentence again, together with the sentence and a half following it: "Man is timid and apologetic; he is no longer upright; he dares not say 'I think,' 'I am,' but quotes some saint or sage. He is ashamed before the blade of grass or the blowing rose . . . they are for what they are; they exist with God today." We can locate Emerson's proposed therapy in this vision of so-called man's loss of existence if we take the successive notations of this vision as in apposition, as interpretations of one another: being apologetic; being no longer upright; daring not to say, but only quoting; being ashamed, as if for not existing today. There are, as Wittgenstein is once moved to express himself, a multitude of well-known paths leading off from these words in all directions. Let us take, or at least point down, two or three such paths.

To begin with, the idea that something about our mode of existence removes us from nature and that this has to do with being ashamed of course alludes to the romantic problematic of self-consciousness (or the post-Kantian interpretation of that problematic), a particular interpretation of the fall of man. But put Emerson's invocation of shame in apposition to his invocation of our loss of uprightness, and he may be taken as challenging, not passing on, the romantic interpretation of the fall as self-consciousness, refusing to regard our shame as a metaphysically irrecoverable loss of innocence but seeing it instead as an unnecessary acquiescence (or necessary only as history is necessary) in, let me say, poor posture, a posture he calls timidity and apologeticness. I will simply claim, without citing textual evidence (preeminently the contexts in which the word "shame" and its inflections are deployed throughout Emerson's essay) that the proposed therapy is to become ashamed of our shame, to find our ashamed posture more shameful than anything it could be reacting to. One might say that he calls for more, not less, self-consciousness; but it would be better to say that he shows self-consciousness not to be the issue it seems. It, or our view of it, is itself a function of poor posture.

But really everything so far said about existence, preexistence, and so forth may be some function of poor posture—including, of course, our view of what poor posture may be. Bad posture Emerson variously names, in one passage, as peeping or stealing or skulking up and down "with the air of a charity-boy, a bastard, or an interloper in the world which exists for him"; in another, he finds men behaving as if their acts were fines they paid "in expiation of daily non-appearance on parade," done "as an apology or extenuation of their living in the world—as invalids and the insane pay a high board. Their virtues are penances." This vision of human beings as in postures of perpetual penance or self-mortification will remind readers of *Walden* of that book's opening pages.

Good posture has two principal names or modes in "Self-Reliance": standing and sitting. The idea behind both modes is that of finding and taking and staying in a place. What is good in these postures is whatever makes them necessary to the acknowledgment, or the assumption, of individual existence, to the capacity to say "I." That this takes daring is what standing (up) pictures; that it takes claiming what belongs to you and disclaiming what does not belong to you is what sitting pictures. Sitting is thus the posture of being at home in the world (not peeping, stealing, skulking, or, as he also says, leaning), of owning or taking possession. This portrayal of the posture of sitting is, again, drawn out in *Walden*, where what Thoreau calls acquiring property is what most people would consider passing it by. Resisting the temptation to follow the

turnings of these paths, I put them at once in apposition to the no-
tation that in not daring to say something what we do instead is to
quote.

There is a gag here that especially appeals to contemporary sensibilities. Emerson writes, "Man dares not say . . . but quotes." But
since at that moment he quotes Descartes, isn't he confessing that
he too cannot say but can only quote? Then should we conclude
that he is taking back or dismantling (or something) the entire
guiding idea of "Self-Reliance"? Or is he rather suggesting that
we are to overcome the binary opposition between saying and quoting, recognizing that each is always both, or that the difference is
undecidable? That difference seems to me roughly the difference
between what Thoreau calls the mother tongue and the father
tongue, hence perhaps makes the difference between language and
literariness. And since I am taking the difference between saying
and quoting as one of posture, the proposal of undecidability strikes
me as the taking of a posture, and a poor one. I imagine being told
that the difference in posture partakes of the same undecidability.
My reply is that you can decide to say so. My decision is otherwise.
(It is helped by my intuition that a guiding remark of Freud's is con-
ceivable this way: Where thought takes place in me, there shall I
take myself.)

Emerson's gag, suggesting that saying is quoting, condenses a
number of ideas. First, language is an inheritance. Words are before I
am; they are common. Second, the question whether I am saying
them or quoting them—saying them first- or secondhand, as it
were—which means whether I am thinking or imitating, is the
same as the question whether I do or do not exist as a human being
and is a matter demanding proof. Third, the writing, of which the
gag is part, is an expression of the proof of saying "I," hence of the
claim that writing is a matter, say the decision, of life and death,
and that what this comes to is the inheriting of language, an owning of words, which does not remove them from circulation but
rather returns them, as to life.

That the claim to existence requires returning words to language, as if making them common to us, is suggested by the fourth
sentence of "Self-Reliance": "To believe your own thought, to believe that what is true for you in your private heart is true for all
men,—that is genius." (One path from these words leads to the
transformation of the romantics' idea of genius: Genius is not a

special endowment, like virtuosity, but a stance toward whatever endowment you discover is yours, as if life itself were a gift, and remarkable.) Genius is accordingly the name of the promise that the private and the social will be achieved together, hence of the perception that our lives now take place in the absence of either.

So Emerson is dedicating his writing to that promise when he says: "I shun father and mother and wife and brother when my genius calls me. I would write on the lintels of the door-post, *Whim*." (I will not repeat what I have said elsewhere concerning Emerson's marking of Whim in the place of God and thus staking his writing as a whole as having the power to turn aside the angel of death.) The point I emphasize here is only that the life-giving power of words, of saying "I," is your readiness to subject your desire to words (call it Whim), to become intelligible, with no assurance that you will be taken up. ("I hope it may be better than Whim at last, but we cannot spend the day in explanation.") Emerson's dedication is a fantasy of finding your own voice, even if that voice makes others angry, so that they, even some mothers and fathers, may shun you. This dedication enacts a posture toward, or response to, language as such, as if most men's words as a whole cried out for redemption: "Conformity makes them not false in a few particulars, authors of a few lies, but false in all particulars . . . so that every word they say chagrins us and we know not where to begin to set them right."

Citing authorship as the office of all users of language, a thing as commonly distributed as genius, is the plainest justification for seeing the enactment or acknowledgment of one's existence as the authoring of it and in particular for what we may take as Emerson's dominating claims for his writing: first, that it proves his human existence (i.e., establishes his right to say "I," to tell himself from and to others); second, that what he has proven on his behalf others are capable of proving on theirs.

These claims come together in such a statement as "I will stand for humanity," which we will recognize as marking a number of paths: that Emerson's writing is in an upright posture; that what it says represents the human, meaning that his portrait of himself is accurate only insofar as it portrays his fellows and that he is writing on their behalf (both as they stand, and as they stand for the eventual, what humanity may become); that he will for the time being stand humanity, bear it, as it is; and that he will stand up for it, protect it, guard it, presumably against itself. But to protect and guard someone by writing to and for that same one means to provide them instruction, or tuition.

The path I am not taking at this point leads from Emerson's speaking of "primary wisdom as Intuition," to which he adds, "All later teachings are tuitions." I note this path to commemorate my annoyance at having to stand the repeated, conforming description of Emerson as a philosopher of intuition, a description that uniformly fails to add that he is simultaneously the teacher of tuition, as though his speaking of all later teachings as tuitions were a devaluing of the teachings rather than a direction for deriving their necessary value. Take the calling of his genius as a name for intuition. Marking "Whim" on his doorpost was its tuition, an enactment of the obligation to remark it, to run the risk (or, as Thoreau puts it, to sit the risk) of noting what happens to you, of making it notable, remarkable, thinkable—of subjecting yourself, as said, to intelligibility.

How could we test the claim Emerson's writing makes to be such enactment, its claim to enact or acknowledge itself, to take on its existence, or, in Nietzsche's words, or rather Zarathustra's (which I imagine are more or less quoting Emerson's), to show that Emerson "does not say 'I' but performs 'I'"? (The mere complication of self-reference, of saying "I," the stock-in-trade of certain modernizers, may amount to nothing whatever beyond rumor of my existence.) How else but by letting the writing teach us how to test it, word by word?

"Self-Reliance" as a whole presents a theory—I wish we knew how to call it an aesthetics—of reading. Its opening words are "I read the other day," and four paragraphs before Emerson cites the cogito he remarks, "Our reading is mendicant and sycophantic," which is to say that he finds us reading the way he finds us doing everything else. How can we read his theory of reading in order to learn how to read him? We would already have to understand it in order to understand it. I have elsewhere called this the (apparent) paradox of reading; it might just as well be called the paradox of writing, since of writing meant with such ambitions we can say that only after it has done its work of creating a writer (which may amount to sloughing or shaking off voices) can one know what it is to write. But you never know. I mean, you never know when someone will learn the posture, as for themselves, that will make sense of a field of movement, it may be writing, or dancing, or passing a ball, or sitting at a keyboard, or free associating. So the sense of paradox expresses our not understanding how such learning happens. What we wish to learn here is nothing less than whether Emerson exists, hence could exist for us; whether, to begin with, his writing performs the cogito he preaches.

He explicitly claims that it does, as he must. But before noting that, let me pause a little longer before this new major path, or branching of paths: the essay's theory of reading, hence of writing or speaking, hence of seeing and hearing. The theory, not surprisingly, is a theory of communication, hence of expression, hence of character—character conceived, as Emerson always conceives it, as naming at once, as faces of one another, the human individual and human language. The writing side of the theory is epitomized in the remark: "Character teaches above our wills. Men imagine that they communicate their virtue or vice only by overt actions, and do not see that virtue or vice emit a breath every moment." The reading side of the theory is epitomized in: "To talk of reliance is a poor external way of speaking. Who has more obedience than I masters me, though he should not raise his finger."

On the reading side, the idea of mastering Emerson is not that of controlling him, exactly (though it will be related to monitoring him), but rather that of coming into command of him, as of a difficult text, or instrument, or practice. That this mastery happens by obedience, which is to say, by a mode of listening, relates the process to his dedicating of his writing as heeding the call of his genius, which to begin with he is able to note as Whim. It follows that mastering his text is a matter of discerning the whim from which it follows. On the writing side, the idea of communicating as emitting a breath every moment (as if a natural risk of writing were transmitting disease) means that with every word you utter you say more than you know you say (here genteel Emerson's idea is that you cannot smell your own breath), which means in part that you do not know in the moment the extent to which your saying is quoting.

(Let me attract attention to another untaken path here, on which one becomes exquisitely sensible of the causes of Nietzsche's love of Emerson's writing. I am thinking now of *Ecce Homo*, a book about writing that bears the subtitle *How One Becomes What One Is*. Its Preface opens with the declaration that the author finds it indispensable to say who he is because in his conversations with the educated he becomes convinced that he is not alive; the Preface continues by claiming or warning that to read him is to breathe a strong air. This book's opening part, "Why I Am So Wise," closes by saying that one of its author's traits that causes difficulty in his contacts with others is the uncanny sensitivity of his instinct for cleanliness: the innermost parts, the entrails, of every soul are *smelled* by him.)

So the question Emerson's theory of reading and writing is designed to answer is not "What does a text mean?" (and one may accordingly not wish to call it a theory of interpretation) but rather "How is it that a text we care about in a certain way (expressed perhaps as our being drawn to read it with the obedience that masters) invariably says more than its writer knows, so that writers and readers write and read beyond themselves?" This might be summarized as "What does a text know?," or, in Emerson's term, "What is the genius of the text?"

Here I note what strikes me as a congenial and fruitful conjunction with what I feel I have understood so far of the practices of Derrida and of Lacan. Others may find my conjunction with these practices uncongenial if, for example, they take it to imply that what I termed the genius of the text, perhaps I should say its engendering, is fatal to or incompatible with the idea of an author and of an author's intention. This incompatibility ought to seem unlikely since both genius and intending have to do with inclination, hence with caring about something and with posture. J. L. Austin, in a seminar discussion at Harvard in 1955, once compared the role of intending with the role of headlights on an automobile (he may have included the steering mechanism). An implication he may have had in mind is that driving somewhere (getting something done intentionally) does not on the whole happen by hanging a pair of headlights from your shoulders, sitting in an armchair, picking up an unattached steering wheel, and imagining a destination. (Though this is not unlike situations in which W. C. Fields has found himself.) Much else has to be in place—further mechanisms and systems (transmission, fuel, electrical), roads, the industries that produce and are produced by each, and so on—in order for headlights and a steering mechanism to do their work, even to be what they are. Even if some theorists speak as though intention were everything there is to meaning, is that a sensible reason for opposite theorists to assert that intention is nothing, counts for nothing in meaning? Is W. C. Fields our only alternative to Humpty Dumpty? *

But I was about to locate Emerson's explicit statement, or performance, of his cogito. In his eighth paragraph he writes: "Few and mean as my gifts may be, I actually am, and do not need for my own assurance or the assurance of my fellows any secondary testimony." Earlier in the paragraph he had said: "My life is for itself and not for a spectacle. . . . I ask primary evidence that you are a man, and refuse this appeal from the man to his actions." And two paragraphs later he will promise: "But do your work, and I shall know you."

In refusing the evidence of actions, or say behavior, Emerson is refusing, as it were before the fact, the thrashing of empiricist philosophy to prove the existence of other minds by analogy with one's own case, which essentially involves an appeal to others' behavior (and its similarity to our own) as all we can know of them with certainty. But how does Emerson evade and counter the picture on which such a philosophical drift repeatedly comes to grief, namely the picture according to which we cannot literally or directly have the experiences of others, cannot have what he apparently calls "primary evidence" of their existence? Emerson's counter is contained in the idea of what I called his promise: "But do your work, and I shall know you." Your work, what it is yours to do, is exemplified, when confronted with Emerson's words, by reading those words—which means mastering them, obeying and hence following them, subjecting yourself to them as the writer has by undertaking to enact his existence in saying them. The test of following them is, according to Emerson's promise, that you will find yourself known by them, that you will take yourself on in them. It is what Thoreau calls conviction, calls being convicted by his words, read by them, sentenced. To acknowledge that I am known by what this text knows does not amount to agreeing with it, in the sense of believing it, as if it were a bunch of assertions or contained a doctrine.

---

* In linking W. C. Fields's suffering of convention with Humpty Dumpty's claim to be master, by his very wishes, of what words shall mean, I find I have not forgotten a passage during the discussion of "Must We Mean What We Say?" the day I delivered it in 1957 (at Stanford, it happens). Against a certain claim in my paper, one philosopher cited Humpty Dumpty's view of meaning (by name) as obviously, in all solemnity, the correct one. This was, I think, the first time I realized the possibility that parody is no longer a distinguishable intellectual tone since nothing can any longer be counted on to strike us in common as outrageous.

To be known by it is to find thinking in it. That would prove that a human existence is authored in it. But how will you prove thinking? How will you show your conviction?

One possibility Emerson presents as follows: "The virtue in most request is conformity. Self-reliance is its aversion." This almost says, and nearly means, that you find your existence in conversion, by converting to it, that thinking is a kind of turning oneself around. But what it directly says is that the world of conformity must turn from what Emerson says as he must turn from it and that since the process is never over while we live—since, that is, we are never finally free of one another—his reader's life with him will be a turning from, and returning from, his words, a moving on from them, by them. In "Fate," Emerson will call this aversion "antagonism": "Man is a stupendous antagonism," he says there. I can testify that when you stop struggling with Emerson's words they become insupportable.

But why does self-reliance insist that it will know its other, even create its other, meaning authorize the other's self-authorization, or auto-creation? Because it turns out that to gain the assurance, as Descartes had put it, that I am not alone in the world has turned out to require that I allow myself to be known. (I have called this subjecting myself to intelligibility, or, say, legibility.) But doesn't this beg the question whether there *are* others there to do this knowing?

I would say rather that it orders the question. The fantasy of aloneness in the world may be read as saying that the step out of aloneness, or self-absorption, has to come without the assurance of others. (Not, perhaps, without their help.) "No one comes" is a tragedy for a child. For a grown-up it means the time has come to be the one who goes first. To this way of thinking, politics ought to have provided conditions for companionship, call it fraternity; but the price of this companionship has been the suppression, not the affirmation, of otherness, that is to say, of difference and sameness, call these liberty and equality. A mission of Emerson's thinking is never to let politics forget this.

In declaring that his life is not for a spectacle but for itself, Emerson is not denying that it is a spectacle, and he thus inflects and recrosses his running themes of being seen, of shame, and of consciousness. A last citation on this subject initially will join "Self-Reliance" with Poe's "Imp of the Perverse."

In his fifth paragraph, Emerson says: "The man is as it were clapped into jail by his consciousness. As soon as he has once acted or spoken with *éclat* he is a committed person, watched by the sympathy or the hatred of hundreds, whose affections must now enter into his account. There is no Lethe for this." The idea is that we have become permanently and unforgettably visible to one another, in a state of perpetual theater. To turn aside consciousness, supposing that were possible, would accordingly only serve to distract us from this fact of our mutual confinement under one another's guard. The solution must then be to alter what it is we show, which requires turning even more watchfully to what it is we are conscious of and altering our posture toward it.

For example: "A man should learn to detect and watch that gleam of light which flashes across his mind from within, more than the lustre of the firmament of bards and sages. Yet he dismisses without notice his own thought, because it is his. In every work of genius we recognize our own rejected thoughts; they come back to us with a certain alienated majesty." Here I find a specification of finding myself known in this text; in it certain rejected thoughts of mine do seem to come back with what I am prepared to call alienated majesty (including the thought itself of my rejected thoughts). Then presumably this writer has managed not to dismiss his own thoughts but to call them together, to keep them on parade, at attention.

Yet he speaks from the condition of being a grown-up within the circumstances of civil (or uncivil) obedience he describes, so he says all he says clapped into jail by his consciousness—a decade before Thoreau was clapped into jail, and for the same reason, for obeying the wrong thing. How is he released? If, going on with Emerson's words, there were Lethe for our bondage to the attention of others, to their sympathy or hatred, we would utter opinions that would be "seen to be not private but necessary, would sink like darts into the ear of men and put them in fear"—that is, my visibility would then frighten my watchers, not the other way around, and my privacy would no longer represent confinement but instead the conditions necessary for freedom. But as long as these conditions are not known to be achieved, the writer cannot know that I am known in his utterances, hence that he and I have each assumed our separate existences. So he cannot know but that in taking assurance from the promise of knowing my existence he is only assuming my existence and his role in its affirmation, hence perhaps shifting the burden of proof from himself and still awaiting me to release him from his jail of consciousness, the consciousness of the consciousness of others. When is writing *done*?

That "Self-Reliance" may accordingly be understood to show writing as a message from prison forms its inner connection with Poe's "Imp of the Perverse." (The thought of such a message of course forms other connections as well—for example, with Rousseau's *Social Contract*, whose early line, "Man is born free and everywhere he is in chains" names a condition from which the writer cannot be exempting his writing, especially if his interpretation of his writing's enchainment is to afford a step toward the freedom it is compelled, by its intuition of chains, to imagine.) I can hardly do more here than give some directions for how I think Poe's tale should, or anyway can, be read. This is just as well because the validation of the reading requires from first to last that one take the time to try the claims on oneself. The claims have generally to do with the sound of Poe's prose, with what Emerson and Nietzsche would call its air or its smell. Poe's tale is essentially about the breath it gives off.

The sound of Poe's prose, of its incessant and perverse brilliance, is uncannily like the sound of philosophy as established in Descartes, as if Poe's prose were a parody of philosophy's. It strikes me that in Poe's tales the thought is being worked out that, now anyway, philosophy exists only as a parody of philosophy, or rather as something indistinguishable from the perversion of philosophy, as if to overthrow the reign of reason, the reason philosophy was born to establish, is not alone the task of, let us say, poetry but is now openly the genius or mission of philosophy itself. As if the task of disestablishing reason were the task of reconceiving it, of exacting a transformation or reversal of what we think of as thinking and so of what we think of as establishing the reign of thinking. A natural effect of reading such writing is to be unsure whether the writer is perfectly serious. I dare say that the writer may himself or herself be unsure, and that this may be a good sign that the writing is doing its work, taking its course. Then Poe's peculiar brilliance is to have discovered a sound, or the condition, of intelligence in which neither the reader nor the writer knows whether he or she is philosophizing, is thinking to some end. This is an insight, a philosophical insight, about philosophy: namely, that it is as difficult to stop philosophizing as it is to start. (As difficult, in Wittgenstein's words, as to bring philosophy peace. Most people I know who care about philosophy either do not see this as a philosophical problem or do not believe that it has a solution.)

A convenient way of establishing the sound of Poe's Tales is to juxtapose the opening sentence of "The Black Cat" with some early sentences from Descartes's *Meditations*. Here is Descartes:

> There is no novelty to me in the reflection that, from my earliest years, I have accepted many false opinions as true, and that what I have concluded from such badly assured premises could not but be highly doubtful and uncertain. . . . I have found a serene retreat in peaceful solitude. I will therefore make a serious and unimpeded effort to destroy generally all my former opinions. . . . Everything which I have thus far accepted as entirely true and assured has been acquired from the senses or by means of the senses. But I have learned by experience that these senses sometimes mislead me, and it is prudent never to trust wholly those things which have once deceived us. . . . But it is possible that, even though the senses occasionally deceive us . . . there are many other things which we cannot reasonably doubt . . . —as, for example, that I am here, seated by the fire, wearing a winter dressing gown, holding this paper in my hands, and other things of this nature. And how could I deny that these hands and this body are mine, unless I am to compare myself with certain lunatics . . . [who] imagine that their head is made of clay, or that they are gourds, or that their body is glass? . . . Nevertheless, I must remember that I am a man, and that consequently I am accustomed to sleep and in my dreams to imagine the same things that lunatics imagine when awake. . . . I realize so clearly that there are no conclusive indications by which waking life can be distinguished from sleep that I am quite astonished, and my bewilderment is such that it is almost able to convince me that I am sleeping.

Now listen to Poe:

> For the most wild, yet almost homely narrative which I am about to pen, I neither expect nor solicit belief. Mad indeed would I be to expect it, in a case where my very senses reject their own evidence. Yet, mad am I not—and very surely do I not dream. But to-morrow I die, and today I would unburthen my soul. My immediate purpose is to place before the world, plainly, succinctly, and without comment, a series of mere household events. In their consequences, these events have terrified—have tortured—have destroyed me. Yet I will not attempt to expound them.[4]

The juxtaposition works both ways: to bring out at once Poe's brilliance (and what is more, his argumentative soundness) and

Descartes's creepy, perverse calm (given the subjects his light of reason rakes across), his air of a mad diarist.

Moreover, the *Meditations* appear within the content of "The Imp of the Perverse," as indelibly, to my mind, as in "Self-Reliance." Before noting how, let me briefly describe this lesser-known tale. It is divided into two parts, each more or less eight paragraphs in length. The first half is, as Poe said about certain of Hawthorne's tales, not a tale at all but an essay. The essay argues for the existence of perverseness as a radical, primitive, irreducible faculty or sentiment of the soul, the propensity to do wrong for the wrong's sake, promptings to act for the reason that we should not—something it finds overlooked by phrenologists, moralists, and in great measure "all metaphysicianism," through "the pure arrogance of the reason." This phrase "the pure arrogance of the reason," to my ear, signals that Poe is writing a *Critique* of the arrogance of pure reason— as if the task, even after Kant, were essentially incomplete, even unbegun. (This characterization is not incompatible with the appreciation of Poe as a psychologist, only with a certain idea of what psychology may be.) The second half of "The Imp of the Perverse," which tells the tale proper, begins:

> I have said thus much, that in some measure I may answer your question—that I may explain to you why I am here—that I may assign to you something that shall have at least the faint aspect of a cause for my wearing these fetters, and for my tenanting this cell of the condemned. Had I not been thus prolix, you might either have misunderstood me altogether, or, with the rabble, have fancied me mad. As it is, you will easily perceive that I am one of the many uncounted victims of the Imp of the Perverse.

Since we have not been depicted as asking, or having, a question, the narrator's explanation insinuates that we ought to have one about his presence; thus it raises more questions than it formulates.

The tale turns out to be a Poe-ish matter about the deliberately wrought murder of someone for the apparent motive of inheriting his estate, a deed that goes undetected until some years later the writer perversely gives himself away. As for the means of the murder: "I knew my victim's habit of reading in bed. . . . I substituted, in his bed-room candlestand, a [poisoned] wax-light of my own making, for the one which I there found." The self-betrayal comes about when, as he puts it, "I arrested myself in the act." That act is murmuring, half-aloud, "I am safe," and then adding, "yes, if I be not fool enough to make open confession." But "I felt a maddening

297

desire to shriek aloud. . . . Alas! I well, too well understand that, to *think*, in my situation, was to be lost. . . . I bounded like a madman through the crowded thoroughfare. At length, the populace took the alarm, and pursued me."

To the first of my directions for reading "The Imp" I expect nowadays little resistance: both the fiction of the writer's arresting himself and wearing fetters and tenanting the cell of the condemned and the fiction of providing a poisonous wax light for reading are descriptions or fantasies of writing, modeled by the writing before us. There is, or at least we need imagine, no actual imprisoning and no crime but the act of the writing itself. What does it mean to fantasize that words are fetters and cells and that to read them, to be awake to their meaning, or effect, is to be poisoned? Are we being told that writer and reader are one another's victims? Or is the suggestion that to arrive at the truth something in the reader as well as something in the writer must die? Does writing ward off or invite in the angel of death?

I expect more resistance to, or puzzlement at, the further proposal that the fiction of words that are in themselves unremarkable ("I am safe") but whose saying annihilates the sayer specifies the claim that "I well, too well understood that, to *think*, in my situation was to be lost"—which is a kind of negation or perversion of the cogito. Rather than proving and preserving me, as in Descartes, thinking precipitates my destruction. A little earlier Poe's narrator makes this even clearer: "There is no passion in nature so demoniacally impatient, as that of him, who shuddering on the edge of a precipice, thus meditates a plunge. To indulge for a moment, in any attempt at *thought*, is to be inevitably lost; for reflection but urges us to forbear, and *therefore* it is, I say, that we *cannot* . . . we plunge, and are destroyed." If the Whim drawing on Emerson's "Self-Reliance" is to say "I do not think, therefore I do not exist," that of Poe's Imp is to say, "I think, therefore I am destroyed." This connection is reinforced, in this brief passage, by the words "meditates" and "demoniacally." Poe's undetected, poisoned wax light may even substitute for, or allude to, Descartes's most famous example (of materiality) in the *Meditations*, the piece of melting wax whose identity cannot be determined empirically, but only by an innate conception in the understanding. (That in Poe's tale the act of thinking destroys by alarming the populace and turning them against the thinker and that perverseness is noted as the confessing of a crime, not the committing of it—as if the confessing and the committing were figurations of one another—mark paths of parody and perverseness I cannot trace here. That thinking will out, that it inherently betrays the thinker—(th)inker—is a grounding theme of *Walden*. Its writer declares that what he prints must in each character "thus unblushingly publish my guilt." He says this upon listing the costs of what he ate for the year. It is as if his guilt consists exactly in his existing, as he exists, and his preserving himself, for example by writing.)

My third suggestion for reading Poe's tale is that the presiding image collecting the ideas I have cited and setting them in play is given in its title. The title names and illustrates a common fact about language, even invokes what one might think of as an Emersonian theory of language: the possession of language as the subjection of oneself to the intelligible. The fact of language it illustrates is registered in the series of imp words that pop up throughout the sixteen paragraphs of the tale: "impulse" (several times), "impels" (several times), "impatient" (twice), "important," "impertinent," "imperceptible," "impossible," "unimpressive," "imprisoned," and, of course, "Imp." Moreover, "imp." is an abbreviation in English for "imperative," "imperfect," "imperial," "import," "imprimatur," "impersonal," "implement," "improper," and "improvement." And "Imp." is an abbreviation for "Emperor" and "Empress." Now if to speak of the imp of the perverse is to name the imp in English, namely as the initial sounds of a number of characteristically Poeish terms, then to speak of something called the perverse as containing this imp is to speak of language itself, specifically of English, as the perverse. But what is it about the imp of English that is perverse, hence presumably helps to produce, as users of language, us imps?

It may well be the prefix "im-" that is initially felt to be perverse, since, like the prefix "in-," it has opposite meanings. With adjectives it is a negation or privative, as in "immediate," "immaculate," "imperfect," "imprecise," "improper," "implacable," "impious," "impecunious"; with verbs it is an affirmation or intensive, as in "imprison," "impinge," "imbue," "implant," "impulse," "implicate," "impersonate." (It is not impossible that "per-verse," applied to language, should be followed out as meaning poetic through and through.) In plain air we keep the privative and the intensive well enough apart, but in certain circumstances (say in

dreams, in which, according to Freud, logical operations like negation cannot be registered or pictured but must be supplied later
by the dreamer's interpretation) we might grow confused about
whether, for example, "immuring" means putting something into
a wall or letting something out of one, or whether "impotence"
means powerlessness or a special power directed to something special, or whether "implanting" is the giving or the removing of life,
or whether "impersonate" means putting on another personality or
being without personhood.

But the fact or the idea of imp words is not a function of just
that sequence of three letters. "Word imps" could name any of the
recurrent combinations of letters of which the words of a language
are composed. They are part of the way words have their familiar
looks and sounds, and their familiarity depends upon our mostly
not noticing the particles (or cells) and their laws, which constitute
words and their imps—on our not noticing their necessary recur-
rences, which is perhaps only to say that recurrence constitutes familiarity. This necessity, the most familiar property of language
there could be—that if there is to be language, words and their cells
must recur, as if fettered in their orbits, that language is grammatical (to say the least)—insures the self-referentiality of language. When we do note these cells or molecules, these little moles
of language (perhaps in thinking, perhaps in derangement), what we
discover are word imps—the initial, or it may be medial or final,
movements, the implanted origins or constituents of words, leading lives of their own, staring back at us, calling upon one another,
giving us away, alarming—because to note them is to see that they
live in front of our eyes, within earshot, at every moment.

But the perverseness of language, working without, even against,
our thought and its autonomy, is a function not just of necessarily
recurring imps of words but of the necessity for us speakers of language (us authors of it, or imps, or Emperors and Empresses of it) to
mean something in and by our words, to desire to say something,
certain things rather than others, in certain ways rather than in
others, or else to work to avoid meaning them. Call these necessities the impulses and the implications of the saying of our words.
There is—as in saying "I am safe," which destroyed safety and de-
feats what is said—a question whether in speaking one is affirming
something or negating it. In particular, in such writing as Poe's has
the impulse to self-destruction, to giving oneself away or betraying

oneself, become the only way of preserving the individual? And does it succeed? Is authoring the obliteration or the apotheosis of the writer?

In the passage I cited earlier from "The Black Cat," the writer does not speak of being in fetters and in a cell, but he does name his activity as penning; since the activity at hand is autobiography, he is penning himself. Is this release or incarceration? He enforces the question by going on to say that he will not expound—that is, will not remove something (presumably himself) from a pound, or pen. But this may mean that he awaits expounding by the reader. Would this be shifting the burden of his existence onto some other? And who might we be to bear such a burden? Mustn't we also seek to shift it? Granted that we need one another's acknowledgment, isn't there in this very necessity a mutual victimization, one that our powers of mutual redemption cannot overcome? Is this undecidable? Or is deciding this question exactly as urgent as deciding to exist?

I will draw to a close by forming three questions invited by the texts I have put together.

First, what does it betoken about the relation of philosophy and literature that a piece of writing can be seen to consist of what is for all the world a philosophical essay preceding, even turning into, a fictional tale—as it happens, a fictional confession from a prison cell? To answer this would require a meditation on the paragraph, cited earlier, in which Poe pivots from the essay to the tale, insinuating that we are failing to ask a question about the origin of the writing and claiming that without the philosophical preface—which means without the hinging of essay and tale, philosophy and fiction—the reader might, "with the rabble, have fancied me mad," not perceiving that he is "one of the many uncounted victims of the Imp of the Perverse." The meditation would thus enter, or center, on the idea of counting, and it is one I have in fact undertaken, under somewhat different circumstances, as Part I of *The Claim of Reason.* There I interpret Wittgenstein's *Philosophical Investigations,* or its guiding idea of a criterion, hence of grammar, as providing in its responsiveness to skepticism the means by which the concepts of our language are *of* anything, as showing what it means to have concepts, how it is that we are able to word the world together. The idea of a criterion I emphasize is that of a way of count-

ing something as something, and I put this together with accounting and recounting, hence projecting a connection between telling
as numbering or computing and telling as relating or narrating.
Poe's (or, if you insist, Poe's narrator's) speaking pivotally of being an
uncounted victim accordingly suggests to me that philosophy and
literature have come together (for him, but who is he?) at the need
for recounting, for counting again, and first at counting the human
beings there are, for reconceiving them—a recounting beginning
from the circumstance that it is I, some I or other, who counts, who
is able to do the thing of counting, of conceiving a world, that it is
I who, taking others into account, establish criteria for what is
worth saying, hence for the intelligible. But this is only on the condition that I count, that I matter, that it matters that I count in my
agreement or attunement with those with whom I maintain my
language, from whom this inheritance—language as the condition
of counting—comes, so that it matters not only what some I or
other says but that it is some particular I who desires in some specific place to say it. If my counting fails to matter, I am mad. It is
being uncounted—being left out, as if my story were untellable—
that makes what I say (seem) perverse, that makes me odd. The surmise that we have become unable to count one another, to count
for one another, is philosophically a surmise that we have lost the
capacity to think, that we are stupefied.* I call this condition living
our skepticism.

Second, what does it betoken about fact and fiction that Poe's
writing of the Imp simultaneously tells two tales of imprisonment—in one of which he is absent, in the other present—as if
they were fables of one another? Can we know whether one is the
more fundamental? Here is the relevance I see in Poe's tale's invoking the situation of Hamlet, the figure of our culture who most
famously enacts a question of undecidability, in particular, an undecidability over the question whether to believe a tale of poison-
ing. (By the way, Hamlet at the end, like his father's ghost at the
beginning, claims to have a tale that is untellable—it is what makes
both of them ghosts.) In Poe's tale, the invocation of *Hamlet* is
heard, for example, in the two appearances of a ghost, who the first

*I find it hard not to imagine that this surmise has to do with the history of the
frantic collection of statistical tables mentioned in Ian Hacking's paper in this volume, because Emerson's essay "Fate" self-consciously invokes the new science of
statistics as a new image of human fate—a new way in which others are finding us
captured by knowledge and which Emerson finds a further occasion for ignorance.

time disappears upon the crowing of a cock. And it is fully marked in the second of the three philosophical examples of perversity that Poe's narrator offers in order to convince any reader, in his words, "who trustingly consults and thoroughly questions his own soul" of "the entire radicalness of the propensity in question":

> The most important crisis of our life calls, trumpet-tongued, for immediate energy and action. We glow, we are consumed with eagerness to commence the work. . . . It must, it shall be undertaken today, and yet we put it off until to-morrow; and why? There is no answer, except that we feel *perverse*, using the word with no comprehension of the principle. To-morrow arrives, and with it a more impatient anxiety to do our duty, but with this very increase of anxiety arrives, also, a nameless, a positively fearful because unfathomable, craving for delay.

These words invoke Hamlet along lines suspiciously like those in which I had recently been thinking about what I call Hamlet's burden of proof—but no more suspiciously, surely, than my beginning to study Poe while thinking about Hamlet.

Hamlet studies the impulse to take revenge, usurping thought as a response to being asked to assume the burden of another's existence, as if that were the burden, or price, of assuming one's own, a burden that denies one's own. Hamlet is asked to make a father's life work out successfully, to come out even, by taking his revenge for him. The emphasis in the question "To be or not" seems not on whether to die but on whether to be born, on whether to affirm or deny the fact of natality, as a way of enacting, or not, one's existence. To accept birth is to participate in a world of revenge, of mutual victimization, of shifting and substitution. But to refuse to partake in it is to poison everyone who touches you, as if taking your own revenge. This is why if the choice is unacceptable the cause is not metaphysics but history—say, a posture toward the discovery that there is no getting even for the oddity of being born, hence of being and becoming the one poor creature it is given to you to be. The alternative to affirming this condition is, as Descartes's *Meditations* shows, world-consuming doubt, which is hence a standing threat to, or say condition of, human existence. (I imagine that the appearance of the cogito at its historical moment is a sign that some conditions were becoming ones for which getting even, or anyway overcoming, was coming to seem in order: for example, the belief in God and the rule of kings.) That there is something like a choice or decision about our natality is what I take Freud's idea of the diphasic structure of human sexual development to show—a provision of, so to speak, the condition of the possibility of such a decision. The condition is that of adolescence, considered as the period in which, in preparation for becoming adult, one recapitulates, as suffering re-birth, one's knowledge of satisfactions. This is why, it seems to me, one speculates about Hamlet's age but thinks of him as adolescent. These matters are represented in political thought under the heading of consent, about which, understandably, there has from the outset been a question of proof.

Finally, what does it betoken about American philosophy that Emerson and Poe may be seen as taking upon themselves the problematic of the cogito (Emerson by denying or negating it, Poe by perverting or subverting it) and as sharing the perception that authoring—philosophical writing, anyway, writing as thinking—is such that to exist it must assume, or acknowledge, the proof of its own existence? I have in effect said that to my mind this betokens their claim to be discovering or rediscovering the origin of modern philosophy, as sketched in Descartes's *Meditations*, as if literature in America were forgiving philosophy, not without punishing it, for having thought that it could live only in the banishing of literature. What does it mean that such apparent opposites as Emerson and Poe enter such a claim within half a dozen years of one another?

Let us ask what the connection is between Emerson's ecstasies (together with Thoreau's) and Poe's horrors (together with Hawthorne's). The connection must be some function of the fact that Poe's and Hawthorne's worlds, or houses and rooms, have other people in them, typically marriages, and typically show these people's violent shunning, whereas Emerson's and Thoreau's worlds begin with or after the shunning of others ("I shun father and mother and wife and brother when my genius calls me") and typically depict the "I" just beside itself. The interest of the connection is that all undertake to imagine domestication, or inhabitation—as well, being Americans, they might. For Emerson and Thoreau you must learn to sit at home or to sit still in some attractive spot in the woods, as if to marry the world, before, if ever, you take on the burden of others; for Poe and Hawthorne even America came too late, or perhaps too close, for that priority.

A more particular interest I have in the connection among these American writers is a function of taking their concepts or portrayals of domestication and inhabitation (with their air of ecstasy and of horror turned just out of sight) to be developments called for by the concepts of the ordinary and the everyday as these enter into the ordinary-language philosopher's undertaking to turn aside skepticism, in the pains Austin and Wittgenstein take to lay out what it is that skepticism threatens. In the work of these philosophers, in their stubborn, accurate superficiality, perhaps for the first time in recognizable philosophy this threat of world-consuming doubt is interpreted in all its uncanny homeliness, not merely in isolated examples but, in Poe's words, as "a series of mere household events."

I end with the following prospect. If some image of marriage, as an interpretation of domestication, in these writers is the fictional equivalent of what these philosophers understand to be the ordinary, or the everyday, then the threat to the ordinary named skepticism should show up in fiction's favorite threat to forms of marriage, namely, in forms of melodrama. Accordingly, melodrama may be seen as an interpretation of Descartes's cogito, and, contrariwise, the cogito can be seen as an interpretation of the advent of melodrama—of the moment (private and public) at which the theatricalization of the self becomes the sole proof of its freedom and its existence. This is said on tiptoe.

POSTSCRIPT

During the discussion period at Stanford, Professor David Wellbery asked about how I conceive the relation of what I have been doing over the years to what deconstructionists have been doing. It is not the first time I have been asked something like this question. Indeed the issue first arose in 1969, in the months after the publication of my *Must We Mean What We Say?*, when a friend who had spent a decade and more of sabbatical leaves and summer vacations in Germany and France studying philosophy announced that what I wrote bore surprising and specific resemblances to the writing of Jacques Derrida, a name that I was hearing for the first time. Mostly, I guess, I feel that to locate and trace out these resemblances, along with their companion disparities, is not my business, that if this work of contrast has profit in it, others are better placed to realize it than I. But Professor Wellbery's full and detailed question was so courteous, and so clear and specific, that I have recalled it several times in the months since the conference, each time with regret at how little I was able to say in

response. I take the occasion of these printed proceedings to acknowledge that fact and to give at least a better account of the poverty of my answer.

Careful not to deny the immeasurable, perhaps incommensurable, distance of provenance and style between such work as
Derrida's and such work as my present essay, Wellbery noted certain affinities between them: for example, in turning philosophy
upon philosophy, especially by refusing to favor the philosophical
or the literary over one another, in content or in form; in attending
to the endlessness of language's responsiveness to (even origin in)
language, a responsiveness pervading bits and pieces of words; and,
not least, in my having found my way to Poe, whom Wellbery
informed me Derrida has also taken up with philosophical respect.
In the light of these and other affinities, Wellbery asked about my
impatience with the idea of the "undecidable" at several points in
my paper. If impatience is what it was, it was directed not toward
Derrida but toward a conjunction of writings by those who adopt
his terms and whose papers and chapters I characteristically find
myself unable to finish. I am not proud of this, any more than of
how difficult I find it to study Derrida. It perfects my bafflement
that those who follow him seem to find what he writes *easy* to follow and summarize and assess. I feel subjected to a family discussion, not mine, yet mine, impertinent and pertinent (as Thoreau
almost characterizes his neighbors at the opening of *Walden*), the
prevailing issues of which, too many of the voices of which, are not
among the rumors of my past, not up to me to turn; someone is
refusing, and someone is getting, satisfactions that I am not alive
to. This certainty alone is apt to make one impatient, to make one
look for an exit. At the conference I responded by saying that the
deconstructionist use of the term "undecidable," so far as I have encountered it, tends to sound like a soft literary pretension to hard
philosophy, to be invoking Gödel's world-historical proof of un-
provability only to (mis)describe issues concerning discontinuities
or undercontinuities between grammar and rhetoric, or supercon-
tinuities between narrations of fact and of fiction, or of reality and
of dreams. ("The coffee is hot" may be an observation, a hint, a
request, an explanation, an excuse, a warning—or hallucinated.)
So what?

This kind of objection—to the soft putting on hard clothing—
might play itself out otherwise in terms of differences between

what I say about Emerson's accusation of quotation and what I know, or must guess, of deconstructionist accounts of the matter. This is for another occasion, perhaps. But the issue, if I understand, promises to be a pretty one. It turns on a shared sense of the fatefulness of the fact that language is inherited, learned, always already there for every human. This sense can prompt divergent responses or emphases. One (I take it the deconstructionist emphasis) will see the fact of inheritance as undermining the distinction between quoted words and their originals: since all words are learned, you may say all are imitated or quoted; but then none are quoted, since there are no originals for them to contrast with. The other emphasis (represented by Wittgenstein, but also, I take it, by Emerson and Thoreau) will not wish to deny the truth in the first emphasis, but it will see that emphasis as deflecting attention, as rushing too quickly away, from the act or encounter entailed in the historical and individual process of inheriting. This second, practical emphasis falls not on the acquisition of the grammar or structure of a language but on the scene of instruction in words. The *Philosophical Investigations* opens with a (quoted) scene of instruction from Augustine's *Confessions*, and the ensuing 693 sections constituting Part I of the *Investigations* can be understood as following out implications of that scene. The scene is explicitly, repeatedly invoked with each recurrence in the *Investigations* of the figure of the child. I sometimes find this figure to represent the most distinctive of all Wittgenstein's departures in philosophy. Something the recurring figure means to me is that the inheritance of language is essentially never over and done with—though any number of accidents, or say fixations, inner or outer, may put an end to it. The play of the literary is one field on which the contest of inheritance is shown to be continued, or continuable, within each breast, each text; the play of philosophy, as in the humor or frivolity of Austin and of Wittgenstein, is another—as if inheriting language itself is formed of the willingness for play, and continues as long as that willingness continues. (It is an essential piece of the inheritance I seek of Wittgenstein and Austin.) By contrast, the play in deconstructionist flights more often feels, to my ear or for my taste, somewhat forced, willful, as if in reaction to a picture of a completed inheritance, as if to undo its trauma. (A comparatively unforced text, perhaps, to work with here is Derrida's marvelously interesting "Coming into One's Own," which contains a study of the

"Fort/Da" scene in the second section of Freud's *Beyond the Pleasure Principle*, another scene of instruction, inheritance of language, and a game.[5])

When Emerson notices, in "Self-Reliance," that "every word they say chagrins us," he is responding to the sound of quotation, imitation, repetition (conformity, confinement, etc.), but for him this sound sets a task of practice, not (merely) a routine for metaphysics—rather, it criticizes metaphysics not as a necessary defeat of thought but as a historical defeat of practice. (This sounds familiar. But Emerson may call undefeated practice, as he calls undefeated thought, "abandonment," which should not sound familiar; it combines bereavement and ecstasy.) And when Wittgenstein finds the task of philosophy to be the bringing of our words back to (everyday) life, he in effect discerns two grades of quotation, imitation, repetition. In one we imitatively declare our uniqueness (the theme of skepticism); in the other, we originally declare our commonness (the theme of acknowledgment). (Individuality, always to be found, is always at the risk of loss.) What you might call philosophy can be in service of either possibility; hence philosophy is never at peace with itself. Too often deconstructive procedures (like analytical procedures) seem to me readily used to bring philosophy a false peace, which may well present itself in the form of bustling activity.

This sense of philosophy's opposite possibilities is, at any rate, why I am drawn (and take the likes of Emerson and Wittgenstein to be drawn) not to undermine but to underline such distinctions as that between quoting and saying. I can imagine that this might be said of deconstruction too. Then style and its obligations become the issue—what I might call the address of language, or the assumption of it, perhaps the stake in it. I have most consecutively followed the consequences of (something like) the distinction between saying and quoting in my *The Senses of Walden*, which can as a whole be taken as a meditation on Thoreau's distinction between what he calls the mother tongue and the father tongue. (This is something like the distinction between speaking and writing. In *The Claim of Reason* it is at one point registered as the difference between what I call the first and the second inheritance of language [p. 189]. By the fourth and last part of that book the pressure of this question takes precedence of the presiding theme of the earlier parts, which is, within the first inheritance, how and when one speaks inside and outside language games.) Because the mother and the father are not two tongues but name two addresses to or assumptions of or stakes in whatever language we have, and because the father tongue is said by Thoreau to be a "reserved and select expression," which is the "maturity and experience" of the mother, it follows that the father tongue is both later and at the same time more original than the mother tongue. Accordingly there is a locale in which quotation becomes more original than its original. Does this deconstruct the distinction between words as quoted and as originally said? It seems to me (rather?) to invite the question whether words such as "quotation" and "original" are being used in the mother or in the father tongue; hence of course to invite the further question whether the differences of the mother and the father (in us) are to be erased or erected.

Go back to my sense of literary softness posing as philosophical hardness. We may postpone the question whether that distinction is itself soft or hard by taking particular cases. What harm would be done if someone wished to characterize the shifting duck-rabbit as undecidably a duck or else a rabbit? This might be harmless, even charming, so long as it did not rule out wishing (with straightforward accuracy) to describe the same figure as *decidably* a duck or else a rabbit. But unless the concept rules something out, what is the point of applying it? What harm if one wished, taking an even colder cliché, to characterize Duchamp's exhibited urinal, entitled "Fountain," as undecidably a work of art or else not a work of art? Although this might do less harm than the arguments Duchamp's nasty brilliance has so far inspired, it might do worse harm, since it would instill the thought that the idolized urinal is decidably art or the reverse. (I do not claim that this is impossible for some minds to think, but I expect they will be ones who would like to decide whether others are human or not.) But isn't the characterization "undecidable" at minimum a helpful antidote to the philosophical craving for essence? Now I wish to take on Wittgenstein's suggestion that "Essence is expressed by grammar" (*Investigations*, section 371), that in other words the philosophical craving for essence has been not so much directed to the wrong goal (seeing an explanation to its end somewhere) as wrongly addressing the goal (seeing the somewhere all explanations end).

Where, then, in a constellation of duplicitous objects and layered intentions shall we locate Poe's "Imp of the Perverse"? In my paper I said that the two readings, one focusing on the narrator, the other on the writer, are not on a par: the fictional prisoner is unmistakable, the actual writer is not; the narrator of this story may not exist apart from this story, but the writer must. So what sense is there in saying that there is duplicity here at all? In what sense are there two prisoners, two poisonings, two confessions, two disappearances? If we say that one is an allegory of the other, would that constitute an answer? Would it repudiate the question? I imagine someone might wish to say that the difference between one and two is undecidable. You might as well tell me that the existence of marriage is undecidable (on roughly the same ground, that it is undecidable whether two have become one). I would not wish to deny the conclusion, but I would feel that you are theorizing in the wrong place. And how can I, as a reader of the writer of *Walden*, remembering him describing himself as "caged in the woods"—which is to say, as penned in America—take the view that whether this is fiction or fact, allegory or event, is undecidable? Such a claim seems to me the place of what there is to decide. If it is allegory then he (who?) *is* penned; that is, he is whatever (else) his being caged allegorizes. Here I must come to a decision about what this makes me. A visitor or spectator? His keeper? Is he my adornment? Who domesticated him? Can I threaten to let him loose? Upon whom? What is his difference from me?

I use the doubleness of the Poe stories, as interpreting the structure of skepticism, to ask, to begin, investigations: of the extent to which writing as telling allegorizes our apparent fate of projecting ourselves as fictions, of appealing to others by theatricalizing ourselves, so that I can never be satisfied that their response is to *me* (Poe's world has advanced beyond Descartes's in having to consider that the author of myself and the narrator of myself may no longer be different persons, if still different selves); hence of the extent to which the resulting dissatisfaction may be a function, or price, of the satisfaction of projecting imaginary characters as real; and finally of what writing as penning is, what there is in it that can be represented as imprisonment, as deserving confinement, even as accepting it (perhaps all too easily).

I end this postscript by relating its issues more generally to the work my paper is intended to extend.

Whether when you say "I'll see you at home" you mean your words as a prediction, an agreement, a promise, an aspiration, or a decision is not a matter for decision, but a matter of the responsibility you bear—or take, or find, or disclaim—for your words. To call the matter undecidable may be just a way of affirming that the words "can" be taken these various ways (which is important, but not news) or a way of denying that you have this responsibility (which is not a fact; it may be a blindness, a posture, or perhaps a decision). In a more radical vein, "There is my home" may be said while pointing to your home or in a dream of pointing to your home (which may or may not resemble anything you now say is home). Nothing in the words will distinguish the real (referential?) from the dream (nonreferential?) occasion, and this difference is again not up for decision. (If it were up for decision, it would follow that life is as a matter of fact a dream, because only in a dream can you *decide* whether you are dreaming or awake.)

That such a thing is not up for decision is the pivot on which skepticism turns. In *The Claim of Reason* I describe this pivot as the limit of criteria, as criteria coming to an end (too soon, as it were), as there being no criteria (say marks or features) for distinguishing dreams from reality (or the animate from the inanimate, or the natural from the artificial). Knowing one from the other is not a matter of telling differences between them. To conclude that such issues are undecidable would be to decide that the conclusion of skepticism is true, that we never know so certainly but that we can doubt. This, to my mind, trivializes the claim of the skeptic, whose power lies not in some decision, but in his apparent discovery of the ineluctable fact that we cannot know; at the same time it theatricalizes the threat, or the truth, of skepticism: that it names our wish (and the possibility of our wishing) to strip ourselves of the responsibility we have in meaning (or in failing to) one thing, or one way, rather than another. Perhaps our most practical courses against the impositions of philosophy are indeed either to trivialize or to theatricalize them. But to me such courses seem to give up the game; they do not achieve what freedom, what useful idea of myself, there may be for me, but seem as self-imposed as the grandest philosophy—or, as Heidegger might almost have put it, as unself-imposed.

To indicate how far down the road a satisfying allocation of these matters is likely to take us, I would like to quote the last paragraph of Part II ("Skepticism and the Existence of the World") of *The Claim of Reason*.[6] The paragraph invokes the issue of logical positivism's abusive or prejudicial idea of decision, which I had thematically taken to task in a section of "The Availability of Wittgenstein's Later Philosophy" in *Must We Mean What We Say?*, written about the same time. It suggests accordingly that today's advanced literary use of the idea of the undecidable is produced by the same distortion or prejudice as yesterday's advanced philosophical use of the decidable. So to me it appears that I am fighting the same battle, but now on an opposite flank.

> If the existence of the world, and our knowledge of its existence, becomes a real, a sensed problem, is it enough to say, with Carnap, "To accept the thing-world means nothing more than to accept a certain form of language, in other words, to accept rules for forming statements and for testing, accepting, or rejecting them"? ("Empiricism, Semantics, and Ontology," p. 211.) We might feel: Accepting the "thing-world" is just accepting the world, and what kind of choice do we have about that? (I don't say there isn't one.) And what kind of choice do we have about accepting a form of language? We can accept or reject whatever in language *we* can construct. . . . If we can't *decide* that (we will say that) the things of our world exist, shall we say that we *believe* they exist? That is something a philosopher will say in the course of that rehearsal of our beliefs with which he begins his investigation of their validity as a whole. But that rehearsal does not *express* belief in anything; it contains no claims. Or shall we say that we have *faith* that the things of our world exist? But how is that faith achieved, how expressed, how maintained, how deepened, how threatened, how lost?

I have been made aware that although *The Claim of Reason* is long it is still compressed. Let me, then, briefly decompress the final sentence I have quoted. It is not vaguely rhetorical or vaguely psychological. It asks for particular opening pieces of the grammar (in Wittgenstein's sense) of "faith." (It is part of the grammar of "faith" that *this* is what we call "to lose one's faith," etc.[7]) The implication is: if these pieces of grammar have no clear application to the case of the existence of the things of the world, then the concept of faith has no clear application to this case. Then what is our relation to the case of the world's existence? Or should we now see that there is nothing that constitutes this relation? Or see that there is no one something? What would it be to see such things?

The Individuality of the Individual: Historical Meanings and Contemporary Problems

NIKLAS LUHMANN

Reconstructing individualism is not an easy task. It is not easy because it has been tried before. The question of how to conceive individuality has a long scholastic tradition, characterized by what we now tend to see as outmoded sophistication. Even if we concentrate on the human individual, we must travel back at least two hundred years if we want to survey the full array of theories and discover why they failed or lost their power of persuasion.

It would be unwise to begin without casting at least a superficial glance at what has already been done. Sociological theory, however, will not prove very helpful. It conceives history as a process of increasing individualism. Its classics contain an important theory built around this point: increasing social differentiation leads to increasingly generalized symbolic frameworks, which make it increasingly necessary to respecify situations, roles, and activities, which results in increasingly individual human beings. Traditional societies had to restrict the number of possible role combinations because families were located unambiguously in a hierarchical system of status groups. Modern society no longer situates families in this manner. Stratification has lost its former importance, and, as a consequence, the choice of role combinations must be left to the individual.

This is one of two currents of mainstream sociology, represented at its best by Durkheim. Within the other tradition, stemming from Simmel and Mead, the individual is conceived as an emerging unit—emerging not from history but from social encounters. Simmel sees the identity of an individual as a collage, glued together by the viewpoints and expectations of other individuals.

The fragmented self of one's own self-impressions becomes continuous and reliable only in and through social situations. Similarly, Mead thinks of the individual mind as an emerging unit, an inner copy of social interaction.[1] Here we have the beginnings of a social theory of the individual, a theory that decomposes and recomposes the individual with reference to social conditions. The social, however, is seen solely as interaction, not as society, and as a more or less present occasion, not as history.

Sociology has reacted unsympathetically to the ideological antithesis between individualism and collectivism (or between the individual and society), trying to bridge the gap yet give each side its due. It has not taken up the difficult task of formulating a theoretically relevant concept of individuality. Fortunately, we do not depend upon sociology alone. European intellectual history contains a long series of attempts to define and promote individuality. For our purposes, this history provides a double perspective. First, it serves as a pool of intellectual resources and, above all, of warnings: there are many traps on the way to a theory of the individual, traps that we can avoid if we know about them in advance. And second, it allows us to reconstruct the history of reconstructing individualism in the style of the sociology of knowledge, relating the history of ideas to that of social structure. The first perspective, *historia magistra vitae* (history teaches life), may be sociologically naive, but we should not judge it prematurely.[2] The second reminds us that every reconstruction of individualism must be carried out within society, by people who think of themselves as individuals and set out, so to speak, to reconstruct themselves.[3]

By Descartes's time, medieval scholastic debate had settled one thing about the individuality of the individual: individuality cannot be defined by pointing to some special quality of the individual in counterdistinction to other qualities; it is not something given to an individual from the outside. An individual is itself the source of its own individuality; the concept of individuality therefore has to be defined by self-reference.[4] All kinds of individual beings, not only humans, are defined by self-reference.* The scholastic theory of individuality was, of course, written by and for humans who had

---

*Indeed, until the late eighteenth century, human individuals were only a special kind of individual thing (*res*), characterized by their rational substance. And *res* meant simply a constraint on possible combinations of traits.

314

to make up their minds about themselves and their social conditions. Thus, the special importance of self-reference for defining the human individual is not surprising. Amid religious schism, political wars, emerging sovereign states, and economic progress and decline, self-reference, which reconstructs the individual on the basis of its own problems and resources, must have seemed an attractive refuge.[5]

One of the most interesting results was the devotional movement of the seventeenth century, which privatized the attempt to achieve salvation. On the basis of a religious world view, the movement fought against a competing tendency to associate individuality with libertinage, with a *fort esprit* that defied religion. The difference between salvation and damnation remained decisive.[6] But religious care was no longer care for others. It did not require praying for others, monastic conditions, or supererogatory works.[7] Instead, it was care for one's own sole salvation. "Etre devot, c'est vouloir se sauver et ne rien negliger pour cela" (to be devoted means to care for one's own salvation and to neglect nothing in view of this aim)—that is the Jesuit view of the job, and it seems compatible with, even similar to, other jobs.[8]

Today, such self-centeredness is no longer à la mode, but at least two effects of the devotional movement should be kept in mind. First, except for alms and charity, necessary for his own salvation, the individual's orientation toward the experience of others was remarkably devalued. The social self, the "me" of James and Mead, received bad marks like "pride" and "vanity." If you took the role of the other, admiring your devotion, you were already on the wrong track: devotion cannot be communicated, at least not intentionally.[9] This led to a second recognition: real and false devotion become indistinguishable. Sincerity and authenticity cannot be communicated; but if others cannot know his sincerity, the individual will feel unable to trust himself.[10] The same problem arises in love affairs.[11] Whoever tries to convince another of his love becomes insincere by attempting to do so. The only escape seems to be a profession of insincerity.[12]

To sum up: within the devotional movement, self-reference—the very essence of individuality—was judged to be the ruin of individuality, at least if an individual tried to stay on the path to salvation and professed to do so. Salvation presupposes something to be saved, whereas, an individual, in the literal sense, is a being with an

indivisible, indestructible soul. If we drop this religious or ontological warrant of individuality, we arrive at the *homme aimable*,
the sociable person of the eighteenth century. He too has lived his
life, and he too has left a clear record of his experiences.

In the eighteenth century, two resources alone remained available for reconstructing the individual as sociable person: the reevaluation of nature and the reevaluation of sociality. Thus a new
cult of sensitivity and friendship replaced religion; self-love expanded to include concern for others. (We are approaching Simmel
and Mead.) Symbolic interactionism was tested for the first time
during the eighteenth century. Social interaction requires superficial conversation without risks or consequences. Its essence is to
take the role of the other and to avoid bothering others with one's
own problems or peculiarities; not to speak about oneself is one of
its central norms.[13] The results were disappointing, particularly for
the self-conscious individual: somehow, the individual withdrew
from interaction. By the end of the eighteenth century, the *homme
du monde*, the *homme de bonne compagnie*, was no longer an individual. If he dies, observes Sénac de Meilhan, what do we know
about him? That he had a seat in the Opera, that he liked to play
lotto, that he took his supper in the city.[14]

Given that this was an age of *lumières et dégoûts* (enlightenment and disgust),[15] how could the individual maintain his individuality? Two ways were open to him. Each required a new distinction, a new guiding difference (in German I could say *Leitdifferenz*),
which replaced the difference between salvation and damnation.
In the first, the individual was guided by the difference between
nature and civilization. Since there was no way back to nature, men
must come to terms with lost innocence and with property. Thus
conceived, the social order retained and even reinforced some of the
bad characteristics of false devotion, such as pride and vanity. In it,
self-interest was given a civilized disguise. It was an order of hy-
pocrisy and, above all, of visible injustice—in which, for example,
property was distributed unequally. In the decades before the French
Revolution, social theories characterized civil society (in contrast
to the state of nature) in terms of the difference between property
and indigence and of a law of necessarily unequal distribution.[16]
The individual might identify with opulence or with misery, according to his situation. Labor became the only link connecting these
extremes, and social analysis showed (as a kind of comfort?) that

both the rich and the poor were slaves of civil society. They were not really individuals. They did not really belong to themselves.[17]

Fortunately, property was only one way to reconstruct the individual within a framework of social interdependencies. The other way used the concept of art and, later, the theory of aesthetics. Nature was said to produce, from time to time and in exemplary individuals, what came to be called "genius."[18] The social was introduced with concepts such as "taste" (*gusto, goût*) and "the public," which judges not by reason but by heart and sentiment. The self-reference of an individual is the self-reference of his heart, and the work of art is, like nature itself, an outside condition that stimulates the heart to act upon itself.[19]

The problem is that all this depended on social stratification. Taste was a qualified taste, and the public was a restricted public.[20] Swiss and German authors (Crousaz, Bodmer, Gottsched, Baumgarten, Kant) tried to eliminate taste as the ultimate judge, replacing it by a new guiding distinction: the difference between the particular and the general. They tried to find, within the realm of concrete particularities, general criteria for the beautiful. If a rational proof for such criteria could be provided, it would be possible to desocialize the judgment of individuals. No longer would the public (of connoisseurs) define the criteria (without reason), but the criteria would define the competence of the public. In making a judgment, the individual would no longer depend on his social stratum but on the realization of the general within himself.

Only the results of the long and complicated dispute over general criteria for judgment and taste are of interest here.[21] They lead to a reconstruction of the individuality of the individual at a new intellectual level. After Kant, a new kind of subjective individualism became possible; given the turn to the "transcendental," the facts of consciousness had to be evaluated by a kind of double standard: empirical and transcendental. This difference parallels that between the particular and the general. As a result, the individual (not only the Cartesian mind) emerged as the subject, as subject of the world. Experiencing the world, the individual could claim to have a transcendental source of certainty within himself. He could set out to realize himself by realizing the world within himself. Education, which bourgeois theory saw as suffocating the voice of nature,[22] now became a liberating process, for which the French revolution had changed the scene.[23]

The individual as the subject? This cannot be surpassed. We can only forget what it meant and then try to salvage one or another of its secondary meanings—say, emancipation, reasonable self-determination, or understanding of the subjective point of view in everyday life.

The history of the individuality of the individual does not continue beyond this point. Or rather, it continues only as a history of ideologies, as a history of "individualism," a term invented in the 1820's.[24] I hope that the title of this book, despite its formulation, is not meant to suggest a reshuffling of ideologies. So I shall stop my historical report here and return to a theoretical analysis of the individuality of the individual.

Within the general framework of the theory of society—society being conceived as the encompassing social system—I propose to characterize modern society as a functionally differentiated social system.[25] The evolution of this highly improbable social order required replacing stratification with functional differentiation as the main principle of forming subsystems within the overall system of society. In stratified societies, the human individual was regularly placed in only one subsystem. Social status (*condition, qualité, état*) was the most stable characteristic of an individual's personality. This is no longer possible for a society differentiated with respect to functions such as politics, economy, intimate relations, religion, sciences, and education. Nobody can live in only one of these systems. But if the individual cannot live in "his" social system, where else can he live? As *homo viator* on his way to heaven or hell?

I would suggest that the change from stratification to functional differentiation as the basic principle for subdividing society explains the successive historical attempts to reformulate the basic problems of individuality. "Explains," of course, is a strong term, but we can discern a remarkable correspondence between structural and semantic changes.[26]

At first, the increasing pressure to live an individual life might have led, in Protestant and Catholic churches alike, to a privatizing of the path to salvation. This ended by increasingly differentiating religion from other social domains. At court and in high society, to be religious or not, according to prevailing opinion, came to be

318

a fashion, even to be described as fashion. This made devotion visible and identified it as a social phenomenon; thus it ruined the devotional movement that had flourished during the seventeenth century by opening to question two of its major tenets. The alliance between the court and religion was no longer structurally important, but a matter of the day, of caprice, of being à la mode.

As a sociable person, the individual could survive, finding in his present life not heaven or hell, but pleasure or ennui. This solution, however, was in turn undone by new differentiation. Society, transforming itself into a functionally differentiated system, could no longer be represented on the level of social interaction, not even by or within its highest strata. The interaction of high society, still representing the "good society" within the societal system, became an island of social rationality, isolated from all serious business. In consequence, the difference between pleasure and ennui collapsed, making a meaningful life impossible. The depersonalization of social interaction desocialized the individual.

There is, after all, a hidden relation between the functional differentiation of the societal system and the individual's self-proclamation as subject. Given the traditional connotations of *hypokeimenon/subiectum*—something "lying under" and supporting attributes—"subject" means something that underlies and carries the world, and, therefore, something that exists in its own right as a transcendental and not as an empirical phenomenon. The guiding difference is no longer pleasure and ennui, or self and other; it is the difference between empirical particularities and transcendental generality. The individual leaves the world in order to look at it. I interpret this extramundane position of the transcendental subject as a symbol for the new position of the empirical individual in relation to a system of functional subsystems. He does not belong to any one of them in particular but depends on their interdependence. But is this a good symbol? Is it an adequate semantic correlate of functional differentiation? What about its traditional connotations, its exaggerations, its internal plausibility, its ideological, political, and motivational feedback?

Today the subject is again fashionable, at least in sociology. Partisans of the subject attack behaviorism, systems theory, information technology, survey research, and ask for the recognition of the subject. They no longer understand, however, what the word means. They recite outworn philosophical terminology in an erroneous way. We should drop the term "subject" ("psychic system," "consciousness," "personal system," perhaps even "individual" would do the job) if we are simply referring to a part of reality. How can we conceive of a part of reality as underlying or supporting reality? Can a part simultaneously be the base of the whole? Can the subject be the *subiectum* of itself and of everything else? Can we conceive the subject as *sphaera se ipsam et omnia continens* (as containing itself and everything else)? This, of course, was the old definition of the world.[27] Can we conceive of the subject as a duplication of the world? The transcendental theory of consciousness was at least aware of this problem and tried to solve it by claiming extramundane status for self-referential conscious experience. But if we refuse to accept this transcendental solution, and of course we do, we are again faced with the old paradox of privileged parts supporting a whole.

For all these reasons, reconstructing individualism today cannot mean reaffirming the subject. We should honor the subject by finding it adequate successors, adequate both in terms of the problem and in relation to the social structure of contemporary society. To make concrete proposals, of course, is risky and difficult. Nevertheless, we can begin with a simple but far-reaching observation concerning the recent boom in research on what have come to be called "self-referential systems." Summing up what has been done and anticipating what can still be done, we can characterize this movement in a few statements:

1. Self-referential systems are empirical and have no transcendental status whatsoever. They are normal objects of normal science, but recognizing their existence has important epistemological consequences.

2. There are several types of self-referential systems, which differ according to their basic operation. This can be life (or possibly some other, or even any, material or energetic operation), consciousness, or communication. Mixing such operations is impossible, because they presuppose closed systems. Conscious systems are not living systems, social systems are not conscious systems. The different domains may, of course, be causally interconnected, yet they are not simply relations between facts but are always organized as a relation of a system to its environment. In this sense, living sys-

tems and conscious systems are parts of the environment of social systems, whereas social systems are part of the environment of living systems and conscious systems.

3. The term "self-reference" refers not only to the identity of the system (as does "reflection" in its classic sense, e.g., as used in the philosophy of consciousness of German idealism) and not only to the structure of the system, that is, to its morphogenesis and its self-organization. It refers also, and primarily, to the constitution of its basic elements. The elementary units of self-referential systems can be produced and reproduced only as self-referential units. They combine self-identity and self-diversity (to use Whitehead's formulation),[28] and their status and function as elements mean that this combination cannot be dissolved by the system itself. This means also that the system cannot distinguish its own basic elements from its own operations.

4. Such systems are called, following Maturana, "autopoietic."[29] Autopoietic systems are closed systems in the sense that they cannot receive their elements from their environment but produce them by selective arrangement. We could also say—and this reminds us that we are operating very close to our background in transcendental theories—that everything used as a unit by the system, whether its elements, its processes, or the system itself, has to be constituted by the system. Units, of course, are complex facts and can be analyzed by an observer. The system itself, however, has to rely on self-constituted reductions to link and reproduce its own operations. The unity of the system, therefore, is nothing but the autopoietic process of constituting units for itself within itself.

5. Producing units requires reducing complexity, namely, the complexity of a domain in which distinguishing between system and environment makes no sense. The autopoietic system has to use distinctions and indications as basic operations (in the sense of Spencer Brown's logic).[30] It realizes the closure of its own operation by self-indication, but to identify itself it needs to distinguish system from environment. It does not necessarily need knowledge about its environment, but it needs to be distinct from that environment.

6. Autopoietic systems produce their elements within temporal boundaries, depending on a beforehand and a thereafter. Many of them, certainly conscious systems and social systems, consist of

events only, of thoughts, for example, or of actions. Events happen at specific moments, and they vanish as soon as they appear. In this sense disorganization is a continuous and necessary cause of being. The system has to manage its own *creatio continua*. Thanks to God, Descartes would have said, structures have evolved that make it possible to interconnect events and to limit the choice of the next event.

7. Self-referential systems are paradoxical; their existence implies the unity of different logical levels, of different logical types.[31] To say their unity produces their unity is not tautological but paradoxical. It is paradoxical because "production" presupposes a difference between cause and effect, and the autopoietic theory states that the different is the same. The analysis of such a situation requires us to ask how a self-referential system itself handles the paradox of its existence; how it tackles such problems as the different is the same, the same is different; how it observes itself as unitary yet multiplex, as a manifold unity; how it simplifies and prepares itself for logical and ontological cognition. This may be seen as an elaboration, by existing, of sufficient identity—or, in the less-technical formulation of Paul Valéry, "Je suis né plusieurs, et je suis mort un seul" (Born as several, I die as one).

By now, this may be ununderstandable enough. But whoever gets this message will at least see the possibility of defining the individuality of an individual as autopoiesis. This leads us back to the late scholastic position with which I began. There is no individuality *ab extra*, only self-referential individuality. But this means that cells and societies, maybe physical atoms, certainly immune systems and brains, are all individuals. Conscious systems have no exceptional status. They are a particular type. There is no ultimate, all-encompassing unity. We have a world only in the sense that some autopoietic systems, certainly conscious systems, can conceive of the identity of the difference between themselves and their environments—that the difference is always *one* difference (in distinction to others). Of course, this again does not deny interconnections between systems. As interconnections, however, they have no immanent, natural, or cosmological unity. They are only ecological *relations*. There is no ecological *system*.

This, as it stands, may be a successful scientific theory or even a paradigmatic revolution in systems theory. But does it give an adequate account of what we would like to be when we observe and describe ourselves as individuals? Does it acceptably redescribe our social environment as an autopoietic, self-referential, circular societal system? And is this theoretical reformulation emotionally adequate to the present human condition? We may, of course, define emotions as the autopoietic immune system of the autopoietic psychic system; but again: is this emotionally adequate? Don't we want to need at least a special place, if not the highest rank, for ourselves in the ecology of autopoietic systems—something like "the highest and richest" of all structures of self-reflection, as Gotthard Günther referred to the self-awareness of man? [32]

I see no way to answer these questions with a clear yes or no. But at least we can trace some possibilities, or rather, impossibilities, that may influence future attempts to reconstruct individualism. The most important consequence might well be that the theory of autopoietic systems seems to bar all ways back to an anthropological conception of man.[33] It precludes, in other words, humanism. The reason is simple: there is no autopoietic unity of all the autopoietic systems that compose the human being. Certainly mind and brain never will build one closed, circular, self-referential autopoietic system, because thoughts, as elements of the mind, cannot be identified with single neurophysiological events, as elements of the brain. This is not to deny that we are all human. But to want to be human has no scientific basis. It amounts to sheer dilettantism.

This means that we have to invent new conceptual artificialities in order to give an account of what we see when we meet somebody who looks and behaves like a human being. How do we know that he is one? Because we are self-observers and able within our own self-reference to assume that the other is a self-observer too? [34] Or—the explanation I prefer—because we interpenetrate in a social system that presupposes the other ego? [35]

Moreover, two consequences emerge: first, all observations of individuals (and theories are programs for observation) must focus on difference, not on unity. Otherwise we would not be able to perceive identity. And second, all observations have to choose system references, self-observation being a special case. This means accepting relativism without exception, without any kind of ontological base, without any kind of *a priori*. The counterbalancing argument can only be that relativism does not preclude, and even is presupposed by, universalism.

Given these constraints, we are free to choose conscious systems as the system reference most appropriate for what we want to express if we claim to be individuals ourselves. This comes very close to what has been done under the heading "transcendental reduction" (Husserl). We drop, however, the distinction between empirical and transcendental. It contradicts the essential unity of the autopoietic process reproducing thoughts out of thoughts (as elements out of elements). Transcendental theory was, after all, a desperate attempt to avoid circularity. The theory of self-referential systems accepts circularity as a basic necessity.

This insight destroys the formula of the individual as the subject. My guess is that the traditional experience (and I say intentionally: "experience") of ennui will provide better clues for a theory of the autopoiesis of conscious systems than the concept of subject did. The seventeenth century made a twin discovery: the subject and its boredom. In other words, the subject has to occupy itself with something, be it economic or aesthetic.* Motives, then, are to be thought of as filling the inner void, the empty circularity of pure autopoiesis, of the reproduction of the elements of consciousness by elements of consciousness; and boredom corresponds to the thinking of thinking. During the seventeenth century, both the subject and its ennui became socially acceptable self-descriptions.

Only the theory of autopoietic, self-referential systems seems to be able to formulate this latent unity of the subject and its ennui—a theory of the self-despairing subject, a theory of dynamism achieved through self-desperation—and to formulate it in acceptable terms. At the moment, however, we cannot find even the slightest approach in this direction. We cannot walk a beaten path. We can foresee, however, that it will no longer be possible to use the venerable distinctions between reason, will, and feeling.† They have to be replaced by the distinction between autopoiesis and structure. The whole body of knowledge about consciousness, meaning, language, and, above all, "internal speech" will have to be reformulated. There is no dual or even pluralistic self, no "I" distinct from "me," no personal identity distinct from social identity. These conceptions are late-nineteenth-century inventions, with-

---

*It is, however, characteristic of the bourgeois drift, which had just begun, that only aesthetic interests were based directly upon the problem of coping with ennui, whereas economic motives were based upon such more "natural" and acceptable sources of motives as uneasiness, restlessness, unlimited drives.

†Then, of course, sociologists would have to admit that there is no reference for "voluntaristic action theory."

out sufficient foundation in the facts of consciousness. We simply do not live and do not experience ourselves that way. Moreover, these dualistic or pluralistic paradigms are themselves semantic reactions to the facts of a complex society.[36] We can drop as futile all attempts to reintegrate a decomposed self. If consciousness operates at all, it does so as an individual system, using its own unity and its own conscious events to reproduce its own unity and its own conscious events.

This is the reason why an autopoietic system cannot produce its own end. Humans can commit suicide because the conscious system can interfere with the organic system. But the autopoietic system of consciousness cannot think of death as the last autopoietic element. Autopoiesis is reproduction of elements that take part in the reproduction of elements, and all attempts to think of a last moment will only produce a *re*productive element.[37] We can be sure that all this presupposes and has reference to individuality in the sense of a closed, circular, self-referential network, in which the elements of the system are produced by the elements of the system. But beware: this is not a nice theory, neither a theory of perfection nor even of the perfectibility of the human race. It is not a theory of healthy states. Autopoietic systems reproduce themselves; they continue their reproduction or not. This makes them individuals. And there is nothing more to say.

Notes

Notes

Freccero: Autobiography and Narrative

1. Paul de Man, "The Rhetoric of Temporality," in Charles S. Singleton, ed., *Interpretation: Theory and Practice* (Baltimore, 1969), pp. 173–209.

2. St. Augustine, *Confessions*, trans. R. S. Pine-Coffin (London, 1961), Book 2, chap. 6, p. 49. All citations are from this edition. Hereafter they will be noted in the text.

3. St. Augustine, *On the Trinity*, 9.8.13. I have used the translation of A. W. Haddan in *A Select Library of the Nicene and Post-Nicene Fathers of the Church*, vol. III (reprint: Grand Rapids, Mich., 1956).

Greenblatt: Fiction and Friction

NOTE: I am indebted throughout to Thomas Laqueur, who has been boundlessly generous with his learning and his ideas. Catherine Gallagher and Steven Knapp read earlier drafts of this paper and made valuable suggestions, which I have gratefully incorporated. I make the usual declaration freeing these friends from the imputation of complicity in whatever faults remain.

1. Jacques Duval, *Des hermaphrodits, accouchemens des femmes, et traitement qui est requis pour les releuer en santé, et bien éléuer leurs enfans. Où sont expliquez la figure des laboureur, & verger du genre humain, signe de pucelage, defloration, conception, & la belle industrie dont vse nature en la promotion du concept & plante prolifique* (Rouen, 1612), p. 394. Unannotated further citations will be identified by page number in parentheses in the text.

2. In the only remotely comparable case that I know of, the court seemed similarly perplexed, though their decision was significantly different. This is the case of Thomasine Hall, born in the 1570's near Newcastle-upon-Tyne. At age twelve, Thomasine was sent by her mother to live with an aunt in London, where she remained for ten years. At the time of the Cadiz action, we are told, she cut her hair, renamed herself Thomas, and enlisted as a soldier. Afterwards, she returned to London and resumed her life as a woman, only to abandon her needlework again and sail as a man to

Virginia, where she became Thomasine once more and served as a chambermaid. Hauled before the Council and General Court of Virginia in 1629 and asked "why hee went in weomans aparell," Thomasine gave the unforgettable, if enigmatic, reply, "I goe in weomans aparell to gett a bitt for my Cat." The court evidently felt that unresolved sexual ambiguity was more tolerable than dizzying sexual metamorphosis; they preferred a figure frozen in acknowledged androgyny to one who passed fluidly and unpredictably from one state to another. Accordingly, they ordered that it be published that Hall "is a man and a woman," and they insisted upon this doubleness in the clothes that they required him to wear: "hee shall goe Clothed in mans apparell, only his head to bee attired in a Cyse and Croscloth [?] wth an Apron before him." (H. R. McIlwaine, ed., *Minutes of the Council and General Court of Colonial Virginia, 1622–1632, 1670–1676* [Richmond, Va., 1924], p. 195.)

3. Pierre Bourdieu, *Outline of a Theory of Practice*, tr. Richard Nice (Cambridge, 1977), p. 86.

4. Michelle Z. Rosaldo, *Knowledge and Passion: Ilongot Notions of Self and Social Life* (Cambridge, Eng., 1980), p. 231.

5. Jacob Burckhardt, *The Civilization of the Renaissance in Italy*, tr. S. G. C. Middlemore (New York, 1958), I, 143.

6. Such stories are by no means limited to literary fictions. Thus, for example, the sixteenth-century chronicler Robert Fabian writes of three New World savages presented to Henry VII that they "were clothed in beasts skins, & did eate raw flesh, and spake such speach that no man could understand them and in their demeanour like to bruite beastes." "Of the which upon two yeeres after," he continues, "I saw two apparelled after the maner of Englishmen in Westminster pallace, which that time I could not discerne from Englishmen, til I was learned what they were." (See my "Learning to Curse: Aspects of Linguistic Colonialism in the Sixteenth Century," in Fredi Chiappelli, ed., *First Images of America: The Impact of the New World on the Old* [Berkeley and Los Angeles, 1976], II, 563.)

7. Jean Céard, *La Nature et les prodiges: L'Insolite au XVIe siècle, en France* (Geneva, 1977).

8. Nathaniel Highmore, *The History of Generation* (London, 1651), pp. 92–93.

9. See, for example, *The Workes of that Famous Chirurgian Ambrose Parey*, tr. Thomas Johnson (London, 1634): "When the husband commeth into his wives chamber hee must entertaine her with all kinde of dalliance, wanton behaviour, and allurements to venery: but if he perceive her to be slow, and more cold, he must cherish, embrace, and tickle her, and shall not abruptly, the nerves being suddenly distended, breake into the field of nature, but rather shall creepe in by little and little intermixing more wanton kisses with wanton words and speeches, handling her secret parts and dugs, that she may take fire and bee enflamed to venery, for so at length the wombe will strive and waxe fervent with a desire of casting forth its owne seed, and receiving the mans seed to bee mixed together therewith. But if all these things will not suffice to enflame the woman, for women for the most part are slow and slack unto the expulsion or yeelding forth of their

seed, it shall be necessary first to foment her secret parts with the decoction of hot herbes made with Muscadine, or boiled in any other good wine, and to put a little muske or civet into the neck or mouth of the wombe" (p. 889).

10. *Ibid.*, p. 126. Unannotated subsequent citations of this source will be identified by page number in parentheses in the text.

11. Galen, *On the Usefulness of the Parts of the Body*, ed. and tr. Margaret May (Ithaca, N.Y., 1968), II, 628–29.

12. *Ibid.*, II, 629. Elsewhere in his work, Galen observes that although the mole's inability to bring forth its eyes is entirely a defect, the female's comparable inability to bring forth her genitals is of great use, since it enables her to bear children. (*De semine*, II, 5, in *Libri novem* [Basel, 1536], pp. 173–74.)

13. Paré, p. 128. Paré does not make the connection between his two explanations and argue for a "providential defect." Instead the contradictory theories exist side by side and speak to different aspects of the same problem.

14. Ambroise Paré, *On Monsters and Marvels* (1573), tr. Janis L. Pallister (Chicago, 1982), pp. 31–32.

15. *Montaigne's Travel Journal* (1580; first pub. 1774), tr. Donald M. Frame (San Francisco, 1983), p. 6. Montaigne or his secretary adds, "they say that Ambroise Paré has put this story into his book on surgery."

16. Duval, p. 63. The clitoris, he says, is a source of such violent sexual pleasure that even the most modest of women will, if they once agree to allow it to be touched by a finger's end, be overcome with desire: "amorcées et rauies, voire forcées au déduit venéréen" (*ibid.*). "Donnant l'exact sentiment de cette partie, pour petite qu'elle soit, vne tant violent amorce au prurit et ardeur libidineux, qu'estant la raison surmontée, les femelles prennent tellement le frain aux dents qu'elles donnent du cul a terre, faute de se tenir fermes et roides sur les arcons" (pp. 63–64). Hence in French, Duval writes, the clitoris is popularly called "tentation, aiguillon de volupté, verge femininine [*sic*], le mépris des hommes: Et les femmes qui font profession d'impudicité la nomment leur *gaude mihi*" (p. 64). On the displacement of the structural homology from the uterus to the clitoris, see Ian Maclean, *The Renaissance Notion of Woman: A Study in the Fortunes of Scholasticism and Medical Science in European Intellectual Life* (Cambridge, 1980), p. 33.

17. *Aristotle's Masterpiece: or, The Secrets of Generation Displayed* (London, 1690). The first known English edition of this incessantly reprinted anonymous work is dated 1684, though the work was probably circulated in English earlier; it was still circulated widely in the nineteenth century.

18. The notion of the enlarged clitoris is alive and well in the seventeenth and early eighteenth centuries. "Sometimes it grows so long," writes the midwife Jane Sharp in 1671, "that it hangs forth at the slit like a Yard, and will swell and stand stiff if it be provoked, and some lewd women have attempted to use it as men do theirs . . . but I never heard but of one in this Country" (quoted in Audrey Eccles, *Obstetrics and Gynaecology in*

331

Tudor and Stuart England [Kent, Ohio, 1982], p. 34). See also Hilda Smith, "Gynecology and Ideology in Seventeenth-Century England," in Berenice A. Carroll, ed., *Liberating Women's History: Theoretical and Critical Essays* (Urbana, Ill., 1976), pp. 97–114.

19. "Thus the metaphors and the substances of sex," writes Thomas Laqueur, "were intimately related to those of life itself; sexual heat was an instance of the heat which vivified inanimate matter." "Orgasm, Generation, and the Female," *Representations*, 14 (Spring 1986).

20. John McMath, *The Expert Midwife* (1694), quoted in Eccles, p. 40.

21. Thomas Vicary, *The Anatomie of the Bodie of Man* (1586), ed. Frederick J. Furnivall and Percy Furnivall, Early English Text Society, Extra Series 53 (1888; reprint: New York, 1975), p. 79.

22. The phrase "Venus' palace" is from Phillip Stubbes, *Anatomy of Abuses* (1583). On attacks on the theater, see Jonas Barish, *The Antitheatrical Prejudice* (Berkeley and Los Angeles, 1980), chaps. 3–6.

23. William Harvey, *The Anatomical Lectures of William Harvey*, ed. and trans. Gweneth Whitteridge (Edinburgh and London, 1964), p. 175.

24. For a similar argument about stories of cross-dressing in medieval saints' lives, see Caroline Walker Bynum, "Women's Stories, Women's Symbols: A Critique of Victor Turner's Theory of Liminality," forthcoming in Frank E. Reynolds and Robert Moore, eds., *Anthropology and the Study of Religions*.

25. For the idea of the "open secret" I am indebted to a superb unpublished essay on *David Copperfield* by D. A. Miller. There is a further, paradoxical function to the open secret of theatrical cross-dressing, since the all-male cast is used to excuse the theater from any imputation of erotic reality: all of the wooing has been a merely imaginary pageant, since the natural end of that wooing—the union of a man and a woman and the generation of offspring—is quite literally impossible.

Davis: Boundaries and the Sense of Self in Sixteenth-Century France

1. Jacob Burckhardt, *The Civilization of the Renaissance in Italy*, tr. S. G. C. Middlemore (Oxford and London, 1945). Burckhardt's statement was part of his introduction to his Part II, "The Development of the Individual": "In the Middle Ages both sides of the human consciousness—that which was turned within as that which was turned without—lay dreaming or half awake beneath a common veil. . . . Man was conscious of himself only as a member of a race, people, party, family or corporation—only through some general category" (p. 81). Burckhardt describes the discovery of personality as a process of distinguishing oneself from the group (pp. 81–83), without the group having any creative role to play in self-recognition. Karl J. Weintraub's masterly essay "Autobiography and Historical Consciousness" insists on the variety of historical and cultural settings in which the self can be reflected on, but sees the "remarkable form of self-conception as an individuality" emerging in the Renaissance only as a product of a weakening of or a competition between "compelling cultural forms" (*Critical Inquiry*, 1 [1975], 841–42). For studies of self-awareness that emphasize group membership, see John F. Benton, "Consciousness

of Self and Perceptions of Individuality," in Robert L. Benson and Giles Constable, eds., *Renaissance and Renewal in the Twelfth Century* (Cambridge, Mass., 1982), pp. 263–95, and especially Caroline Bynum, "Did the Twelfth Century Discover the Individual?" in her *Jesus as Mother: Studies in the Spirituality of the High Middle Ages* (Berkeley and Los Angeles, 1982), pp. 82–109.

2. Michel de Montaigne, *Essais*, in *Oeuvres complètes*, ed. Albert Thibaudet and Maurice Rat, Bibliothèque de la Pléiade (Paris, 1962), III, 9, pp. 946, 1650; Montaigne is quoting Terence, *Adelphi*, 3.5.9.

3. On families and family culture in sixteenth-century France, see Jean-Louis Flandrin, *Familles: Parenté, maison, sexualité dans l'ancienne France* (Paris, 1976); N. Z. Davis, "Ghosts, Kin and Progeny: Some Features of Family Life in Early Modern France," in Alice S. Rossi, Jerome Kagan, and Tamara K. Hareven, eds., *The Family* (New York, 1978), pp. 87–114; and Barbara B. Diefendorf, *Paris City Councillors in the Sixteenth Century: The Politics of Patrimony* (Princeton, N.J., 1983).

4. Benvenuto Cellini, *The Life of Benvenuto Cellini*, tr. John Addington Symonds (London, 1896), pp. 3, 371; Burckhardt, p. 203.

5. Thomas Platter, *Autobiographie*, trans. Marie Helmer (Paris, 1964), p. 19 and passim.

6. N. Z. Davis, *The Return of Martin Guerre* (Cambridge, Mass., 1983), chaps. 4–5.

7. François Rabelais, *Pantagruel*, chap. 8, in *Oeuvres complètes*, ed. Jacques Boulenger and Lucien Scheler, Bibliothèque de la Pléiade (Paris, 1955), pp. 202–3.

8. Louise Bourgeois dite Boursier, *Observations diverses sur la sterilité, perte de fruict, foecondité, accouchements, et maladies des femmes, et enfants nouveaux naiz* (Rouen, 1626), II, 201–2. Louise Bourgeois had been midwife to Marie de Médicis.

9. Montaigne, II, 8, pp. 365–67.

10. On family law in early modern France, see Paul Ourliac and J. de Malafosse, *Histoire du droit privé* (Paris, 1957–68), III, part 1. On the disorderliness of the female sex, see N. Z. Davis, *Society and Culture in Early Modern France* (Stanford, Calif., 1975), chap. 5.

11. On this world of belief, see *Les Evangiles des quenouilles* (Paris, 1855), an imagined conversation between women spinning thread, composed in the fifteenth century and published in many editions in the sixteenth century; Madeline Jeay, *Savoir faire: Une Analyse des croyances des "Evangiles des quenouilles" (XVe siècle)*, Le Moyen français, 10 (Montreal, 1982); and Jean Benedicti, *La Somme des pechez, et le remede d'iceux* (Paris, 1595), Book 1, chap. 8, pars. 20–36.

12. Charlotte Arbaleste, *Mémoires de Madame de Mornay*, ed. Henriette de Witt (Paris, 1868–69), I, 1: "Mon Filz, Dieu m'est temoing que, mesme avant votre naissance, il m'a donné espoir que vous le serviriez. . . . En ceste intention, nous avons mis pene, votre père et moy, de vous nourrir soigneusement en sa craincte, que nous vous avons, en tant qu'en nous a esté, faict succer avec le laict." Archives d'Etat de Genève, "Recit de La Maizon et origine des des Gouttes," fol. 12v: I thank God that "vous avez

este nourriz des la mamelle en son eglise sans Jamais avoir particippe a Aulcune superstition ny ydollatrie." On Catholic and Protestant body imagery, see N. Z. Davis, "The Sacred and the Body Social in Sixteenth-Century Lyon," *Past and Present*, 90 (February 1981), 40–70.

13. Platter, p. 19.

14. Felix Platter, *Beloved Son Felix: The Journal of Felix Platter, a Medical Student in Montpellier in the Sixteenth Century*, trans. Sean Jeannett (London, 1961).

15. See Stephen Greenblatt, "Fiction and Friction," above, pp. 30–51.

16. Montaigne, I, 28, p. 183; II, 17, p. 625; III, 9, pp. 928–29; II, 8, p. 369. The quote is from III, 13, p. 1079.

17. T. Platter, pp. 51–52; F. Platter, pp. 109–10, 113–14, 120–23.

18. *Bref Discours de la vie de tres sage et tres vertuze dame Madame Claude du Chastel, redigée par escrit par Charles Gouyon son mary, pour servir de memoire à ses enfans et posterité*, in *Mémoires de Charles Gouyon, Baron de la Moussaye (1553–1587)*, ed. G. Vallée and P. Parfouru (Paris, 1901). Part I recounts the adventures of the ancestors of Claude; Part II is devoted to Claude and Charles, one-half of it to his courtship of her.

19. Arbaleste, I, 3–4, 46–71, 89; II, 110–11.

20. Jeanne du Laurens, "La Généalogie de Messieurs du Laurens," in Charles de Ribbe, ed., *Une Famille au XVIe siècle d'après des documents originaux*, 3d ed. (Paris, 1879).

21. Montaigne, II, 8, p. 365.

22. Du Laurens, pp. 61–62, 69–71, 86–91.

23. M. Z. Rosaldo, "The Use and Abuse of Anthropology: Reflections on Feminism and Cross-Cultural Understanding," *Signs*, 5 (Spring 1980), 414–15.

24. Richard M. Douglas, "Talent and Vocation in Humanist and Protestant Thought," in T. K. Rabb and J. E. Seigel, eds., *Action and Conviction in Early Modern Europe* (Princeton, N.J., 1968), pp. 261–98.

25. Du Laurens, pp. 54, 77–78, 61–62.

26. Charles Gouyon described a quarrel between himself and his father that arose when in order to win the approval of his beloved, a Protestant, he decided to leave the king's army for the Reformed army. His father, a Catholic, threatened to disinherit him, saying this would be the ruin of their house. Not long afterward they made up, Charles promising that apart from his conscience and his "maitresse," he would do nothing that was disagreeable to his father (pp. 75–76, 81–82). In fact, the father was very eager for the match, provided that the king's consent could be won. (It eventually was.) We have here the son using the language of love and religion to justify his independence when his aspirations were not ultimately in opposition to his father's.

27. T. Platter, pp. 30, 46, 56.

28. F. Platter, pp. 25, 52, 91–92, 96, 113–15, 128.

29. Montaigne, III, 11, p. 1010; II, 17, p. 626; III, 2, p. 782.

30. Juan Huarte, *L'Examen des esprits pour les sciences. . . . Le tout traduit de l'espagnol par François Savinien d'Alquie* (Amsterdam, 1672),

p. 459. This Spanish physician's much-reprinted book first appeared in 1575.

31. Bourgeois, II, 203. On the general question of female work identity, see N. Z. Davis, "Women in the Crafts in Sixteenth-Century Lyon," *Feminist Studies*, 8 (Spring 1982), 46–80.

32. Nancy L. Roelker, *Queen of Navarre: Jeanne d'Albret, 1528–1572* (Cambridge, Mass., 1968), pp. 54–55; John T. Noonan, Jr., *Power to Dissolve: Lawyers and Marriages in the Courts of the Roman Curia* (Cambridge, Mass., 1972), pp. 27–47.

33. Marguerite de Valois, *Mémoires et autres écrits de Marguerite de Valois, la Reine Margot*, ed. Yves Cazaux (Paris, 1971), pp. 45, 51, 59, and passim.

34. This material is based on the analysis of hundreds of notarial documents from sixteenth-century Lyon in the Archives départementales du Rhône, and will be discussed more fully in N. Z. Davis, *The Gift in Sixteenth-Century France* (Madison, Wisc., forthcoming).

35. Archives d'Etat de Genève, Registres du Consistoire, Annexe 5, fol. 56ʳ, Feb. 26, 1568. See my portrait of Bertrande de Rols for another effort to find cultural resources that would allow a peasant woman to think of disposing of her body in her own way (*Martin Guerre*, chaps. 3, 5–6).

36. Carol Gilligan, *In a Different Voice: Psychological Theory and Women's Development* (Cambridge, Mass., 1982).

Schneewind: The Use of Autonomy in Ethical Theory

BIBLIOGRAPHICAL NOTE: The best complete edition of Joseph Butler's *Sermons* is that edited by J. H. Bernard (London, 1900). Sermons II and III present Butler's views about how we are a "law unto ourselves." There are many other editions.

Immanuel Kant first presented his ideas on autonomy in *Foundations of the Metaphysics of Morals* (1785), translated by Lewis White Beck (1949). In his *Critique of Practical Reason* (1788), translated by Lewis White Beck (Indianapolis, 1964), and in Part II of his *Metaphysics of Morals* (1797), translated by Mary Gregor as *The Doctrine of Virtue* (Philadelphia, 1964), he developed these ideas much further.

John Rawls's *A Theory of Justice* (Cambridge, Mass., 1971) is the basic statement of his view. He supplements his position in a series of papers, among them "The Independence of Moral Theory," *Proceedings and Addresses of the American Philosophical Association*, 47 (1974–75), and "Kantian Constructivism in Moral Theory," *The Journal of Philosophy*, 77, no. 9 (1980).

The literature on personal identity and the nature of the self is enormous. A good introduction is given in the debate contained in Sidney Shoemaker and Richard Swinburne, *Personal Identity* (Oxford, 1984), which also has an extensive bibliography.

Among the many writers who object to Kantian ideas of autonomy are Adina Schwartz, "Against Autonomy," *The Journal of Philosophy*, 78, no. 3 (1981); Robert Paul Wolff, *In Defense of Anarchism* (New York, 1970);

Carol Gilligan, *In a Different Voice* (Cambridge, Mass., 1982); Michael J. Sandel, *Liberalism and the Limits of Justice* (Cambridge, 1982); and Bernard Williams, *Moral Luck* (Cambridge, 1981).

Fried: Courbet's Metaphysics

NOTE: A version of this essay appeared in *MLN*, 99, no. 4 (September 1984): 785–815.

1. The full title of *The Quarry* in French is *La Curée, chasse au chevreuil dans les forêts du Grand Jura.* For recent discussions of *The Quarry* and related works, see Bruce MacDonald, "*The Quarry* by Gustave Courbet," *Bulletin: Museum of Fine Arts, Boston*, 67, no. 348 (1969), 52–71; Hélène Toussaint, *Gustave Courbet (1819–1877)*, exhib. cat., Grand Palais, Paris, 30 Sept. 1977–2 Jan. 1978, cat. no. 53, pp. 144–46; and Peter-Klaus Schuster, "Courbet Gemälde," in *Courbet und Deutschland*, exhib. cat., Kunsthalle, Hamburg, 19 Oct.–17 Dec. 1978, and Städtische Galerie, Frankfurt am Main, 17 Jan.–18 March 1979, cat. nos. 247–48, pp. 243–46.

2. MacDonald, p. 59. See his article for a careful discussion of the formal and physical disparities between individual segments.

3. Michael Fried, "The Beholder in Courbet: His Early Self-Portraits and Their Place in His Art," *Glyph*, 8 (1978), 85–129; idem, "Representing Representation: On the Central Group in Courbet's *Studio*," in Stephen J. Greenblatt, ed., *Allegory and Representation*, Selected Papers from the English Institute, 1979–80 (Baltimore, 1981), pp. 94–127; idem, "Painter into Painting: On Courbet's *After Dinner at Ornans* and *Stonebreakers*," *Critical Inquiry*, 8 (1982), 619–49; and idem, "The Structure of Beholding in Courbet's *Burial at Ornans*," *Critical Inquiry*, 9 (1983), 635–83. The brief remarks in the present essay on paintings by Courbet prior to *The Quarry* are based on more extensive analyses in the above articles; see those articles too for references to discussions of those works by other scholars.

4. The opening stages of that tradition are the subject of my *Absorption and Theatricality: Painting and Beholder in the Age of Diderot* (Berkeley and Los Angeles, 1980).

5. Notably Alfred Sensier, *La Vie et l'oeuvre de J.-F. Millet* (Paris, 1881), pp. 53–54.

6. A critic of the first school is Ernest Chesneau, one of the second, Charles Baudelaire; see my "Painter into Painting," n. 33, pp. 647–49.

7. The photograph is reproduced by MacDonald, p. 66; it is seen as postdating *The Quarry*, perhaps by as much as five years, by Marie-Thérèse de Forges, *Autoportraits de Courbet*, Les Dossiers du département des peintures 6 (Louvre, Paris, 1973), p. 43.

8. See Emile Littré, *Dictionnaire de la langue française* (Paris, 1885), I, 935. Littré also notes that *sonner la curée* is to blow a hunting horn to summon the dogs to such a feeding (*ibid.*).

9. Obvious pentimenti reveal that originally the tail of the black and white dog, farther to the right, was roughly parallel to its partner's; the curving tail appears in its present position in Célestin Nanteuil's litho-

graph after *The Quarry* published in *L'Artiste,* July 18, 1858 (reproduced by MacDonald, p. 60).

10. My suggestion that *The Quarry* calls attention to the roe deer's undepicted genitals and to their exposure to the hunter or at least to his point of view invites further discussion in terms of the Freudian problematic of castration. Now what chiefly characterizes the painting's treatment of these motifs (if I may so describe them) is the absence of any signs of special or excessive affect and in particular of anxiety, which may seem to indicate that for the painter-beholder the implied threat to the roe deer's genitals was simply that, an objective menace, not the expression of a primal insecurity. On the other hand, the absence of affect ought perhaps to be seen as a further expression of the splitting of the painter-beholder into passive hunter and active *piqueur:* that is, it would be a further index of the hunter-painter's manifest passivity, which itself might be described as a sort of castration. My thanks to Neil Hertz for his help in thinking through this question. Cf. in this connection Hertz's "Medusa's Head: Male Hysteria under Political Pressure" and "More about 'Medusa's Head,'" *Representations,* 4 (Fall 1983), 27–54, 63–72, esp. 65–70.

11. MacDonald (p. 64) suggests that the roe deer may have preceded the figure of the hunter, indeed that the latter may not have been part of Courbet's initial conception of the core image. If this is true—we are unlikely ever to be certain one way or the other—we might imagine either that the painter-beholder came to project himself into the core image in response to the outward movement of the dead roe deer, or that an initial relationship of something like mirroring obtained between the painter-beholder and the core segment as such, say the blank canvas, on which both roe deer and hunter were then realized, or perhaps that some conjunction of these operations took place.

12. Félix Ravaisson, *De l'habitude* (1838), ed. Jean Baruzi (Paris, 1927). Baruzi's introduction summarizes Ravaisson's argument and analyzes the sources of his ideas (pp. i–xxxv).

13. Henri Bergson, "The Life and Work of Ravaisson," in *The Creative Mind: An Introduction of Metaphysics,* trans. Mabelle L. Anderson (New York, 1946), pp. 220–52. In a brief biography in Paul Edwards, ed., *The Encyclopedia of Philosophy* (New York, 1967, VII, 75–76), George Boas emphasizes Ravaisson's importance to Bergson and more broadly his place in a spiritualist tradition in French philosophy stemming from Maine de Biran. Accordingly, one implication of the comparison I have drawn between Courbet and Ravaisson is that the conventional view of Courbet's aesthetic as materialist, although by no means simply mistaken, stands in need of refinement.

14. Ravaisson, p. 40.

15. *Ibid.,* p. 49.

16. Its title in French is *Hallali du cerf, épisode de chasse à courre sur un terrain de neige.* The *Hallali* is the name given to the sounding of the horn that signals the kill is near (Littré, II, 1975).

17. Sigmund Freud, "Instincts and Their Vicissitudes" (1915), in James Strachey, ed., *The Standard Edition of the Complete Psychological Works*

of Sigmund Freud (London, 1953–66), XIV, 109–40; Jean Laplanche, "Aggressiveness and Sadomasochism," in *Life and Death in Psychoanalysis*, trans. Jeffrey Mehlman (Baltimore, 1976), chap. 5; and Leo Bersani, "Representation and Its Discontents," in S. Greenblatt, ed., *Allegory and Representation*, pp. 145–62. In the last of these, Bersani sums up Laplanche's and his own reflections on the Freudian scenario as follows: "Thus the genealogy of sado-masochism has somewhat startling consequences. In order to account for the mystery of sadistic sexuality—that is, how we can be sexually aroused by the suffering of others, as distinct from the easier question of why we wish to exercise power over others—Freud is led to suggest that the spectacle of pain stimulates a mimetic representation that, so to speak, shatters the subject into sexual excitement" (p. 149). Or as Laplanche remarks in the course of his discussion of a related essay by Freud, "A Child Is Being Beaten" (1919): "The process of turning round [on the subject] is not to be thought of only at the level of the content of the fantasy, but *in the very movement of fantasmatization*. To shift to the reflexive [i.e., to move from the initial formulation "A child is being beaten" to the construction "I am being beaten by my father"] is not only or even necessarily to give a reflexive content to the 'sentence' of the fantasy; it is also and above all to reflect that action, internalize it, make it enter into oneself as fantasy. To fantasize aggression is to turn it round upon oneself, to aggress oneself: such is the moment of auto-eroticism, in which the indissoluble bond between fantasy as such, sexuality, and the unconscious is confirmed" (p. 102, his emphasis).

18. Two earlier masterpieces of Courbet's Realism, the *Stonebreakers* and the *Burial*, may be seen as representing such a shattering (the smashing of stones in the first of these) and such an introducing and filling in of gaps (the excavation of the grave and ceremony of interment in the second). But the further theme of violence or indeed killing, although by no means wholly absent from these works, seems less explicitly developed in them than in *The Quarry*. Another painting that bears on the issues treated in the final sections of this essay is the *Wounded Man* (ca. 1844–54).

19. L. Bersani and U. Dutoit, *The Forms of Violence* (New York, 1985).

20. See Georges Riat, *Gustave Courbet, peintre* (Paris, 1906), p. 266.

Hamacher: "Disgregation of the Will"

1. G. W. Leibniz, *Philosophische Schriften*, ed. Gerhardt (1880), IV, 18.

2. The entire sentence reads: "Cum entia singularia existant, evidens est, *Ens singulare*, sive *Individuum* esse illud, quod omnimode determinatum est." (Christian Wolff, *Gesammelte Werke* [Frankfurt, 1736], V, 188.)

3. J. W. Goethe, *Gedenkausgabe seiner Schriften*, ed. Beutler, XVIII, 533.

4. Here and in the following, Nietzsche's texts are cited—with few exceptions—from *Werke in drei Bänden*, ed. K. Schlechta (Munich, 1966). The locations of the passages in this edition are placed at the end of quotations in parentheses, roman numerals for volume, arabic for page. Here: I, 222.

5. If these formulations are reminiscent of Heidegger's privileging of

the future as a realm of the authentic capacity for Being, then this is because Heidegger's reflections look back, in part, to Nietzsche: Heidegger
acknowledges the debt in an impressive, brief analysis of Nietzsche's essay
on history in *Sein und Zeit* (§76) but then later fails to repay the debt
when, in the lectures on Nietzsche, he fails to consider worthy of remark
Nietzsche's contribution to a new evaluation of the futurity of Being. On
the problem of the promise and of the discourse that runs out ahead of itself, cf. W. Hamacher, "Das Versprechen der Auslegung—Überlegungen
zum hermeneutischen Imperativ bei Kant und Nietzsche," in N. Bolz and
W. Hübener, eds., *Spiegel und Gleichnis, Festschrift für Jacob Taubes*
(Würzburg, 1984), pp. 252–73.

6. A. Schopenhauer, *Die Welt als Wille und Vorstellung*, ed. A.
Hübscher (Wiesbaden, 1949), II, 563.

7. On the movement of the *Doppelgänger* in Nietzsche, cf. W.
Hamacher, "pleroma—zu Genese und Struktur einer dialektischen Hermeneutik bei Hegel," in G. W. F. Hegel, *Der Geist des Christentums,
Schriften 1796–1800*, ed. W. Hamacher (Berlin, 1978), pp. 306–18. On the
same problem, cf. J. Derrida, *Otobiographie de Nietzsche* (Paris, 1984).

8. In *Human, All Too Human*, one finds, in a different sense: "In mor-
als, the human doesn't treat himself as an *individual*, but as a dividual."
(I, 491). And in yet another sense Novalis writes: "The genuine dividual is
also the genuine individual" ("Das allgemeine Brouillon," no. 952, *Werke,
Tagebücher und Briefe Friedrich von Hardenbergs*, ed. H.-J. Mähl and R.
Samuel, II, 692 [Munich, 1978]).

9. It has been pointed out that *überleben*, as it is read here, bears
a certain similarity to the *survivre* that J. Derrida has read in texts by
Blanchot and Shelley. I assume that certain differences individuate these
readings. So, compare: J. Derrida, "Living On," in Harold Bloom et al., eds.,
Deconstruction and Criticism (New York, 1979), pp. 75–176.

10. F. Nietzsche, *Gesammelte Werke, Musarion-Ausgabe* (Munich,
1922), I, 412–13.

11. In the manner of the early romantics, one could note: individual =
anacoluthon of prosopopoeia.

Clifford: On Ethnographic Self-Fashioning

NOTE: Of the various people who have responded to different versions of
this essay I would like particularly to thank Herbert Phillips, Annette
Weiner, and Ian Watt. Their skeptical comments have much improved its
argument—though I doubt they will fully approve the final result.

1. For the concept "culture" in the nineteenth century, see Raymond
Williams, *Culture and Society: 1780–1950* (New York, 1966). On the transition to the plural, ethnographic definition: George Stocking, *Race, Culture and Evolution* (New York, 1968), esp. pp. 69–90. The novelty and fragility of the Western notion of the individual was noted in 1938 by Marcel
Mauss in what may be the first ethnographic overview of the subject: "Une
Catégorie de l'esprit humain: la notion de personne, celle du 'moi,'" in *So-
ciologie et anthropologie* (Paris, 1950), pp. 333–62.

2. Walter Kaufman, ed., *The Portable Nietzsche* (New York, 1954),
p. 46.

3. Stephen Greenblatt, *Renaissance Self-Fashioning: From More to Shakespeare* (Chicago, 1980).

4. The best critical discussion of Malinowski's fieldwork as innovation and disciplinary model is by George Stocking: "The Ethnographer's Magic: The Development of Fieldwork in British Anthropology from Tylor to Malinowski," *History of Anthropology*, 1 (1983), 70–120.

5. Malinowski to Mrs. B. Z. Seligman, quoted by Raymond W. Firth in *Man and Culture: An Evaluation of the Work of Bronislaw Malinowski* (London, 1957), p. 6.

6. Joseph Conrad, *Heart of Darkness*, ed. Robert Kimbrough (New York, 1971). The interpretation I suggest in this essay owes a good deal to previous explicators of Conrad, most notably Edward Said and Ian Watt. In its biographical dimensions it draws on the standard works: Jocelyn Baines, *Joseph Conrad: A Critical Biography* (London, 1960); Ian Watt, *Conrad in the Nineteenth Century* (Berkeley and Los Angeles, 1979); Frederick Karl, *Joseph Conrad: The Three Lives* (New York, 1979); and Zdzislaw Najder, *Joseph Conrad: A Chronicle* (New Brunswick, N.J., 1983). My focus on *Heart of Darkness* as an allegory of writing and of grappling with language and culture in their emergent twentieth-century definitions is, I believe, a new one, but it draws on many points well established in Conrad studies. I have not cited specific sources for biographical facts, since those I build with are not to my knowledge disputed in the literature.

7. Bronislaw Malinowski, *Argonauts of the Western Pacific* (New York, 1961); *A Diary in the Strict Sense of the Term* (New York, 1967).

8. Zdzislaw Najder, *Joseph Conrad*; and *Conrad's Polish Background: Letters to and from Polish Friends* (Oxford, 1964).

9. The most perspicacious assessment to date is that of George Stocking, "Empathy and Antipathy in the Heart of Darkness," in Regna Darnell, ed., *Readings in the History of Anthropology* (New York, 1974), pp. 85–98.

10. Harry C. Payne, "Malinowski's Style," *Proceedings of the American Philosophical Society*, 125 (1981), 438. (There is an interesting slip between this passage and its footnote, equating functionalist "therapy" with "theory.")

11. For the contrast in functionalist style between the descriptions of Malinowski and of Radcliffe-Brown, see Payne, pp. 420–21.

12. As quoted in Walter Houghton, *The Victorian Frame of Mind* (New Haven, 1957), p. 43.

13. Watt, *Conrad in the Nineteenth Century*, esp. pp. 148–51.

14. Edward Said, *Joseph Conrad and the Fiction of Autobiography* (Cambridge, Mass., 1966), p. 13.

15. Clifford Geertz, *Works and Lives: The Anthropologist as Author* (Stanford, Calif., forthcoming); Paul Rabinow, *Reflections on Fieldwork in Morocco* (Berkeley and Los Angeles, 1977); Vincent Crapanzano, *Tuhami: Portrait of a Moroccan* (Chicago, 1980); Kevin Dwyer, *Moroccan Dialogues* (Baltimore, 1982).

16. The discursive field cannot, of course, be limited to the discipline of anthropology and its frontiers, nor is it adequately captured in terms like "reflexive" or "dialogical." For two provisional surveys, see George

Marcus and Dick Cushman, "Ethnographies as Texts," *Annual Review of Anthropology*, 11 (1982), 25–69; and James Clifford, "On Ethnographic Authority," *Representations*, 1 (1983), 118–46.

Valesio: The Beautiful Lie

1. Cf. André Ernout and Antoine Meillet, *Dictionnaire étymologique de la langue latine: Histoire des mots*, 4th ed. (Paris, 1967).

2. From Gabriele D'Annunzio, *La città morta*, act 2, scene 4. The translation is by Nancy Canepa; for the original, see D'Annunzio, *Tragedie, sogni e misteri I*, vol. 3 of *Tutte le opere*, ed. E. Bianchetti (Verona, 1954–65). The ellipses are in the original text.

3. Stendhal, *Red and Black*, trans. Robert M. Adams (New York, 1969), chap. 4.

4. Sigmund Freud, *The Standard Edition of the Complete Psychological Works*, ed. J. Strachey with Anna Freud (London, 1953–66), XII, 239–54.

5. Gilbert Durand, *Les Structures anthropologiques de l'imaginaire: Introduction à l'archétypologie générale* (Paris, 1960), pt. 1, chap. 1.

6. Louis-Ferdinand Céline, *La Vie et l'oeuvre de Philippe-Ignace Semmelweis* (1818–1865), published together with *Mea culpa* (Paris, 1937), pp. 35–36. (My translation.) The genealogy of "il faut un mâle" reaches back to Nietzschean conceptions, as in section 60 of *The Antichrist*, on Christianity's destruction of Moorish culture in Spain: "Why? Because it owed its origins to noble, to *male* instincts, because it said Yes to life." (Here and elsewhere, the basis for Nietzsche quotes is Walter Kaufman's collection *The Portable Nietzsche* [New York, 1968]. Only chapter or section, not page, will be given.)

7. These are the questions tossed about in the slender pamphlet (reflecting a luncheon talk) by T. S. Eliot, *The Literature of Politics*, with a Foreword by Sir Anthony Eden, Conservative Political Centre, no. 146 (London, 1955). Such usages confuse the literature of politics with two quite different enterprises: discussions of politics and literature, and investigations of the politics *of* literature.

8. My *"Pax Italiae* and the Literature of Politics," *Yale Italian Studies*, 2 (Spring 1978), 143–68 (written before I knew of Eliot's talk), is the beginning of such an investigation.

9. I cite from Robert Brasillach, *Écrit à Fresnes* (Paris, 1967). I owe my acquaintance with these letters to Alice Kaplan.

10. See my "The Practice of Literary Semiotics: A Theoretical Proposal," *Point of Contact/Punto de Contacto*, 5 (April-May 1978), 22–41 (reissued in Working Papers and Pre-Publications, no. 71, Centro Internazionale di Semiotica e di Linguistica, Urbino, February 1978).

11. *Fresnes*, pp. 140–41. José Antonio Primo de Rivera (b. 1903) is the founder of the Falange Española. He was tried and shot in 1936, under the Popular Front government. As "José Antonio" he entered the legend and lore of those years in Spain.

12. For "Chénier" as a pen name, see Brasillach's letter to his sister of November 14, 1944, *Fresnes*, p. 201; for direct comparison, see the first

stanza of his poem "Le Testament d'un condamné" of January 22, 1945, pp. 493–98; the short essay is "Chénier," pp. 471–88. The essay's approach is reminiscent of Renato Serra, an Italian essayist killed in combat in the First World War.

13. George Eliot, *Adam Bede*, chap. 5.

14. Leszek Kolakowski, *Chrétiens sans église: La conscience religieuse et le lien confessionnel au XVIIᵉ siècle*, trans. from the Polish by Anna Posner (Paris, 1968 [1965]).

15. *Aion: Researches into the Phenomenology of the Self* (1951), in *The Collected Works of Carl Gustav Jung*, trans. R. F. C. Hull (Princeton, N.J., 1968), vol. IX, pt. 2, pp. 68–69.

16. See *ibid.*, pp. 46 and 61; the quote is from p. 42.

17. Suffice it to refer here to the thought of Georges Bataille; and consider such surveys as that by Michel Carrouges, *La Mystique du surhomme* (Paris, 1948), with its discussion of "mystical atheism."

18. Chapters 26–28 of Rabelais, *Quart livre*, are one of the most suggestive points in the genealogy of this ante-Christian attitude within what is essentially a Christian context.

19. One can read the episode at the "maison de force" in the fifth part of *Histoire de Juliette ou les Prosperités du vice*, in the Marquis de Sade, *Oeuvres complètes: Édition définitive* (Paris, 1962–64), IX, 383–87, or in *Juliette*, trans. Austyn Wainhouse (New York, 1968), pp. 980–85. Interestingly, in a French paperback edition, *Les Prosperités du vice* (Paris, 1969), in which the monumental text is reduced to "larges extraits," we are spared none of the sexual details, but the religious exhortations uttered by the delirious "Jesus Christ" put to torture are excised—a further proof that the frontier of obscenity is religious, not sexual, discourse.

20. Published in Paris in 1913—also the date of the first production.

21. Nicola Zingarelli, *Vocabolario della lingua italiana* (Bologna, 1983), s.v.

22. *Eros e Priapo: Da furore a cenere* (Milan, 1967).

23. See, for instance, the 1962 novel by Philip K. Dick, *The man in the High Castle* (New York, 1981). I thank Kristin Ross for this reading.

Brooke-Rose: The Dissolution of Character in the Novel

1. John Barth, *Lost in the Funhouse* (New York, 1968), pp. 117–21.

2. Richard Brautigan, *Trout Fishing in America* (New York, 1967), pp. 50, 56, 63, 65.

3. See Philippe Hamon, "Un Discours contraint," *Poétique*, 16 (1973), 411–44; reprinted in R. Barthes et al., *Littérature et réalité* (Paris, 1982), 118–81.

4. Mas'ud Zavarzadeh, *The Mythopoeic Reality* (Urbana, Ill., 1976), p. 39.

5. Barth, *Lost in the Funhouse*, p. 11.

6. See Nathalie Sarraute, *L'Ere du soupçon* (Paris, 1956); and Djuna Barnes, "What Kate Was Not," in *Ryder* (New York, 1979; originally published 1928), chap. 17, p. 108.

7. Alain Robbe-Grillet, *Pour un nouveau roman* (Paris, 1962), p. 45.

8. Jorge Luis Borges, "Pierre Menard, Author of Don Quixote," in *Labyrinths* (New York, 1962), pp. 36–44.

9. John Barth, "The Literature of Replenishment," *The Atlantic Monthly*, 245 (January 1980): 65–71. This itself is a kind of answer to that author's own "The Literature of Exhaustion," *ibid.*, 220 (August 1967): 29–34.

10. Martin Heidegger, *Being and Time* (New York, 1962; originally published 1927); Susan Sontag, "The Aesthetics of Silence," in *Styles of Radical Will* (London, 1969), p. 14; Hayden White, *Metahistory: The Historical Imagination in Nineteenth-Century Europe* (Baltimore, 1973) and *Tropics of Discourse: Essays in Cultural Criticism* (Baltimore, 1978).

11. Roland Barthes, *S/Z*, trans. R. Miller (New York, 1974), p. 67.

12. Philippe Hamon, "Pour un statut sémiologique du personnage," in *Poétique du récit* (Paris, 1977, pp. 411–45).

13. Dorrit Cohn, *Transparent Minds* (Princeton, N.J., 1978); Ann Banfield, *Unspeakable Sentences* (London, 1982).

14. Cited and discussed in Banfield, chap. 5, pp. 208, 218.

15. Ian Watt, *The Rise of the Novel* (London, 1957).

16. 1966 was the date of Lacan's *Ecrits*, 1967 that of Derrida's three seminal books, *De la grammatologie* (trans. Gayatri Chakravorty Spivak as *Of Grammatology* [Baltimore, 1976]); *L'Ecriture et la différence* (trans. Alan Bass as *Writing and Difference* [Chicago, 1978]); *La Voix et la phénomène* (trans. David B. Allison as *Speech and Phenomena and Other Essays on Husserl's Theory of Signs* [Evanston, Ill., 1973]).

17. George Steiner, *Language and Silence* (Toronto, 1958; paperback ed., with additions, New York, 1966; rpt. 1982); Oscar Lewis, *The Children of Sanchez* (New York, 1961); Ernst Bloch, *Das Prinzip Hoffnung* (Frankfurt, 1969; written in the United States 1938–47, revised 1953–59).

18. Walter J. Ong, *Orality and Literacy* (London, 1982); E. M. Forster, *Aspects of the Novel* (London, 1927).

19. Marshall McLuhan, *The Gutenberg Galaxy* (London, 1962); Eric A. Havelock, *Preface to Plato* (Cambridge, Mass., 1963), *Origin of Western Literacy* (Toronto, 1976), and *The Literate Revolution in Greece and Its Cultural Consequences* (Princeton, N.J., 1982); Albert J. Lord, *The Singer of Tales* (Cambridge, Mass., 1960).

20. Northrop Frye, *The Secular Scripture* (Cambridge, Mass., 1976).

21. Robert Scholes, *Structural Fabulation* (South Bend, Ind., 1975); Mark Rose, ed., *Science Fiction: A Collection of Critical Essays* (Englewood Cliffs, N.J., 1976); Kingsley Amis, "Starting Points," in Rose, ed., *Science Fiction*, reprinted from *New Maps of Hell* (New York, 1961).

22. Joseph McElroy, *Plus* (New York, 1977).

23. Northrop Frye, *Anatomy of Criticism* (Princeton, N.J., 1957).

24. Steiner, "The Pythagorean Genre," in *Language and Silence*, pp. 78–91.

25. Steiner, "Night Words: High Pornography and Human Privacy," in *Language and Silence*, pp. 68–77.

26. Steiner, "Literature and Post-History," in *Language and Silence*, pp. 381–92. The allusion is to p. 391.

27. Philippe Muray, "La marquise revint à minuit," *L'Infini* 2 (1983), 26–38.

28. Jacques Lacan, *Le Séminaire 1972–73, Livre XX, Encore* (Paris, 1973).

29. Jean-Claude Milner, *L'Amour de la langue* (Paris, 1978).

Chodorow: Toward a Relational Individualism

NOTE: I am indebted to Ann Swidler and Abby Wolfson for very helpful responses to an earlier version of this paper and to Peter Lyman for general conversations about these issues. The argument in this paper is part of a larger project formulated in various ways over the past several years by Jessica Benjamin, Jane Flax, Evelyn Fox Keller, and myself. I have benefited from discussion and correspondence with all of them as well as from their work. See Benjamin, "The End of Internalization: Adorno's Social Psychology," *Telos*, 32 (1977); "Authority and the Family Revisited, or, A World Without Fathers?," *New German Critique*, 13 (1978); "Rational Violence and Erotic Domination," in Hester Eisenstein and Alice Jardine, eds., *The Future of Difference* (Boston, 1980); and "The Oedipal Riddle: Authority, Autonomy, and the New Narcissism," in John Diggins and Mark Kamm, eds., *The Problem of Authority in America* (Philadelphia, 1981); Flax, "Critical Theory as a Vocation," *Politics and Society*, 8 (1978); "Political Philosophy and the Patriarchal Unconscious," in Sandra Harding and Merrill B. Hintikka, eds., *Discovering Reality: Feminist Perspectives on Epistemology, Metaphysics, Methodology, and the Philosophy of Science* (Boston, 1983); and "On Freud: Narcissism, Gender and the Impediments to Intersubjectivity," unpublished paper; Keller, *A Feeling for the Organism* (San Francisco, 1983); and *Reflections on Gender and Science* (New Haven, 1985). Sherry Ortner first suggested to me the formulation "relational individualism."

1. Sigmund Freud, "Introductory Lectures on Psycho-Analysis" (1915–16), in James Strachey, ed., *The Standard Edition of the Complete Psychological Works of Sigmund Freud* (London, 1953–66), XVI, 285.

2. See Michel Foucault, *The History of Sexuality*, I (New York, 1978), and Fred Weinstein and Gerald M. Platt, *The Wish to Be Free* (Berkeley and Los Angeles, 1969).

3. Sigmund Freud, "Dissection of the Psychical Personality" (1933), in Strachey, ed., *Works*, XXII, 80.

4. The polarity I discuss is found in personality psychology as well as within psychoanalytic theory. See Avril Thorne, "Disposition as Interpersonal Constraint," (Ph.D. diss., University of California, Berkeley, 1983). But for a very different argument, for individualism in personality psychology, see Gordon Allport, *Personality: A Psychological Interpretation* (New York, 1937), who argues in his opening paragraphs not against a more relational conception of personality but against the scientific psychological attempt to cut up the self into nomothetically derived aspects that can be studied across persons without regard to their situatedness in the makeup of the whole person.

5. Sigmund Freud, "Some Psychical Consequences of the Anatomical Distinction Between the Sexes" (1925), in Strachey, ed., *Works*, XIX, 257.

6. See Carol Gilligan, *In a Different Voice: Women's Conceptions of the Self and Morality* (Cambridge, Mass., 1982), and "Remapping the Moral Domain: New Images of the Self in Relationship," in this volume.

7. See Michel Balint, *Primary Love and Psycho-Analytic Technique* (New York, 1965), and *The Basic Fault* (London, 1968); W. R. D. Fairbairn, *An Object-Relations Theory of the Personality* (New York, 1952); Harry Guntrip, *Personality Structure and Human Interaction* (New York, 1961), and *Schizoid Phenomena, Object-Relations and the Self* (New York, 1969); Edith Jacobson, *The Self and the Object World* (New York, 1964); Margaret S. Mahler, Fred Pine, and Anni Bergman, *The Psychological Birth of the Human Infant* (New York, 1976); and D. W. Winnicott, *Collected Papers: From Paediatrics to Psychoanalysis* (London, 1958), *The Maturational Processes and the Facilitating Environment* (New York, 1965), and *Playing and Reality* (New York, 1971).

8. See on the primary creation of internality and externality, Hans Loewald, "Internalization, Separation, Mourning and the Superego" (1962), in his *Papers on Psychoanalysis* (New Haven, 1980), and Jacobson, *The Self*.

9. Sigmund Freud, "Outline of Psychoanalysis" (1940), in Strachey, ed., *Works*, XXIII, 206.

10. Joan Riviere, "The Unconscious Phantasy of an Inner World Reflected in Examples from Literature," in Melanie Klein, ed., *New Directions in Psychoanalysis* (London, 1977), pp. 358–59. This essay and quote came to my attention in Norman O. Brown, *Love's Body* (New York, 1966), p. 147.

11. Riviere, p. 347.

12. I discuss this further in "Beyond Drive Theory: Object Relations and the Limits of Radical Individualism," *Theory and Society*, 14, no. 3 (1985), 271–319.

13. Sigmund Freud, *The Ego and the Id* (1923), in Strachey, ed., *Works*, XIX, 29.

14. See Roy Schafer, "Narrative in the Psychoanalytic Situation," *Critical Inquiry*, 7 (1980), 29–53.

15. See Elizabeth R. Zetzel, "Therapeutic Alliance in the Analysis of a Case of Hysteria," in *The Capacity for Emotional Growth* (New York, 1970), and other papers in that volume; and Ralph Greenson, *Technique and Practice of Psychoanalysis* (New York, 1967).

16. For the most fully formulated account of this position, see Charles Brenner, *Psychoanalytic Technique and Psychic Conflict* (New York, 1976). For a lively account of the debate, see Janet Malcolm, *The Impossible Profession* (New York, 1980).

17. See Balint, *Primary Love* and *The Basic Fault*; Heinz Kohut, *Analysis of the Self* (New York, 1971) and *Restoration of the Self* (New York, 1977); Frieda Fromm-Reichman, *Principles of Intensive Psychotherapy* (Chicago, 1950); Margaret Little, *Transference Neurosis and Transference Psychosis* (New York, 1981); Leo Stone, *The Psychoanalytic Situation* (New York, 1961); Harold Searles, *Countertransference and Related Subjects* (New York, 1979); and D. W. Winnicott, *Maturational Processes* and *The Piggle* (New York, 1977).

18. Elizabeth R. Zetzel, "Current Concepts of Transference," *International Journal of Psycho-Analysis*, 37 (1956), 374. A discussion of gender in the creation of psychoanalytic theory is beyond the scope of this essay. I note, however, that women analysts were particularly central to focusing psychoanalytic interest on the importance of countertransference. See Fromm-Reichman, *Principles*; Annie Reich, "On Counter-Transference," *International Journal of Psycho-Analysis*, 32 (1951), 25–31; Lucia Tower, "Countertransference," *Journal of the American Psychoanalytic Association*, 4 (1956), 224–55; Margaret Little, "Counter-Transference and the Patient's Response to It," *International Journal of Psycho-Analysis*, 32 (1951), 32–40; Paula Heimann, "On Counter-Transference," *International Journal of Psycho-Analysis*, 31 (1950), 81–84; and Mabel Blake Cohen, "Counter-Transference and Anxiety," *Psychiatry*, 15 (1952), 501–39. I noticed this while reading Peter Loewenberg, "Subjectivity and Empathy as Guides to Counseling," unpublished paper.

19. See Josef Breuer and Sigmund Freud, *Studies on Hysteria* (1893–95), in Strachey, ed., *Works* II; and Sigmund Freud, *The Interpretation of Dreams* (1900–1901), in Strachey, ed., *Works*, IV and V. See also Nellie Louise Buckley, "Women Psychoanalysts and the Theory of Femininity: A Study of Karen Horney, Helene Deutsch, and Marie Bonaparte" (Ph.D. diss., University of California, Los Angeles, 1982), who suggests that the dominant psychologies of women emerged from their own life histories, if not their own self-analyses.

20. See the introduction to Harold Searles, *Collected Papers on Schizophrenia and Related Subjects* (New York, 1965); and Little, *Transference Neurosis*.

Meyer: Myths of Socialization and of Personality

1. Max Weber, *The Protestant Ethic and the Spirit of Capitalism* (New York, 1958). The first translation into English, by Talcott Parsons, appeared in 1930; the work was originally published as a series of papers in German in 1904–5. Talcott Parsons presents his own view of the individualist nature of modern society most succinctly in *The System of Modern Societies* (Englewood Cliffs, N.J., 1971).

2. For a recent account, see Perry Anderson, *Lineages of the Absolutist State* (London, 1974).

3. Alexis de Tocqueville, *Democracy in America*, ed. Phillips Bradley (New York, 1945).

4. For comparative data, see Gabriel Almond and Sidney Verba, *The Civic Culture* (Boston, 1963).

5. See John W. Meyer, "The Self and the Life Course: Institutionalization and Its Effects," in A. Sørensen, F. Weinert, and L. Sherrod, eds., *Human Development and the Life Course* (Hillsdale, N.J., forthcoming).

6. See, for example, David Tyack, *The One Best System* (Cambridge, Mass., 1974).

7. John W. Meyer et al., "The World Educational Revolution," in John W. Meyer and Michael T. Hannan, eds., *National Development in the World System: Educational, Economic, and Political Change, 1950–1970* (Chi-

cago, 1979), pp. 37–55; Francisco Ramirez and John Boli-Bennett, "Global Patterns of Educational Institutionalization," in P. Altbach, R. Arnove, and G. P. Kelley, eds., *Comparative Educaton* (New York, 1982), pp. 15–36.

8. John Boli-Bennett, "Human Rights or State Expansion?" in V. Nada et al., eds., *Global Human Rights* (Boulder, Colo., 1981), pp. 173–93.

9. Meyer et al.; Phillip Coombs, *The World Educational Crisis* (Oxford, 1968); Francisco Ramirez and Richard Rubison, "Creating Members: The Political Incorporation and Expansion of Public Education," in Meyer and Hannan, eds., pp. 72–82.

10. Audri Gordon Lanford and Robert Fiala, "Educational Ideology in Cross-National Perspective" (unpublished paper, Department of Sociology, Stanford University, 1980).

11. Meyer et al.

12. Ivar Berg, *Education and Jobs: The Great Training Robbery* (Boston, 1971).

13. Aaron Benavot, "The Rise and Decline of Vocational Education," *Sociology of Education*, 56 (1983), 63–76.

14. See, for example, UNESCO, *Statistical Yearbook* (Louvain, 1983).

15. Stephen Heyneman and William Loxley, "The Effect of Primary-School Quality on Academic Achievement Across Twenty-Nine High- and Low-Income Countries," *American Journal of Sociology*, 88 (1983), 1162–94.

16. Almond and Verba; Alex Inkeles and David Smith, *Becoming Modern* (Cambridge, Mass., 1974).

17. Heyneman and Loxley.

Hacking: Making Up People

1. Arnold Davidson, "Closing Up the Corpses," *I&C*, 11 (forthcoming).

2. Ian Hacking, "Biopower and the Avalanche of Printed Numbers," *Humanities in Society*, 5 (1982), 279–95; "The Autonomy of Statistical Law," in N. Rescher, ed., *Scientific Explanation and Understanding* (Pittsburgh, 1983), pp. 3–20; "How Should We Do the History of Statistics?" *I&C*, 8 (1981), 15–26.

3. Ian Hacking, "The Invention of Split Personalities," *I&C*, 11 (forthcoming).

4. Pierre Janet, *The Major Symptoms of Hysteria* (London, 1906), p. 78.

5. Pierre Janet, "Les Actes inconscients et le dédoublement de la personnalité pendant le somnambulisme provoqué," *Revue Philosophique*, 22 (1886), 581.

6. *The State*, Columbia, S.C., October 4, 1982, p. 3A. I apologize for using a newspaper report, but the doctors involved created this story for the papers and do not reply to my letters requesting more information.

7. Abram H. Dailey, *Mollie Fancher, the Brooklyn Enigma* (Brooklyn, 1894).

8. K. Plummer, ed., *The Making of the Modern Homosexual* (London, 1981).

9. John Marshall, "Pansies, Perverts and Macho Men: Changing Conceptions of the Modern Homosexual," in Plummer, ed., pp. 150, 249, n. 6.

10. Reprinted in Plummer, ed., pp. 30–43, with postscript; originally published in *Social Problems*, 16 (1968), 182–92.

11. John I. Kituse and Aaron V. Cewrel, "A Note on the Uses of Official Statistics," *Social Problems*, 11 (1963), 131–39.

12. Michel Foucault, *Power/Knowledge*, ed. C. Gordon (London and New York, 1980), p. 97. The translation of this passage is by Alessandro Fontana and Pasquale Pasquino.

13. After the conference, my colleague Bert Hansen (who has helped me a number of times with this paper) remarked that the relation of the nominalist/realist dispute to homosexuality is used by John Boswell, "Towards the Long View: Revolutions, Universal and Sexual Categories," *Salmagundi*, 58–59 (1982–83), 89–114.

14. Thomas Hobbes, *Elements of Philosophy*, II, 4.

15. T. S. Kuhn, *The Structure of Scientific Revolutions* (Chicago, 1962), p. 115.

16. G. E. M. Anscombe, *Intention* (Oxford, 1957).

17. Jean-Paul Sartre, *Being and Nothingness*, trans. Hazel E. Barnes (London, 1957), p. 59.

18. *Ibid.*, p. 522.

19. E. Esquirol, "Suicide," *Dictionnaire des sciences medicales* (Paris, 1823), LIII, 213.

20. Ian Hacking, "Suicide au XIXe siècle," in A. Fagot, ed., *Medicine et probabilités* (Paris, 1982), pp. 165–86.

21. C. E. Bourdin, *Du suicide considéré comme maladie* (Batignolles, 1845), p. 19. The first sentence of this book asserts in bold letters: *Le suicide est une monomanie.*

22. Michel Foucault, *The History of Sexuality*, trans. Robert Hurley (New York, 1978), p. 139.

23. A classic statement of this idea is in Jack D. Douglas, *The Social Meanings of Suicide* (Princeton, N.J., 1967), chap. 3.

Gilligan: Remapping the Moral Domain

NOTE: I am grateful to Mary P. Chatfield, my guide to the *Aeneid* and to classical scholarship, as well as to Hilde Hein for her insights about dependence. The study of two moral orientations was supported by a grant from the National Institute of Education. The study at the Emma Willard School was made possible by the Geraldine Rockefeller Dodge Foundation, and I wish to thank Trudy Hanmer and Robert Parker of the school, Scott McVay and Valerie Peed of the foundation, and Sharry Langdale, Margaret Lippard, and Nona Lyons of the Harvard Graduate School of Education for their collaboration. I am indebted to Marilyn Brachman Hoffman, whose generous gifts and encouragement have provided support at critical junctures, and to the Carnegie Corporation for enabling me to spend a year as a Faculty Fellow at the Bunting Institute of Radcliffe College. Susan Pollak's comments on an earlier draft of this paper and Eve Stern's careful reading were most helpful in its revision.

1. Virgil, *The Aeneid,* trans. Robert Fitzgerald (New York, 1983), 6: 463–64, p. 176.
2. *Ibid.,* 6: 458, p. 175.
3. *Ibid.,* 2: 3, p. 33; 4: 85, p. 98.
4. T. S. Eliot, *On Poetry and Poets* (New York, 1957), p. 63.
5. A similar distinction is made by H. Richard Niebuhr in *The Responsible Self* (New York, 1963).
6. *Aeneid,* 6:450–52, p. 175.
7. W. R. Johnson, *Darkness Visible: A Study of Virgil's Aeneid* (Berkeley and Los Angeles, 1975); Marilyn B. Skinner, "The Last Encounter of Dido and Aeneas: A 6.450–476," *Vergilius,* no. 29 (The Vergilius Society, 1983), pp. 12–18.
8. Skinner, p. 16.
9. Johnson, p. 153.
10. The term "object" was first used by Freud in *Three Essays on the Theory of Sexuality* (1905) to distinguish sexual objects from sexual aims. It is now widely used by "object-relations" theorists, psychoanalysts following Melanie Klein and Margaret Mahler who focus on the primacy of relationships. In both contexts, the term refers to a person who has become the object of another's desire.
11. This difference was described in the mid-1970's by Nancy Chodorow, "Family Structure and Feminine Personality," in M. Z. Rosaldo and L. Lamphere, *Woman, Culture and Society* (Stanford, Calif., 1974); by Jean Baker Miller, *Toward a New Psychology of Women* (Boston, 1976); and by Carol Gilligan, "In a Different Voice: Women's Conceptions of the Self and of Morality," *Harvard Educational Review,* 47 (1977). The point has been extended by Chodorow, *The Reproduction of Mothering* (Berkeley and Los Angeles, 1978); Gilligan, *In a Different Voice: Psychological Theory and Women's Development* (Cambridge, Mass., 1982); and Miller, "The Development of Women's Sense of Self," Stone Center Working Paper Series, no. 12 (Wellesley, Mass., 1984); as well as in a variety of other feminist writings.
12. These responses to questions about responsibility were given by students at the Emma Willard School for girls, in Troy, New York. All such quotes in my paper are from these girls.
13. Gilligan, *In a Different Voice.*
14. C. Gilligan, S. Langdale, N. Lyons, and M. Murphy, "The Contribution of Women's Thought to Developmental Theory," report to the National Institute of Education, Washington, D.C., 1982. See also S. Langdale, "Moral Orientations and Moral Development," Ph.D. diss., Harvard Graduate School of Education, 1983, and N. Lyons, "Two Perspectives: On Self, Relationships and Morality," *Harvard Educational Review,* 53 (1983).
15. For this example, I am grateful to Anne Glickman, the mother of the four-year-old boy.
16. Ian Suttie, *The Origins of Love and Hate* (New York, 1935), p. 1.
17. *Ibid.,* p. 2.
18. *Ibid.,* p. 4; emphasis in text.
19. John Bowlby, *Attachment and Loss,* in three volumes: *Attach-*

ment (New York, 1969), *Separation: Anxiety and Anger* (New York, 1973), *Loss: Sadness and Depression* (New York, 1980).

20. Bowlby, *Loss*, p. 44.

21. Sigmund Freud, "Mourning and Melancholia" (1917), *The Standard Edition of the Complete Psychological Works of Sigmund Freud*, ed. James Strachey (London, 1953–66), XIV, 249.

22. *Ibid.*, p. 249.

23. Bowlby, *Loss*.

24. Freud, XIV, 248.

25. Freud, *Three Essays on the Theory of Sexuality* (1905), VII, 227.

26. *Aeneid*, 4:323, 4:421.

27. *Ibid.*, 4:338–39, 4:414, pp. 107, 110.

28. Skinner, p. 12.

29. *Ibid.*

30. *Aeneid*, 4:440, p. 111.

31. *Ibid.*, 12:938, 12:946–47, p. 402.

32. Freud, VII, 227.

33. *Ibid.*

34. The study was conducted at the Emma Willard School for girls and is part of a larger project on adolescent development. For omission of girls in the literature on adolescence, see J. Adelson, ed., *Handbook of Adolescent Psychology* (New York, 1980).

35. Jane Austen, *Persuasion* (New York, 1964).

36. *Ibid.*, p. 140.

37. *Ibid.*, p. 234.

Nussbaum: Love and the Individual

1. Martha C. Nussbaum, "The Speech of Alcibiades: A Reading of Plato's *Symposium*," *Philosophy and Literature*, 3 (1979), 131–72; also chap. 6 of Nussbaum, *The Fragility of Goodness: Luck and Ethics in Greek Tragedy and Philosophy* (Cambridge, Eng., 1985). See also chap. 7 of *Fragility*, an interpretation of Plato's *Phaedrus*.

2. Martha C. Nussbaum, "Flawed Crystals: James's *The Golden Bowl* and Literature as Moral Philosophy," *New Literary History*, 15 (1983), 25–50.

Cavell: Being Odd, Getting Even

NOTE: A version of this essay appeared in *Salmagundi*, 67 (1985): 97–128.

1. Jaakko Hintikka, "*Cogito, Ergo Sum*: Inference or Performance?"; Bernard Williams, "The Certainty of the *Cogito*"; both reprinted in Willis Doney, ed., *Descartes* (Garden City, N.Y., 1967), pp. 108–39, 88–107.

2. This description of the *Meditations* takes up a piece of unfinished business broached in "The Avoidance of Love: A Reading of *King Lear*," in *Must We Mean What We Say?* (New York, 1969; rpt. Cambridge, 1976), p. 336.

3. The translation, here and elsewhere in this paper, is that of Laurence J. Lafleur (New York, 1951).

4. *Collected Works of Edgar Allan Poe*, ed. Thomas Ollive Mabbott (Cambridge, Mass., 1978).

5. In *Psychoanalysis and the Question of the Text*, ed. Geoffrey H. Hartman (Baltimore, 1977). I cite this paper hesitantly, both because I have read it just once and because its translator warns that it is lifted, even somewhat reordered, from a larger work, one I do not know.

6. Stanley Cavell, *The Claim of Reason: Wittgenstein, Skepticism, Morality, and Tragedy* (Oxford, 1979).

7. *Ibid.*, pp. 70ff.

Luhmann: The Individuality of the Individual

NOTE: I am indebted to Stephen Holmes for reading and improving an earlier draft of this essay.

1. The more recent school of symbolic interactionism tends to fuse Mead's behavioralism with phenomenology. This fusion cannot succeed and amounts to an enormous hybridization of incompatible kinds of theory. Husserl clearly rejects the idea of internal communication as a model of conscious self-reference, and this rejection is not a casual remark but a necessary precondition for the founding of transcendental phenomenology. See his *Logische Untersuchungen*, 5th ed. (Tübingen, 1968), II, 1, parts 1–8. For a critique and a different (semiological, but again not behavioralistic) position, cf. Jacques Derrida, *La Voix et la phénomène* (Paris, 1967; trans. by David B. Allison as *Speech and Phenomena: and Other Essays on Husserl's Theory of Signs* [Evanston, Ill., 1973]).

2. Such a perspective may even be historically naive. Cf. Reinhart Kosselleck, *Vergangene Zukunft: Zur Semantik geschichtlicher Zeiten* (Frankfurt, 1979), pp. 38ff.

3. For this point and for a confrontation of American optimism and European skepticism with respect to healthy individuals, see Ray Holland, *Self and Social Context* (New York, 1977).

4. See, within the context of a long discussion about previous theories, Francisco Suárez (1548–1617), *Disputationes metaphysicae*, Disp. VI, esp. VI, 14: "Modus substantialis, qui simplex est et suo modo indivisibilis, habet etiam suam individuationem ex se, et non ex aliquo principio ex natura rei a se distincto." (*Opera omnia* [Paris, 1866; rpt. Hildesheim, 1965], I, 185).

5. Much literature is available on this theme. Cf. Alban J. Krailsheimer, *Studies in Self-Interest: From Descartes to La Bruyère* (Oxford, 1962); Niklas Luhmann, "Frühneuzeitliche Anthropologie: Theorietechnische Lösungen für ein Evolutionsproblem der Gesellschaft," in *Gesellschaftsstruktur und Semantik* (Frankfurt, 1980), I, 162–234.

6. Even for nonbelievers, so runs the argument, it would be too risky to ignore this distinction completely.

7. Cf. Kenneth E. Kirk, *The Vision of God: The Christian Doctrine of the Summum Bonum* (London, 1931).

8. Pierre de Villiers, *Pensées et reflexions sur les égaremens des hommes dans la voye du salut*, 3d ed. (Paris, 1700), II, 93.

9. "Qui voudra être devot pour en faire profession, ne le sera pas. Qui

le sera véritablement, en fera profession sans penser de le faire." (*Ibid.*, p. 98.) But then, what happens if he knows of, or even hopes for, this inadvertent communication?

10. Many reflections on this point can be found in Pierre Nicole, *Essais de morale* (Paris, 1671–74; new ed. in 4 vols., 1682). Jesuits, on the other hand, claim to have the special professional skills necessary for making this difficult distinction.

11. Cf. Niklas Luhmann, *Liebe als Passion: Zur Codierung von Intimität* (Frankfurt, 1982), passim, esp. pp. 112ff., 131ff.

12. So the recommendation of the Comte de Versac in Claude Crébillon (fils), *Les Égarements du coeur et de l'esprit* (Paris, 1961).

13. Cf. Francois-Augustin Paradis de Moncrife, *Essais sur la nécessité et les moyens de plaire* (Amsterdam, 1738), pp. 92ff., and many other authors.

14. "Il avoit un quart de loge à l'Opéra, jouoit au lotto et soupoit en Ville." (Sénac de Meilhan, *Considérations sur l'esprit et les moeurs* [London, 1787], p. 317.)

15. *Ibid.*, p. 41.

16. Perhaps the best theoretical conception can be found in Simon-Nicolas-Henri Linguet, *Théorie des loix civiles, ou Principes fondamentaux de la société*, 2 vols. (London, 1767). Better known, but less revealing, is the line taken by Voltaire, Rousseau, Diderot, Mercier, and others, who use the distinction between nature and civilization as a springboard for purely moralistic discourses about modern conditions.

17. "Son existence cessa, pour ainsi dire, de lui appartenir." But the institution of property manages to deceive individuals, to "les asservir, sans les empêcher de se croire libre" (*ibid.*, I, pp. 198–99). The more optimistic line, and the prevailing one, does not pay any attention to this difference but simply focuses on the institutional unity of property, which gives to all human beings the chance to extend their enjoyment of life. "Die Vergrösserung und Vervielfältigung des Menschenlebens ist der Zweck des moralischen Menschen" (the growth and variation of human life is the aim of the moral man), and individual property is the means necessary to this end. Justice, then, becomes "die unveränderliche Neigung, einem jeden Menschen sein ganzes Eigentum uneingeschränkt zu lassen und unverletzt zu erhalten" (the unchangeable inclination to leave in the unrestricted possession of every man his whole property and to maintain it inviolate). So Johann August Schlettwein, *Grundfeste der Staaten oder Die politische Ökonomie* (Giessen, 1779), pp. 384–85. (Schlettwein was the premier German physiocrat.)

18. Again: descriptions of this process make no reference to religion. Genius is no longer a gift of God and, of course, not a way to salvation but simply an accident of nature, an "arrangement heureux des organes du cerveau" (Jean-Baptiste Dubos, *Réflexions critique sur la poesie et sur la peinture*, new ed. [Paris, 1733], II, 7). See also Lodovico A. Muratori, *Della perfetta poesia italiana* (1706); new ed. (Milan, 1971), I, 217.

19. "Le coeur s'agite de lui-même et par un mouvement qui précède toute déliberation quand l'objet qu'on lui présente est réellement un objet touchant." (Dubos, *Réflexions*, II, 326).

20. Cf. R. G. Saisselin, *Taste in Eighteenth Century France: Critical Reflections on the Origins of Aesthetics, or, An Apology for Amateurs* (Syracuse, 1965).

21. Cf. Alfred Baeumler, *Das Irrationalitätsproblem in der Aesthetik und Logik des 18. Jahrhunderts bis zur Kritik der Urteilskraft*, 2d ed. (Tübingen, 1967).

22. "Étouffer la voix de la nature," says Linguet, *Théorie*, I, 184.

23. To give as much content as possible to humanity within each individual, connecting his ego and the world by the most general, vivid, and free reciprocal action—this is Humboldt's idea of *Bildung*. See "Theorie der Bildung des Menschen," in Wilhelm von Humboldt, *Werke*, 2d ed. (Darmstadt, 1969), I, 234–40, 235 n.

24. Cf. K. W. Swart, "'Individualism' in the Mid-Nineteenth Century (1826–1860)," *Journal of the History of Ideas*, 23 (1962), 77–90; Stephen Lukes, *Individualism* (Oxford, 1973).

25. Cf. Niklas Luhmann, *The Differentiation of Society* (New York, 1982).

26. For further materials supporting the same point see Luhmann, *Gesellschaftsstruktur und Semantik*, 2 vols. (Frankfurt, 1980, 1981).

27. Nicolaus Copernicus, *De revolutionibus orbium caelestium libri sex* (1543), ed. Franz Felles and Karl Felles (Munich, 1949), bk. I, chap. 10, p. 25, for the system of fixed stars.

28. Cf. Alfred North Whitehead, *Process and Reality: An Essay in Cosmology* (New York, 1929).

29. Cf. Humberto R. Maturana and Francisco J. Varela, *Autopoiesis and Cognition: The Realization of the Living* (Dordrecht, 1980); Varela, *Principles of Biological Autonomy* (New York, 1979); Milan Zeleny, ed., *Autopoiesis, Dissipative Structures and Spontaneous Social Orders* (Boulder, Colo., 1980); and Zeleny, ed., *Autopoiesis: A Theory of Living Organization* (New York, 1981).

30. Cf. George Spencer Brown, *Laws of Form*, 2d. ed. (London, 1971).

31. Cf. Yves Barel, *Le paradoxe et le système: Essai sur le fantastique social* (Grenoble, 1979).

32. Cf. "Cybernetic Ontology and Transjunctional Operations," in Gotthard Günther, *Beiträge zur Grundlegung einer operationsfähigen Dialektik* (Hamburg, 1976), I, 313–92, 316.

33. But see Edgar Morin, *La méthode*, 2 vols. (Paris, 1977–80), for the contrary opinion.

34. This is Heinz von Foerster's explanation. Cf. "Kybernetik einer Erkenntnistheorie," in Wolf D. Keidel, Wolfgang Händler, and Manfred Spreng, eds., *Kybernetik und Bionik* (Munich, 1974), pp. 27–46. See also his "On Constructing Reality," in Wolfgang F. E. Preiser, ed., *Environmental Design Research* (Stroudsburg, Pa., 1973), II, 35–46.

35. See also Ranulph Glanville, "The Form of Cybernetics: Whitening the Black Box," in *General Systems Research: A Science, a Methodology, a Technology* (Louisville, 1979), pp. 35–42.

36. See Jan Hendrik van den Berg, *Divided Existence and Complex Society* (Pittsburgh, 1974). The author, however, would not accept my idea of a semantic reaction.

37. Think of the last-minute reports so fashionable in recent years. But think also of the famous analysis of Jean-Paul Sartre, *L'Être et le néant*, 30th ed. (Paris, 1950), pp. 615–38. Or simply of Paul Valéry's "La mort est une surprise que fait l'inconcevable au concevable" ("Rhumbs," in *Œuvres*, ed. Jean Hytier [Paris, 1960], II, 611).

Index

Index

Adorno, Theodor, 12
Aeneid (Virgil), 237–38, 239, 245–46
"Aesthetics of Silence" (Sontag), 187
After Dinner at Ornans (Courbet), 80,
    81 (plate), 82, 98n, 102
After the Hunt (Courbet), 105
Age of Suspicion (Sarraute), 186
Albret, Jeanne d', 61
Allegory, 3, 20f, 27f
Almayer's Folly (Conrad), 144, 148f,
    158
Ambrose, Saint, 26–27
America, 12, 210–15 passim, 224
Amis, Kingsley, 192
Anaphoric signs, 188
Anscombe, Elizabeth, 230
Anthropology, *see* Ethnography
Antichrist (Nietzsche), 178–81
Antichristians/antichrists, 179
Antitheatricality, 77–78, 88, 102
Apollo, 114
Arbaleste, Charlotte, 56, 57–58
Argonauts of the Western Pacific
    (Malinowski), 144–48 passim, 152,
    157–60 passim
Aristophanes, 265
Aristotle, 31, 190, 256, 266, 269–70
Aristotle's Masterpiece (Anon.), 43,
    333
Arnold, Matthew, 154
Asad, Talal, 160n
As You Like It (Shakespeare), 47f, 50
Attachment, 238–51 passim
Augustine, Saint, 3, 16–29 passim,
    218f, 258, 307

Austen, Jane, 188f, 251
Austin, J. L., 284, 291, 305, 307
Authenticity, 10–11, 12
Authority, of conscience, 65f
Authorship, 14, 22, 156, 283–84, 288,
    291, 304. *See also* Writing
Autobiography, 3, 16–29
Automatisms, Courbet and, 97–102
    passim
Autonomy, 3–12 passim, 142, 248; in
    16th-century France, 59–63 passim;
    and morality, 64–75, 117–18, 237–
    42 passim; Nietzsche and, 115, 117–
    18, 123, 138; psychoanalysis and,
    198–203 passim, 207
Autopoietic systems, 321–25 passim

Bakhtin, Mikhail, 189
Balint, Michael, 201, 206
"Baloma" (Malinowski), 145n
Banfield, Ann, 188
Barnes, Djuna, 186
Barth, John, 184–87 passim, 194
Barthelme, Donald, 187, 194
Barthes, Roland, 103, 187–93 passim
Bataille, Georges, 193
Beckett, Samuel, 187, 189, 194, 262,
    273
Behavioralism, 351
Beholder, Courbet and, 77–103 pas-
    sim, 337
Being and Time (Heidegger), 283
Benavot, Aaron, 217
Bergson, Henri, 98, 337
Bersani, Leo, 102, 103–4, 338

Beyond Good and Evil (Nietzsche), 117, 123, 126
Bick, Mario, 149 n
Biographical narrative, 9
Birth of Tragedy (Nietzsche), 114–15
"Black Cat" (Poe), 279, 296, 301
Blake, William, 190
Bloch, Ernst, 190
Boas, Franz, 142
Boas, George, 337
Boli-Bennett, John, 214
Borges, Jorge Luis, 187, 194
Boswell, John, 348
Boundaries, of self, 4, 53, 56, 63
Bourdieu, Pierre, 33
Bourgeois, Louise, 54, 61
Bourgeoisie, 9, 146
Bourget, Paul, 123
Bowlby, John, 243–45
Brasillach, Robert, 169–73, 182
Brautigan, Richard, 184–85, 194
Brecht, Bertolt, 193
Brooke-Rose, Christine, 7, 11
Brooks, Peter, 148 n
Burckhardt, Jacob, 3–4, 35, 53 f
Bureaucracy, 8–9, 213
Burial at Ornans (Courbet), 80, 82, 98 n, 338
Burroughs, William S., 193
Butler, Joseph, 65–74 passim
Butor, Michel, 187

Calvin, John, 65
Calvinists, French, 56
Calvino, Italo, 194
Canary Islands, 159–60
"Cargo cult," 209
Carnap, Rudolf, 312
Carrington, Dora, 259–75 passim
Casement, Roger, 149
Case of Wagner (Nietzsche), 123, 127
Castration, 337
Categorical imperative, 65, 67, 69, 74, 240
Cavell, Stanley, 13 f
Céline, Louis-Ferdinand, 166–67, 172
Cellini, Benvenuto, 54
Central myth tradition, Frye concept of, 191
Chastel, Claude du, 57
Chaucer, Geoffrey, 22
Chénier, André, 172
Children of Sanchez (Lewis), 190

Chodorow, Nancy, 7, 10–11
Christ and Christus, as contrasting terms, 178
Christianity, 17, 27–28, 56, 61, 64–65, 72, 177–80 passim. *See also* Augustine
Cicero, 235
Claim of Reason (Cavell), 301, 308, 311–12
Clifford, James, 7–12 passim, 236
Cohn, Dorrit, 188
Colonialism, 8, 152–53
"Coming into One's Own" (Derrida), 307–8
Communication, 133, 134–35. *See also* Language
Communism, 126, 171 ff, 182
Computer science, 194 f
Confessions (Augustine), 16–29 passim, 307
Confessions (Rousseau), 22 f
Conformity, 285, 288, 293
Congo, 144–50 passim
Conrad, Joseph, 9, 12, 140–62 passim
Conscience, 65–66, 73–74
Consciousness, 132–33, 320–25 passim, 332
"Contributions to a Discussion on Masturbation" (Freud), 165
Conversion, 17–22 passim, 26, 28
Cooley, Charles Horton, 240
Coombs, Phillip, 215
Coral Gardens (Malinowski), 145 n
Counterfeiters (Gide), 21
Countertransference, psychoanalytic, 205, 206–7
Courbet, Gustave, 6–7, 76–105, 337 f
Courcelle, Pierre, 17
Crane, Stephen, 147 n
Crapanzano, Vincent, 161
Critique of Practical Reason (Kant), 69
Croissants, origin of term, 233
Culture and Anarchy (Arnold), 154

D'Annunzio, Gabriele, 11, 164, 172, 175–76, 182 f
Dante Alighieri, 21, 254, 275
Darwin, Charles, 22
Davidson, Arnold, 222, 226, 230
Davis, Natalie Zemon, 3–4
Daybreak (Nietzsche), 139
Death of the Stag (Courbet), 100–104 passim, 100 (plate)

Decadence, 123–25
Deconstructionism, 11, 33, 190–95 passim, 305–10
Deer, *see* Roe deer
Defocalization, 185
Deictics, 188f
Delaroche, Paul, 78
Dependence, 247–50
Depression, 244f
De Quincey, Thomas, 163
Derrida, Jacques, 191, 291, 305–8 passim
Descartes, René, 5, 279–87 passim, 293–98 passim, 303ff, 310
Desgouttes, Jérome, 56
Detachment, 239–40, 244–51 passim
Determinism, 9, 107–8, 116, 133–38 passim
Diary in the Strict Sense of the Term (Malinowski), 144–60 passim
Diderotian mode, and the anti-theatrical tradition, 77–78
"Dionysian affliction," 114
Disgregation, 125–27, 138
Doctrine of Virtue (Kant), 67
Dogs, in Courbet's *Quarry*, 87f, 94, 96
Domestication, in American literature, 304–5
Dualism, 6–7, 14
Durkheim, Emile, 142, 235, 313
Dutoit, Ulysse, 103–4
Duval, Jacques, 31–46 passim, 331
Dwyer, Kevin, 161
Dynamic nominalism, 228f, 236

Ecce Homo (Nietzsche), 119–20, 290–91
Education, 213–19 passim, 317
Ego, 198f, 202
Eliot, George, 154, 174
Eliot, T. S., 192, 237–38
Emerson, Ralph Waldo, 278–308 passim
England, 235
Englishman's Treasure (Vicary), 45
Entitlement principle, 32–33
Equality, 110, 124, 126f, 238–39, 247
Erikson, Erik, 240
Eros, 179–82 passim. *See also* Sexuality
Eros and Priapus (Gadda), 182
Esquirol, E., 234
Ethics, *see* Morality

Ethnography, 140–62
Europe, 211–12, 235. *See also individual countries by name*
Evil, 3, 21–24 passim, 68
Existentialists, 12

Fabian, Robert, 330
Fact, Fiction, and Forecast (Goodman), 228n
Fallopius, Gabriel, 39
Family, 53–63 passim. *See also* Marriage
Fancher, Mollie, 225
Fascism, 11, 163f, 168–77 passim, 182–83
"Fate" (Emerson), 293, 302n
Febvre, Jeane le, 30–31, 45
Félida X (split-personality case), 223–24
Feminism, 194, 195–96
Fiala, Robert, 215
Fichte, J. G., 108
Fiction, 7, 46–52, 191–92. *See also* Novels
Fields, W. C., 292n
Flame of Life (*Il Fuoco*; D'Annunzio), 175–77, 181f
"Flat characters," 190–95 passim
Flaubert, Gustave, 143, 180, 189
Focalization, 185
Ford, Ford Maddox, 147n
Forms of Violence (Bersani and Dutoit), 103
Forster, E. M., 190
Foucault, Michel, 13, 142, 226, 235
France, 4, 53–63, 76–105, 175, 224, 234f
Frazer, J. G., 144
Freccero, John, 3
Free indirect style, 188–89
French Revolution, 175
Freud, Sigmund, and Freudianism, 186, 197–207 passim, 281, 285, 287, 300, 303–4; and Courbet, 6–7, 102ff; and oedipal struggle, 19, 199; and sado-masochism, 104, 338; on masturbation, 165; and loss/detachment, 243–46 passim; "object" used by, 349
Friction/heat, sexual, 39, 44–52 passim, 332
Fried, Michael, 4–7 passim
Fromm-Reichman, Frieda, 206

Frye, Northrop, 191 ff
Functional differentiation, of society, 318 f
Functionalism, 151 f

Gadda, Carlo Emilio, 182
Galen, 38–43 passim, 331
Garçon de café, role of, 231–34 passim
Gautier, Théophile, 104
Gay Science (Nietzsche), 115, 127, 129, 133
Geertz, Clifford, 142, 161
Gender, *see* Hermaphrodites; Men; Women
"Genealogy of Messieurs du Laurens," 58–59
Genealogy of Morals (Nietzsche), 128
Genesis, Book of, 28
Genêt, Jean, 172
Genetic individualism, defined, 33
Genius, 287–88, 291, 317, 352
Germany, 224
Gide, André, 17, 21
Gilligan, Carol, 13, 63, 200
Girls' development, 247–51 passim
God, 127 ff, 135, 230
Gödel, Kurt, 306
Goethe, J. W., 108, 244
Golden Notebook (Lessing), 18, 21
Gombrich, Ernst H., 103
Goodman, Nelson, 228
Gouyon, Charles, Baron de la Moussaye, 57 f, 334
Graham, Malcolm, 225
Gravity's Rainbow (Pynchon), 187, 193
Greenblatt, Stephen, 3–4, 9, 57, 63, 141–42, 220
Grotto (Courbet), 91 n, 92 (plate)
Greuzian mode, and the antitheatrical tradition, 77–78
Guerre, Martin, 54
Gunther, Gotthard, 323

Habit, Ravaisson concept of, 98–99
Hacking, Ian, 13, 302 n
Hall, Thomasine, 329–30
Hamacher, Werner, 9
Hamlet (Shakespeare), 279, 302–3, 304
Hamon, Philippe, 188
Hansen, Bert, 348

Hartmann, Heinz, 199, 200–201
Harvey, William, 48
Havelock, Eric A., 191
Hawthorne, Nathaniel, 304
Heart of Darkness (Conrad), 144–62 passim
Heat/friction, sexual, 39, 44–52 passim, 332
Hegel, G. W. F., 108, 137
Heidegger, Martin, 187, 278, 283, 311, 338–39
Henri III, 61
Henri IV (Henri de Navarre), 61–62
Hermaphrodites, 32–42 passim, 227
Hérodias (Flaubert), 180
Heyneman, Stephen, 218
Highmore, Nathaniel, 38
Hintikka, Jaakko, 280
Hippocrates, 43
History, 33–34, 35, 45–46, 138–39, 169–73 passim, 183, 187, 313 f, 318; autobiography and, 3; Nietzsche and, 108–11, 116 f
Hitler, Adolf, 164 n
Hobbes, Thomas, 65 f, 228
Homology, human, 39–43 passim, 331
Homosexuality, 225–26, 233 f, 348
"Homosexual Role" (MacIntosh), 226
Human, All Too Human (Nietzsche), 110, 115
Humanism, 13, 178, 323
Humboldt, Wilhelm von, 353
Hume, David, 228 n, 235
Hunter on Horseback (Courbet), 93 n
Hunters and hunting, in Courbet's art, 84–105 passim, 337
Husserl, Edmund, 351
Hutcheson, Francis, 66
Huxley, Aldous, 185

Id, 198 f
Identity, 13, 31–46 passim, 142, 146, 152, 250
"Imp of the Perverse" (Poe), 279, 293–303 passim, 309–10
Individualism, 1–13 passim, 33–34, 63, 138–39, 165–68 passim, 173–82 passim, 239–40, 318; Augustinian tradition and, 3, 29; Renaissance and, 32–34, 35, 45–46; Charlotte Arbaleste and, 58; psychoanalysis and, 198 f, 207; socialization and, 208–21

Individuality, 1–4 passim, 9–16 passim, 21, 106–8, 140, 166, 267, 313–25; in 16th-century France, 4, 60, 62; Nietzsche on, 9, 16, 108–39; psychoanalysis and, 198, 201f, 207; threat to, in society, 278–312. *See also* Autonomy; Identity
Inequality, 238–39, 247
Infini (journal), 193–94
Inkeles, Alex, 218
"Instincts and Their Vicissitudes" (Freud), 102, 104
Intelligence quotient (I.Q.), 213, 218
Interactionism, symbolic, 316, 351
Irony, 11–12; and ethnography, 12, 141f, 148, 153, 161, 180, 192, 246; saints' autobiographies and, 19f, 22, 28

James, Henry, 147n, 184, 253, 265
James, William, 244, 278
Janet, Pierre, 223–25
Jeanroy, Marie Henri Gustave Alfred, 16
John, Book of, 28
Johnson, W. R., 239
Joyce, James, 21, 192
Jung, C. G., 167, 177f

Kant, Immanuel, 5, 64–74 passim, 107–8, 132–33, 317
Kierkegaard, Sören, 108, 180f, 190
Klein, Melanie, 202
Kleist, Heinrich von, 235
Kohut, Heinz, 199n, 206
Korzeniowski, Konrad, *see* Joseph Conrad
Krafft-Ebing, Richard von, 230
Kristeva, Julia, 193
Kuhn, T. S., 229

Labeling, 226, 233f, 236. *See also* Nominalism
Lacan, Jacques, 195–96, 291
Lanford, Audri Gordon, 215
Language, 130–37 passim, 196, 299–302 passim, 306–9 passim; ethnography and, 142f, 148, 149–50, 155–60 passim; Emerson and, 287f, 299, 308; Poe and, 299–302 passim. *See also* Reading; Writing
Language and Silence (Steiner), 193
Laplanche, Jean, 102, 338

Laurens, Jeanne du, 58–59
Leibniz, G. W., 68, 106–7, 112, 115
Lessing, Doris, 18, 21
Lewis, Oscar, 190
Literature, 7, 46–52, 167–72 passim, 281–82, 287, 301–9 passim. *See also* Autobiography; Novels
Little, Margaret, 206
"Lived body," 95–96
Locke, John, 62, 236
Logical positivism, 311–12
Lord, Albert J., 191
Lost in the Funhouse (Barth), 184, 185–86
Louis, Morris, 82
Love, 12, 55, 67, 237–77 passim
Loxley, William, 218
Loyalty conflicts, 237–40 passim, 247, 250
Luhmann, Niklas, 13f
Luther, Martin, 65
Lysias, 266

McElroy, Joseph, 192
MacIntosh, Mary, 226
McLuhan, Marshall, 191
MacNish, Robert, 223
Maeterlinck, Maurice, 181
Magister Augustinus, 17
Making of the Modern Homosexual (Plummer), 225–26
Malinowski, Bronislaw, 8, 12, 140–61 passim, 236
"Malinowski's Style" (Payne), 152
Man, Paul de, 20, 22f
Manet, Edouard, 77
Man with a Hoe (Millet), 78
Man with the Leather Belt (Courbet), 79, 80 (plate), 82–87 passim
Man with the Pipe (Courbet), 83f
Marcis, Marie/Marin le, 30–52 passim
Marie-Magdeleine (Maeterlinck), 181
Marlowe, Christopher, 141
Marquis de Sade, 230
Marriage, 55, 61–62, 159f, 252, 305
Marrou, Henri, 16
Marx, Karl, 285
Marxism, *see* Communism
Masks, 129–37 passim
Masturbation, 165–66, 181–82
Mattheissen, Wilhelm, 178n
Maturana, Humberto R., 321
Mead, George Herbert, 240, 313f

Mead, Margaret, 158
Médicis, Catherine de, 61–62
Meditations (Descartes), 279–83 passim, 296–97, 298, 303 f
Meilhan, Senac de, 316
Mein Kampf (Hitler), 164 n
Melancholia, 244 f
Melodrama, 305
Melville, Herman, 21
Men, 18–19; in Renaissance, 30–52 passim; in 16th-century France, 53–63 passim. See also Sexuality
Metahistory (White), 187
Metaphysics, 6–7, 76–105, 282, 284, 308
Meyer, John W., 7 f
Middle Ages, 3–4, 17, 35, 332. See also Augustine
Midsummer Night's Dream (Shakespeare), 48
Mill, John Stuart, 285
Millet, Jean-François, 78, 97–98
Milner, Jean-Claude, 196
Milton, John, 44 n
Mimetic modes, 192–93
Mirroring, 91–94, 240
Modernism, 3, 7, 12, 124–25, 161, 192, 194
Mollie Fancher (Dailey), 225
Monologue, 128 f, 138
Montaigne, Léonor de, 57
Montaigne, Michel de, 41, 53–63 passim
Morality, 64–75, 117–18, 237–52
More, Thomas, 141
Mornay, Philippe de, 57–58
"Mourning and Melancholia" (Freud), 244
Much Ado About Nothing (Shakespeare), 48
Multiple personalities, 223–25, 229, 233 f
Muray, Philippe, 193–94
Mussolini, Benito, 170
Must We Mean What We Say? (Cavell), 305, 312
"Mutabilitie Cantos" (Spenser), 37
Myth, 191 ff

Najder, Zdzislaw, 146
Naming, *see* Nominalism
Napoleon I, 166–67
Narcissism, 44 n, 200–201

Narrative, 7, 9, 103–4, 148 n; autobiographical, 3, 16–29; biographical, 9; ethnographic, 152, 161–62; of love, 256, 272–73. See also Literature
Nation-states, 213–17 passim
"Natives of Mailu" (Malinowski), 145 n
Nature, 98–99, 316 f; in Renaissance thought, 36, 41, 47 f; in 16th-century France, 59–60, 61; and morality, 67–71 passim, 75
New Introductory Lectures on Psychoanalysis (Freud), 244
Newton, Isaac, 69
Nicodemus, 20
Nietzsche, Friedrich, 9, 16, 58, 108–42 passim, 190, 226, 281, 285, 289 f; Heidegger and, 339; *Thus Spake Zarathustra*, 176–82 passim
Nominalism, 225–29 passim, 233 f, 236, 348
Nonfiction genres, 190
Notebooks of Malte Laurids Brigge (Rilke), 165
"Note on the Uses of Official Statistics" (Anon.), 226
Novels, 7, 9, 144–62 passim, 184–96
Nussbaum, Martha C., 11 f

Object-relations psychoanalysis, 200–204, 240, 349
Oedipal struggle, 18–19, 26–27, 199
Onanism, 165–66, 181–82
Ong, Walter J., 190 f
On Habit (Ravaisson), 98
On Hermaphrodites, Childbirth, and the Medical Treatment of Mothers and Children (Duval), 32, 34–35
"On Narcissism" (Freud), 200
"On the Affection of Fathers for Their Children" (Montaigne), 54–55, 58
On the Trinity (Augustine), 24
On the Use and Disadvantage of History for Life (Nietzsche), 108
"On Truth and Lie in an Extra-Moral Sense" (Nietzsche), 141
Orality, Ong's concept of, 190–91
Outliving, Nietzsche's concept of, 118–26 passim, 130

Painter-beholder, in Courbet's art, 79–103 passim, 337
Painter's Studio (Courbet), 82–83, 85 (plate), 86, 91, 98 n, 102

Paré, Ambroise, 39f, 43, 331
Paris, Gaston, 16
Patriarchal family, 53–63 passim
Paul, Saint, 64–65
Payne, Harry, 152
Peasants of Flagey Returning from the Fair (Courbet), 80, 82
Personality, 212–13, 214, 221, 332; multiple, 223–25, 229, 233f. *See also* Self
Persuasion (Austen), 251–52
Perversion, 222, 230
Petrarch, 17, 21
Phaedrus (Plato), 255, 265f, 268, 272, 275
Phenomenality, 131–36 passim
Phenomenologies, 5ff, 19, 95–96, 351
Philosophical Investigations (Wittgenstein), 301, 307
Philosophy, 64–75, 113, 167–68, 179, 181, 281–82, 295–96, 301–11 passim. *See also individual schools and philosophers by name*
Philosophy of Sleep (MacNish), 223
Piqueur, in Courbet's *Quarry*, 86–89 passim, 94–97 passim, 98n
Plato, 253, 255, 265–75 passim
Platter, Felix, 56–57, 60
Platter, Thomas, 54–60 passim
Pleasure of the Text (Barthes), 190, 193
Plus (McElroy), 192
Poe, Edgar Allan, 279, 293–310 passim
Point Counter-Point (Huxley), 185
Poland, 145–46, 149
Politics, 4, 8–14 passim, 70, 126, 163–77 passim, 182–83, 213–17 passim
Pollock, Jackson, 82
Pope, Alexander, 68f
Popular fiction, 191–92
Poradowska, Marguerite, 148–49, 150
Portrait of the Artist as a Young Man (Joyce), 21
Positivism, 9, 311–12
Possession vs. multiple personality, 224
Postmodernism, 7, 184–96
Poststructuralism, 12–13, 188
Pound, Ezra, 192
Primary orality, Ong's concept of, 190–91
Prinzip Hoffnung (Bloch), 190
Prodigies, 4, 36–41 passim, 47, 57

Proust, Marcel, 21, 271–72, 273
Psychoanalysis, 10–11, 189, 197–207, 240, 349. *See also* Freud and Freudianism
Psychology, 214f, 239, 241, 346
Pufendorf, Samuel, Baron von, 67
Puits noir (Courbet), 91n, 92 (plate)
Pynchon, Thomas, 185, 187, 194

Quarry (Courbet), 76–105, 77 (plate), 90 (plate), 337f

Rabelais, François, 54
Rabinow, Paul, 161
Ravaisson, Félix, 98f, 337
Rawls, John, 70–74
Reading, 156f, 165, 182, 289, 290–91
Realism, 103–4; Courbet's, 79–80, 94–105 passim, 338; ethnographic, 161; in novels, 192, 194; ir science fiction, 192; and nominalism, 227–28, 348
Reconstruction, 2
Red and Black (Stendhal), 166–67, 175
Reed, Ishmael, 194
Relativism, 141, 323
Religion, 315, 318–19. *See also* Christianity
Remembrance of Things Past (Proust), 21
Renaissance, 4, 7, 17f, 142, 224, 332; sexuality in, 30–52 passim, 330–32 passim
Renaissance Self-Fashioning (Greenblatt), 141
Responsibility, 237–41 passim, 250
Revolution, 11, 175
Reynolds, Mary (split-personality case), 223
Rilke, Rainer Maria, 165
Rivers, W. H. R., 144
Riviere, Joan, 202–3
Robbe-Grillet, Alain, 186, 189
Roe deer, in Courbet's *Quarry*, 87–97 passim, 98n, 337
Romans, Book of, 64–65
Romantic fiction, 191–96 passim
Romanticism, 167, 175
Room of One's Own (Woolf), 195
Rosaldo, Michelle Zimbalist, 34, 59
Rose, Mark, 192
Rothstein, William, 225

Rouge et le noir (Stendhal), 166–67, 175
"Round" characters, 190f, 195
Rousseau, Jean-Jacques, 21–25 passim, 295

Sade, Marquis de, 230
Sadomasochism, 104f, 230, 338
Said, Edward, 154
Saints, 21–22, 113
Sarraute, Nathalie, 186f, 189
Sartre, Jean-Paul, 21, 231–32, 234
Saussure, Ferdinand de, 142
Sauvages (predecessor of Esquirol), 234
Scheler, Max, 95
Schlegel, Friedrich, 108
Schneewind, J. B., 4–5, 7
Scholasticism, 314–15, 322
Scholes, Robert, 192f
Schopenhauer, Arthur, 114f, 132
Schopenhauer as Educator (Nietzsche), 112–13
Science fiction, 192f, 195
Science Fiction Encyclopedia, 195
Searles, Harold, 206
Secondary orality, Ong's concept of, 190–91
Secular Scripture (Frye), 191
Secular tradition, Frye concept of, 191
Self, 10–12, 104, 167, 190, 236; transcendental/moral, 3, 5–6, 67, 69, 72–75 passim, 117, 168, 224, 237–52, 317, 319f, 324; in autobiography, 3, 16–25 passim; 16th-century sense of, 4, 53–63, 332; psychoanalysis and, 10–11, 197–207; and socialization, 213, 218–21 passim
Self-consciousness, 188–89, 285–86
Self-legislation, 65, 69, 72
Self-portraits, Courbet's, 79–103 passim
Self-reference, 314–15, 317, 321, 351
Self-referential systems, 320–25
"Self-Reliance" (Emerson), 279–98 passim, 308
Semio-history, Valesio's category of, 170
Senses of Walden (Cavell), 308
Separation, 18–22 passim, 201, 203, 207, 237–47 passim. *See also* Autonomy
Sexuality, 153, 179–82 passim, 193, 220, 338, 349; Augustine and, 24–27 passim; in Renaissance, 30–52 passim, 330–32 passim; in Courbet's art, 102–3; nominalism and, 225–29 passim. *See also* Homosexuality; Transvestism
Shakespeare, William, 34, 46–52, 141
Simmel, Georg, 313–14
Skepticism, 281, 284, 302, 305, 310f
Skinner, Marilyn B., 239, 246
Smith, David, 218
Social Contract (Rousseau), 295
Socialism, 212, 214–15
Socialization, 117, 208–21
Social Problems, 226
Social responsibility, 237–41 passim, 250
Society, 7–9, 208–13 passim, 317–22 passim; Renaissance, 34–36; and morality, 70–71, 74, 117; Nietzsche and, 117, 131, 285; novels and, 189f; and threat to individuality, 278–312
Sociology, 313–14, 319
Socrates, 255ff, 263, 266
Sollers, Philippe, 193
Sontag, Susan, 187
Source (Courbet), 91, 92 (plate)
Spencer Brown, George, 321
Spenser, Edmund, 37, 141
Stanford University, 212, 214
State organization, 8–9, 213–17 passim. *See also* Politics
Steiner, George, 190, 192f
Stendhal (M. H. Beyle), 167
Stone, Leo, 206
Stonebreakers (Courbet), 80, 81 (plate), 82, 338
Stratification, social, 317f
Structuralism, 7, 10, 187f
Subjectivity, 7, 14, 117, 137; ethnographic, 12, 141ff, 150, 155. *See also* Self
Suicide, 234–35
Superego, 198f, 202
Surrealists, 186
Suttie, Ian, 243
Symbolic interactionism, 316, 351
Symposium (Plato), 253, 255, 272

Taming of the Shrew (Shakespeare), 48
Technology, 194f
Teleological individualism, defined, 33
Tel Quel (journal), 194
Terence, 53
Teresa of Avila, Saint, 18f
Theater, 46–52

Theatricality, in painting, 77–79, 88, 102f
Theory of Justice (Rawls), 70
Thief's Journal (Genêt), 172
"Thing body," 95–96
Thoreau, H. D., 278, 286–94 passim, 304–9 passim
Thus Spake Zarathustra (Nietzsche), 176–82 passim
Tilh, Arnaud du, 54
Tocqueville, Alexis de, 210f
"Toward a Semiotic Law of Character" (Hamon), 188
Tractatus (Wittgenstein), 190
Transcendental phenomenology, 351
Transcendent self/subject, 3, 5–6, 67, 69, 117, 168, 224, 317, 319f, 324
Transference, psychoanalytic, 205
Transparent Minds (Cohn), 188
Transvestism, 41–42, 47–52 passim, 329–30
Trobriand Islands, 143–52 passim, 158
Troilus and Criseyde (Chaucer), 22
Tropics of Discourse (White), 187
Trout Fishing in America (Brautigan), 184–85
Twelfth Night (Shakespeare), 47–51 passim
Tyndale, William, 141

Ulysses (Joyce), 186
Undecidability, 287, 302, 306–12 passim
United Nations, 216; UNESCO, 215, 217
Universalism, 72–73, 323
Unspeakable Sentences (Banfield), 188
Untimely Meditations (Nietzsche), 108–15 passim
Utilitarianism, 66

V (Pynchon), 185
Valéry, Paul, 186, 322
Valesio, Paolo, 11
Valois, Marguerite de, 61–62
Vicary, Thomas, 45

Virgil, 237–38, 239, 245–46, 275
Vocation, in 16th-century France, 59–60, 61

Wagner, Richard, 123–27 passim, 134
Waiters, role of, 231–34 passim
Walden (Thoreau), 286, 299, 306
Watt, Ian, 154, 189
Ways of Worldmaking (Goodman), 228n
Weber, Max, 209
Wellbery, David E., 305–6
Wells, H. G., 147n
Wheat Sifters (Courbet), 82f, 83 (plate), 98n
White, Hayden, 187
Whitehead, Alfred North, 321
Wholeness, 131, 135, 138, 207
Will, 66–69 passim, 98–99, 123, 125–27, 138
Williams, Bernard, 280
Williams, Raymond, 141n, 154
Winnicott, D. W., 201
Witkiewicz, Stanislas, 149
Wittgenstein, Ludwig, 190, 257, 278, 284f, 296, 301, 305–9 passim
Wolff, Christian, 107
Women, 18, 63, 241–42, 346; in 16th-century France, 4, 55–63 passim; in Renaissance, 30–52 passim; Shakespeare's actors for, 47, 50–51; and feminism, 194, 195–96; and detachment, 247–51 passim. *See also* Sexuality
Woolf, Virginia, 195
Words (Sartre), 21
Writing, 22, 165, 182, 262; ethnographic, 155–59 passim; and character, 190; Emerson and, 288–91, 295, 304; Poe and, 295–304 passim, 310. *See also* Literature
Wyatt, Thomas, 141

Zavarzadeh, Mas'ud, 185
Zetzel, Elizabeth, 207

cosmopolitanism — 140ff

Library of Congress Cataloging-in-Publication Data

Main entry under title:

Reconstructing individualism.

Bibliography:
Includes index.
1.Individualism—Addresses, essays, lectures.
2.Individuality—Addresses, essays, lectures.
3.Self—Addresses, essays, lectures.   I.Heller,
Thomas C.   II.Sosna, Morton.   III.Wellbery, David E.
B824.R43   1986   141'.4   85-27678
ISBN 0-8047-1292-1 (alk. paper)
ISBN 0-8047-1291-3 (pbk.)